THE FREE SOCIETY IN CRISIS

ALSO BY DAVID SELBOURNE

An Eye to China

An Eye to India

Through the Indian Looking-Glass

In Theory and in Practice

The Making of A Midsummer Night's Dream

Against Socialist Illusion

Left Behind: Journeys into British Politics

Death of the Dark Hero: Eastern Europe 1987–90

The Spirit of the Age

Not an Englishman: Conversations with Lord Goodman

The Principle of Duty: An Essay on the Foundations of the Civic Order

Moral Evasion

The Losing Battle with Islam

EDITED BY DAVID SELBOURNE

A Doctor's Life

TRANSLATED BY DAVID SELBOURNE

The City of Light

THE
FREE SOCIETY
IN CRISIS

A History of Our Times

DAVID SELBOURNE

Prometheus Books

59 John Glenn Drive
Amherst, New York 14228

Published 2019 by Prometheus Books

Cover image © Onischenko Natalya / Shutterstock
Cover design by Liz Mills
Cover design © Prometheus Books

Inquiries should be addressed to
Prometheus Books
59 John Glenn Drive
Amherst, New York 14228
VOICE: 716–691–0133 • FAX: 716–691–0137
WWW.PROMETHEUSBOOKS.COM

23 22 21 20 19   5 4 3 2 1

Library of Congress Cataloging-in-Publication Data

Identifiers: LCCN 2018042239 (print) |
ISBN 978-1-63388-531-8 (ebook) | 978-1-63388-530-1 (hardcover)

Printed in the United States of America

CONTENTS

PREFATORY NOTE

This is a work neither of the "left" nor of the "right" but influenced by both, and it is addressed principally to readers in the United States and in Britain. Without deference to nonjudgmentalism and political correctness, it was written out of the necessity to record and try to make sense of the disintegration of Western free societies in the last two or three decades, and to point to the principles of the "true commonwealth" as an alternative to today's political, ethical, and social disorders. One of the book's governing ideas is that market freedom and moral freedom are two sides of the same coin, and that between them they are bringing down civil society itself.

I have drawn on a wide variety of sources past and present. In addition to citations of the findings of governmental and intergovernmental organizations, and of social institutions of many kinds, I have used contemporary media coverage of the subjects with which the book deals. Available daily in the public domain, such material serves to illustrate the extent to which bad faith chooses to ignore whatever is unwelcome to it.

I have also sidestepped the work of academics whose writings shed too little light on our times, and many of which are overburdened by scholastic theories without practical utility and lacking in genuine substance. Instead, I have often preferred Greek, Roman, and Hebraic thinkers and the writings of America's Founding Fathers as guides to the truths we need.

The book is dedicated to my wife, without whose inspiration and ideas it could not have been written. I would also like to thank Bryony Hall of the Society of Authors; my daughter, Emilie, for her encouragement and bibliographical help; my son, Raphael, for his advice and moral support; my former student, Dr. Geoff Andrews of the Open University, for reading an early draft of the book; Stefano Volponi for his technical assistance; Steven L. Mitchell, Hanna Etu, Jade Zora Scibilia, Mark Hall, Lynn Pasquale Gresch, Liz Mills, Catherine Roberts-Abel, Jake Bonar, and others at Prometheus Books for the publication of this work; and Laura Shelley for her analytical skills in compiling the index.

CHAPTER 1

AS OTHER POWERS ADVANCE

These are convulsive times for Western democracies, times of turmoil. On the horizon other political and moral forces are advancing, benefiting from the free society's gradual fall. These are times, too, of gross disproportions of poverty and wealth under the pressures of globalization, greed, and growth; times of the breaking of many moral bounds, of the perpetual motion of migrants crossing lands and seas in search of work or refuge from strife, and of deepening environmental harm.

Metropolises increase to unprecedented size, and the prospect arises of a world population of some 11 billion by the century's end.[1] Interplanetary travel beckons; one billion tourists are on the move each year—more than 100 million passengers traveled through Atlanta airport in 2016,[2] over 75 million through Heathrow[3]—and Americans drive their vehicles more than three trillion miles in a single year.[4] At the same time, the flux of humanity is so great as to constitute a new and advancing world force in its own right.

The number of migrants living in countries other than those in which they were born had reached over 250 million by 2017,[5] an increase of nearly 50 percent since 2000, with prophecy of an even greater "exodus of biblical proportions" to come.[6] Such motion is in itself no new thing. "When there be great Shoales of People without Meanes of life and Sustentation," wrote Francis Bacon in 1639, "it is of Necessity that once in an Age or two, they discharge a Portion of their People upon other Nations."[7] But today's "discharge" is on an unprecedented scale.

Asylum seekers, refugees (real or pretended) from war and civil conflict, and economic migrants flow in their tens of millions from place to place in search of sanctuary, food, and work, with many in flight from encroaching famine as climate change takes an increasing toll on the teeming populations of Africa and elsewhere. They are rescued, or drown, by the thousands in foreign seas, are blocked at borders, or enter their havens as "undocumented" illegals. If subsequently caught, they may suffer arrest and deportation; find guarded welcome or arouse hostility as communities struggle to absorb them, house them, feed them, and educate their children; or "disappear" without a trace.

Today's instabilities are on a larger scale than in the 1930s, with uncountable numbers lost to civil society in the labyrinths of electronic limbo. It is also a hard fact that neither discredited socialist nor amoral libertarian prescriptions can deal with the free society's multiplying dysfunctions. In disintegrating Western democracies, the instinct for self-harm to "left" and "right," and the illusions which accompany it, reign largely unchecked. Belief in the supreme virtues of free choice, and large indifference to the consequences of its exercise, flourish. Freedom from moral restraint is seen as a right, even as a human right, and limits placed upon it are perceived as authoritarian or worse. Even mere transgression is regarded by some as progressive, while in the freest societies that have ever existed "progressives" believe—or pretend to believe—that they are living in "police states."[8]

In this chaos of perceptions, a mirror of our times, the belief reigns in many (or most) that a market-driven liberal democracy resting upon free moral choice and individual entitlement in liberty's name is the culmination of the historical process and stands at the summit of political evolution. But Francis Fukuyama in *The End of History*[9] was wrong.

Instead, there is a new and suicidal dialectic at work within free societies which is bringing them to disorder and disintegration. Many of their supposed strengths are weaknesses; the failure to grasp this a source of further debilitation. Meanwhile, "freedom and liberty" in market and moral choices are undoing the social order, while internal disparity and division grow. "During my stay in the United States," wrote Alexis de Tocqueville, "nothing struck me more forcibly than the general equality of condition among the people."[10] He would not find this today, yet de Tocqueville saw such condition as American democracy's premise. But, now, all that is required for Western democracy's survival, so some think, is the preservation of economic and moral laissez-faire from erosion, diminution, or regulation.

Historical knowledge, on the wane in Western democracy's educational systems, is necessary for true perspective and informed judgment. Its increasing lack prevents us from seeing that our freedoms, many of them now put to antisocial ends, are mutations of the freedoms fought for in the Reformation and in the revolutionary overthrow of the *anciens régimes*. Where abused, such liberties also parody those for which the nineteenth-century emancipationists and the suffragettes struggled. Moreover, many lack the means to exercise today's freedoms, whether those freedoms be real or false.

It is a paradox, too, that many of Western democracy's present-day libertarians—"progressive" human rights libertarians and free-market libertarians alike—are deeply authoritarian. Both are swift to condemn any institution, ethic, or legal decision which runs counter to their dogmas, and each assumes that its principles and prohibitions are conducive to the common good.

In the bypassing or subverting of alternative notions about where the true interests of civil society lie, the scope of public debate has shrunk to the harm of democracy itself. Moreover, neither the one type of libertarian nor the other possesses an ethic capable of protecting the free society from increasing self-harm. Indeed, few libertarians of whatever stripe, and whether market or moral free-choosers, believe in much more than doing what one wants.

If in the "Soviet bloc" civil society was wrecked by state socialism, in Western democracies it is being brought down in freedom's name. This is therefore not the "end of history"—far from it—but a time in which the dialectic is quickening as free societies unravel, with

American sway reduced and other powers advancing. Yet because the "left" has been disabled by state-socialist failure and because market nostrums are productive of great injustice, few can now tell the truth about Western democracy's decomposition.

Nor has it been grasped that new times such as these require a new understanding of what constitutes "progress." Today's political class in free societies, and those who furnish it with its increasingly impoverished thoughts and words, are incapable of it. But it is clear enough that a "pro-enterprise and pro-competition agenda" on the one hand, and a moral free-for-all on the other, are insufficient for true progress.

Moreover, the word *progress* has no fixed sense other than that of a "going forward." It is a sense which demands new interpretation in times such as these. Thus, to make a stand against much of what presently passes for "progressive"—such as the abuse of the liberties that the free society provides—could be regarded as urgent, and as itself a "going forward" in the general interest.

However, candor about the free society's woes is also stopped in its tracks by nonjudgmentalism, holding its tongue, and by political correctness, an orthodoxy of mind born of fear of the truth. Such fear is the true Reaction of our times, since without moral judgment of our mounting ills there can be no real progress in social reform, while self-censorship blocks Reason with taboos about what we can say, and (almost) about what we should think. Between them, nonjudgmentalism and political correctness help "progressives" to fill the hole where the "socialist project" once stood and are surrogates for genuine belief.

There are many optimists who still believe that the heart of the free society is essentially sound. "Hope," Edward Gibbon tells us in *The Decline and Fall of the Roman Empire*, is "the best comfort of our imperfect condition."[11] But growing distresses of every kind in the free society do not encourage hope, social orders are easily damaged, and the time span of empires is short and becoming shorter; indeed, few have lasted as long as has Western dominion. Unsurprisingly therefore, and like other poorly led Western democracies, America is under challenge by notions of right different from its own, with those of Islam leading the way.

The United States once judged the world. It is now increasingly judged by it, the biter bit, its change of fortune a familiar one in the histories of power. As Roman Seneca asked, "What realm is there whose ruin is not already in preparation?"[12] Gibbon similarly warned that "apparent security" can be undone by "new enemies."[13] As an example of it, he drew attention to an earlier rise of Islam when the Saracens, who had formerly "languished in poverty and contempt," "spread their conquests from India to Spain" under the inspiration of their prophet. Such warnings are salutary. Nevertheless, illusions about American prowess continue to hide its condition. Thus in the late 1980s it was declared that "this is the American moment in world history,"[14] and similarly by President Trump in January 2018 that "this is our American moment."[15]

But for all such assertions, the waning of America's strategic influence in world affairs has been clear for some time. Its former secretary of state John Kerry could travel "more than 1.4 million miles in 596 days"[16] and have little to show for it in benefit to the United States, while for all Trump's bluster, and with his own secretary of state vowing in May 2018 to help America "get back" its "swagger,"[17] its reach remains a limited one in many fields of conflict. "Mexico is going to pay for the wall," declared the president about his southern border project.[18] "Not now, not ever," the Mexican president responded,[19] and laughter greeted President Trump's assertion at the UN General Assembly in September 2018 that "in less than two years, my administration has accomplished more than almost any administration in the history of our country."[20]

Moreover, despite the worsting of US armies in foreign fields from Vietnam to Afghanistan and the reduction of its influence in the Asia-Pacific region, its military arsenals have been depleted. The US Navy has fewer vessels now than in the mid-nineties,[21] its Second Fleet—previously deployed in the North Atlantic—was dismantled in 2011, its "rapid reaction force" in Europe has been described as "undermanned and poorly equipped,"[22] it took almost twenty years of "testing problems, delays and cost-overruns" before its F-35B supersonic fighter jet made a first combat airstrike,[23] while its intercontinental ballistic missiles are aging. Even the US space program's Atlas V launch vehicle relies upon Russia's RD-180 rocket engine to get off the ground.[24]

In February 2018, the Trump administration announced a $700 billion Pentagon budget in order to "begin to rebuild."[25] But Russia's modernization of its armed forces with new jets, tanks, submarines, and missiles—as well as allegedly "invincible" nuclear weapons[26]— started in 2008.[27] Moreover, "the quality of people willing to serve" in the US forces was said in June 2014 to have been "declining rapidly,"[28] with many applicants overweight, without a high-school diploma, or with "behavioral shortcomings," including drug use[29]; and by 2018 less than 30 percent of American 17-to-24-year-olds met the "physical, mental and moral requirements" for the military,[30] which found itself short of 6,500 new recruits[31] despite increasing resort to "moral waivers" for criminal offenses "from drug convictions to arson."[32]

"Tonight," nevertheless declared President Obama after the killing of Osama bin Laden in May 2011, "we are once again reminded that Americans can do whatever we set our minds to."[33] It cannot. "US leadership will continue to be unrivalled" and "the US will remain the most influential, powerful and important country in the world," similarly declared the White House's national security adviser in June 2013.[34] Other Americans, "progressive" but equally wrong, have held the United States to be "totalitarian" and even "fascist."[35] It is neither.

But it is not the land it was. In old Europe in March 1778, Louis XVI's minister Turgot described America as "the hope of the human race,"[36] while president Obama called it "the envy of the world."[37] It is so no longer. Similarly reduced, Britain's navy, with no ships that can fire cruise missiles,[38] was described in 2016 as "way below the critical mass required for the tasks that could confront it,"[39] and its army—"twenty years out of date"[40]—as approaching its smallest size since the American colonies were lost. "Living a lie" about their imagined strength,[41] its armed forces were also said in April 2018 to lack 8,000 full-time military personnel, 700 intelligence analysts, 2,400 engineers, and 800 pilots.[42]

"There is a cycle in human affairs" the rich Croesus is reported to have told Cyrus, the sixth-century BCE ruler of Persia, "and in its turning it does not permit any people to find permanent good fortune."[43] No, but there is little to match the modern free society's lost sense of direction. Meanwhile, the alleged or real military and cyber strengths of Russia—with its robot tanks, new hypersonic missiles, "nuclear-powered underwater drones armed with an atomic weapon," and "mobile laser system capable of destroying satellites in space"[44]—increase. It invades the Ukraine, seizes the Crimea and weathers the sanctions imposed upon it, intrudes upon and hacks into an American presidential campaign, "infiltrates the social media" with "robot accounts,"[45] carries out a nerve-gas attack in Britain on a turncoat agent, conducts large-scale military exercises with China,[46] and has military dominance in the Arctic, while its influence in the civil war-torn Middle East grows as US decision in the region becomes more random. By September 2018, Russia's foreign minister even felt able to mock "several Western nations" for their "self-proclaimed status as world leaders."[47]

At the same time, Turkey resumes its Ottoman and Islamizing ambitions; its ties with Russia deepen; it controls parts of northern Syria, gives refuge to members of Egypt's outlawed Muslim Brotherhood, plans to produce its own long-range missiles;[48] and its autocratic president vows to "rip the heads off" those plotting against him[49] and to "break the hands" of Turkey's foes.[50] President Trump's imposition of tariffs against it, exacerbating its economic problems, was similarly denounced as a "plot to make Turkey kneel,"[51] while the European democracies were described by Turkey's leader as having "failed,"[52] a judgment—whether premature or not—made in times when a new world order is being constructed before our eyes.

Meanwhile Iran, also aided by Russia and attempting to repress internal dissent, suffered economically from the re-imposition by President Trump of sanctions against its energy, petrochemical, and financial sectors after he rejected the 2015 international accord by which its nuclear ambitions were sought to be curbed, a rejection made on the grounds of Iran's "malign behavior" as a "sponsor of terrorism" and its "aggressive development of long-range missiles."[53] Iran nevertheless maintained and even increased its grip (with the help of political proxies) upon Syria, Iraq, and Lebanon, its reach thus extending to the eastern Mediterranean, while remaining a threat to Yemen and the Gulf States and posing a challenge to Saudi Arabia. Moreover, even Afghan Taliban fighters were being trained in Iran in 2018,[54] while the Teheran regime, its ties with China growing closer, has also collaborated with and been aided by North Korea[55] in its nuclear ambitions, with Iran's centrifuge and enrichment programs continuing despite the 2015 accord which sought to curb them.[56]

In this changing balance of forces, in which new advancing powers are swift to challenge the United States, the Iranian president thus warned Trump in peremptory terms to remain in the nuclear deal— which had relieved Iran of some of the burden of sanctions—or "face severe consequences";[57] the US flag was burned in the Iranian parliament in May 2018; and Iran's foreign minister declared that the United States needed to engage in a "respectful dialogue" with his country.[58] The United States did not have "the courage for face-to-face war with Iran," a senior Iranian military officer even asserted,[59] and "would regret what it had done" in withdrawing from the accord;[60] to negotiate with President Trump would itself be a "humiliation," announced the Iranian parliament's deputy speaker;[61] while the head of Iran's Revolutionary Guards' Special Forces mocked Trump's warnings as "cabaret-style rhetoric."[62] "You may begin the war, but it will be us who will end it," he added, the Iranian president also advising the United States to "think again" about its "presence in the Persian Gulf, in the Sea of Oman, in Afghanistan, in Iraq and other places."[63]

For its part, impoverished North Korea, burdened by UN sanctions for its own nuclear proliferation efforts and thought to have produced enough fissile material for up to sixty warheads,[64] in 2017 threatened to inflict on America "the greatest pain and suffering it has ever gone through,"[65] to turn it to "ashes and darkness,"[66] and to "remove it from the world"[67] while describing Trump's threats against it as "the sound of a barking dog."[68] Nevertheless, after his meeting with Kim Jong-un, the US president was persuaded in June 2018 that there was "no longer a Nuclear Threat from North Korea,"[69] that Kim was "very open and honorable"[70]—investing him with a status he had not possessed before—and even declared that he had a "very special bond"[71] with North Korea's leader.

But the regime's claims to have shut down or disabled its nuclear test site were soon disbelieved,[72] with allegations that plutonium was still being produced at its nuclear facility at Yongbyon,[73] that the reactor was being upgraded,[74] that new ballistic missiles were under construction,[75] and that there were as many as "20 undeclared missile operating bases."[76] By mid-July 2018 President Trump had himself declared that there was now "no time limit" for North Korean "denuclearization,"[77] while North Korea, in exchange for such "denuclearization," sought "corresponding measures" from the United States[78] and threatened to strengthen its nuclear arsenal if the United States did not lift economic sanctions against it.[79] Thus another new power advances.

Meanwhile, in teeming free societies today, anxious millions fear for their futures even as their freedoms are held to be the precondition of the good life, while what seems like progress to some is regarded with abhorrence by others. In the French Revolution of 1848, "men's minds were in a state of utter confusion. They knew neither what to hold on to nor where to stop," wrote de Tocqueville of another period of turmoil.[80] Nor do we today, as floundering democratic politicians in their own confusions search for a "center ground" on which to get a footing.

"What is to be done?" is an old political question, the oldest. Such is the scale of the free society's disorders, it is also a question which most cannot now answer, while the far right's knocking at democracy's door seems destined to grow louder. Even the sense that we belong to a civil society is evaporating, with what was once a polity now largely comprised of rights-bearing isolates wheeling their shopping carts through shopping malls in single file. The very word *citizen* has been displaced by *customer* or *consumer*, while market-thought, not Marxist thought, promises humanity's salvation.

This development has come full-term in today's suicidal free societies. But it has had a long gestation. Adam Smith himself complained that eighteenth-century Britain had established "a great empire for the sole purpose of raising up a nation of customers,"[81] while in 1807 the poet Robert Southey declared that "this nation offers a perpetual reward to those who will discover new wants for them."[82] Today's shallowness of huckster-thought has deep roots. Calling it "our latest Gospel yet preached," Thomas Carlyle objected to what he called the "vague janglement of laissez-faire, Supply and Demand, Cash Payment . . . Free Trade, Competition and Devil take the hindmost."[83]

Carlyle's "janglement" is no longer "vague." Its sound in free societies is now deafening, overwhelming Reason itself, with a governing purpose of *Homo sapiens* held by market-thought to be that of producing ever more "goods and services to consume."[84] This ethos is again a reductive betrayal of the political liberties gained in the Enlightenment itself. Old slavery and darkness of mind have been replaced in free societies by servitudes equally great, with deferences to "the market" overshadowing the many desires that cannot be met by "products" and on which no money price can be set. Meanwhile, the thinning out of knowledge of the past has disabled judgment, while on the horizon stand the advancing political and moral forces of the future, watching and benefiting from the free society's self-harms.

There is also widespread naiveté, or ignorance, in Western democracies about the beliefs and purposes of rival powers as the latter's reach and confidence grow. In this new dialectic China, the re-ascendant Middle Kingdom—more than a billion strong, its three largest cities (Shanghai, Beijing, and Guangzhou) each with a population of over 20 million[85]—similarly sees the United States as a declining force. It has also not hidden its view of President Trump as his tariff trade war with China has proceeded. "The wise man builds bridges, the fool builds walls," its official news agency declared in June 2018,[86] the Great Wall of China notwithstanding, while American criticism of China's trade policies was described in October 2018 as a "symptom" of the "insecurities" of the United States.[87]

Manufacturing and multiplying—it ceased its "one-child" policy in 2016—modernizing and militarizing, China has been the world's largest trading nation since 2013. In 2016 the yuan became a reserve currency; China is the biggest net oil importer and biggest automobile market; it leads the field in the making of supercomputers; and it could be the world's largest economy by 2029.[88] It also has a vast internal security apparatus, tens of thousands of state enterprises, and the world's largest communist party with more than 80 million members, and it is at the same time a substantial holder of US government debt, one of "America's bankers."[89]

With the world's biggest standing army at over two million strong, as well as the world's largest navy, and with military spending lavish—including on a new generation of ICBMs, stealth fighters, combat drones, and an unmanned tank—it has installed cruise missiles in disputed islands in the South China Sea,[90] expressed its "common military concerns" with Russia,[91] and supplied Pakistan with weapons. It has also pledged security cooperation with Turkey,[92] grown closer to North Korea,[93] set up a satellite and space-mission-control station in Patagonia,[94] and banned the promotion of overweight soldiers in its army.[95] China also has tens (and even hundreds) of millions living in poverty, tens of millions on the move from rural to urban areas, 20,000 kilometers of high-speed rail track, and over 700 million internet users.[96]

In addition, while reconstituting the ancient Silk Route's maritime and overland routes, it is engaged in many transcontinental railway, highway, pipeline, and telecom projects, with infrastructure investments—some of potential military use—across the African continent; in aerospace plants in Burma, Pakistan, and Saudi Arabia; and in strategically well-placed ports from Sri Lanka to the Greek Piraeus. It also has a stake in nuclear-power generation in Britain,[97] invests in and gains access to US technologies (including by cyber-espionage[98]), and is making advances toward creating limitless energy by means of nuclear fusion[99] while simultaneously exerting ideological control over its mass media and seeking to stifle opposition to one-party rule.

Thus, in November 2013 the Chinese authorities published a new version of Mao's *Little Red Book*, and in March 2015 a party newspaper described "Western values" as a "ticket to hell";[100] "resolutely resist the influence of erroneous Western thought," declared the president of China's Supreme Court.[101] Likewise, in December 2016, President Xi Jinping ordered higher education to "adhere to the correct political orientation"; human rights activists are arrested; websites are shut down; Facebook is banned;[102] the need for "iron discipline" is asserted;[103] and "unity in thinking" is called for.[104] At the same time, it takes from the West whatever ideas and innovations serve it best, while its tech companies stand to challenge those of the United States.[105] Indeed, in July 2017 its government promised that "by 2030" China would reach a "world-leading level in artificial intelligence technology and application,"[106] and it plans to launch a Mars probe by 2021.[107]

With its acrobats adept on the high wire, the Chinese, despite intermittent economic and social tribulations of their own—including mounting national debt, increasing capital outflow, fluctuating growth, and the spread of corruption and labor unrest—have so far succeeded in running a giant marketizing society under communist direction. Or as Xi Jinping, made president for life in March 2018, expressed it, "China took a brave step forward to embrace the world market"[108] in the "long march of our generation."[109] But at the same time "Chinese socialism" was "entering a new era."[110] "Our land radiates with enormous dynamism," he also declared in October 2017,[111] while "every inch of its territory" would be "protected."[112]

Given China's phoenixlike rise as a political and economic force, and America's declining influence and status in the world, the "pest-holes of Asia"—in Ayn Rand's phrase[113]—are not what they were. Nor is the "Atlantic skyline of New York" any longer to be jeeringly contrasted with the "mystic muck of India";[114] its first manned space mission is planned for late 2021 or 2022.[115] In *Atlas Shrugged*, published in 1957, Rand also has her hero, John Galt, express contempt for "barefoot bums" and "jungle females," inquiring "who will provide them with their electrical refrigerators, their washing machines and vacuum cleaners?"[116] It is a misplaced contempt now.

As Western democracies, their liberties increasingly misused, lose their way, the boot is on the other foot. In June 2014, Britain was described in a Chinese party publication, once more, as an "old declining empire" which a "rising country" like China "should understand."[117] But, in the "old declining empires" themselves, these are times of many-sided evasions of unwelcome truths of every kind, whether about their own condition or about the forces at work in the wider world.

This is especially so in relation to Islam's third and potentially greatest historical upsurge. It is being carried forward with particular boldness and skill against free societies weakened by their lack of insight into what afflicts them. This is compounded by their even greater confusion about the nature of Islam. Perceived by "Islamophobes" as bringing impenetrable darkness of mind to the modern world, it is seen by its hundreds of millions of the faithful as a source of salvation and light, while the politically cowed and the nonjudgmental walk on eggshells to avoid giving offense on the subject.

With "Islam," "radical Islam," "Islamism," and even "Islamofascism" as alternative descriptors, some hold that Islam's militancies and violences are fully sanctioned by its sacred writings. Others argue that the same militancies and violences represent a perversion of an essentially pacific faith. Meanwhile, Islam's adherents already constitute around one-quarter of the world's population and are projected to outnumber Christians by 2070.[118] As Christian faith in free societies weakens, Islam's defiance of the "infidel" who invades its lands is, or ought to be, easily understood.

But Western democracies, handicapped by nonjudgmental restraints on free thought itself, cannot truly measure the strength of a transnational political and ethical movement—barbarous as are many of the acts done in its name—which believes that it is in humanity's interests to be subdued under Islam's rule. With several of old colonialism's map-drawn countries in the Levant, in Mesopotamia, and in the Maghreb ceasing to exist as states, the West has been in increasing disarray during the half century of the current Islamic advance. It is the new dialectic once more.

Low levels of leadership, especially in the United States, have compounded the non-Muslim world's problems. Or as Edmund Burke expressed it in March 1775, "a great empire"—as was Britain in the past—"and little minds go ill together."[119] Today, Western democracy's confusions, some of them understandable, have brought ambivalence, impotence, and improvisation in the face of civil wars and mutual slaughters in internecine conflicts in Muslim lands. At the same time, Trump-like attempts at deal making with Islamic interests are being made from positions of declining influence. Moreover, a combination of fear of Islam and ignorance of it, together with alternations of belligerence, "outreach," and compromise with its rising force, have increasingly disabled the West.

Revived Islam is a force which has many guises and disguises. It has created a labyrinth, made more complex by sectarian division within Islam between Sunni and Shia, which Western reason, such as it now is, has been unable to master either by diplomacy or with hell-fire missiles. Instead, as time passes, the Islamic world of some fifty-seven nations gains in confidence and strength. "Islam is advancing according to a steady plan. I have no doubt that America is on its way to destruction," cries a voice from Saudi Arabia;[120] "Europe is sick and collapsing," announces Turkey's leader;[121] and "the West is becoming much weaker," declares the Syrian dictator,[122] refusing security cooperation with it in favor of alliance with Russia and Iran. "Our power is growing each day," asserts the Iranian president in turn,[123] as memories of the historic Persian empire quicken and a nuclear-armed future beckons.

Meanwhile, from Algeria to Afghanistan, from Pakistan to the southern Philippines and Indonesia, from Syria and the Sinai to Somalia, from the mountains of Xinjiang to the eastern Mediterranean and even in Mexico and Brazil[124]—and whether Islamic State, al-Qaeda, al-Shabab, the Taliban, al-Mourabitoun, Boko Haram, Hamas, Ansar al-Sharia, or other—Islam's soldiers, secretly funded by Arab states such as Qatar and Saudi Arabia, wage their battles against local powers and intruding forces, and are joined in combat by "foreign fighters" from Western lands. And when, after some half a million deaths, the "caliphate" which had been proclaimed in Syria and Iraq in June 2014 was optimistically said to have been defeated in 2017, its surviving warriors and their networks moved on, while others remained to fight another day. There are Islamic State cells and affiliated groups now in Egypt, Libya, Tunisia, Turkey, western Europe, and elsewhere; al-Shabab has moved southward from Kenya into Tanzania and northern Mozambique; while al-Qaeda remains a "disciplined" threat in North Africa, Somalia, Yemen, and beyond[125] as messaging apps continue to recruit fighters to the cause of the international jihad.

The Muslim Brotherhood has likewise made no bones about its aspiration for "mastership of the world,"[126] its leadership declaring in 2011 that the United States "does not champion moral and human values and cannot lead humanity."[127] Indeed, as the Islamic world's disdain for the Western free society increases, doctrines of market and moral choice are decreasingly a match for the ethics of Islam and sharia, like them or not. Yet in the "battle for hearts and minds" in Iraq, the US First Cavalry Division saw fit in 2005 to set up "Operation Adam Smith" in order to teach marketing skills, among other things, to local entrepreneurs.[128] There can be no victory on that terrain.

Further disabling is the vicarious satisfaction felt by "progressives" at the West's reverses. A cavalry of Trojan horses whose number is growing, their principle—or antiprinciple—is that "my enemy's enemy is my friend," while the naiveté of those who see jihadis as a "minority of fanatics" adds to the prevailing confusion. At the same time, the West is over a barrel in its dependencies on the oil resources of Arab and Muslim countries. Together, such factors have made for divided judgment and decision. Indeed, they have so debilitated Western democracy's responses to the many-sided challenge it faces that Islam's own sectarian divisions, often murderous, have not impeded its progress.

In the fourth century BCE, between 357 and 338, the aggressive and cunning Philip II of Macedon and his army were advancing upon Athens and its allies in the comparably disordered Hellenic world. With a mixture of guile and stealth, threat and violence, the Macedonian took control of Thessaly and Illyria, invaded Thracia, and seized Athenian possessions. But he was also aided by the gullibility, wishful thinking, and mutual hostilities of those who might have fought him, and Athens fell.

Responses to Islam's revival have been similar, with alternations between warfare and the search for compromise, between advance and retreat, and with global market interests today exerting their own pressures. In this new dialectic once more, and as memories of its past triumphs reawaken in the Muslim world, there can be no comparable doubts about Islam's ambitions. "The time has come for the disappearance of the West," the speaker of the Iranian parliament asserted in July 2012,[129] while in March 2015 Iran's Ayatollah Khamenei declared the "American system" to be in a condition of "internal disintegration."[130]

In this perspective, 9/11 was a "towering day in history" to a Muslim cleric,[131] with some 3,000 deaths, similar in number to those of Pearl Harbor in December 1941, reduced to a mere nothing. "As we ascend in this new era"—a characterization beyond the grasp of most of the non-Muslim world—"we smell our victory over the West," declared a jihadi in January 2013.[132] "The black flag of jihad will fly over Downing Street" and "we will conquer Rome by Allah's permission," the voices proclaim;[133] while amid democracy's responses have been a British prime minister's "I want London to stand as one of the great capitals of Islamic finance in the world,"[134] and "I will make London a beacon of Islam," in the words of a former mayor.[135]

Islam's upsurge has been both pacific and aggressive. It is being achieved by democratic and diplomatic means as well as with the aid of roadside bombs, with vote-bank gains in free societies as well as by resort to carnage. Bewilderment shakes its head over it, the politically correct look away, and freethinkers—Muslim and non-Muslim alike—put themselves at risk, while jihadis promote their cause on the "deep web."

But the future of Islam in its third renaissance will in large part be shaped not in the Muslim world but in disordered Western free societies, whose frailties and self-harming excesses, atrophied ethics, and growing social discontents invite decline. Such decline, as Gibbon demonstrated, is a slowly unfolding, not a cataclysmic, process. But in the Western democracies the decline is under way, even if many keep silent about it and others prefer to deny that it is occurring, with weariness and depression playing their parts.

Much of the "apathy" is more seeming than real. Nevertheless, moral disengagement from democracy's social disorders, recurrent economic crises, and political frailties, together with the widespread loss of sense of identity and place, are contributing to the free society's plight. Above all, the fear that resistance to the decline might be considered "reactionary" in the old pejorative sense is misplaced. For if the civic and moral orders of democracy are to be recomposed and are to survive, there is a need to relearn, or to teach ourselves, certain principles that are fundamental to democracy itself. Those of civic consciousness, not class consciousness, are among them.

Moreover, it is truly "reactionary" in today's circumstances to be naively optimistic about the free society's fate. Such fate might be considered a small matter in the order of things. But we are the heirs of historic notions about what constitutes a "true commonwealth," notions that transcend belief in the autonomy of the individual. It is an ethical and political inheritance whose squandering is among the greatest of our self-harms.

CHAPTER 2

RICH AND POOR

The disproportionate partition of wealth between nations and within them is an historic constant. "Everywhere the rich are few and the poor are many," as Aristotle observed of his times.[1] In the "developing" world, and out of the free society's sight, hundreds of millions live in often extreme poverty, with hunger and undernourishment—said to affect "one-third of humanity"[2]—exacerbated by strife, climate change, and the rising market price of staple foods.

But with the cheap labor of Bangladesh's sweatshops providing clothes for British retailers, expensive Louis Vuitton shoes marked "Made in Italy" produced at Cisnadie in Transylvania,[3] and Ivanka Trump's fashion "brand"—until it closed down in July 2018[4]—the work of the low paid in southeast China;[5] with cobalt mined in the Congo for smartphone batteries and laptops[6] and with Kindle tablets assembled by "underpaid" and "exhausted" workers in Hunan province;[7] with indentured hirelings building skyscrapers and malls in the Gulf states, and slave-manned trawlers in Thailand supplying prawns to Western democracy's supermarkets, the demands of the global economy drown the complaints and cries of the indigent in conveniently faraway places. And while deprivations of every kind, including growing water scarcity,[8] cut their annual swath through the ranks of the distant poor—with hundreds of millions "chronically hungry"[9] and three-quarters of the world's blind children, themselves unseen, living in the poorest regions of Africa and Asia[10]—market interests turn a pretty penny on food futures and on other primary materials.

The "world food crisis" was thus said in April 2008 to have

"turned rice into gold,"[11] with advice given in democracy's press on how to "make money from increased food-prices";[12] to the historian Arnold Toynbee a "perverse impulse" which prevented humanity from cooperatively organizing effective world food production. "We have become defenseless against ourselves," he added.[13] But in similar "perversity," Western "big pharma's" property rights—with patents more important than patients—have served to impede the generic production of cheap drugs to treat HIV. Similarly, rich nations deploy their industrial trawlers in the "Third World's" seas, depleting their fish stocks and impoverishing the local communities which rely upon them. The ancient world knew this phenomenon too. "With our own seas trawled through and failing, and with gluttony raging," wrote the Roman poet Juvenal, "we scour our neighbors' waters to their depths for the market."[14]

But ancient Rome did not know the scale of contradictions in the world today. Thus, benevolence dispatches food aid far and wide to feed the hungry while one-third of food produced on the Earth for human consumption is said to be "lost or wasted" every year;[15] and at the same time corporate interest targets poor populations with its synthetic "food and drink products." Similarly in the United Kingdom, millions of tons of household food—an estimated one-fifth of what is bought—is discarded annually into landfills and other means of disposal[16] (with bread, potatoes, milk, and more than a million eggs a day leading the way[17]), and at the same time over one million food parcels are distributed each year in Britain by charitable food banks. A third of the parcels go to households with children,[18] with demand increasing in July and August when school provision ceases.

At the same time, the number of hospital beds in England taken up by patients being treated for "primary or secondary malnutrition"—attributed to "rising poverty" and "inadequate social care"—has almost tripled in the last decade,[19] with malnutrition an "underlying cause or contributory factor" in some 350 deaths in hospitals in England and Wales in 2016.[20] Meanwhile in the United States food aid is provided annually to over 40 million people, almost half of whom are under the age of eighteen.[21] even as the obese and overweight spend increasing sums on gastric bypasses and similar measures.

Self-harm in free societies comes in many forms, the deepening of inequality arguably the most disabling, and with the rich benefiting greatly more than the poor from "growth." The disproportions of it in Western democracies are reflections of those of the globe itself. The wealth of the richest forty-two individuals in the world was asserted in 2018 to be equivalent to the wealth of the planet's poorest 3.7 billion people,[22] while in Britain the richest 1,000 were estimated in 2017 to have more wealth than the poorest 40 percent of households between them,[23] a degree of inequality incompatible with democracy itself. "Money," thought Francis Bacon, "is like Mucke, not good except it be spread."[24] It is a wisdom unheeded.

Despite the scale of it, there is nothing new in phenomena of this kind nor in the destruction of a civil society at its own hand. Injustice and inequality, and the bitternesses they arouse, are constants of the human order. So, too, is greed. To some, or many, "money smells sweet wherever it comes from" and the "majesty of riches" is "the most revered of all," in Juvenal's words.[25] In John Bunyan's *The Pilgrim's Progress*, "Madam Bubble," a universal figure, is described as "wear[ing] a great purse by her side" with "her hand often in it, fingering her money as if that was her heart's delight."[26] "A bold and impudent slut," Bunyan continues, she has "given it out that she is a goddess" but has brought uncountable numbers to "Hell."

Ayn Rand, avatar of the free market, dissented. In *Atlas Shrugged*, she has one of her characters, Francisco d'Anconia, assert that "to love money is to know and love the fact that money is the creation of the best power within you."[27] To Bunyan, "the fatter the sow is, the more she desires the mire";[28] in Rand's work, money is called the "product of virtue" and the "base of a moral existence," while greed is termed "radiant."[29]

In similar spirit, London's mayor Boris Johnson in November 2013 pronounced inequality to be "essential for the spirit of envy and, like greed, a valuable spur to economic activity."[30] "But for top traders' enterprise, their ambition and, yes, their greed," declares a similar voice, "the country would be considerably worse off" ;[31] "we should not outlaw bankers' greed," cries another;[32] while opposition to inequity could be described by "one of the City's wealthiest entrepreneurs" as itself "reeking of envy."[33]

The Roman philosopher Seneca did not concur, referring with disgust to those who "throw themselves headlong into the pursuit of money and possession,"[34] while Longinus, as early as the first century CE and without the benefit of modern psychological insights, thought that the desire for riches was "a sickness which diminishes the mind."[35] Such preoccupation has also made possible conscienceless falsehoods about the sources and nature of wealth, among them the claim that America "started with an empty continent to conquer."[36]

Truth is similarly mocked by the notion that those who fall by the wayside in the welter of Madam Bubble's market are presumptively "losers" incapable of standing on their own feet. "Forty-seven per cent of Americans believe that they are victims, and that the government has a responsibility to care for them. They believe they are entitled to health-care, to food, to housing, you name it,"[37] declared Mitt Romney during the 2012 American presidential campaign, implying that personal well-being is a private matter and that public welfare— in a notional democracy—saps the individual will.

This premise is spoken out loud in Milton Friedman's *Free to Choose*, where the "winding down of social security" is recommended and "national health" is described as a "meaningless phrase."[38] "Drop it, fast," says the steelmaker Hank Rearden in *Atlas Shrugged*, interrupting a government scientist who had raised an issue with him of the public good.[39]

"I don't speak that language," declares Rearden.

"But surely questions of social welfare . . ."

"Drop it." "But what then is your chief concern?"

"The market," Rearden replies.

At the heart of recoil from the troubles of others is the moral approval that is given by market-thought to the "spur of self-interest."[40]

Or as Rand's Francisco d'Anconia puts it, "You have no duty to anyone but yourself."[41] Rand, to whom selfishness was a "virtue,"[42] goes further. In *Atlas Shrugged*, her alter ego Dagny Taggart sneers at "charity lust," the "champions of need," and the "lechers of pity."[43] The Good Samaritan is made an object of contempt.

Even the utilitarian argument that self-interest may be served by serving the interests of others has no purchase here. Demosthenes in the fourth century BCE was more intelligent, even if cynical, in suggesting that aid to the poor and the old was "advantageous to the rich," since to deprive anyone of the necessities of life by public decision served only to "make many enemies of the state."[44] "My own good was my purpose," Rand has her Rearden instead declare, baring a truth of which Bunyan's Madam Bubble would have approved.[45] "If I was asked to serve the interests of society apart from, above and against my own, I would refuse. . . . The public good be damned." It is a dismissiveness which mocks democracy itself but has been made easier by socialist failure.

To hold Rand's now-commonplace views "extreme," or to attribute them to an author's imaginative skills, are evasions. "I have always lived by the philosophy I present in my books, and it has worked for me as it works for my characters," she wrote in a 1957 postface to *Atlas Shrugged*.[46] "I trust that no one will tell me that men such as I write about don't exist," she added. Indeed, the "philosophy" Rand shared with her characters has increasingly made battlefields of public provision—the assaults upon it by the Trump administration were nothing new—with welfare cuts driving the poor into greater poverty, even as economic, educational, housing, health, and other inequalities in rich free societies deepen and as need increases. In the United States, over 40 million people are estimated year upon year to be living in poverty;[47] the life expectancy of the wealthiest, with American provision for healthcare in growing disorder, exceeds that of the poorest by "ten to fifteen years";[48] and in Britain, too, the differential in life expectancy between rich and poor is increasing.[49]

Meanwhile, globalization and automation have destroyed millions of manufacturing jobs in Western democracies, its domino effect forcing many skilled workers into lower-paid or part-time employment, if they can find employment at all. Under such pressures, there have come internal migration and depopulation, and a growing divide between poor and prosperous areas. In microcosm, it brought civic bankruptcy to Detroit in July 2013, its auto industry in collapse, with thousands of vacant, abandoned, and derelict buildings needing to be cleared by the city's "blight task force."[50] Other "postindustrial centers" from which the global economic tide has retreated have suffered in similar fashion.

But even in many areas of prosperous Western metropolises, living standards have fallen. For "growth" has brought great benefit to some—and "gentrification" of once run-down areas—but economic insecurity and job obsolescence to others. It is not only in the "developing" world that the noses of the poor are pressed to the window glass behind which the cornucopias of market plenty stand. Among the submerged in free societies are also the millions in debt in a "borrowing culture," the armies of young jobless, and in Britain and the United States the millions of children living in poverty.[51] Even paupers' funerals are on the increase in Britain.[52]

Solon, the ancient Greek lawgiver, tried to put a gloss on such things; there is as long a history of the avoidance of truth as the telling of it: "Many of the rich are very unhappy, many of the poor are lucky to be so," he pretended.[53] Old people surviving in poverty on the free society's small state benefits, and even without enough food,[54] might not agree; nor the millions in Britain said to be living in inadequate housing conditions, and unable properly to heat their homes.[55]

Among the ranks of the most impoverished in prosperous free societies there are not only permanent or semipermanent dependents on welfare, Ayn Rand's "moochers." There are also the working poor or "cheap labor," often doing "the world's most needful work"[56] in low-paid or part-time jobs, engulfed by rising prices and rents, and reliant on housing benefits despite being in work; 60 percent of the British in poverty, and 58 percent of the London poor, were estimated in June 2016 to live in households where someone was in work.[57] Indeed, some of the largest corporate employers pay their workforces, with migrants the most exploited, the minimum wage or close to it—"the living wage would destroy jobs," a voice declares[58]—while "zero-hours contracts," which give no guarantee of regular work or stable income and which provide no benefits of employment, are spreading far and wide. There have been estimated to be perhaps a million people in Britain employed on such terms.[59]

At the same time, many of the rich grow richer, their assets of all kinds accumulating. In the United States, the gap between the richest 1 percent and the rest is the widest since the 1920s[60] and widening, with the average incomes of the lowest quintile one-tenth or less of the average incomes of the highest quintile.[61] In some New York condos today, there are even side entrances or "poor doors" for rent-regulated tenants, while higher "market-rate" residents, living in the same building, pass through the front entrance. In addition, the wealthiest in the United States have been found to be giving a smaller share than in previous years to charity, and the poor and middle-income earners a larger,[62] even as the income gap increases.

With "potent men breaking through the Cob-web Lawes of their Country," as Thomas Hobbes put it,[63] tax evasion has also become more widespread and complex. "What use are laws where money rules?" the Roman satirist Petronius asked.[64] In today's free societies, it has led to "trillions of dollars"[65] being hidden away by US corporate giants and others in "black-hole" tax havens, as the worlds of the rich and the poor in ostensible democracies become more distant.

Now a "top soccer star" in Britain can earn more in a few days for kicking a ball than a nurse earns in decades for the care of the sick; in May 2018, a player joined Manchester United for a weekly remuneration of almost €400,000 and another was "bought" by Italy's Juventus for over €100 million.[66] Again, CEOs of Britain's one hundred major companies were reported to have earned €3.9 million on average in 2017; a full-time worker on a median salary in Britain would have to work 167 years to earn an equivalent sum.[67] Or, put another way, the average FTSE chief executive "earns more in three days than the average full-time British worker earns in a year."[68] Similarly, the median annual "pay package" in 2017 of the heads of America's five hundred major companies was over $11 million[69]—salaries in the healthcare "industry" can reach $100 million[70]—with "typical CEOs" making over one hundred and sixty times the median pay of their own employees.[71]

The scale of all this is new, even if in 1909 Charles Masterman was already complaining that "money power" was "more and more concentrated in the hands of enormous corporations."[72] But today's stellar salaries, stock options, and bonuses reward the United States' leading corporate executives and hedge fund managers with multiple millions of dollars a year, the net worth of Facebook's founder said to rise at "$4 billion a day,"[73] Yahoo's CEO receiving $127 million in severance pay and stock awards on his departure,[74] and Amazon's founder and chief executive said to have a $100 billion fortune.[75] Likewise, some $25 billion in bonuses can be shared annually by the employees of Wall Street banks,[76] while in Britain executive salaries, pension contributions, retention payments, incentive payments, bonuses—sometimes paid despite company losses and failures—and golden handshakes fulfill Rand's ideal, represent Madam Bubble's triumph, and hasten democracy's fall.

For at the free society's ground level is another world. It is one in which "food poverty" increases and, as earlier mentioned, millions in the United States depend on food stamps for their rations; where over 12 billion pounds' worth of clothes are allegedly thrown away each year in Britain;[77] where a London pediatrician could say in 2017 that he was "seeing kids with rickets on a fairly regular basis";[78] a world in which 12 million in Britain were said to be "too poor to take part in all the basic social activities" that concerned them,[79] and with almost 700,000 households unable to "afford to eat properly, keep clean, or stay warm and dry."[80] It is also a world, again that of a notional or theoretical democracy, in which poor children are increasingly handicapped before they arrive in the classroom. It is a handicap that accompanies many into a life of social dysfunction in disabled communities hard to escape, and now even harder to redeem.

Meanwhile, the populations concentrated in democracy's conurbations rise, and housing shortages, housing costs and the numbers of over-crowded homes grow. So do the numbers of tenant evictions, with over 40,000 households evicted from rented accommodation in England and Wales in a single year,[81] despite "discretionary payments" of tens of millions of pounds annually by local authorities to help the cash-strapped pay their housing costs. At the same time, millions of young adults in employment cannot acquire a home of their own and are driven to live with their parents or to leave the metropolis behind them.

Likewise, a diminishing number of families can afford a mortgage on the earnings of a single breadwinner, with homeownership in Britain at its lowest in decades.[82] Simultaneously, second-home ownership by the prosperous is increasing; in Britain, over five million people own second homes, but 40 percent own no property at all;[83] and tens of thousands of the "working homeless," a total that has almost doubled since 2013, live in "temporary accommodation."[84] Moreover, gamblers in real estate make ever-larger profits on their properties, while police, teachers, nurses, and others can no longer afford to live in the communities they serve.

At the same time, as families in the free society fragment and personal relationships become more unstable, the numbers of single people seeking accommodation rise, a problem compounded by the increasing numbers of migrants who require to be housed. Yet in the name of the "right to buy," and in private ownership's cause, much of the stock of social housing in Britain—once in the community's hands—has been sold off at a relatively cheap price but at always higher cost. The true commonwealth is not this, and a democracy cannot survive it.

Above all, it is homelessness that challenges the very concept of a civil society; a civil society cannot be called so unless its members find adequate shelter in it, and a citizen without a home is a contradiction in terms. But while "the market" talks up "house values" and competition becomes more intense among the prosperous for the most desirable places to lay their heads, homelessness in the free society, as in Britain,[85] is rising. In the United States, with budget cuts to homeless assistance proposed by President Trump but rejected,[86] over half a million are homeless, with more than 120,000 under-18s among them.[87] The young, the derelict old, families broken or whole, poor migrants, and even veterans of the armed forces—some 40,000 were said to be homeless in 2017[88]—are driven to seek refuge in emergency shelters, which are full to capacity in the cold, or in increasing numbers they sleep rough in parks, underpasses, subway carriages, vacant lots, sheds, and on the pavement. "Many older homeless people," reported the US Department of Housing in 2016, "have been on the streets for almost a generation,"[89] while in Britain there have been over three hundred deaths of the homeless in the street or in temporary shelters since 2013, their average age forty-three.[90]

With 60,000 "in and out of shelters" in New York City,[91] young children among them, and 168,000 homeless in California, Oregon, and Washington State—including over 17,000 "chronically homeless" in Los Angeles[92]—private charity and public provision do what they can, as in the setting up of storage centers on skid rows where those without homes can keep their belongings;[93] a "special cart" equipped with "handbrakes, shelving and locks" was designed in 2018 at the University of British Columbia for the use of the Canadian homeless.[94] But others see only blight and harm in the presence among them of the destitute, if they see them at all, with growing complaint about "petty crime, public defecation, and people sleeping on sidewalks."[95]

In downtown US cities, often where "gentrification" is in progress, increasing numbers of local laws ban living in vehicles, forbid begging, make it a crime to sit on the sidewalk, and restrict or prohibit the charitable feeding of the poor in public places, finding the Good Samaritan and the beggar guilty together. Among the arguments against such charity is that feeding places become "magnets for the homeless,"[96] or that the presence of the poor harms local property values. Thus, the city council in Oxford threatened rough sleepers with fines of up to £2500 for having a "detrimental effect" on the quality of life of those living nearby,[97] while over fifty local authorities in Britain have issued "Public Space Protection Orders" which ban the homeless from town centers.[98]

The "hand-built structures" of the homeless in rich Silicon Valley are likewise torn down by police; homeless camps in downtown Cincinnati are "sanitized" and "cleaned out";[99] and rough sleepers on the streets of Tucson, Arizona, are restricted to three items of personal possession each on the sidewalk,[100] or they have their belongings— including tents, stoves, medication, and documents—seized. Other sanctions have included the placing of "anti-homeless spikes" in a store entrance in London's Regent Street, metal cages put over public benches in a southern French city, and water jets installed above each of the doorways of San Francisco's main cathedral to deter rough-sleepers.[101] There have also been arson attacks on encampments and individuals in Berlin, San Diego, and Seattle,[102] and a San Antonio police officer was dismissed from the force for giving a homeless man a sandwich filled with feces.[103]

At the same time, in that other world of the property market where Bunyan's Madam Bubble rules, housing shortages, soaring house prices, and excessive mortgage lending—with low "teaser" interest rates and no down payments—were to threaten the global financial system itself. On overvalued property, mountains of high-risk (or "sub-prime") mortgage debt, unrepayably "toxic," were "packaged up" and sold on as bonds and securities to investment trusts, pension funds, and other financial institutions.

A ramshackle edifice, it was to bring down banks, property values, and aspiring homeowners in its fall, leaving "shattered lives and livelihoods around the world," as a US attorney general was to describe it.[104] But the investment bankers themselves, free of regulation in a free market, made stellar profits by betting on the market's collapse, a hunger for gain which inflicted further harm on the self-destroying social order as a whole, and for which Goldman Sachs, Morgan Chase, Citigroup, Barclays, and Bank of America had to pay billions in penalties for the losses that had been caused.[105] But it did not prevent their subsequent access to President Trump's White House and to positions of continuing power.

Civil society in the Western democracies has been further harmed as inequalities between city and country increase. With many small farmers, especially dairy farmers and fruit growers, crushed by the agribusiness and supermarket worlds, and by the low prices they pay, three-quarters of the "economically distressed" areas of the United States are said to be rural,[106] and farmers in the United States take their own lives at a higher rate than any other occupation.[107] Meanwhile, the prosperous seek "places in the country," romanticizing the rural and the summer resort, and purchasing their second homes where locals cannot find or afford a first one.

The needs of dissolving rural communities also have ever-lower priority in public-policy decision; President Trump's declaration in January 2018, mere rhetoric as it may have been, that "farm country is God's country"[108] was a politically rare one. More typical was the assertion even by a US agriculture secretary in December 2012 that "rural America, with a shrinking population, is becoming less and less relevant to the politics of this country,"[109] despite the disproportionate electoral strength it retains in the US voting system. Indeed, it has been estimated that by 2030 two-thirds of the world's population will be living in cities.[110]

Far beyond the metropolis, village schools, libraries, loss-making post offices—held to be no longer commercially viable as "outlets"—and police stations close, with public service seen as a business like any other. Subsidy of rural public transport is reduced or ceases, further isolating the aged and car-less, and access to healthcare shrinks. Even gas stations disappear. And so the permanent population declines further and village shops, already squeezed by supermarkets, close in turn, with life expectancy itself reported to be falling in isolated areas in Britain.[111] "There used to be butchers, fishmongers, bakers, grocers but they have all gone," a lost voice declares.[112] Thus community dies, and local democracy also.

For rural communities are microcosms of the polity as a whole, each a component of the larger body. But such microcosms in Western free societies are now subordinate to market interest. It is a galvanizing and self-harming power, engine of production and innovation, and promoter of gross inequity and injustice. Moreover, in the cost-benefit analyses made by market-thought, much that a civil society—and especially a democracy—require for its well-being and survival has little or no worth at all, being unquantifiable in cash terms.

After visiting America in the 1830s, Alexis de Tocqueville did not think that "democracy in future would retreat before capitalists," as he optimistically put it.[113] He was to be proved wrong, with the failure of socialism leaving the way wider open to the engulfing tide of "market forces." "I see no danger," says Simple in *The Pilgrim's Progress.* "Yet a little more sleep," says Sloth.[114]

CHAPTER 3

SOCIALISM'S DEFEAT

There was an abyssal silence in the streets of Bucharest. It was November 1987 in Nicolae Ceausescu's Romania, with not even *Pravda* on sale. "Sometimes we hear of a strike or a demonstration, or of some poor worker trying to do something on his own and being liquidated. There is no real information, only rumors. Everyone is isolated," said the dissident intellectual who was to become minister of culture when the regime fell in December 1989.[1] "Even Marx would have ended up under interrogation in Czechoslovakia if he had opened his mouth in public," I was told in Prague in February 1987, when the country was still "building an advanced socialist society based on the principles of class-consciousness, socialist patriotism and proletarian internationalism."[2]

"What is socialism?" I inquired of a down-at-heel Bulgarian, Zhelyu Zhelev, who had been banished to the provinces for his anti-regime writing. It was April 1989, sixteen months before he became the nation's president. "I do not know," he answered.[3] "What do you have here?" I asked him. "A police-dominated system of bureaucratic human domination which is called 'socialist.'" "By whom?" I asked. "By its own agit-prop department," he replied.

In Bucharest, dissenters fearful of surveillance—including by family members—spoke of an "atomistic society where social morality has been forgotten"; in Prague, of a "political fake" where "to get by without trouble you have to be both stupid and silent"; in Budapest, of a system that had "destroyed the notion of a citizen."[4] "To you," said Gaspar Tamas, a former philosophy teacher at Budapest University sacked in 1982 for "oppositional activity," "it is theory. To us it is practice. We have been through this damned thing of socialism. We don't share the Western left's illusions."[5] "People feign outward loyalty to the system while inwardly ceasing to believe in anything," the future Czech president Vaclav Havel told me in February 1988.[6]

The collapse of state-socialist dictatorships in economic and political ruin exacted its price in Western democracies too. Despite the fact that free-market societies were themselves floundering in crises once dear to the old left's diagnoses, it made the word *socialist* a term of reproach and taboo for many. It was even argued in September 1996 by a "left-wing" British Labour MP and former student radical that the word *socialism* should be "humanely phased out."[7]

Alternatively, having become an electoral liability, the term was redefined to near-meaninglessness. "My kind of socialism is a set of values based around notions of social justice," declared Tony Blair, also in 1996,[8] his nonsocialism a winning formula in successive elections. "We have everything to gain for our people," he told the Trades Union Congress,[9] as other notionally left parties in Western democracies "rebranded" to avoid the socialist stigma. "We are intensely relaxed about people getting filthy rich," a British Labour government trade and industry secretary declared in 2008.[10]

Against such backsliding there have been varieties of left response. For example, the post-Blairite Labour leader Jeremy Corbyn complained in December 2016 in Prague (of all places) that the "message of what socialism is" had been "diluted."[11] But by then the party was itself confused and divided over the doctrinally unpalatable choice between membership of a supranational "common market" and the reclaiming of sovereign powers for the country; a choice between the capitalist devil and the deep blue nationalist sea. Instead, under the influence of metropolitan entrants into the party, it made a bid for the motley youth and student vote in times when class is decreasingly a determinant of political choice. Indeed, with traditional working-class organizations having lost membership and purchase in Britain as in the United States—less than a quarter of the workforce is unionized in the former[12] and less than 11 percent in the latter[13]—"labor movements" have become shadows of their former selves, while the old history of socialism in Britain is at an end.

Instead, to be on the "left" is to be a protester for this and that serviceable cause or interest, and to be opposed to this or that serviceable foe. France's defeated Socialist Party primary candidate in the 2017 presidential election not only offered the politics of the 32-hour week and a universal monthly basic income but the legalization of marijuana; while in the United States the self-described "democratic socialist" Bernie Sanders, promising a "political revolution,"[14] called for "no more wars,"[15] a "moral economy,"[16] and "respect" for "people's choices to love whomever they choose."[17] Defeated in his contest with Hillary Clinton after spending $270 million on his socialist campaign,[18] he asserted that "the struggle continues,"[19] with the Democratic Socialists of America pledged among other things to "empower ordinary people," to "restructure gender and cultural relationships," and to establish "popular control of the resources of production," its slogans including, "No Borders, No Nations."[20]

But despite such surviving idealism—and despite increasing inequality and declining social mobility in Western democracies—state-socialist failure has made it possible, across much of the political spectrum in our new "postideological" times, to assert that the common good is synonymous with the good of the market, while market-thought alone is given the imprimatur of Reason. Moreover, the dream of sharing the market's cornucopia also turned out, after the Fall of the Berlin Wall, to have been the dream of many (or most) of those who experienced, and suffered under, the rigors and privations of communist rule.

In the event, the passage from communism to consumerism—or from Marx to the market—not only brought political and economic liberty to the citizenries of the fallen regimes but also predations by corrupt private interests upon the former public domain and its assets. This has been the case even where, as in China and Vietnam, communist party rule has continued. In the former, the unleashing of market forces—translated by the Chinese president into the "developing of the forces essential to socialism" and the "adaptation of Marx to the Chinese context"[21]—saw corruption flourish, with death sentences for leading malefactors and tens of thousands of party officials punished for violating the Chinese Communist Party's "frugality code."[22] In the latter, as the general secretary of the Vietnamese party explained, "a country without discipline would be chaotic and unstable."[23]

But whatever such "discipline," throughout the former state-socialist world there have come the deepening of inequality and the visiting of old harms upon the poorest; and where the "bourgeoisie" had once been "expropriated" in socialism's name, new business oligarchs seized hold of public goods. In this upheaval, a woman blogger in Vietnam could be sentenced to ten years in jail for "defaming the Communist regime,"[24] and human rights activists imprisoned for advocating a multiparty democratic system,[25] while golf courses, devouring local rice fields, were being created for the elite in rural areas of the country. The transformation also brought a Rolls-Royce showroom to Cambodia's capital Phnom Penh, a McDonald's to Saigon (from which the Americans had fled in April 1975), and a combination of homelessness[26] and Starbucks to Hanoi, with the Vietnamese prime minister's son-in-law gaining the franchise. Similarly, the house in Shanghai in which the young Mao Tse-tung had lived became part of a luxury mall of fashion boutiques, and one of the mall's attractions.

Quick to appear in postcommunist countries, most notably in Russia, were also the flaunting of new fortunes, rising rates of alcoholism and drug use—the grandson of Albania's former communist dictator, Enver Hoxha, found himself on trial in Tirana for cocaine trafficking to Western countries[27]—and increasing familial breakdown. It was a recognizable pattern. With a third and more of Russia's newfound wealth reported by 2013 to be in the hands of some one hundred individuals,[28] and with President Putin's circle discovered to have hundreds of millions of dollars in offshore tax havens,[29] there also came a large "underclass"—similar to that in Western democracies—of over 20 million people, around 14 percent of the population, living below the official poverty line in a daily struggle to get by on less than $180 per month.[30]

However, the barons of the New Order in Russia have prospered, with Western capital making hay with ex-communism's cheap and abundant labor in globalizing freedom's name. At the same time, in a country divided, statues of Lenin still abound and one-third of a sample poll in 2017 chose Stalin as "the most outstanding person in history."[31] Yet the Kremlin itself was absent from the centenary celebrations of the Russian Revolution,[32] while thousands marched in Ekaterinburg to commemorate Tsar Nicholas the Second, who was executed with his family in 1918 after the Bolsheviks seized power.[33]

The Fall of the Wall was the outcome of domestic revolt against the extremes of socialist illusion. But, as mentioned, it also struck hard blows at the old Western left's "socialist project." Many, or most, of those for whom the "free play of market forces" is no better than the law of the jungle had this "project" in mind, even if they differed about the means by which it might be attained. Under it, the capitalist system would be superseded or overthrown, "wage slavery" would be abolished, and an egalitarian order—harmonious and fair—would be established. In more modest versions of the same general aspiration, welfare cuts would be reversed, taxes on the rich increased, and public ownership restored.

Although such aspirations remain, the "class struggle" has been largely overtaken in Western democracies by the struggle to gain access to, and to consume, the market's "products" and "brands." Moreover, the contribution of manufacturing to democracy's national economies has shrunk, and attempts to limit the right to strike have spread. In the United States, employers can prohibit their employees from taking collective action on their pay and conditions,[34] while in Britain in 2017 the smallest number of workers was involved in strikes since records began in 1891.[35] Mrs. Thatcher was also able to cancel May Day, and even a Labour government felt no need to restore it. Meanwhile, unease over the deteriorating condition of the Western democratic social order has grown, even as the free-marketeer continues to pose as the holder of the keys to the true Utopia.

In this void of representation, the way has opened for the maverick newcomer to speak to fears and angers which in the last decades have been increasingly ignored in government policy and decision. Marchers, squatters, and "occupiers" of public spaces have protested and even rioted against social and economic injustices of many kinds but have largely gone unheard. They have objected to privatizations of state assets, foreclosures, job losses, low wages, zero-hours contracts, labor-law reforms, and austerity measures which have struck hardest at those who can least afford them. But in the shadow of socialist failure—"we have been through this damned thing of socialism"— such protests have had little impact. At the same time, the political, economic, and cultural issues raised by the large-scale migration of incomers to free societies have provoked those negatively affected by it but their unease has generally been dismissed as merely xenophobic.

Into the vacuum, varieties of "populism" have unsurprisingly stepped. Some are potent and perilous, others ephemeral and lightweight. With the French socialist movement in near collapse, the thirty-nine-year-old Emmanuel Macron, a former banker and economy minister seen as "power-hungry and inexperienced,"[36] created a "nonparty" "centrist" movement *ex novo*—called République En Marche—"broke down the right-left wall"[37] created by "dying old parties,"[38] and urged his rivals to defect. Recruiting half his candidates from "civil society" rather than from the political world, within months in May 2017 he became French president with 20 million votes, 60 percent of the seats in the French Assembly, and with the "left," among others, worsted. In September 2017, the routed Parti Socialiste put its Parisian Left Bank headquarters up for sale.[39]

Similarly the Italian Five-Star Movement, founded in 2009 by a comedian and operating in a political space created by socialism's failures—and with the Italian left a waning force—aspired to create a grassroots "civic movement" composed of those who had abandoned their political allegiances, "left," "right," and "center." Offering a fluctuating bill of fare "neither of the right nor of the left,"[40] its maverick policies included a "citizen-wage" for those in difficulty, raising the pensions of the poor and reducing the pensions of the rich, the cancelation of "useless" infrastructure projects, tax reductions for small businesses, and even the "abolition of trade unions."[41] "There is no further need for them," the comedian had argued,[42] before retiring from the leadership of a party which in March 2018 gained over 10 million votes in Italy's general election, with the left ousted from rule and only half of the members of Italy's largest trade union confederation voting for candidates of the left.[43]

Although *populism* is an empty word, and begs questions about its content and true purpose, in one respect it is just. It points to the intensifying competition in a postsocialist world to speak for "the people," a many-headed hydra which old socialists divided into classes. Now, with class no longer an organizing principle on the left, Labour's Corbyn also argued that his party was "founded to stand up for people"[44] and, again, that it was the party's "historic duty to make sure that the people prevail."[45] Similarly, from the right, France's defeated Front National presidential candidate declared herself to be "the candidate for the people";[46] while in his campaign for the US presidency, Donald Trump also appropriated some of the ground which the old left once considered its own.

Claiming to have created a "great movement,"[47] as once the labor movement was, he pilloried the "conspiracy against you, the American people."[48] Asserting that they had been betrayed by "special interests"[49]—before appointing Exxon Mobil's president as Secretary of State, placing an ex–Goldman Sachs partner at the Treasury, a fast-food executive at the Department of Labor, and a venture capitalist at Commerce while moving to curb welfare spending and to reduce the taxes of businesses and high earners—Trump pledged to "return power" to the "forgotten men and women of our country."[50] They would "never be ignored again."[51] But the appropriation of the old left's constituency by the victorious Trump and his advisers—before some were driven from the White House by internal faction-fighting—went further. He thus pledged to make the Republican Party the "party of the American worker,"[52] and in the name of "putting the American worker first"[53] imposed heavy protectionist tariffs on foreign goods, while his working-class supporters were derisively described by some as the "trumpen-proletariat."[54]

In France, the Front National's Marine Le Pen likewise urged the diminished left to vote for her against the world of "global finance" and the "reign of money,"[55] but (unlike Trump) offered worker control of companies, limited working hours, and wealth taxes. Again, on becoming prime minister in July 2016, Tory Theresa May promised to "fight against" the "burning social injustices of poverty, educational inequality and discrimination."[56] She also declared at the World Economic Forum in Davos that "many feel left behind by capitalism,"[57] and undertook in June 2017 not only to "enhance workers' rights and protections" but to be "guided by what matters to the ordinary working families of this nation,"[58] or those "working around the clock."[59] In October 2016, she had further described the Conservative Party as a "party for the public good," committed to ensuring that "markets serve ordinary working people."[60]

But despite these sub-socialist gestures, market-driven thought and policy, legitimated for many by the failure of the fallen "classless" societies, command the field; a Mrs. May, for all her invocation of "workers' rights," is no match for Madam Bubble, who has been too long at her market stall to be dislodged by rhetoric alone. Even the commonplace ways in which market-thought and policy are expressed are nothing new. In a discussion about how a Sunday school in the fictional city of Zenith could attract more support, Sinclair Lewis in his satirical novel *Babbitt*—published in 1922, now almost a century ago—has Babbitt, a realtor, declare that "if you analyse the needs of the school, going right at it as if it were a merchandising problem, of course the one basic fundamental need is growth."[61] To achieve this, Babbitt recommends "real he-hustling, getting out and drumming up customers—or members, I mean."

For her part Ayn Rand, who left her native Soviet Union for

America in 1926, challenged the absolutism of state-socialism with the equal absolutism of the free market. In *Atlas Shrugged*, even a composer of symphonic music exclaims "Emotions be damned! When I find a customer"—that word again—"my performance is a mutual trade. An artist is a trader."[62] And today, similarly, firearms enthusiasts are termed "consumers" of ammunition,[63] a concert pianist's hands are "worth more than $15 million,"[64] winning an Olympic gold medal is said to have a "potential value of £600,000,"[65] newspapers are called "print products,"[66] "gender fluidity" is seen as a "marketing opportunity,"[67] cannabis "promises high returns for investors,"[68] and the detention of immigrant children is described as a "billion-dollar industry."[69] Similarly, market interest calculated (even in a "left-wing" newspaper) that the wedding of Prince Harry and Meghan Markle "could give an £80 million lift to Britain's economy," or asserted that the "magic of Meghan" had "widespread selling-power."[70]

With the building of the "advanced socialist society" buried in the ruins of communism's party-led regimes, and with Cuba, North Korea, and Venezuela not inviting emulation, innocent socialist ideals—the ideals of mutuality, equity, and cooperation—have also suffered. Indeed, even modest attempts at economic regulation and social intervention can now be decried as "socialist," and some (or many) agree with Milton Friedman that a welfare state "threatens our freedoms."[71] Moreover, the marketization of perception and even of language knows no boundary of party, and is no longer a Babbitt satire.

In an Oxford lecture in December 1999, a British Labour prime minister could therefore describe "entrepreneurial universities" in the "knowledge economy" as "wealth-creators in their own right, in the value they add through teaching and research."[72] The civil service "should be run like a business," says a second;[73] "we must shop our way out of crisis," declares a third;[74] deportations of illegal migrants from the United States "would be bad news for the housing market,"[75] argues a fourth; while the French president reassured the world after bomb attacks in March 2016 that it was "safe to invest in France."[76] Even sperm can be considered a "valuable asset."[77]

In the face of such mind-set, to boost public spending or to increase the minimum wage raises the specter of a discredited ideology that would be "anti-business" and hostile to "wealth creation," rather than a possible means of rescuing the disintegrating free society from itself. Instead, "value for money" reigns in Britain as a criterion, even the only criterion, of the worth of public institutions, from the BBC and the prison system to the British royal household. Or as the Keeper of the Privy Purse declared in 2005 on the publication of the royal finances, "we believe this represents a value-for-money monarchy."[78] "More than ever the Royal Family is worth every penny," said a similar voice in July 2011.[79]

Thus, despite the cyclical failure of the market's nostrums—and whatever the rhetoric of aspirant politicians—even modest measures of redistributive justice can suggest to free-market absolutists that "Marxism" is alive and well. Likewise, despite the passing attempts to revive its passions, the discrediting of socialism has made the placing of limits upon the exercise of economic self-will appear to many to be against the natural order of things, whatever sympathy may be expressed for "ordinary working people."

Moreover, state-socialism's failures have served those who see "public ownership" as uncompetitive, retrograde, and inefficient. In the last decades it has paved the way for the large-scale privatization of public goods. Calls to "open up" this and "free up" that, including institutions which were the tax-funded property of the citizen body as a whole, have therefore had an emancipatory ring. "Progress" has been identified with the expansion of market values into hitherto un-marketized areas of public life, while objections to such "freeing up" are seen as the mark of Reaction, and re-nationalization as threatening a return to the world of Stalin.

Forgotten is the Winston Churchill who argued in 1906—a decade before the Russian Revolution sealed the fate of such views—that "for some purposes" it was necessary to be "collectivist." "Collectively," he wrote, "we have an Army, a Navy, a Civil Service; collectively we have a Post Office, a police and Government; collectively we light our streets and supply ourselves with water. . . . The ever-growing complications of civilization create for us new services which have to be undertaken by the state," he added, declaring that there was "a growing feeling, which I entirely share, against allowing those services to pass into private hands."[80]

But in these postsocialist times, the trade unions themselves have had little choice but to surrender to the dismantling of large areas of the public sector, even as the social order unravels. It has been no contest between "multiple public-service providers" in a "competitive market" and the haunting memory of socialist dirigisme under single-party rule. This has helped make possible the fatal breaking up and dispersal of many public institutions of the state and civil society, accelerating the latter's dissolution.

There have thus been asset sales of national and local government "real estate"—and even of army barracks, naval sites, and airfields[81]— some of it mere spoliation by corporate interests based in extraterritorial tax havens. Cato, the stern Roman, could be said to have anticipated the essence of it. While thieves of private goods run the risk of imprisonment, he wrote in the second century BCE, "thieves of public goods live in gold and purple."[82] Today, private interest's profits from the "contracting out" to them of public property and (often) of essential public services have in addition been guaranteed by government, but without adequate democratic debate and local consultation.

With privately funded schools and hospitals in Britain often proving more costly to run than when they were in the hands of the state,[83] taxpayer subsidies paid to private interests in command of what was formerly in the public domain are generally larger than they were under nationalization, even as prices to the citizen increase. High rents and other charges will also be owed for decades to come in Britain for the use of buildings and services which were once the property of the public. Some terms of the deals between government and private interest—for example, guarantees of the latter's profits—have even been concealed from view, with off-balance-sheet accounting hiding the extent of the obligations incurred by the state, while a major private supplier of public services, accused of a "reckless pursuit of growth," collapsed in January 2018 in a "sea of debt"[84] and with pension liabilities to its workforce which it could not meet.

These large-scale schemes of private investment in public goods, launched in theoretically democratic societies with the postsocialist finger of blame pointed at the "overgoverned society," have been devices of market-thought. They were introduced in the name of efficiency savings and reduced public subventions, and out of a proclaimed need for a "smaller state," less bureaucracy, and wider "choice." Only some of these benefits have materialized, and at disproportionate cost.

There is a vicious circle in it. For private interest's rights have been established over once-public utilities which met the citizen's basic needs for heat, light, water, and much else, at the same time as citizen identity has waned in the free society from other causes. Under such conditions, it has been even less in the public interest for private interest—promoted by lobbyists, including former public servants and out-of-office politicians—to swallow so much of the public domain. But it has served the interests of democracy least of all. For the primary loyalty of "private enterprise" is not to the polity but to shareholders. Yet it is the taxpayer who has borne the costs of the subsidies paid to the new owners and leaseholders of public goods, as well as the costs of privatization's failures.

Now private contractors collect taxes, operate key areas of the social-security system, manage and mismanage confidential citizen databases, gather military intelligence, and conduct army recruitment; "it is a competitive market out there," declared a spokesman for the British Ministry of Defence as recruiting was "outsourced."[85] They also train secret services, supply interrogators, patrol borders, control air traffic, make deliveries to the NASA space station, protect military installations, preside over (and even own) prisons, run immigrant detention facilities and deport illegal migrants, all for profit. In Western free-market societies, large numbers of consultants and managers, most placed in post by private interest whether open or concealed, are also installed at the policy-making heart of central government. Here they are largely immune from public accountability and, once more, from democratic oversight.

In education, private trusts linked to business interests and with access to government advisers have taken over failing state schools in Britain and set up new "academies." At a cost of £745 million to the taxpayer for the conversion of some 7,000 such schools,[86] these takeovers were carried out in the names of greater parental choice, independence from local authority, higher standards, freedom from bureaucratic imposition, and the need for market competition. For education, too, has been described by a Milton Friedman as a "vast market," and a state-run education system disparaged as an "island of socialism in a free market sea."[87]

But the "contracting-out" of public education to private interest—in which school buildings, financed by private capital, are leased back to the state and high sums charged to the latter for their maintenance—has driven some schools in Britain to economize even on staff numbers in order to meet its costs. Moreover, in the case of "academies" subsequently closed down for failing performance,[88] declining numbers, and even structural building flaws, local authorities must discharge the debts to private interests which they have incurred, and again use public funds to do so.

Health provision has likewise been "freed-up." It is again a freedom of a particular kind. Contractual service agreements, some with thirty- to sixty-year terms, have been struck in Britain between public authority and international corporate investors, with (for example) two billion pounds' worth of National Health Service contracts in England awarded to Richard Branson's Virgin Care, including in district nursing, prison dentistry, and children's health provision.[89] Whether for new hospital construction or for "delivery" of medical care, with private agencies "supplying" hospitals with doctors and nurses, health is now a "product" in a new "market environment." "Productivity" in patient care is measured, and there is a "choice agenda" for patients.

With these agreements have again come crippling repayment obligations, to the point of bankrupting some health authorities. There have also been overcharging by corporate providers, intensified lobbying and corruption of hospital bureaucrats by drug firms, raised running costs, mismanagement, and bailouts by the taxpayer. Moreover, it has brought control by private interest over local health decision and administration, once more weakening the community's participation in its own affairs.

License for such "public-private partnerships" in which private hands grasp hold of public provision at the taxpayer's expense has been easily gained, such was the discredit of "this damned thing of socialism." Yet rule by corporate money power and market-thought over Western democracy's dissolving social orders has many things in common with the rule of party apparatuses and of their dogmas in the failed "socialist republics." But in the free society there is no need for Five-Year Plans or single-party rule. The command over a market economy by corporate interest is enough. Increasingly reshaped to its prescriptions, the free society has become a command economy in all but name, over which the citizen body has little or no control. Whatever term be used for such polity, "democracy" is not among them.

Market dogmas, like communist dogmas, also distort everyday judgment. It can thus be asserted that "nowhere is the gap between rich and poor wider than in those societies that do not permit the free market to operate,"[90] or that "the market is the surest guarantor of social justice."[91] In the state-socialist utopias, party apparatchiks spoke in this way too; in the free society there is a different set of shibboleths, but they are equally self-harming.

In Britain, they permitted a formerly national railway system—a public property of routes, tracks, and stations—to be broken up and offered to "private enterprise" as separate commodities for franchise, lease, or sale, with three-quarters of Britain's railway companies ending in foreign hands.[92] Although carried out notionally for the common good, the breakup was followed by managerial, financial, service, and safety failures, with government even driven to "temporary re-nationalization" of the London-to-Edinburgh rail service when its private provider failed.[93] But executive salaries and bonuses soared,[94] dividends to shareholders rose, taxpayer subsidies continued or increased, and fare charges climbed to unprecedented heights. Over many routes it became less expensive to travel by air than by privatized rail, with some commuters having to change their jobs in order to reduce the cost of getting to work.[95] The public had paid for its own expropriation.

Serious opposition to the privatizations of healthcare, education, national rail transport and other areas of public provision would have required the courage and cast of mind of dissidents in Eastern Europe in the late 1980s. There was no such resistance, and organic parts of civil society were disposed of in competition's name. In Britain, the "opening up" and "selling-off" from October 2013 of the "business" of the almost five-hundred-year-old Royal Mail to the "free market"—described by the Tory prime minister of the day as "popular capitalism"[96]—was another depredation. Moreover, it was sold off on the cheap, bringing further loss to the taxpayer, while the investment bank which had fixed the flotation price too low by some £1 billion or more—underestimating the value (in all senses) of a national postal service—made a profit of millions on the first day of trading when the share price rose by almost 50 percent.

In the name of free choice and in objection to the "overpowerful state," Milton Friedman expressed scorn for the idea that a "postal monopoly" could help "cement the nation together."[97] But the citizen body's sense of community was once formed by the local presence of national institutions of this kind. To rigid dogmatists of the free market, they offend the principles of enterprise and competition. Yet the individual's "freedom to choose" between this and that "service provider"—often a freedom without substance—cannot compensate for the loss of key public institutions to private interest. For it is a civic loss.

More serious in its longer-term implications for civil society in Britain has been the advance of private security firms upon the criminal justice system. Some of the functions of the probation and prison services—and even of the police—have been "sold off" and "outsourced." Maladministration, as in the case of the probation system for young offenders in Britain,[98] has often been the outcome, while a Birmingham prison was taken back into public hands in 2018 after inspectors found that inmates had effectively "seized control" of the jail.[99] Above all, such divestments have taken private enterprise into the heart of the body politic in its most sensitive public functions: those of the restraint and punishment of the citizen, and noncitizen, on behalf of the community as a whole. Only a public servant can properly carry out such functions. Above all, it is a challenge to the rule of law itself for the employee of a private company to lock the prison door upon a fellow citizen, or noncitizen, for profit. It hands the keys of the *polis*, the city, to those who should not have them.

Nevertheless, many kinds of public service in Western democracies are now seen as inferior to the services of the private sector, despite the latter's failures. This perception is the work of market-thought, and it has harmed the ethos of public service itself, dispiriting many who still give their all to it. Disparagement of public servants is a commonplace of satire upon officialdom in every culture and at all times. In *Little Dorrit*, for example, Charles Dickens's absurd "Circumlocution Office"—the "most important Department under government"—is shown "muddling" and "addling" everything it touches.[100]

But today the worthiest of the free society's public servants, the old "uniformed working class" among them, have paid a high price for the reduced moral status of the "public sector." In England there were more than 56,000 reported physical assaults on National Health Service staff in twelve months;[101] in Scotland, violence against the staff of public bodies was said in October 2017 to have reached "epidemic" proportions;[102] in New York City, transport authority bus drivers suffer abuse and attack;[103] and in Britain again, even firefighters encounter aggression.[104] Moreover, the principle of civic duty, since it cannot be measured in cost terms, is not a market value and has therefore been left to fend for itself, while the liberty of the individual in a market society is seen as the commonsense precondition of personal well-being and wider progress.

Today, the same degree of wishful thinking is therefore attached to "free enterprise" and the virtues of "choice" as once attached to the old socialist belief that "planning" was a cure-all for human ills, or that the day of the "universal dictatorship of the proletariat" was nearing and would usher in a Golden Age. Now the illusions of the market rule the free society, while the "left" no longer has models for emulation. Moreover, even when socialist prospects still seemed bright, most "left" intellectuals needed "the working class" more than it needed them.

The unjustly forgotten nineteenth-century social critic Thomas Wright, a journeyman engineer and son of a blacksmith, saw through this. To him, the "professional friends of the people"[105] and the "champions of the working man"[106] were out to "flatter"[107] working people, and were therefore not to be trusted. But today most "progressives," abandoning their old proletarian poses and leaving the "working man" to the care of the aspirant for political office, have moved to other ground.

With the working class no longer its principal constituency, much of today's "left" instead espouses a pick'n'mix of causes and issues, those of "identity," gender, "diversity" and "lifestyle choice"—"choice" here too—among them. To an extent it was always so. As George Orwell described it in 1937, "one sometimes gets the impression that the mere words 'socialism' and 'Communism' draw towards them with magnetic force every fruit-juice drinker, nudist, sandal-wearer, sex-maniac, Quaker, 'Nature Cure' quack, pacifist and feminist in England."[108]

Occupying much of the ethical void created by socialist failure, today's "progressive" libertarian similarly seeks the expansion of whichever freedoms-to-choose are in fashion—often mere abuses of liberty—and like the free-marketeer does so without regard to the well-being of the social order as a whole. And as the free society gradually collapses under the strains imposed upon it by these combined libertarianisms, both the moral free-for-all and the market free-for-all can be regarded as forms of Reaction. Moreover, individualistic "progressives" who seek the unimpeded satisfaction of a choice, a claim of right, or an arbitrary caprice—from most of which market interest itself turns a profit—cannot easily object to the rights of capital to make its money as it sees fit, and without interference.

It is a libertarianism with deep roots. In *Culture and Anarchy*, Matthew Arnold—Thomas Wright's contemporary—thus objected to those who equated the "desires of the ordinary self" with the "laws of human progress."[109] "Our prevalent notion," he wrote in 1869, "is that it is a most happy and important thing for a man to be able to do as he likes," which he not only called "our national idea" but a "fetish."[110] But he did not live to see the "left" also make a "fetish" of "doing as one likes," nor hear it claim the status of "human rights" for the "desires of the ordinary self," and in the name of Progress.

CHAPTER 4

BREAKING THE BOUNDS

The rights-armed individual created by past struggles for human emancipation is now a free-chooser, even if without means. His or her freedom has been harnessed to market interest and endowed with virtue. The consequences have proved dire. For it is a form of liberty which invests the individual's right to act as he or she sees fit with greater legitimacy than any ethic which sets bounds to choice. Moreover, such choices are exercised with little or no regard for their effects upon the social order. In its essence this is again not new. "Licentiousness, or rather the frenzy of liberty," wrote the philosopher David Hume in 1768, "has taken possession of us and is throwing everything into corruption."[1]

In a sea of inequality, new norms of human conduct and new moral goods of widening range are available in liberty's name. Some of these goods are beneficent, and some are trivial—"No Pants Day" is celebrated annually across the world from New York to Warsaw and beyond—but others are hastening civil society to destruction. Indeed, as the range of "choices" increases, sense of citizen-belonging and of personal identity in Western democracies is waning. But the connection between increased "choice" and lost identity is sidestepped or denied, while the age-old distinction between liberty and license is decreasingly made. There can be "moral slavery" in some forms of freedom, as Hawthorne pointed out;[2] and there is no true emancipation to be found in a clothing-optional "naked restaurant" in London,[3] or in a television "nude dating show" with "repeated genital close-ups."[4]

Until now, the need for bounds to "choice" in the interests of all has been a commonplace of political thought across the spectrum. It is not only a Thomas Hobbes who asserts that for individuals to "judge what is lawful and unlawfull" by their own "private judgments" is a "weak and false Principle."[5] To Alexis de Tocqueville also, "institutions and customs" were required to "prevent men running wild."[6] Today, such restraints are seen by many as threats to liberty itself, even as individual choices overwhelm the common good and particular wills rule the social order. With new norms of entitlement established, the range of the permissible also widens. Not much quarter is now given to such wisdoms as that of the Roman historian Livy. "A people cannot coalesce into a single body," he argued, "except by means of laws, which is to say norms established by authority."[7] A single body? Norms? Authority? Perish the thought.

Instead, as normlessness increasingly becomes the norm, pressures grow in liberty's name to legitimate each new breaking of bounds, and the abuse of liberty comes to be a mark of liberty itself. In the ostensibly liberatory process, a world has been created in the free society remote from that of family, old democracy, and nation, with de Tocqueville's "institutions and customs" hollowed out, and many of them reduced to a cosmetic shadow of their former selves.

For there are attributed to most "choices"—whatever they may be—values which have little or nothing to do with previous notions of the common interest, while the idea of the "good life" mutates and expands in a marketplace of options. In particular, if the servicing of a "choice," however aberrant or self-harming by previous moral criteria, is a source of market profit, its legitimacy gradually ceases to be questioned, or is questioned only by killjoys and the "old-fashioned." Indeed, the "good life" is increasingly felt to be one that is untrammeled by self-control or external judgment, and in which the individual becomes his or her own legislator.

And as the social and moral order unravels under the blows which free choice rains down upon it, alarm itself is thought (by many) to be aberrant. De Tocqueville's old assertion that "the evils which freedom sometimes brings" are "apparent to all"[8] is no longer true. Moreover, the liberty, or license, which is today claimed equally by the free-marketeer and the moral free-chooser—birds of a feather—has little room for self-restraint, since self-restraint is a value of less market worth than self-indulgence. At the same time, economic and ethical bound-breaking in liberal democracy is opening the way wider to Reaction, that of puritan Islam included.

With personal distresses growing in the free society's merry-go-round, the search for palliatives also becomes more despairing, but Botox and a gastric staple are poor alternatives to the devout Muslim's vision of Paradise Garden. Moreover, to teach that "morality is a matter of choice"[9] is to teach a cruel principle to those who have lost their bearings in the market's free-for-all. Leaving isolates more isolated, the "right to choose" is in essence the market-stall-holder's contribution to political thought, dwarfing the sense of duty both to self and to the community at large. In the eyes of an Ayn Rand, the latter is a value only among "losers," while the placing of limits upon what may be chosen is perceived as a fetter on enterprise and an obstacle to "progress."

Freedom from restraint has played an historic part in the conquests made by Reason over obscurantism, by energy over sloth, and by invention over inertia. But today's free-chooser and bound-breaker is less an embodiment of the Enlightenment, or heir to the French Revolution's "rights of man," than an often lone and unhappy consumer with a sense of large entitlement but without the means to fulfill it. And into the deepening void between a market society's promise and the unhappy reality of it, the increasingly solitary and those with too little "disposable income" can only stare. To lack the means for consumption of the market's goods, tawdry as many of them are, bears particularly hard on the out-of-pocket young. For to possess such means is for many the measure of individual worth and personal "self-esteem."

Market-thought and interest are naturally wary of the argument that they have contributed to the distresses of body, mind, and spirit which afflict so many. Nonetheless, these ills are multiplying. Some are age-old, as is the understanding of them. Or as Sophocles has a character in *Oedipus Rex* declare, "from the exercise of free choice come the disasters which cause the greatest grief."[10] Indeed, today's forms of "free choice" have brought a normlessness in moral conduct which has contributed both to the undermining of the social order and of the individual's sense of direction, while the anxieties, depressions, angers, and other "behavioral" problems of growing numbers of the population have inflicted further harm on society as a whole.

Consumption rates of antidepressants, sleeping pills, tranquillizers, and similar solaces are growing. Promoted by pharmaceutical corporations and dispensed by psychiatrists and medical practitioners with abandon, they are also used by millions without supervision. Resort to such amount of pills and potions is making for a therapy society composed not of citizens but of patients, many in anomic retreat from family, community, and self. Moreover, as the "products" available to the diagnosticians of mental distress increase, so do the many millions who have recourse to them. The totals of those who are taking antidepressants in Britain have been described as "staggering,"[11] with more than 60 million antidepressant tablets prescribed in the year 2015–2016, a total which had almost doubled in a decade, and with of them over 7 million individuals prescribed them in 2017–2018.[12]

Market demand seeks supply, and market supply meets and encourages demand, with daily life medicalized on prescription. But in a disintegrating social and moral order, "neurosis" and a sense of emotional impoverishment, together with anxiety over the individual's present condition or future prospects, have a real basis. It is one that medication can palliate but not cure, with suicide rates in the United States—nearly 45,000 Americans killed themselves in 2016[13]—rising sharply in the last decade, especially among the middle-aged, and attributed to "social isolation," "gray divorce," "substance abuse," and "economic crisis,"[14] while in Britain in 2016 the Samaritans charity received over half a million calls for help[15] and there were over 4,000 male suicides in 2017.[16] At the same time, as more lose their balance in the whirlpool of Western democracy's costly supermarket of liberties and choices, the abuse of alcohol and food has also increased in scale. But the self-harming drug-and-pill addict, the binge drinker, and the compulsive eater are themselves to the taste of the market. It is in its interest to meet need, whatever the need may be.

Sometimes a prelude to harder drug addiction, the appetite in particular for opioid "painkillers"—a resonant term—has been insatiable especially in the United States. In five years, pharmaceutical companies shipped some 780 million "painkilling" pills to West Virginia alone—with its population of under two million,[17] an average of over four hundred pills per person[18]—and opioid prescription in England is increasing, as is the death rate from "opioid misuse."[19] Mimicking the effects of heroin and morphine and available by mail order,[20] legal opioids such as oxycodone constitute a "nearly $10 billion US market,"[21] with 1.35 million "low-income" Americans estimated to have an "opioid use disorder";[22] and despite a reported "leveling off" in overdose deaths, more than 11 million people in the United States were said to have "misused opioids" in 2017.[23] Even doctors, nurses, and pharmacy staff are said to steal opioids from hospitals "for their own use or street sales,"[24] while "big pharma" lobbyists spend millions to prevent legal restriction on their supply and to protect their patents,[25] despite the fact that between 1999 and 2016 prescription opioid overdoses cost the lives of over 200,000 people in the United States,[26] and some 200 per day in 2017.[27]

There has similarly been an explosion in the market-driven variety of "legal highs," or "designer drugs," which mimic the effects of amphetamines, cannabis, and heroin; even rural areas in Britain have seen a surge in their use.[28] But resort is also had to potentially lethal synthetic alternatives to the legal opioids, fentanyl among them. Many times more potent than heroin or morphine, and powerful enough to be used as a nerve agent in war, China is one of its main sources of supply in the United States,[29] including by online purchase and dispatch by mail.[30] With growing numbers in its grip, two "on-site addiction counselors" working at a "recovery lodge" in suburban

Philadelphia themselves died of an opioid overdose while counseling other addicts,[31] and in May 2018 the members of a native Sioux tribe in Montana were said to be "battling methadone addiction."[32]

Whether mind-changing or painkilling, whether hallucinogens or opiates, whether heroin or cocaine, whether amphetamines or solvents, and whether ingested or injected, sniffed, or snorted—there is even a "snortable chocolate powder" made from cacao beans[33]—resort to drugs is widespread and increasing, especially among the young. The ranks of drug users have swelled, the market vast, with the supply of some drugs exceeding demand and falling prices[34] stimulating greater use. A bag of heroin is said to cost as little as $6 to $10 in New York[35] and is cheaper than prescription opiates; methamphetamine is available at "$5 a hit" and "has never been purer, cheaper or more lethal";[36] while cocaine addiction—Colombia is producing more cocaine for the market than ever before[37]—is a commonplace barely worth notice, with London, Barcelona, and Antwerp sewers containing the highest concentrations of it in Europe.[38]

No-fly zones have also had to be imposed over jails in Britain to "stop drones being used to smuggle drugs into prison grounds";[39] around five hundred British soldiers a year were dismissed from service in the decade to 2015 for drug taking[40] until the rules were relaxed and a "second chance" given;[41] and the bodies of two track-maintenance workers who were killed by a passing train in Philadelphia tested positive for cocaine in one, and for morphine, codeine, and oxycodone in the other.[42] In March 2017 alone, San Francisco municipal workers also collected up more than 13,000 discarded needles left in parks and on sidewalks,[43] while antidepressant drug traces have been found in the brain tissue of fish in the Great Lakes region[44] and oxycodone in mussels in Puget Sound.[45]

Resorted to as mitigators of pain, as aids to confidence, as stimulants of energy, or as a mere fashionable habit, drug use brings varieties of relief and grief. With a rising volume of hospitalizations for addiction,[46] including in Britain for "mental and behavioural disorders" due to cocaine use,[47] deaths from drug overdoses have continued to increase in the United States—as in other Western societies, Britain included[48]—to over 70,000 in 2017,[49] while in 2016 fentanyl "killed at least 220 people on Long Island."[50] Meanwhile, the use of methadone can lead to loss of teeth and hair; psychotic reactions to heavy cannabis use are common; spice, a cheap synthetic cannabis substitute known as the "zombie" drug, can cause a catatonic state of collapse; and intravenous drug users are vulnerable to HIV infection from nonsterile needles. Moreover, with many addicts incapacitated for work, the commission of crime to fund a drug habit has become an everyday matter, while drugs such as cocaine and ecstasy have grown stronger and purer as a result of inter-gang "competition in the market."[51]

Yet drug taking is again perceived by some as no more than an exercise of "choice." At the same time, calls by "progressive" civil libertarians for the decriminalization of possession and use of drugs, including on "human rights" grounds, and whether hard or soft, chime with drug users' claims of entitlement in a free society to do as they see fit with their bodies. Meanwhile, medically supervised "self-injection rooms" or "shooting galleries," with clean syringes and freedom from arrest, have been provided in some "ninety cities" around the world.[52] But the costs of the "drug culture" to civil society as a whole are largely discounted, with harm and self-harm serviced by the market and having to be treated by the medical profession as each new bound is broken.

In addition, over 30 million Americans have been estimated to smoke pot, the percentage having almost doubled in three years,[53] and many billions of dollars a year are spent on it.[54] With legalization of the possession and sale of "recreational" marijuana helping to drive the increase—the first commercial marijuana stores opened in the United States in Colorado in January 2014, and nine states had legalized it by 2018, with other states to follow—political and other interests were quick to point to the millions of dollars in new tax revenue which would be generated by the "pot market."[55] "High quality" marijuana was described by Madam Bubble as a "valuable product,"[56] the producing of it an "industry"[57] with "extreme growth potential,"[58] the sale of it as a "business," and its vendors as "entrepreneurs."[59] But the labor unions also saw "growth potential in California pot workers"[60] when "recreational" marijuana became legal in the state, with the "pot economy" estimated to be "worth $7 billion,"[61] while in Michigan and in civil liberty's name the Democrat proponents of a ballot measure for its legalization in the state argued that the "lure of legal weed" would "bring out the youth vote" and aid the party.[62]

By March 2017, Colorado had some five hundred licensed pot growers, and in Nevada there was so great a demand for it—long queues formed outside the state's forty-seven newly opened retail stores where it was on sale—that its governor ordered the issuing of more licenses to vendors.[63] In California a marijuana company bought a small desert town, a relic of the Gold Rush, in order to turn it into a "marijuana tourist destination" and a "production hub for cannabis-based products,"[64] while in Oregon so much marijuana was grown that its market price fell sharply,[65] and in Canada, within twenty-four hours of its legalization in October 2018, an Ontario cannabis store had received some 100,000 orders.[66]

Binge drinking or the "alcohol crisis" also has uncountable numbers in its grip, with market interest serving the customer whatever his or her age, even as alcohol-related death rates rise in the United States, especially in the 25–34 age cohort,[67] and take the lives of many thousands a year in the United Kingdom.[68] But market interests drive on despite the scale of alcohol-related hospital admissions, estimated at several hundreds of thousands a year in England alone.[69] These interests have secured longer opening hours, strengthened the alcohol content of their "products," sought to reduce the prices of their already-cheap supermarket "brands," and made access to alcohol easier, including by children. And notwithstanding a reported decrease in teenage drinking in Britain[70]—as drug taking rises—the challenge to public health posed by the "drinking culture" grows, with Madam Bubble again at the till.

Indeed market-thought perceives alcohol as a commodity like any other. Meanwhile, the rates of liver disease and other drink-related disorders—some physical and others "behavioral"—rise. But the merriments and convivialities of the old tavern are increasingly remote from today's scene. It is one in which uncountable numbers seek to alleviate their loneliness, anxiety, and "low self-esteem" by whatever means, and who can no longer find their way amid the rights, choices, and liberties, both real and imagined, which they possess.

De Tocqueville believed that democracy "encourages a taste for physical gratification."[71] However, the increase in overweight and obesity in free societies has again broken previous bounds. Millions of all ages and conditions, especially among the already disadvantaged, are affected or afflicted by it. In the United States, where obesity has been posited as one of the factors in the decline of life expectancy,[72] some 40 percent of adults and approximately 20 percent of teenagers and children—including 14 percent of those aged between two and five—are obese,[73] a percentage which is rising year by year. Long gone are the days when a Nathaniel Hawthorne could describe the typical American as "lean of flesh."[74]

In Britain the orders of magnitude are similar, with nearly two-thirds of adults obese or overweight.[75] This total includes almost three million 16-to-24-year-olds and one-quarter to one-third of children,[76] with more than 22,000 leaving primary school "severely obese," a tenfold increase since 1990,[77] and with diagnoses of type-2 diabetes in young people on the rise.[78] By 2030, or in other estimates as soon as 2025, more than a third of all men and women in Britain, millions in total, are expected to be "clinically obese" and "the fattest in Europe,"[79] and by 2045 this could rise to almost half.[80] Similarly, if current trends continue, over half of today's American children will be obese by the time they reach the age of thirty-five.[81]

Consumption is here made flesh, the ill health that obesity brings—the amputation of limbs in type-2 diabetes cases is at an "all-time high" in Britain[82]—costing the social order billions to treat,[83] while obesity in women is one of the causes of the increase in miscarriage and in the maternal mortality rate.[84] Again, potential recruits to the armed forces are too heavy for service or, once recruited, fail fitness tests for being overweight, with some 7 percent of US combat forces said to be so in 2016,[85] as earlier indicated. This is no longer the army to whose "superior physical condition" William Cobbett attributed America's victory in the War of Independence.[86]

The "economic and societal impact" of obesity has been described as "deep and lasting."[87] Yet market interest again shows little or no scruple in the mass selling of high-fat, high-sugar, and high-salt processed foods to the entire world, with obesity rates rising from Mexico to China.[88] Corporate food scientists work sedulously to achieve addiction to their products,[89] and controls are resisted as an incursion upon market freedom, whatever the consequences for public well-being. Thus in Britain, where many school playing fields have been sold off to developers, cheap calorific "products" of low nutritional value are peddled to sedentary children by the "food and beverage industry," insatiable itself; 11-to-18-year-olds are said to drink on average over two-hundred sugary drinks a year, or "one bathtub full";[90] and, as mentioned in a previous chapter, even rickets has reappeared.

Cravings for food and other "eating disorders," such as bulimic overeating and purging, are at the same time pathologized by professional experts. Obesity surgery, including for teenagers and children, supplies rising market demand for liposuction of "unwanted fat deposits," "sleeve gastrectomies," bypass procedures, and gastric-band operations. By means of stomach stapling, for instance, a narrow passage is created which slows the food as it moves from the upper to the lower stomach, helping the patient to feel full more quickly and to eat less. In the private clinic's operating rooms, bounds are thus re-imposed by surgery which self-will, fast food, and compulsive behavior have broken, while Madam Bubble in nurse's uniform rakes in her profits.

Meanwhile, fire services need special lifting gear for the "super-sized," and health services require larger ambulances, stretchers, wheelchairs, toilets, trolleys or gurneys, beds, operating tables, body bags, and bariatric fridges. In treating the grossly obese, hospitals in the

United States have even turned to zoos in order to use MRI scanners "built for lions, gorillas, horses and cattle."[91] Cinemas, theaters, sports arenas, and road vehicles likewise need bigger seats, and airlines extra fuel. The automobile industry builds wider cars, overweight children need bigger safety seats, schools (and cruise ships) install reinforced chairs, and clothing manufacturers increase their sizes. Mortuaries need more capacious coffins, crematoria larger furnaces, and cemeteries bigger grave plots. Even an execution by lethal injection was made impractical in the United States when the veins of a convicted murderer—said to weigh 480 pounds—could not be found. His sentence was commuted to life imprisonment.[92]

Gluttony, obesity, and overweight are again hardly new; "gluttony kills more than either the Plague, Famine or Sword," an anonymous seventeenth-century voice declares.[93] "Once shortage of food led to death from the body's wasting. Now excess overwhelms it," similarly wrote the Roman poet Lucretius,[94] while Ovid advised his contemporaries to "desist when you feel full and eat less than you could."[95] Dickens's corpulent and "purple"-faced Major Bagstock, described as "gasping," "blowing," and "panting," had to be "hoisted into a railway-carriage";[96] the Roman emperor Caligula had an "enormous body";[97] the composer Handel thought a goose a "most inconvenient bird, too much for one and not enough for two";[98] and the playwright Ben Jonson weighed more than twenty stone, or almost three hundred pounds.[99] Likewise, Henry the Eighth in his later years is said to have measured fifty-two inches around the waist and to have weighed nearly four hundred pounds at his death.[100] They were none of them sylphlike figures, but today's extent of obesity and overweight is without historical equal.

For a culture of "consumption" and "growth" has had its due effect on the body mass index. The plenty in supermarket aisles and fast-food outlets—there are over 50,000 in England, disproportionately located in the "most deprived areas,"[101] while some 85 million people in the United States are estimated to eat fast food on any given day[102]—has taken its toll, as have flavor dips; tasty snacking ideas; "new meal sensations"; sundaes which combine fudge, caramel, bacon, and vanilla ice cream; and chocolate-covered fries. In 2013 the Heart Attack Grill in Las Vegas, with its slogan "Taste Worth Dying For" and its waitresses dressed as nurses, had a 10,000-calorie "Bypass Burger" on offer,[103] while in the United States "competitive eaters" swallow lobsters, hot dogs, hamburgers, chicken wings, pies, pastries, and oysters for prizes.

In a hot-pepper-eating contest in New York State, a competitor was hospitalized with "excruciating thunderclap headaches,"[104] and there are fatalities too. A young woman choked to death in Connect-icut during a pancake-eating contest,[105] and after "downing dozens of roaches" in a roach-eating contest a Florida man—who had also eaten worms—was said to have died of "asphyxia due to choking and aspiration of gastric contents."[106] But in a consumer society an ethic of restraint is no virtue, and greed no vice, while in a free society each may claim the right to indulge it. Hence, as natural bounds are broken, walls and stairs must be brought down and hoists and winches used to extricate the immobilized obese from their homes—fire crews in Britain were called out more than nine hundred times in 2017 for the purpose[107]—and take them to the hospital or the morgue. Meanwhile the human frame, once sung by art but now lost in fat, tries to make its arduous way with hips paining and knees metal-braced. More than half a million knees and over 300,000 hips are said to be replaced in the United States each year.[108]

At the same time those fixated upon "righteous eating," today diag-nosed as orthorexics,[109] pursue their obsessions for "pure" foods guar-anteed—by market interest—to be "additive-free"; even the desire for the natural now breaks natural bounds. Others, made anxious by the marketing of the perfect form by underweight, air-brushed, and photo-shopped models, starve themselves to a spectral thinness, driving them-selves to another breaking of bounds and sometimes into the grave.

But since the logic of free choice dictates that choice be untram-meled, all bounds in a free society are subject to attempts to break them. In March 1976, Britain's National Council for Civil Liberties campaigned for the age of consent to be lowered to fourteen;[110] the Department of Education's 2014 guidelines for the sex education of 13-to-17-year-olds described sex with "the same or opposite gender" as part of a "safe and healthy sexual development";[111] and the German Ethics Council in September 2014 declared that laws banning incest between brothers and sisters were expressions of a "social taboo" and offended the "fundamental right of adult siblings to sexual self-determination."[112]

Moreover, in June 2015 and in equity's name, same-sex marriage was held by the US Supreme Court in a narrow majority verdict to be a constitutional right for all Americans, and its denial to be a "grave and continuing harm."[113] At issue for Justice Anthony Kennedy was "equal dignity in the eyes of the law,"[114] while the decision was similarly described by President Barack Obama—with the White House illuminated in celebratory rainbow colors—as affirmation that "all Americans are created equal."[115] But California's representative Nancy Pelosi described the verdict, more accurately, as "about freedom."[116] Indeed the freedom to marry, which homosexuals had gained in the face of often cruel prejudice and pronouncement, also came to possess market value as a "brand" in itself.

The Empire State Development Corporation was quick to estimate that over a period of three years the legalization of gay marriage in New York would "generate about $400 million economic benefits state-wide,"[117] including revenue from holding gay weddings. Likewise, there was swift public acknowledgment of the "boost" to the "state economy," and to the "wedding trade," which gay marriage would bring to the state of Maine after its approval of same-sex unions.[118] When France took the same step, gays were described as a "new newlywed market";[119] the mayor of Minneapolis in September 2013 urged same-sex couples to come to his state to get married and to "spend lots of money on weddings";[120] and it was estimated that to permit gay marriage in Illinois would "pump more than $100 million into the state and local economy."[121] Conversely, "corporate leaders" in Indiana warned that the failure of the state legislature to enact a law protecting

LGBT individuals from discrimination "could rebound on business" by making it "harder to sell the state as an attractive place to live."[122] The P&O shipping company had more business sense, becoming the first British cruise line to offer same-sex weddings at sea.[123]

Meanwhile, in the face of hostilities to which I will return in a later chapter, the entitlement of same-sex partners to marry or to enter into a formal civil union (or, thereafter, to obtain a divorce) was claimed before many parliaments and at law, including as a fundamental human right; and by 2017 the right to marry had been gained in some two dozen free societies.

But even before the US Supreme Court decision, same-sex weddings were being solemnized in Washington's National Cathedral, its dean declaring that to do so was "being faithful to the kind of community that Jesus would have us be."[124] The Presbyterian Church, the largest protestant group in the United States, similarly recognized same-sex marriage in March 2015 after years of debate on the subject, as did the Scottish Episcopal Church but with a "conscience clause" permitting its clergy to opt out of performing same-sex weddings,[125] while the American Episcopal Church decided to allow same-sex marriages from December 2018.[126] In Britain, with the Anglican church divided and some clergy defying church rules by blessing same-sex couples, the Dean of St. Albans in July 2012 expressed himself in favor of gay marriage "because I'm sure that God is too,"[127] while a Church of Ireland canon described his church's ban on gay marriage as "un-Christian."[128]

Other churches disagreed. The United Methodist Church in the United States held same-sex relationships to be "incompatible with Christianity,"[129] while the Vatican—torn between the desire to be "inclusive" and the pressure to uphold established doctrine—declared in April 2016 that "same-sex unions may not simply be equated with marriage," but that "such families should be given respectful pastoral guidance."[130] Nevertheless, in the eyes of many, an anomaly which had confined marriage to individuals of the opposite sex had been corrected. Above all, in defense of same-sex marriage, it is held that the law must come to terms with change, convention must adjust to modernity, and tradition bow to natural progress. Indeed, in the free society's public debates on the issue, distinctions in law and ethics between homosexual and heterosexual unions were often presented as offenses not only against concepts of justice but against rationality itself. Moreover, such scruples run counter to the market principle of choice, whether ethical or material. Meanwhile, aided by surrogacy and surgery, the exercise of the right to homosexual marriage has created forms of the family hitherto unknown, while gender reassignment has similarly been made possible in correction of what are now seen as Nature's errors.

But such developments could be considered minor matters in times when scientists and technologists are, for various purposes, physically changing—and playing with—the entire natural order. These purposes include the gratification of idle curiosity and the meeting of real need, the cure of ailment or defect, and once more the provision of wider choice. Calls for the ethical control of such developments have had little effect. For some, "whatever is, is right" as Alexander Pope put it.[131] But even if held to be wrong, the existence of the means to secure an end increasingly overwhelms recoil from the uses to which it may be put. This is so whether the object of expert attention be plant, animal, or human. If the techniques exists, it is almost certain that in collapsing social orders dominated by largely uncontrollable market interests they will sooner or later be used.

As human powers reach unprecedented heights, anxiety over their potential misuse also grows. This is particularly so when the re-ordering of Nature, as by the genetic modification of its forms of life, is being commanded by corporate interest on an industrial scale. While driving real advances in medical treatment, human genetics research is big business. In part-consequence, ethical restraint among scientists is on the wane, with many regulatory bodies retreating as new bounds are broken.

For some, the attempt to impose a moral limit upon experiment is itself wrong and invites challenge as a matter of intellectual principle. The scientist's freedom to explore the natural order is also seen as an expression of liberty as such, whether the outcomes or "products" be benign, life-enhancing, and disease-curing, or perilous and grotesque. Ethical objections to the manipulation of natural laws are also perceived, especially by those hostile to moral judgment itself, as obstacles to human progress, while the market's interest in new technologies is threatened by excessive scruple.

In science's (or technique's) shop window, there is therefore every kind of groundbreaking and bound-breaking innovation and device on offer or in arrival, both for good and ill. They include synthetic body parts "custom-made" from a person's own stem cells by "tissue engineering"—blood vessels and a bladder here, a windpipe and nostrils there, with more complex organs such as kidneys, lungs, and livers yet to come to market—as well as genetically modified fish, a bug-free vine, and a brand-new face. Some of these contrivances come at a larger price than others, including a moral price. But their range is widening, since the laws of the market privilege "products" which are new, while little or no regard is paid, in notional democracies, to public anxieties about the direction in which the social, moral, and natural order is being taken.

Market interest and the license of the free take every breaking of bounds in their stride. Indeed, certain advances can only be made if bounds are broken. They have led, among other things, to the exertion of technical power over almost every aspect of reproduction in plants, animals, and humans. New means are available not only to overcome physiological obstacles to normal conception, but by resort to surrogates to avoid the stretch marks of pregnancy which diminish "self-esteem." The ethic, or anti-ethic, of free choice makes little or no distinction between the satisfaction of a whim and the creation of a human child spared a fatal gene-defect. Moreover, "interventions" in the "heritable genome" make it possible by DNA "editing" not only to prevent inherited disease but to enhance a child's ability or appearance.[132] It has even been argued that there is a "moral obligation" to screen embryos for genetically inherited "personality flaws" in order to produce "ethically better children."[133]

Even without such eugenics, the effects upon civil society and upon the moral order of advances in the technologies of reproduction have been substantial. On the one hand, late maternity by means of the "harvesting" and freezing of a woman's ova has been facilitated, and a uterus can be transplanted to a woman born without one; on the other, the purchase and sale of motherhood has been made possible in new "niche trades" over which market interests once more preside. Appropriate payments will secure the implantation in surrogates of ova of varying origin and methods of fertilization, the resulting children having no relation to the women who have gestated them and given them birth. Moreover, such freedoms may be employed equally by heterosexual or homosexual couples who wish to "have a child," while in 2015 a gay couple fathered three children by three different surrogate mothers, two with the sperm of one of the partners, and a third child with the sperm of the other.

Sperm donation or the purchase of sperm from a "sperm bank"— an appropriate term—has also made possible the bearing of a child by a heterosexual woman without a male partner, as well as by one partner in a lesbian couple. In the sperm market, intelligence, athleticism, and tallness are among the virtues which command the fertilization trade's highest prices, while leading sperm banks export their "products" far and wide, so that a child born by anonymous sperm donation can have dozens of unknown siblings. "I'm grateful to the sperm-donor but he isn't really a person to me," said a sperm bank customer who bore a child by these means.[134] There has also been a developing trade in "private" sperm provision, where donors "find their clients through Facebook," "charge a fraction" of the price asked by "regulated sperm banks," and "hand over vials of sperm in pubs and cafes."[135]

In times when the "conventional" family in free societies is under great stress from other causes, such erosion of previously existing physiological, sexual, and ethical bounds has led to familial relations of again unprecedented kinds, yet with relatively little public engagement in the profound issues they raise. Thus, breaking new familial ground have been cases where a father who donated his sperm for use by his daughter-in-law and infertile son became both grandfather and genetic father to the resulting child;[136] where a mother, serving as a surrogate for her daughter and carrying her child, gave birth to her own granddaughter;[137] where, conversely, a daughter served as a surrogate for her post-menopausal mother and gave birth to her own brother;[138] and where the parents of an only son, who was unmarried and killed in a road crash, "retrieved" his sperm postmortem, purchased the services of a surrogate, and created a grandchild.[139]

Again, a post-menopausal lesbian whose donated ovum from a stranger was fertilized in vitro by her brother—but without committing incest—became the parent of a child biologically related to her through her own sibling.[140] Likewise breaking all previously known bounds, a mother, acting as a surrogate for her gay son and pregnant with a donor ovum fertilized in vitro by him, gave birth to a male child who was not only her son's son but also, in law, her son's brother. In March 2015, the British High Court permitted her son to adopt the child.[141]

On this previously unknown terrain where the free-chooser increasingly holds sway, the law has had difficulty in adjudicating conflicts arising from the new range of possibilities for parenthood, a foundational relationship of civil society in all previous times. There have thus come before the courts disputes over who owns sperm donated to a sperm bank, the donor or the woman who has paid for it; and over the issue of whether a sperm donor is or is not the legal parent of a resulting child, and therefore owes it support. It has also had to be decided whether the vendor of her ova on the market has superior parental rights to those of the implanted surrogate mother, and whether a husband whose frozen sperm was taken by his estranged wife—and who then bore two children conceived by IVF with their aid—should be forced to pay his wife for their upbringing.[142] Again, a surrogate mother in California who gave birth to seeming twins, and subsequently discovered that one of them had been naturally conceived with her boyfriend after the implant of the donor embryo, had to go to court in order to recover her own child,[143] while an Australian court held that a woman can use a donor's sperm in IVF without her husband's consent.[144]

Having to be weighed in the judicial balance, too, is whether a surrogate mother, after successfully claiming custody of her (biologically unrelated) child, is obligated to repay the fee given to her by the biological father for her hire.[145] It has also had to be determined whether both members of a gay couple can be registered under the law as the "parents" of a child born to a surrogate mother with the aid of the sperm of one of them, and whether unmarried gay couples can adopt. Further dispute has arisen when a fertility clinic has used the "wrong" sperm from its sperm bank, and a customer has given birth to a child with different characteristics from those for which payment had been made,[146] while in Indiana and Ottawa "fertility doctors" were accused of using their own sperm to inseminate patients.[147]

Even wilder shores have come into view, not seen before, as the science and technology of reproduction have advanced. They include the possibility of a womb transplant into a transgender male-to-female; of "growing" synthetic sperm and ova from stem cells in service of the infertile; and of producing by genetic cloning a child who is biologically related to both members of a male or a female couple. Already arrived, or beckoning, are the modification—or "editing"—of the DNA of the human embryo in order to combat disease, referred to earlier; the fashioning of a three-parent child freed of the mutations present in the mother's ova; and even the fertilization of an ovum without the use of sperm. Foreseeable, too, is the technology by which both sperm and ovum will be provided by a single person, male or female.

On a more modest technical level, to plump the lips, iron out wrinkles, and lift the eye or buttock; to pin the ear or improve the smile; to diminish or enlarge the breast; to remove the veins and reduce the nose, the belly, or the thigh; to reshape the labia and tighten or "rejuvenate" the vagina; and (seemingly) to change sex is a vast market business, its "revenue streams" a cosmetic Niagara. Now, too, clinics which offer costly "stem-cell treatments" for a variety of diseases and conditions, but with too little evidence of their utility or safety, have opened across the United States.[148]

At the same time, the "human tissue industry" "harvests" the body parts of cadavers for transplant, the penis included, and on a further shore makes available the entire replacement of the disfigured human face—skin, muscles, teeth, lips, nose, cheekbones, and jaw—by donation from the dead. "It's not me," said the first individual to undergo the "procedure" in 2005, a woman who had been savaged by her own dog as she lay comatose from a drug overdose. "A part of me and my identity has disappeared forever,"[149] she declared, but her body rejected the transplant. On a still further shore await the "cryogenic" freezing of the human brain for future transplant,[150] the graft of a living person's head onto a donor body—described as a "procedure" that "would change the course of human history"[151]—and the possibility of reversing the aging process.[152]

The existence in the free society of the technical means to meet a need or satisfy a want—the need or want of the experimenter included—now carries almost all before it, overriding or bypassing public sanction, and seemingly without concern for wider consequence, whether good or ill. "There arrives a point in time when the procedure should simply be done," a "bio-ethicist" declares.[153] "Someone has got to push the envelope," says a "reconstructive surgeon" in the same spirit.[154] Today, a "near-complete" human brain "comparable with that of a five-week-old fetus" has been made from "re-programmed adult skin cells";[155] a beef burger can be "lab grown" using stem cells from cow muscle;[156] Chinese research scientists by resort to "gene-editing" have created healthy mice from two female parents;[157] white rhinoceros embryos have been produced in vitro to save the species from extinction;[158] brains from the severed heads of pigs have been kept "alive" outside the body using pumps, heaters, and artificial blood;[159] the means to grow human transplant organs in sheep and pigs is being developed;[160] and an animal ovum could perhaps be fertilized by human sperm.

Undeterred by the mutations of the natural order, the artificers of new possibilities and newly patented "products," competing fiercely with one another for fame and fortune, press on, dancing to the market's tune. As technologies advance, and with "science alone" unable to provide the values that might check them,[161] the increasing resort to "smart machines" and other robotic devices which fulfill human tasks and displace those who hitherto carried them out—in China, robot TV newsreaders nod their heads, blink, and raise their eyebrows,[162] while a novel written by a Japanese computer program even reached the second round of a national literary prize in 2016 [163]—also raise fears of "species obliterating risks"[164] and of "things that could go wrong." Among them is the possibility of "self-aware" computers capable of independent decision-making and beyond human intelligence to control,[165] as well as of "autonomous" weapons systems[166] which could "cause war on a vast scale."[167]

Meanwhile, cloned animals replicated in laboratories—a sheep in Scotland in 1996, pigs in Virginia in 2000, and monkeys in Shanghai in 2018[168]—walk the Earth. Beyond lie the possibilities of a full-term human clone and the artificial manufacture of life-forms not yet known, from genetically engineered viruses to variants of the human being; a part-pig and part-human embryo, or chimera, has already been created,[169] and human brain cells have been transplanted into the heads of mice and rats.[170] At the same time, suffering is meted out to existing animal creation on increasing scale, and death dealt out to humankind with diminishing conscience. While the fertilization "industry" creates new means of fecundation, rates of abortion—as a right, a need, or again a "lifestyle choice"—rise, and discreet or open euthanasia is winked at or encouraged. "Assisted dying" by means of lethal medication administered to the knowing, and whether or not terminally ill,[171] is also decreasingly thought a breach of the Hippocratic oath. Rather, it is a final fulfillment of the freedom to choose.

The free society does not command these processes. It is driven on its path by its notions of what liberty is, with the questioning of such notions regarded as the mark of the "judgmentalist" or worse. Instead, bound-breaking is seen as a precondition for the free society's progress. In our false commonwealths it is one of the few rules that cannot be broken.

CHAPTER 5

THE HOME FRONT

As moral choice has widened, the home has not prospered. In a moral free-for-all, "family values" and family relationships fare badly. Marriage becomes a growing restraint, and the notion of filial obligation an anachronism. The free moral agent has increasingly taken the place of husband and wife, of father and mother, of son and daughter. Once, as in ancient Athens, the household or *oikos* stood at the heart—not the periphery—of the social order, while for Aristotle the domestic hearth was where amiability, a sense of justice, and concern for the good of others were taught and learned.[1] But home is often a cold place now.

The casualties of family breakdown and the escapees from it grow in number, heaping burdens on civil society, and with men, women, and children equally the victims of the free-chooser. One such is vividly portrayed in Rand's *Atlas Shrugged*, individualism's exemplary text. With love described as a "celebration of one's self," Rand has her model of the self-made man express a dismissive contempt toward family members, for whom Hank Rearden "felt nothing but the merciless zero of indifference."[2] Ruthless with his wife, Rearden had the "shining guiltless knowledge that it did not matter to him what [she] felt" and tells his younger brother that "I haven't the slightest interest in you, your fate or your future."

Although such sentiments are extreme and even parodic, they express a recoil from the moral ties that bind, ties that may obstruct the free society's go-getter. With the number of unmarried couples living together doubling in Britain in twenty years, "growing the fastest," and now the "second largest family type,"[3] the speed of "relationship failure" in marriage, in re-marriage, and in short-term cohabitation has also accelerated. The declining predisposition to make long-term commitments, the increase in single-parenting, the quickening rate of marriage collapse, and the rising total of solitary households are together helping to undo the ostensible commonwealth to which we all belong.

As marriage gradually ceases to be the social norm or preferred "lifestyle choice," in the United States and the United Kingdom the married gradually become a minority,[4] and less than half of American children live in a home with two married heterosexual parents in their first marriage.[5] Indeed, despite some fall in the divorce rate among the newly married,[6] almost half of marriages in Britain fail, the effect and further cause of social dissolution, with over 20 million people divorced, widowed, or who have never married,[7] and with marriages lasting an average of only twelve years.[8] Moreover, again in Britain, one-fifth of the married who divorce have divorced before, and even among the over-60s the rate of separation and divorce has been rising since the 1990s,[9] while "digital divorce proceedings" or divorces online—"to save time, paperwork and stress"[10]—are available both in Britain and in the United States; in Britain the application process takes some twenty-five minutes and a "quickie divorce" can be obtained in three months or less.[11] And where divorce rates fall, it is in large part because the number of the married has fallen too, while the "re-partnering" of the divorced and widowed, without further marriage, is a growing phenomenon in the United States,[12] and the numbers of gay couples rise.[13]

The variety of domestic entities, many precarious, is therefore multiplying as "conventional" family ties and obligations weaken. Ex-husbands and ex-wives bring their children to new relationships with stepfathers, stepmothers, and unrelated siblings, and almost one in three families in Britain now has a stepchild from a previous relationship, some two million children in all.[14] These new relationships are often short-term themselves; in Britain, more unmarried than married couples with children broke up in 2016.[15]

Amid this dissolution, there are growing numbers of adults, male and female, who are living alone or who are still in the parental home, if there is such. In Western free societies, increasing numbers of young adults and in general more males than females—tens of millions in total—live with their parents, a "record level of dependency."[16] In the United States, some one-third of 18-to-34 year-olds were still living at home in 2016,[17] more than those living with a spouse or partner; in Italy, two-thirds of the same age group and almost three-quarters of the males—some 8.5 million individuals in all—were in the same condition in 2016;[18] and, in Britain, one-third of men aged 20 to 34 were still living with their parents.[19]

Some have been unable or unwilling to find permanent or temporary partners, or are intermittently partnered. But in Britain there are also rising numbers of couples living under the same roof as their parents.[20] Many are prevented from finding homes, and from forming independent families, by unemployment or poorly paid work, and by rising rents and house prices; the percentage of families headed by 25-to-34-year-olds owning their own homes has more than halved in many parts of Britain in the last three decades.[21] It has also led in the United States to what has been called the lowest level of "mobility" among young adults in half a century,[22] again attributed to low-paid jobs, non-marriage, debt, housing shortage, and inability to buy a home, in turn held responsible (by some) for the greater proneness of "millennials" to suffer at middle age from "lifestyle" diseases—such as diabetes and cardiac disorders—than were their parents.[23] Moreover, almost half of Americans aged 18 to 30 are without savings and have no access to a pension.[24]

While many young adults thus continue to live in the parental home, the millions of lone elderly and isolate old, too often neglected by their offspring if they have them, also bear the scars of the disruptions in free societies of previously normative human relations. "Agism," too, makes its amoral contribution to their plight, as regard for old age—"to which we shall all come if we survive," in the words of an Athenian of the fourth century BCE[25]—declines. Today, to describe a British public figure after she had suffered a stroke as a "pampered, self-indulgent, gin-soaked geriatric"[26] brings no Athenian "dishonor" to the author of it. Indeed, in defiance of the wisdom of the ages and of democracy itself, the "elderly" have never been more excluded from the public square, even as populations grow older and birth rates fall; and it is in China, not in Western free societies, that an "elderly rights" law prescribes that adult children must visit their parents, or face the risk of fines and jail.[27]

Moreover, unprecedented numbers of older people in free societies are being "left to fend for themselves."[28] About one-third of the over-65s and over half of the over-85s in the United States live alone,[29] while the number of older men living alone in the United Kingdom is expected to total 1.5 million by 2030.[30] And as the population ages—with the British state-pension scheme set to run out of funds by the mid-2030s[31] and the pension-fund deficit for public employees in the United States standing at $1.4 trillion in 2016[32]—there is also a growing shortage of local community provision, and residential care is increasingly beyond reach. In the United States, the average cost of a private room in a nursing home is some $89,000 a year,[33] while in Britain nine out of ten over-55s have put nothing aside for care costs in old age.[34]

It has been estimated that by 2040 one in seven of the population of Britain will be over seventy-five;[35] and by 2066, the over-65s will number more than 20 million.[36] Similarly the United States will have more over-65s than under-18s by 2035;[37] and today's 50 million over-65s[38] could number more than 80 million by 2050,[39] over 20 percent of the citizen body, and more than double the percentage of 1970. Likewise in Canada, there are already more people aged 65 years and over than there are people aged 14 and under;[40] while in Japan in 2018 almost 30 percent of the population was over-65—more than 35 million people[41]—and there were some 70,000 centenarians, whereas in 1963 there were only 173.[42] As life expectancy improves in Britain, despite some faltering as the rate of dementia-death increases,[43] the numbers of people aged over-65 who will need care could reach nearly three million by 2025.[44]

Yet the social care system in Britain is already under stress, with council taxes having to be raised to pay for it, demand rising,[45] some local authority care homes closing, many hundreds of thousands not getting the help they need,[46] and with the "family hearth" as a refuge receding from sight. Now, aging Americans increasingly "home-share" with nonrelatives for companionship and cost savings, and "seniors look after seniors."[47]

The partner-less mother and child are also representative figures of our times. Alongside them are the women who do not have children at all—a percentage which is rising—and those who give birth ever later. In the United States, the birth rate among women aged thirty to thirty-five is today higher than among the cohort aged twenty-five to twenty-nine,[48] while in Britain the average age of women giving birth is over thirty, the highest since records began,[49] with women in their forties the only cohort in which the birth rate is increasing both in the United States and Britain.[50] At the same time, the rising median age—over thirty-five in Britain[51]—of women who choose to marry or who succeed in finding long-term partners brings its own consequences for the birth rate as it declines, while at the same time the neonatal death rate increases in Britain and is attributed to causes which include maternal smoking, obesity, poverty, and midwife shortage.[52]

Meanwhile, some (or many) women whose maternity is delayed, or who remain childless, rationalize their circumstances as matters of liberated choice or of unwillingness to compromise a career. But often their childlessness, despite new reproductive technologies and techniques, including the freezing of ova, is involuntary and a source of private despair; whether falling sperm counts" are also a factor in Western societies is a matter for debate.[53] Simultaneously, in the chaos, the rate of "out of wedlock" births continues at high levels: over 40 percent in the United States, one-third of births in England and Wales,[54] and one-third of births in notionally Catholic Italy also.[55]

To some, this combination of phenomena demonstrates the diversity of the social order and the emancipatory options gained by women in their decades-long struggle for social justice, moral autonomy, and individual rights. Yet despite such advance, ground has been lost too. With the wider freedom to choose, market interest—which is no respecter of persons or their bodies—has made large profits from the license of our pornographic times. Moreover, as exploitative pressures of all kinds upon women and girls increase, there have been female self-abandon and self-abasement too, corrupting feminism's cause in liberty's name. It has been a form of self-harm, compromising the efforts of other women to combat male oppressions of many kinds, efforts which by October 2018 were said in the United States to have "brought down" more than two hundred "powerful men" after accusations against them of sexual misconduct.[56]

But despite the increase in female vulnerabilities, the number of teen pregnancies in the United States and Britain has declined in recent years, as has the number of abortions among the pregnant young, with both declines attributed to the greater use of contraceptives.[57] But the consequences for the over 200,000 children born to teenagers in America in 2016,[58] for example, remain. The teen mother is unlikely to have a partner for long, or at all—and even less likely to be married—and be driven to parent her child alone, or with the help of her own parents. But they are often no standby, whether for economic reasons or because their own relationships are fractured, or both. Thus in the United States, as elsewhere, "full-time grand-parenting" has become increasingly common, with over 2.5 million grandparents responsible for their grandchildren.[59] This is not least because younger mothers are in many cases little more than children themselves, with rising levels of drug addiction also a factor in the transfer of responsibility to grandparents.[60] Yet, for many, the "right to a child" weighs as heavily as parental duty to it in the moral scales of the free social order.

Indeed, even as such order unravels, some see "family values" as both regressive and oppressive. At the same time, gays and lesbians have fought for the right to marry, often with the support of heterosexuals who themselves avoid it. Moreover, although the "conventional" heterosexual marriage is now sidestepped by many, some gay and lesbian spouses imitate its formalities to the last detail; even the *in vitro* fertilization of a lesbian partner may be postponed until after marriage lest, among other consequences, the resulting child be considered "illegitimate" according to scruples which most heterosexuals have abandoned.[61] The drive for equity has also exacted a price in falsehood; in February 2004, the Massachusetts Supreme Court described as a "mere prejudice" the proposition that there is a "natural relation" between heterosexuality, procreation, and childbirth.[62]

Nevertheless, the rate of failure of "conventional" families has helped bolster the argument that they are not models for emulation, even if they once constituted humanity's norm. Given such families' mounting troubles, rights to marry, to have a child, and to adopt have almost inevitably widened. Indeed, distinctions between the "natural" and the "unnatural" have themselves been placed under a new taboo by many, as the assertion by the Massachusetts court indicated. Moreover, to the moral free-chooser there is a presumption in favor of nondiscrimination and the expansion of individual rights, as well as increasing distaste for distinctions between right and wrong.

Today, the extension of choice as to how a family may be created, and of whom it may consist, has therefore reached the boundary of what mind and body can conceive, as the previous chapter illustrated. A grandmother, after falling in love with her own grandson and paying for a donor ovum to be inseminated with his sperm and implanted in a surrogate, can bring up the child as if she were its natural mother. Or a lesbian mother, after being artificially inseminated with the sperm of a gay friend, can now share the parenting of the offspring with her female partner, her gay friend—the child's biological father—and his male partner.

But on these new home fronts the rights of children, some of them mere purchases on the market, have narrowed, and with scant regard to their interests. As the means of fertilization have widened, the supposition that a child benefits from the presence of its male father and female mother has come to be regarded by some (or many) as anachronistic. Meanwhile, as the forms of the family—microcosms of the social order—multiply in accord with the ethic of free choice, it has again been left to the courts to adjudicate upon domestic issues not previously known to the law, and on novel moral ground. Even the question of whether a male-to-female transgendered person— with a birth certificate retrospectively amended—may legally marry a man and "start a family" has come to court as an issue of human rights and natural justice; while a female-to-male who gave birth to a child before "he" became a "man" also went to court in Britain seeking registration as the child's father.[63]

A gay sperm donor has also challenged a lesbian birth mother for parenting rights over the resultant child and won the case, a family-law expert describing the decision in the Glasgow Sheriff Court as evidence that "the courts are coming to terms with the changing nature of society."[64] In addition, a biological mother can now lose custody of her own children to her lesbian ex-partner after a court held the latter to be the children's "psychological parent."[65] "We have moved into a world where norms that seemed secure twenty or more years ago no longer run," said the judge. Still more complex was the case heard in the San Francisco Appeal Court of one partner in a lesbian couple who had given her ova, artificially fertilized, for implant into the other. After the pair became estranged, the ova donor challenged the birth mother for custody of the resulting twins and lost, even though the children were biologically hers, at least in part.[66]

In some of this there is logic, too, even if it is a logic previously unknown. Extramarital same-sex infidelity during same-sex marriages and unions has thus become adultery, and a ground for legal separation and divorce. In Britain, to declare oneself "single" when entering a formal same-sex union or marriage, and to conceal the fact of already being (heterosexually) married, is—again logically—to commit the crime of bigamy and even risk a custodial sentence. "I didn't know she was married," said the deceived woman in a lesbian couple, complaining—logically once more—that the deception had "made a mockery" of the same-sex partnership ceremonial. The bigamist was given a suspended jail term by Shrewsbury Crown Court and ordered to do one hundred hours of community service.[67] In a similar case in Virginia, a bigamist lesbian who had married her female partner without first divorcing her (male) husband was sentenced to two years' probation.[68]

And what of the children on these home fronts old and new? The answer is that the child of today's moral and social confusions may be fostered, adopted—including by same-sex couples—grandparented, stepparented, single-parented, parented by same-sex parents with technological help, or parented by its biological parents; and be born to its own mother or a surrogate mother. In England in 2018, the child may also be among the more than 75,000 in local authority care—ninety young people enter the care system each day—after being removed from their homes because of abuse, neglect, or other "family dysfunction."[69] Today, in addition, some four million young children in Britain, one-third of the cohort, do not live with both of their parents.[70] It has also been estimated, again in Britain, that "half of all children born today will not see their parents together by the time they reach 16,"[71] while one in eight divorced fathers has lost all touch with them.[72]

Against the odds, many young people survive as moral and social beings. But ever-larger numbers do not, their education, health, and conduct harmed by familial change and household disorder. Moreover, as the costs of raising a child mount—to an estimated £60,000 in Britain in the first four years[73]—two incomes are often needed to meet such costs even as the scale of lone-parent upbringing increases. Unsurprisingly, some two-thirds of Britain's lone parents—the large majority of them women—are said to be in financial difficulty,[74] with half of such parents having to borrow to pay for the upbringing and care of their children.[75] Single parents with dependent children are also more likely than couples to be in poorly paid work, or unemployed; over one-third of lone-parented children in Britain live in a workless household.[76] Moreover, "child poverty" increases as low wages, rising household debt,[77] and welfare cuts take their further domestic toll.

Some four million children in the United Kingdom—nearly a third of the total, and a proportion which is said to be rising[78]—are estimated to live in poverty,[79] two-thirds of them in working families;[80] almost 20 percent of under-15s suffer from "food insecurity";[81] and "up to three million" are at risk of "going hungry during school-holidays."[82] In the United States, child homelessness, referred to in a previous chapter, has been said to be at an "all-time high";[83] in 2018, there were over 10,000 children aged six and under living in New York's shelters.[84] In the New York City school system, over 110, 000 students—a rising number—have also been found to be homeless at some point during the school year, whether living in the "shelter system," in "temporary living quarters," or in "other makeshift living situation," with two-thirds of the young people in the city's shelters said to be "chronically absent" from school or who "just disappear."[85] Even in East Palo Alto in California's Silicon valley, one-third of school students were defined in 2016 as homeless.[86] Likewise in Britain, over 120, 000 children—again a rising total, with more than 25,000 under-5s among them—were living in temporary accommodation at Christmas in 2017.[87]

In the thick of it there is also parental abuse of children, with more than 1,700 domestic fatalities in the United States from such cause reported in a single year,[88] but with many other cases thought to go unrecorded.[89] In addition, "problem families," often in chronic trouble with the law, cause other harms to those around them, with which civil society attempts to deal. Directed to the disarray are parenting classes, child-support payments ordered against absent fathers, and other measures. Some of the sanctions attached to these measures are morally unjust—for example, the imprisonment of errant single mothers—most are ineffectual, and many are directed against the neglected, abused, and wayward young people themselves.

Family failure bears heavily upon them in all free societies, bringing them disadvantage and harm. In Britain, over a thousand infants each year are born addicted to drugs taken in pregnancy by their mothers,[90] while in the United States neonatal drug dependency, accompanied by withdrawal symptoms, has increased more than fourfold in a decade, and costs more than $1 billion a year to treat.[91] In Manchester, New Hampshire, as many as one hundred children were said to have witnessed an adult overdose in their homes in 2016–2017;[92] and in Delaware in October 2014 a four-year-old, who had been given the "wrong backpack" by her mother, handed out heroin—she had 250 bags of it—to her friends at a daycare center, "thinking they were candy."[93] Similarly, in Utah, a grandmother put her "meth pipe" in her eight-year-old granddaughter's backpack, where it was found by her teacher,[94] while a five-year-old in Trenton, New Jersey, mistakenly brought thirty packs of heroin to school in her lunchbox.[95]

Moreover, with drugs negligently kept in the home, there were some fifty accidental drug deaths of children under age five in the United States in 2015.[96] In Akron, Ohio, a one-year-old was taken to hospital unable to breathe from an opioid overdose;[97] in Pennsylvania, a child aged twenty-two months who "got into a bag of the drug" was hospitalized after consuming methamphetamine;[98] in Virginia, a three-month-old was admitted to hospital "in respiratory distress" after a mother tried to "calm" the child with the opiate methadone, orally administered;[99] and again in Pennsylvania, a five-month-old was found dead in its crib from dehydration and starvation three days after her parents had themselves died from drug overdoses.[100]

With the lack of bonds and bounds now bearing heavily upon them, the cries for help of the unhappy young, often unheard, grow more insistent. Whether expressed in contempt for self, eating disorders, or violence, and with drug addiction reported at ever-earlier ages, eight hundred under-16s in Britain were treated in hospital in 2015 alone for overdoses of heroin, cocaine, ecstasy, and other substances;[101] and in the same year in the United States there were over seven hundred teenage drug-overdose deaths,[102] with even thirteen-year-olds found to be dealing in addictive antianxiety medications at school.[103] Parental self-preoccupation and neglect also bring attention-deficit hyperactivity disorders. Diagnoses of it in children and adolescents in the United States now run to many millions, while central nervous-system stimulants, harm-causing themselves, are provided by market interests to treat it. They are given in the United States and Britain even to preschoolers.

At each new mark of disaffection in the young, psychiatrization is on hand with its diagnoses and "products." It prescribes equally for "poor cognitive development" and aggression, for "lack of concentration" and depression. In England, tens of thousands of under-18s, including almost 2,000 primary-school children, were given antidepressants in 2017.[104] Other young people are fobbed off with distractions for their absence of nurture, and fashionable "brands," for those who can afford them, take the place of care. Many—"almost a third"—set out for their first day at school in Britain "not ready for the classroom,"[105] with rising numbers of children lacking "speech and language skills."[106] Casualties of domestic disarray, they are variously unable to "communicate in full sentences," to "respond to questions," "control their behaviour," or "make relationships with other children."[107] "They can swipe a phone but have no idea of conversation," a primary-school teacher declared.[108]

Against the odds, many make the best of their reduced life chances, while others are delivered to the healthcare, welfare, and criminal-justice systems, with half the children in youth custody in England and Wales coming from foster or residential care.[109] But those diagnosed as "delinquent" are often merely acting out the governing ethic of the collapsing free society itself: that limits upon liberty of "choice" are unacceptable impositions, whatever the "choice" may be.

Others, more innocent, worry about their clothing and appearance, their sense of inadequacy having been induced early by market-driven images of fashionable perfection; in France, under a law designed to help combat anorexia in young people, photoshopped images that make models look thinner than they are must (in theory) carry the warning "retouched photograph."[110] Moreover, an inert virtual existence, much of which is spent in the electronic void, adds to the solitudes of the growing but not always maturing child. British children, for example, are said to be "among the most housebound in the world,"[111] their levels of physical activity in decline[112]—12 percent of a sample of 2,000 18-to-24-year-olds had never seen a cow[113]—with many parents of teenagers "not monitoring their activities, not ensuring their healthcare, nor taking interest in their education."[114]

"Problems with food" also accompany some anxious children into adolescence and beyond, and the number of young people in Britain admitted to hospital with "eating disorders" rises, girls leading the way.[115] Depressive underweight follows some into adult life, while in others overweight has been fed at home—to the point of obesity—on junk and compensatory treats, sometimes provided by hard-pressed mothers who may themselves be obese. Inheriting the sense that restraint in the free society brings little reward, other young people cast themselves away sexually in search of well-being and find new distress. For some girls, often already harmed, seduction and child-birth promise care, esteem, and love. But early pregnancy and early abortion are the outcomes for many—in England and Wales, half of all pregnancies in the under-18s end so[116]—although, as already mentioned, the numbers have seen some decline. At worst, sexual violence is rife in the inner city's gang-land world, with young girls "offering sex in return for status and protection."[117]

In Britain in June 2016, a quarter of a million young people under eighteen, almost 54,000 of them between the ages of six and ten, and 12,000 aged five and under, were receiving mental-health help,[118] while in the 2017–2018 school year in England there were over 30,000 referrals of pupils for mental-health treatment.[119] Similarly, in a single year over 1,000 university students abandoned their studies with "mental health problems."[120] A total that is increasing, more female than male students disclosed that they had such problems.[121] In a 2015 survey of British girls and women aged eleven to twenty-one who had needed mental-health help, a large majority also held the view that adults did not recognize the pressures they were under—including of cyber-bullying and sexual harassment—with "self-harm" found to be the "most serious health issue."[122]

A symbol of civil society's wider self-destruction, it takes many forms in the young, suicide included. Almost six hundred young people between the ages of ten and twenty-four took their lives in England and Wales in a single year,[123] ninety-eight children between ten and fourteen in the decade to 2014,[124] with "teen suicides" and attempted suicides increasing in the United States also.[125] In addition, rising totals of self-harmers, some in their early teens and even younger—as young as seven[126]—and with girls far outnumbering boys,[127] slash their arms and cut their bodies with scissors, razor blades, and glass; bruise and burn themselves; and pull out their hair.

The turning of the self upon the self, short of suicide, is again not new. "I should be glad to hurt myself as a relief to my feelings," Dickens has a young unrequited lover declare.[128] But the character is depicted as absurd. The phenomenon is not absurd today. In England in 2017, more than 13,000 females and over 2,000 males under the ages of eighteen were treated in hospital accident-and-emergency departments for injuries that had been self-inflicted, a total that has doubled in twenty years.[129] Similarly, those between the ages of thirteen and seventeen were the largest cohort in 2015,[130] with almost 1,000 children in the year to 2016 aged twelve and under,[131] while in the United States some one in four teenage girls were found in a 2015 sample survey of high-school students to have committed "non-suicidal self-injury."[132]

For this degree of anomic distress, psychiatry again offers its diagnoses and prescriptions. By such route, increasing numbers of the young join the massed ranks of the "consumers" of painkillers, amphetamines, and other mind-altering or antipsychotic medications. But few parents or carers, whether innocent or guilty of the failures that bring the young to such a pass, could be expected to fathom its causes. Deep-rooted in lost identity and direction, they are symptoms of the dissolving free society itself.

Bearing much of the brunt of the failure of family, nurture and the home are the teacher and the school. Decreasingly a matter of the eternal rebelliousness of the youthful spirit, such failure has brought growing hostility and anger to the classroom. Children in all times have suffered deprivation and neglect, and turned their frustrations on others. At a "Ragged School" visited by Dickens in 1852 in the then-poor Faringdon district of London, the teachers "knew little of their office; the pupils, with an evil sharpness, found them out, got the better of them, derided them, made blasphemous answers to scriptural questions, sang, fought, danced, robbed each other; seemed possessed by legions of devils."[133] Today, such children may be diagnosed as hyperactive and be medicated. But in a collapsing social order, they also possess a sense of right.

From families in varieties of difficulty and dysfunction there have always emerged into the light not only battle-hardened survivors but optimistic and ethically self-aware individuals. But in free societies many young people now appear to have been irreparably harmed at home. The psychologizer can thus find a "coldness" in those denied affection which "leads to aggression," and in children with limited expressiveness "bitterness towards those who know how to speak."[134] Arguably disabling, too, is that single-mothered children, and others who have lost contact with their fathers, find ever fewer male teachers when they reach school age. In Britain, a quarter of primary schools have no male teachers at all,[135] and in Ireland almost 90 percent of primary teachers are women.[136] At the same time teachers, put under increasing physical and mental strain by pupils' problems and behavior, come and go in a replication of the impermanence which growing numbers of children already know.

Nevertheless, despite the rate of "under-achievement"—especially of boys—and the contempt for education formed early and growing during school years, many children learn or, in flight from home and school, acquire the arts of survival on the street. Meanwhile, hard-pressed teachers strive to educate the morally innocent along with the precociously experienced and even vicious, the responsive learner sitting beside the resistant, the socialized with the asocial. In such conditions, with early-retirement rates rising, the function of teachers is increasingly that of policing not pedagogy. There falls to them the task of grappling with the "behavior problems" brought from home by the harmed child, so that all may learn.

In some schools, as in Dickens's Faringdon, teachers run the gauntlet in class of verbal abuse, harassment, and even physical assault by their pupils; four in ten teachers in Britain were said to have suffered assault in 2015,[137] while teaching assistants reported similar levels of abuse and attack.[138] Teachers are also subjected to new forms of bullying and insult online. In addition, they may suffer parental blame and sometimes violence for their disordered children's failures. In small worlds of threatening language, derision, and blows, brought from home to school, anger-counseling—sometimes for children as young as seven—and in Britain "behaviour support teams" seek to pacify the victims of familial failure and social breakdown.

In England and Wales, over 2,000 weapons, including axes, airguns, and knives, were seized by police in schools in thirty-two police areas between April 2015 and January 2017.[139] Four dozen children under the age of ten were among those who had them; acid and ammonia hidden in drinking bottles have been found in schools in London for potential use as weapons;[140] and in West Virginia opioid antidotes can be administered to students who have overdosed, without the need first to contact parents.[141] Where the school has become a true battlefield, as in the American inner city, it has also brought the installation of metal detectors for weapons, police patrols—with armed officers present at least once a week in over 40 percent of all US public schools[142]—and even on-site police posts.

"Safety guards" in Chicago's most dangerous gang-ridden neighborhoods accompany children to school, while even in rural Colorado,[143] and from Texas to California, teachers and other school employees have gained the right to be armed. In-school violent crime has been committed in the last years by both boys and girls, using weapons such as blades, sharpened metal combs, scissors, and (especially in the United States) handguns. These crimes, again especially in the United States, have included homicides of teachers and of pupils, in the latter case often driven by varieties of jealousy, rivalry, and hatred. Thus in a fight in a suburban Detroit high-school classroom, a sixteen-year-old was stabbed twice in the chest with a "kitchen-style steak-knife" by another teenage girl and died during surgery at a hospital nearby.[144]

The jeering contempt of the delinquent for the dutiful student can also turn everyday mischief-making and bullying to murder, again including girl-on-girl killings. Moreover, in the United States there can be "mass killings" by school students, or former school students, as at Columbine High School in Colorado in 1999, at Sandy Hook Elementary School in Connecticut in 2012, and at high schools in Parkland, Florida, and Santa Fe, Texas, in 2018. Often enough, aggressors are found to be on medication, including for "attention-deficit" and "bipolar" disturbances of mind; in Wisconsin, a girl of twelve stabbed a classmate to death in order to appease a character in a horror-film that she was in the habit of watching.[145] In their backgrounds, brought from home, may also be found histories of insensate anger for trivial reasons—over teasing, noise, or the interruption by a parent or sibling of a video game—with depression and other ailments offered as diagnoses.

Meanwhile, in Britain "pupil-referral units" (themselves said to have become "recruiting-grounds for gangs"[146]) segregate troublemakers; there were more than a third of a million "fixed period" exclusions of disruptive pupils in the 2015–2016 school year;[147] and nearly half of a sample of 3,000 teachers reported in 2017 that they removed children from their classes at least once a week.[148] Or they are permanently excluded from primary and secondary schools for "persistent disruptive behaviour," as well as for attacks on teachers and fellow pupils, sexual assaults included; more than two-hundred rapes were committed by young people on their fellow pupils in England and Wales between 2013 and 2016.[149]

In England, the number of such permanent exclusions has been rising every year since 2012, with 6,700 excluded from primary, secondary, and special schools in the year to 2016. Several hundreds of them were aged seven or under, and fifty a mere four years old; the most common ground for expulsion is that of "persistently disruptive behavior," and one-third for assaulting an adult.[150] Putting both teaching and learning under siege, their conduct is of a kind that teachers can barely manage or cannot manage at all; one-third of a sample of 4,000 British secondary-school students said that their classes had been interrupted ten times and more in a week.[151] Schools in Kentucky and Florida were even driven to handcuff unruly pupils;[152] in New Jersey, a preschool director was found guilty of child abuse after brandishing a knife at two four-year-olds;[153] and in Massachusetts during the 2016–2017 school year students had to be "physically restrained" on more than 9,000 occasions, with more than 240 injuries sustained by students and staff.[154]

Although still minorities in number, the totals of the already-harmed arriving in the education system, and of those who fail to benefit from it or who drop out of school in their teens, are growing. Counsel, much of it again psychologized and some of it naive, is no match for the strength of will that counters it, and sanctions are increasingly ineffective. Punishment of the young in Britain for "anti-social behavior" even gains "street-cred" and becomes a badge of honor, and rights are swiftly held to have been infringed.

Today, millions of school students in the United States are also classed as "chronically absent"[155]—with "improper steps" found to have been taken by teachers at a Washington, DC, high school to conceal it[156]—and in Britain, likewise, there is a 10 percent proportion of "persistent" absentees,[157] with some 50,000 classed as "missing education" or as "off the radar" entirely.[158] At the same time, tens of thousands of parents are prosecuted and fined each year in the United Kingdom for taking their offspring on "unauthorized family holidays" during the school term.[159] But fines have been found to have had "no effect on overall absence rates," which rose in some local authority areas after the penalties were introduced.[160] Moreover, parents are "increasingly bold"[161] in protesting against such sanctions. They thus argue for the "educational value" of term-time vacations[162] or claim—in a further abuse of liberty—that to be fined for it is an infringement of "parents' rights."[163] Many parents also refuse to accept moral responsibility for the community-wrecking conduct of their young, or are unable to check it. In Britain, parental-training orders, drug-treatment orders, child curfews, police dispersal of youth gangs, child-support orders against absconding fathers, and court-ordered removals of "disruptive" families from their homes continue to do battle with circumstances as best they can.

Meanwhile, several thousand young people in Britain aged between ten and seventeen come before the courts each year for knife possession. The total is rising,[164] with the numbers of young victims of knife attacks growing,[165] the severity of wounds increasing,[166] and with "spikes in violent activity" when students "come out of the school gates."[167] With youth firearms offenses also on the increase,[168] many thousands of young people become the victims of armed robbery and violence themselves.[169]

Inadequately secured guns in American homes have also led to rising numbers of deaths of children, with nearly four hundred deaths between January 2015 and September 2018 in "accidental shootings" of young people, sometimes very young.[170] A two-year-old shot himself with his police-officer father's gun in Cleveland, Ohio;[171] a two-year-old in Baton Rouge, Louisiana, shot its one-year-old sibling in the face; and another Louisiana two-year-old climbed on a stool at home, found a gun "on the counter," and shot himself dead;[172] a child of five "picked up her dad's gun and shot herself in the head";[173] and a four-year-old boy in South Carolina shot himself with his mother's .38 caliber gun after "finding it in her purse." His parents were arrested.[174]

Similarly, a Californian father was arrested for child endangerment after his six-year-old son brought a gun to his elementary school in a backpack, having had access to the gun at home,[175] while an eight-year-old boy was arrested in Maryland for bringing a loaded semiautomatic to elementary school in his bookbag.[176] In January 2018, a girl of twelve likewise brought a loaded semiautomatic to a Los Angeles middle school in her backpack. The backpack fell, the gun went off and shot a fellow pupil in the head, an event described as "accidental" by local police.[177] Or a young person may find a parent's gun and with it shoot the parent, as when a three-year-old girl in Indiana, playing with her father's gun, shot her pregnant mother in the stomach.[178]

Thus the free society is undermined in liberty's own name, as also in the failure of attempts in the United States to curb the access by minors to sadistic videos. A legislative effort to prohibit the sale or rental to under-18s of violent video games which give players the options of "killing, maiming, dismembering or sexually assaulting an image of a human-being" was declared by a federal appeals court to be a violation of minors' constitutional rights under the First Amendment. Aristotle would have disapproved. "We must keep all that is of low quality unfamiliar to the young, particularly things with an element of wickedness in them," he warned long ago.[179] But the US Supreme Court in 2011 concurred with the appeals court decision. It did so on the grounds that the "power to protect children from harm" did not include the right to "restrict the ideas"—including of sadistic violence—"to which children may be exposed."[180] The video-game "industry" celebrated the victory; unsurprisingly, since in Madam Bubble's reckoning, hand in purse, the "industry" is worth some $20 billion a year.[181]

Meanwhile, sanctions drive the disaffected young further into the wilderness, where purpose can be found in crime and identity in a gang. With "more than three-hundred teen crews" in New York alone, they have been said to be responsible for "about 40 per cent of the city's shootings."[182] The Roman historian Tacitus might have understood it. "Enmities," he wrote in 98 CE, "are more dangerous in conditions of freedom."[183] The number of such gangs—all-girl gangs or "sister gangs" too—is rising; and although some youth crime is driven by perennial forms of hardship and need, other crime is committed for gang prowess, intimidation, and entertainment. It may also be driven by contagious destructiveness and predation, as in the riots of August 2011 in British cities which saw vandalized stores ransacked and looted by thousands of mostly young people, children included.

With weapons an increasing commonplace in adolescent hands, with gangs fearless of the police and heedless of penal sanction, and with gang honor a surrogate for other achievement, familial, educational, and wider social failure is creating ever more unfit recruits for a democratic citizen body. "A crew to me is family. They're going to be there for me like my parents was never there for me" is the voice of it.[184] Freed in his teens from education and parental ties to become petty king of some mean street, the inner-city malefactor, child of wrecked home and disappearing social order—and made violent if "disrespected"—may become a hero to his peers; he may even be honored with a pavement shrine of graffiti messages, candles, and flowers, should he be knifed or shot dead.

In murders and manslaughters carried out by adolescents, assailants will be typically described as of "troubled background," as "loners," or as "obsessed with violence." They will often have a history of drug and substance abuse, and at worst—as in numbers of American cases—the violence they commit can be extreme, and include the emotionless stabbing, beating, and even kicking to death of victims. To Demosthenes, *philanthropia*, or a liking for one's fellows, was an attribute "brought from home,"[185] which at its best is the miniature commonwealth of the social order. For many, "home" now teaches no such lessons. Even attacks on the vulnerable elderly and the homeless by "disturbed" young people, females included, intermittently make the news, above all in the United States. "The assault by a younger man on an older man is a disgusting sight. The gods hate to see it," declared Plato, his moral recoil reaching us from other times.[186]

When a child or adolescent kills or seriously wounds a grandparent, parent, or other close relative, another new depth is reached; in a suburb of Tulsa, Oklahoma, for example, two adolescent brothers stabbed to death their parents and three siblings in July 2015.[187] These events occur most frequently in the United States once more. But in Britain, too, the extent of violence against parents is growing, with some 1,400 cases of assault and injury being recorded in a single year in London alone.[188] With the police increasingly called out to help embattled parents cope with abuse and violence directed at them, the large majority of offenders are male, and mothers the large majority of victims.[189] To Demosthenes, fear of being "shamed" by such deeds was the "greatest of compulsions upon all free men."[190] In the moral wilderness we have made of our freedoms, it is so no longer.

Instead, as in the United States, a difference, a restraint, a denial, or a reproach can lead to the wounding or killing of a family member by a young person, aided by the presence of weapons in the home. Sometimes carried out on swift impulse, sometimes with seemingly careful premeditation, remorse in such crimes is significantly rare. Routinely found once more are "psychiatric disorders," hard and soft drugs, antidepressants, parental neglect, and addiction to violent video games.

Parricide and matricide have hitherto been considered the most heinous of crimes and the worst of sins. The Greek historian Herodotus tells us that the Persians found it impossible to credit that anyone could take the life of a parent,[191] while Plato believed that the "deliberate murder of relatives" occurs "in states that have a defective system of education."[192] Hobbes, too, thought that to kill a parent was "a greater crime than to kill another; for the parent ought to have the honor of a sovereign."[193] But in free societies where ordinary familial duties are seen by many as impositions, this is an alien judgment. The loss of civic rights imposed in ancient Athens for harming a parent[194] is equally unthinkable now.

Although the numbers of murders of parents and other close relations are relatively small—with woundings and assaults much more frequent—they are recurrent now in the United States, and revealing. For the court evidence often suggests that attacks on family members are punishments as well as crimes, meted out for the harms done to young people in failing social and moral orders. Moreover, the youthful assailants can be seen as the free society's natural offspring, born to its ethic of self-will, injured by familial breakdown, damaged by their own sense of right, and indifferent to consequences.

In the free society, such indifference is learned early.

CHAPTER 6

IN LIMBO

To grasp the range and scale of the problems which bedevil today's free society is getting harder, despite the growing resources for the dissemination of knowledge about it. In the best of circumstances—not ours now—it is difficult to take a just measure of events, while fear for the future that awaits us is perennial. "There is a cycle in human affairs, and in its turning it does not permit any people to find permanent good fortune," the wealthy Croesus is said to have observed in the sixth century BCE.[1] The Greek historian Polybius thought much the same: "In every human body, in every polity, there is a natural growth, a crowning moment, then a decline."[2]

During a century and more of technical progress and social disaggregation in the modern free society, unease has been growing. Charles Masterman, a sensitive observer of early twentieth-century Britain, saw the society of his time as "complicated and baffled," and in 1909 thought that "most people" felt "confused in a world of confusion," with "life making ever more difficult demands on body and soul."[3]

Adding to today's confusion, some see vice and others virtue in the same things, while new expressions of self-will in moral conduct and material acquisition bring both benefit and harm. With "change" made a leading principle of social policy and ethical judgment, broader liberty and greater license are empowering for some and give new occasion for pleasure. But they also inflict growing pain upon the self and others, and that which for some is emancipatory and right is perceived as plain wrong by others. At the same time, new possibilities— keeping millions on the run—are beyond the reach of many, while those within reach seem rarely to satisfy for long, deluding hopes that this or that new "product" or moral choice will bring contentment.

Humanity, as it tries to make sense of the world, also has a long history of staring at Plato's shadows on the wall.[4] Today's shadows are increasingly electronic, with a widening range of market-driven "products" to benefit, console, inform, and distract the solitary individual. Severed from a sense of real place and canceling unwelcome truth about their own and others' condition, many in our "digital age" thus turn their faces to a screen and to the shadows which play upon it. With the door closed on the real world and surfing cyberspace as the hours pass, here is Milton's fathomless limbo "large and broad,"[5] remote from the truly-lived life among fellow human beings and in sentient contact with them.

In limbo today, prodigious numbers are held in thrall to the web, tablets, smartphones—the iPhone dates from 2007—and TV, and with tens of millions of tons of discarded computers, monitors, cell phones, and other electronic waste now dumped around the world.[6] Facebook, founded in 2004 and whose mission statement was "to make the world more open and connected,"[7] had over two billion users in 2018,[8] more than one quarter of the planet's population. With only 12 percent of Americans not having a Facebook account,[9] and the average daily time spent on it in the United States "nearing an hour"—or three times more than is spent reading or exercising[10]—it was described by a company spokesman as a "good measure of whether we're delivering value."[11]

But political and commercial interests were discovered in 2018 to have gained access to tens of millions of Facebook users' personal data.[12] Fined half a million pounds in Britain for the breach[13]—equivalent to its revenue every five-and-a-half minutes[14]—and losing $120 billion in market value in a single day following the discovery,[15] growth slowed, the number of "daily active users" in Europe showed some decline,[16] and profits fell, but use of it and revenue from it continued to run in the billions. Similarly, there are over 330 million Twitter users[17]—the Pope and a US president included, the latter "bypassing" both the "dishonest media"[18] and government decision-making procedures—with hundreds of thousands of "tweets" sent every minute, and hundreds of millions per day.

In this limbo, millions check their messages by day and night, billions of "apps" are downloaded each year, almost half of the world's population use the internet,[19] and there were some five billion mobile-phone users in 2018,[20] over 60 percent of the world's population. In Britain, almost 80 percent own a smartphone—95 percent of 16-to-24-year-olds—on average check it every twelve minutes of the waking day, and are online for an average of twenty-four hours a week.[21]

It has also been estimated that the "average household" in the United Kingdom has more than eight "devices" linked to the internet, its members often sitting together in the same room and looking at different ones.[22] Nearly half of all British children get a mobile phone before they leave primary school,[23] two-thirds even of preschoolers use tablets[24]—some 20 percent of whom spend one to four hours a day online[25]—while the electronic void is home to the neglected child; and over six million people in Britain, including one in five 18-to-24 year-olds, do not own a book.[26] In the United States, similarly, an average of twenty-four hours a week is spent online;[27] 95 percent of teens own a mobile device; 70 percent use it "multiple times" per day, and over a third "prefer texting to talking" as their favorite way to communicate with friends.[28]

In consequence, the rule over limbo of "tech giants" armed with their weapons of mass distraction made Apple, with its over 50 million iPhone sales in a quarter, [29] the first US public company to be worth $1 trillion.[30] As the revenues of the leading firms reach billions of dollars a week, they also have poor records of compliance with tax laws. Thus Apple was itself made to pay back billions after a European Union tax investigation into the diversion of its profits through Ireland;[31] Amazon, the beneficiary of an illegal tax deal in Luxembourg, where it had based much of its European operations, was similarly ordered to pay €250 million in evaded taxes;[32] while Google was fined $2.7 billion in an antitrust ruling for the abuse of its dominant position in the "electronic market" as search-engine leader,[33] and $5.1 billion for forcing cellphone makers to install Google apps.[34]

Meanwhile, electronic limbo's shop window has become ever more lavishly supplied by Madam Bubble with advanced devices; as Thucydides pointed out even in the fifth century BCE, "it is inevitable that in technical activity the more recent prevails."[35] Electronic "products" multiply in sophistication and range; how they are made and by whom are questions rarely asked. With e-commerce, web buying, and internet shopping causing increasing harm to civil society's high streets and town centers—"in the future all companies will be internet companies, or they won't be companies at all,"[36] says a department-store boss—such devices include "internet-enabled smart TV" giving "consumers" the ability to "turf," or watch TV and surf the Web at the same time; tablets described as a "snacking version" of the home computer;[37] and "wearable tech" of many kinds.

Already arrived or in near prospect are "gaze-interaction software," glance-controlled, that permits the wearer to consult the Web, send an email, watch a film, or shoot a video with the blink of an eye (or at voice command), and to distribute to fellow dwellers in limbo whatever the wearer sees, hears, or says; GPS technology which can "layer digital images" onto real-life settings;[38] satnav footwear connected to a mapping system and sending directions to the wearer's feet on which way to go; digital spectacles projecting the Web onto our eyeballs; "electro-encephalography headsets" combined with "smart glasses" which permit the playing of video games by mind control alone; "direct brain interfaces" which, similarly, will one day "let you communicate using only your mind";[39] and sex-at-a-distance, with vibrators and other devices triggered electronically by a known or unknown partner.

Such devices have also been described as an "extension of the self."[40] It is a "self" which, despite its enhanced powers, inhabits a world, or limbo, of associative make-believe in a cyberspace which is un-peopled, with heavy use of digital media by young people also linked by researchers to behavioral problems,[41] and with the decreasing ability outside the electronic sphere to relate to, or communicate with, others. In "chat rooms" which are not rooms—"suicide chat rooms" included—"chat" is not the conversational exchange of those present to one another; in "crowdfunding" there is no crowd; and in "cyber hangouts" where no one hangs out or in electronic "meeting places" where no one meets, we are "linked in" only to the ether, the very term "social media" a misnomer. Above all, failing democracy can find no salvation in political "assemblies online"[42] or in a "contract of government" ratified by an online vote,[43] and no new "digital socialism"[44] is in prospect, while "communities" of bloggers cannot recover the spirit of a true commonwealth nor create a new civic order.

In "interactions" abstracted from the reciprocity of real human contact but in which the techno-isolate finds a seeming place, harm-doing has been better served, with Facebook having to take down millions of posts containing graphic violence, sexual activity—the largest category—and hate speech.[45] Electronic technology also provides the means for the state to pry on the unwary, and for the state's foes to disable civilian and military administration by cyber-attack, while social media platforms were allegedly used by Russian interests, assuming American identities, to disparage Hillary Clinton and promote Donald Trump in the 2016 US presidential election.

This or that interest can also hack into the banking system, blow state secrets, and steal personal data; can demand ransom, groom the young for sexual predation, and purchase or distribute fake passports, drugs, and guns, while in the furthest recesses of the "dark web" bomb-making instructions are exchanged and "terror" is promoted. Such resource has even made decapitations a "form of theater"[46] for home consumption, and put sophisticated encryption and its messaging services at the disposal of recruits to the advancing jihad. Once, the "electric telegraph whose silent speech even kings cannot control"[47] aroused premonitory alarm. This, however, is of an entirely new order.

But even if the web is not the "gift from God" proclaimed by Pope Francis,[48] there are also illuminations to be had from it on every topic under the sun, opportunities for lightning-swift communication and exchanges of information, and new resources by which to see, hear, speak, and learn. However, true knowledge—not the same as information—appears to advance proportionately little. Attention spans become briefer, ease of resort to search engines diminishes and darkens memory, and loss of expressiveness together with other ills accompany thraldom to the screen.[49]

Indeed, for most, there is less a mastery of the digital world than a burdensome subordination to its demands, and a filtering away of identity and time in what Lewis Mumford called the "unlived life."[50] To be wired for sound and plugged in to other worlds than this, lost to physical place and surfing the electronic waves, or casting endless messages into solitude's high seas, is to enter a limbo which has no bounds and in which to be deprived of "access" or to lose a mobile brings anxiety and stress. As the absorbed texter walks, head lowered, the real world—the world of Nature included—goes unseen, the term "waking day" another misnomer.

In the mid-eighteenth century, Chesterfield also complained that "many young people see and hear in so superficial and inattentive a manner that they might as well not see or hear at all."[51] But now the motorist at the wheel uses a mobile phone and surfs the net; a texter steps into the path of a truck or oncoming train, off a pier in Melbourne harbor,[52] or into a shopping-mall fountain in Beijing;[53] a New Jersey woman on her cell phone falls into a basement cellar;[54] and in Antwerp (and Xi'an in northwest China[55]) "text walking-lanes" are set up to "prevent collisions."[56] Similarly, while taking "selfies," a girl fell off a railway bridge in Russia onto high-voltage cables;[57] a couple plunged to their deaths from a wall above a Portuguese beach;[58] and a child in a stroller fell into a southern Italian harbor while its parents were taking a photo of themselves.[59] There is also an underclass of non-selfie-takers and non-users of the internet—almost five million in Britain[60]—who are not "connected," and "lacking basic digital skills"[61] are perceived by those who are themselves in limbo to be living in a lost world of their own. An elderly New Hampshire doctor unable to use a computer even lost her license to practice.[62]

Meanwhile, self-absorbed "interactive" communications make their own comment on the free society's isolations, while electronic messages from screen to screen using techno-speak's abbreviations are dumb-show versions of true conversation. "It is amazing to observe the way men write, talk and jabber away without a jot of meaning," Satan declares in a nineteenth-century satirical fable.[63] But this Satan did not know our times, times in which mutual estrangement is digitally transmitted.

Moreover, today, millions search in electronic limbo for a sense of personal significance they cannot find in the actual world and in its daily round. Ironically, much of this addictive searching amid the babel of the blogosphere is conducted under the cover of anonymity or in a false persona. It is little surprise, therefore, that in the electronic arena—no bricks and mortar of the real arena here—rumor and gossip, abuse and cruel spite, plagiarism, idle defamation, race hatred, "revenge porn," and threats of violence flourish. The world of the "tweet" and the "Twitter" is less infantile than the words suggest.

In addition, low levels of analysis, self-expression, and polemic on many blogsites make for a form of mob rule, not debate, in matters of opinion and judgment, with websites driven to use "moderators" or to ban comment entirely. Moreover, anonymity—which has been described as a "major appeal" of "online life"[64]—gives further license to electronic "trolling" and stalking. Many young people in Britain between the ages of eleven and sixteen who use social networking sites are said to suffer from malice and bullying,[65] with some "targeted daily"[66] and the numbers rising sharply.[67] Each year, among the teenagers who take their own lives, are many who do so after being pursued in limbo by rivals and foes, while hundreds of thousands of British teenagers are caught up in "casino-style" video-gambling.[68] Others, children included, are entrapped in a world of "sexting" and "sextortion," as "naked selfies" and other compromising images of them circulate beyond control.

But whether it be a matter of cruelty or license—a casual dating site for British students called "shag at Uni" quickly attracted 150,000 members online[69]—a growing habituation to limbo's freedoms carries all before it. Some offenders even film their crimes as they commit them and distribute the videos via "social media," while secret Instagram groups foment gang warfare,[70] and YouTube, at Metropolitan police request, deleted dozens of rap music videos with violent lyrics and images, including of street stabbings.[71] Moreover, with personal identity increasingly an electronic confection and not a real self—which "selfies" do not restore—many attribute to the electronic void the virtues which actual social orders have lost.

They thus find (or pretend to find) in limbo the democratic *polis* itself. But even though politicians may resort to tweeting and through parties use electronic "micro-targeting" of voters, as in American electoral campaigns, cyberspace is beyond the reach of political domestication. Above all, there can be no true democracy without participant social beings, as already argued. Cyphers, often without habitation or name and in contact with other worlds than the living one around them, cannot serve.

Nevertheless, many think they have found a place for themselves and community with others in electronic limbo. There has thus come a "deluded sense of intimacy"[72] with the shadows they see before them. On the death of a British TV chat-show host, "millions" were said to feel that they had lost "their own special friend,"[73] or to have lost a "special mate" when a TV comedian died.[74] Indeed, many see more materiality in the shadow on the wall than in the actual materiality before them.

A ferry sinking in Indonesia, a plane skidding off a runway, the aftermath of a Japanese earthquake, a fire in the Philippines, a machete attack in south London, a hurricane in the Caribbean, and the collapse of an Italian motorway bridge could therefore be described by witnesses and survivors as "like something from a Steven Spielberg scene," a "surreal experience," "like a disaster movie," "so bad it didn't seem real," "like something from a film," "like a movie I never want to see," and "an apocalyptic sight like a film."[75] The jihadi attack in New York in October 2017 was also called "surreal."[76] None was what it was. Even congressional hearings on the radicalization of Muslims in the United States were compared with "reality TV" by an American politician,[77] the 2016 Republican race in the United States had a "real life *Game of Thrones* plot,"[78] while the theft from the Vatican of a Pope's papers was called a "sensational Hollywood-like scandal."[79]

Moreover, as the need for public response to actuality grows more urgent—in a democracy above all—ever-greater claims on attention are made by the seeming verities of the screen. Indeed, even Osama bin Laden is said to have ended his days looking at videos of himself in his Abbottabad lair before an irruption of Reality in May 2011 shot him down; and to the sofa-bound millions without sense of place in a social order, electronically created celebrities seem more real than they. At the same time, addicted "internet activists," blogging their websites into "market brands," think themselves the equivalents of genuine actors in the public domain. They may even become so for a while. But their *personae* remain electronic confections, not actual selves.

The desire for distraction from the way things are is easily under-stood; the surfer's roaming in cyberspace, the texter's messaging, and the restless switching-of-channels are part of the spirit of the age. Yet these are times when truth-telling about the free society's plight has never been more necessary. Instead, in the further limbo we have made, instant opinion supplants analysis, shorter attention spans are fed by half-truths and by sound-bites, while falsehood serves the political place-seeker or a newspaper proprietor's ambition.

As need for reason and judgment grows, hectic headlines and deadlines crowd out measure in the shallow competition for "market share," and last week's sensation is soon overtaken. Despite the valu-able information which some of the press and the press agencies provide, a form of show business has been made of news itself—the more catastrophic the better. Media "packages" combine notice of massacre with the latest fashions, non-events without meaning are daily news, and the shooting stars of celebrity flash across the media heavens and are gone.

The worlds of the chat-show host, the television pundit, the newspaper columnist, the blogger, and the journalist have gradually converged. At the same time, the question of which version of actuality and which opinion sees the light is increasingly a market decision. In the (often misjudged) interests of circulation and audience share, other deteriorations follow. Vocabularies atrophy, semiliteracy is streamlined, and crudity of word and thought commands the greatest attention. Although the degree and extent of it are unprecedented, this is again no new theme; long ago, de Tocqueville disparaged what he regarded as the "vulgar turn of mind" of American journalists of the day, and their "coarse appeal" to the "passions" of readers.[80] In our time such "appeal" has brought to the competitive newspaper market in Britain, and in other free societies, wares of ever-lower grade.

The demotic terms and seeming swagger of it, again as if in "progress's" name, are not the work of bold freethinkers and liberated spirits but once more a form of self-harm. With women writers often leading the way, approval can therefore be expressed—by no Swift or Rabelais—of those who "piss" in the alleys of London, calling it a "decisive break from bourgeois manners and mores."[81] "Drop your knickers to half-mast, the Erotic Review is no more," pronounces the Times;[82] "feminism is more than just capitalism with tits," declares a writer in the Guardian;[83] "all women's bums are not created equal," says another;[84] "you look better with meat on your arse," reads a Telegraph feature title;[85] and "why farting is a feminist issue" was explained in the New Statesman.[86]

Similarly, a woman writer in the Telegraph described the "sheer joy" of "having one's pubes poking out of the side of one's swimsuit and not caring."[87] "All hail Lily Allen and her baggy vagina," the Telegraph also proclaimed;[88] "look between your legs before you pick a career," recommended a contributor to the Times;[89] " I pee in the undergrowth. I enjoy being a criminal," declared a female voice in the Guardian;[90] and "a little something that can do the job well," wrote another woman columnist on the subject of vibrators, "is never going to be the same thing as shagging a real person. Yet having something to fill the hole—literally and metaphorically—can only be a good thing."[91]

"Don't tell me to put my boobs away," cried a *Telegraph* writer in November 2016;[92] "if only my vagina could speak," a *Times* contributor exclaimed;[93] and "every penis tells a story," read a *Guardian* sub-head in May 2017.[94] "What happens when you flush a plane loo?" and "is body odor the last taboo?" articles in the *Guardian* and *Telegraph* have inquired;[95] "our politicians shouldn't be judged by the contents of their underwear," the *Telegraph* told its readers in July 2016;[96] "Theresa May's job is not to wipe Britain's bottom," thought another *Telegraph* writer in September 2016;[97] and "the perils of talking dirty with your flies open" was the subject of a *Times* column in July 2018.[98] "The crotch of the matter: to bulge or not to bulge,"[99] "are scrotal lifts the next trend in male grooming?"[100] and "should I shave my pubic hair?"[101] were again dilemmas raised by the *Telegraph* and the *Guardian*, while "songs about bodily fluids" and the "fart-filtering failure of underwear" were further subjects of articles in the *Guardian*.[102] "It's vulgar, I love it!" confirmed a contributor to the *Times* in October 2016.[103]

These limbo coarsenesses of mind and witless metaphor, beyond any that a de Tocqueville could have anticipated, disclose a will to violate feeling, sordid as it is to rehearse the matter. An object of disparagement can be called a "swivel-eyed horse-shitter" and an "industrial-strength knob-end" in the *Observer*,[104] a "thieving toe-rag" in the *Times*,[105] or a "rent-a-gob" in the *Guardian*.[106] Infantilism finds its thrills with words like *ass* and *asshole*, *boobs*, *bollocks*, and *bums*, *crap*, *fart*, *piss*, *shit*, or *wank*, including in titles or sub-headings. Labour Party members of a previous generation can be called "hairy-arsed sons of toil,"[107] and Trump can be described as dominating the news "like a fart in a car."[108] "To pee or not to pee" can also pass as wit.

With pointless transgression—at Madam Bubble's command— now a fixed part of limbo's media diet, falsely democratic vulgarities of simile and image abound in internet and print editions of the once "up-scale" British press. A writer in the *Observer* can object to the "early morning smell of a stranger's armpit on a crowded train,"[109] untruths are called the "fat turds of falsehood" in the *Guardian*,[110] and

the "disgusting truth about running" is said to be "permanently drip-
ping snot."[111] Even the defects of a computer program may be gratu-
itously compared with the "faint smell of piss in a subway,"[112] "Bums
on Seats" can now be the title of a *Times* leader,[113] and 2017 could be
described in a headline as "the year of the asshole."[114]

Much of this tawdriness in free expression's name is trivial. But
other self-harming sentiments are less so. We can therefore be told
by a writer in London's *Evening Standard* that "politeness is for timid
mice who cannot keep up in the rat-race. Instead of vainly trying to
soften up a tough world, they should either grow a thicker skin or else
sod off into a monastery. What does the bottling up of your hatred
beneath a painted smile give you?" he asks. "Cancer of the colon,
that's what," he answers.[115]

A vicarious pleasure may also be vulgarly—or again pseudo-
democratically—expressed in harm done to, or suffered by, others.
In an election, a politician is not defeated but "given a smack in the
mouth,"[116] or (more frequently) a "good kicking." All British "quality"
newspapers employ the kicking metaphor. "There is no getting away
from the viciousness of the kicking Mr. Blair has suffered," says the
Telegraph with relish;[117] "could anything be more joyous?" asked the
Observer of a similar "kicking" meted out to a politician.[118] "This one
is winnable," declared the *Telegraph* on rival bids for the 2012 Olym-
pics, "but only if our leaders get their kicking boots on,"[119] a hooligan
image. Poor financial news can similarly be described as "a knee in
the nuts to bankers"[120] or "a boot in the groin to the Chancellor of
the Exchequer."[121]

The metaphor of giving an opponent a "kicking" is not new. "I do
not know any nation from whom we can afford to accept a kicking,"
said the British colonial secretary Joseph Chamberlain in December
1895.[122] But today there are few bounds to the use of such type of
image. Tory politicians could therefore be recommended by a *Times*
columnist, as an electoral contest with Labour approached, to "kick
the living daylights out of them, humiliate them, knock them all over
the shop. . . . Pile in, fists flailing, jump up and down on their heads,

kill."[123] Even in a literary dispute a rival can be described as having received a "good kick in the face,"[124] a "philosopher" can declare that the objects of his disapproval "merit a good kicking,"[125] a chat-show host is said to have a "poundable face,"[126] and an actor is given space to announce that "when I die I want the chance to hit God in the face."[127] Women are again in the thick of this fray. "I'm in Edinburgh [at the festival] and I want to kick something to death," a female voice declares.[128] And one woman can even say of another that the latter has given "her feminist sisters" a "good kicking."[129]

In the breaking of bounds, media metaphor in the British "quality" press has gone further. "When a politician is on the floor, bleeding heavily, it's hugely tempting for his political opponents to kick him to death," a commentator in the *Telegraph* assures us,[130] while it was asserted in the *Guardian* that it is a "normal human impulse to watch two people kick the hell out of each other."[131] Likewise, we can be told that "we all want revenge"—do we?—and that "to take an eye for an eye" is "our national urge."[132] In limbo, there are few limits to these excesses. "Violence against women" could therefore be said in the *Times* to have the "thrill of any great taboo," that "we love to watch women suffer"—do we?—and that "each time their agony is racheted [*sic*] up a notch, we crane our necks with interest in its effect on the lovely victim."[133]

These emanations from the void are dismissible as excrescences for notice's sake. But they are also expressions of what Bunyan might have called the "Spirit of Demolition," directed equally from "left" and "right" at institutions and principles, customs and rites of passage, articles of faith, reputations, and moral distinctions. They are all objects now of the urge (in some) to disable and destroy the given, good with bad, and once again in a false liberty's name.

With educational standards falling, contributors to British "quality" newspapers can therefore claim that "traditional grammar-teaching is a waste of time,"[134] that mathematics is "the core subject that we should drop,"[135] and that "there's nothing wrong with unqual-ified teachers."[136] Likewise, when the problem of school absenteeism was under debate, the *Telegraph* in August 2016 offered its readers guidance on the "ten ways to have a guilt-free family holiday in term-time."[137] "Our ignorance is gaining mass. Embrace it," the title of a *Times* article read in July 2012.[138]

In such fashion, what Thucydides called "cleverness coupled with license"[139] is increasingly aimed by the Spirit of Demolition at the social order. When a (woman) judge called a defendant a "bit of a cunt" in court and faced a "judicial conduct" inquiry for it, "three cheers for a judge who sounds like normal people," exclaimed a contributor to the *Times*;[140] "I was a middle-class shoplifter, where's the harm?" inquired a *Telegraph* headline on New Year's Eve[141] in similar fashion. Using the limbo media as their instruments, such wilderness voices seem to call out to us to join them. Or in Simone Weil's words, "the uprooted seek to uproot others."[142] The Roman philosopher Seneca also understood it. "If we live focused only upon ourselves," he wrote two thousand years ago, "we begin to raise edifices of our own, and to bring other edifices down."[143]

"Marriage is a sham" and a "costume drama," thus declared a contributor to the *Guardian*.[144] "Forget the hot air on family values,"[145] "why it's OK to be seen as a bad mother,"[146] and "on Mother's Day let's celebrate the pleasure of watching mums failing badly,"[147] other wilderness voices tell their readers. The "thesis" that "families form the bedrock of social stability" was similarly dismissed as "absurd" by a columnist in the *Times*.[148] Family meals together? No, they "would greatly accelerate the breakdown of the family," says one;[149] "far easier to knock the kitchen and the dining-room into one huge space and let the children use it as a football pitch and a grazing ground," says another.[150]

Further and further such Spirit of Demolition enters into the heart of personal life, speeding the vortex of harm and self-harm as it goes. In one place, the Spirit advises that teenagers should be "encouraged to have sex";[151] in another, that "our children urgently need less self-esteem";[152] and in a third declares that it is "good" if "your child is lying to you."[153] "I wish my mother had aborted me," reads a feature title;[154] "there's nothing normal about giving birth," declares a woman columnist in the *Guardian*;[155] and "breastfeeding is creepy," asserts the editor of a parenting magazine.[156] The Spirit of Demolition can likewise claim that "parental neglect" is a "precious gift to children";[157] "idle parenting" is said to "make happy children";[158] and "why you should leave your kids in the pub" is explained to us in the *Times*.[159]

"Who needs fathers?" the same paper asks, and "Get out and stay out, Dad!" shouts its headline.[160] "What should we do with mother?" The *Times* also inquires,[161] with a pair of wizened hands to illustrate the query, and age itself disparaged. "How to live with an aging parent and not go totally mad," explains the *Telegraph*,[162] while "the ageing population" was described as a "creaking liability for the working population."[163] In "20 reasons it's okay to hate Valentine's Day"—with an accompanying image of decapitated red roses—even the expression of love can be soiled by the Spirit of Demolition.[164] "Valentine's Day is an ugly business," the *Guardian* repeated in February 2015.[165]

The range of attempted harm-doing at the Spirit's hands thus widens as the free-chooser's sense of entitlement grows. It can be expressed in the assertion that "it doesn't mean anything to be a 'man'";[166] more grimly, in the explanation of "why it's OK to hate other people's children";[167] and in the condemnation of "normality perverts."[168] "Self-improvement is a waste of time. Embrace the lazy under-achievers you really are"[169] was infantile, and likewise the claim that "addiction to social media can be good for you."[170] But the assertion that "violence should be seen as a sign of a healthy democracy"[171] was a different matter. A true perversity can be aroused even by the largest moral challenges that we face, as with the possibility—earlier referred to—that human-animal chimeras may one day walk the earth. "They pose grave questions about the future of mankind," a *Times* leader averred.[172] "All the more reason to press on with the science," it declared.

With its will to harm, the Spirit of Demolition makes idle play with civil society's many wounds. "Have drug-scandals actually made sport more interesting?" the Spirit therefore asks;[173] tells the reader of the British "quality" press that "I took mephedrone and I liked it";[174]

claims that "taking drugs can be fun and the law should reflect that";[175] calls "cocaine, the perfect drug for a brittle and anxious Britain";[176] and says that "Prozac can be a beautiful thing";[177] while the fact that a leading politician had used cocaine and dope is said to "prove that times have changed for the better."[178]

In this way the self-harming Spirit of Demolition has marched on, assaulting all manner of virtues and values, large and small. "Good sports don't make champions," the Spirit announces,[179] and "Go on, waste your time in court," a headline on the duty of jury service jeers.[180] Its stride is long, especially in Britain, and there are no limits to what it would sully or seek to destroy. "The British high street is dead, let's celebrate";[181] and "Good news—foreigners are buying up Britain,"[182] it declares. And the seasons' round? "Why I hate summer (and you should too)," it replies;[183] and "summer is dead, so let's dance on its grave."[184]

And when we would ascend the ethical scale, the pitiless Spirit of Demolition is again on hand to push us down. "We should make a virtue out of being mean";[185] and "Of all our moral nonsenses, patriotism is the dumbest," the Spirit asserts;[186] while "Truth? Give me cheats and fibbers any day" read the headline over a *Times* column.[187] "This obsession with ethics is the curse of our time," pronounces the same Spirit;[188] exclaims "to Hell with the foolish idea of forgiveness";[189] and declares that "Mammon not God should rule on Sundays."[190] "Faith and Hope, yes—but ditch Charity," a *Times* article proclaimed even on Christmas Day.[191]

All voices from limbo, they seem to urge the free society to a quicker fall. Yet, as it dissolves, many remain immobilized at their screens. There are also more active responses and reactions, some to be welcomed, others to be feared.

CHAPTER 7

REACTIONS

Anxiety at the free society's condition, an anxiety which is growing, is variously expressed, including by contempt for the political class and the media, and by depressive retreat into self or into the shadows of a half-lived life in technology's arms. Unconcern has also played its part. In the *Inferno*, Dante locates just inside the gates of Hell those who have spent their days in a state of indifference both to good and evil, and were "for themselves only."[1]

But some of the seeming public passivity and personal self-absorption is deceptive. Describing the "general ruin" of ancient Athens, Thucydides complained that events were "passing unobserved."[2] They are not so today, even if dismay, weariness, and feelings of helplessness are common. "What will the future be," the first-century Roman writer Petronius has one of his characters ask, "if neither gods nor men take pity on this society of ours?"[3] Many ask the same question now, often in silence.

Nevertheless, the forms of reaction—again dialectical—to the self-destruction of the free society are wide-ranging. Some are ethical and rational, others mere rabble-rousing, and others again are paranoid, with scapegoats old and new being sought for public fears, angers, and despairs. In the 1920s and '30s, similar feelings found their outlets in mounting xenophobia, and disillusionment with the political class paved the anti-democrat's way.

Today, free-society governments again flail in the face of economic and social problems of halting "growth," reckless deficit spending, and recurrent bank crises. At the same time, proposals for austerity measures on the one hand, or increased welfare spending on the other, provoke varieties of hostility across the political spectrum. As insecurities of different kinds deepen, animus also increases against the "alien" and the "financial sector," against supranational interest and the stranger next door. Meanwhile, mavericks of various stripes—beating new and old drums—try to harness the depressed and despairing to their causes with promises of redemption if their banners are followed into battle.

In some disabled democratic societies, still-surviving national temperament has acted as a brake upon excesses of public fervor. Despite the antiquity of its inequalities and divisions, Britain has been one such, its radical tradition notwithstanding. "There is little danger in England of any general popular uprising against a system which has concentrated in few hands so disproportionate a percentage of the national accumulation," Charles Masterman thought a century ago. "But there may be a danger of a kind of internal collapse," he warned, long before today's unraveling of the civic order began to provoke deepening unease.[4]

As this unraveling has proceeded on its course, many have continued to dance to Madam Bubble's piping tunes. At the same time, in both Britain and the United States, the unequal and the excluded have continued to make their voices heard, however poorly organized their movements and however various the issues that have provoked them. Protesters have "occupied Wall Street" and picketed banks, and foreclosed homes have been reclaimed by the dispossessed. Trade unionists, a shrinking proportion of the workforce, have downed tools and briefly marched to a past rhythm, while masked youths out for arson and pillage have set cars on fire, as in France. Undemonstrative discontent has also grown, with hankerings for a revival of the sense of nation, and—among the often less benign—for a new "discipline" and a new "order."

Moreover, in the United States and Britain, despite their relative political quiescence, the election of Donald Trump on the one hand, and the majority vote to leave the European Union on the other, pointed to impulses which the established political class had largely ignored. Thus, after his repeated cries from the hustings to "Make America Great Again!" Donald Trump (in a tweet) described his election to the US presidency in January 2017 as "the day the people became the rulers of this nation again,"[5] signed a proclamation for a "National Day of Patriotic Devotion" in his first moments in office,[6] and planned a "really great parade to show our military strength."[7]

In his campaign and thereafter, he and his speechwriters also promised "Americanism not globalism,"[8] "fair trade" in place of "free trade,"[9] and the restoration of "safety," including by means of a "great border wall" to keep out illegal immigrants "roaming free to threaten innocent citizens."[10] "I am your voice," he told the latter.[11] He also undertook to bring millions of jobs back to the United States,[12] tilted the Supreme Court balance in a conservative direction, and part-militarized the security apparatus. "You know what I am?" he asked a crowd in Houston in October 2018. "I'm a nationalist," he replied.[13]

The decision of over 17 million people in the British referendum of June 2016 to leave the European Union "super-state," and to regain "control of its borders,"[14] was the expression of desires similar to those which propelled Trump to office. With English (rather than British) patriotism said to be "on the rise,"[15]—and "Eurosceptic" movements stirring elsewhere—the prime minister told the president of the European Council that the referendum result was a vote to "restore our national self-determination";[16] even, in the words of Britain's then foreign minister, a "liberation."[17] And as with much of the support garnered in Trump's campaign, the Brexit referendum result—described by a commentator as a "grassroots insurgency"[18]— was said to have been "fueled by poorer voters" who felt they had "very little control over immigration"[19] and were powerless in face of the social and economic challenges posed by the free movement of labor under EU treaty rules; indeed, two-thirds of the areas of Britain where there had been a marked increase in foreign-born residents between 2007 and 2016 voted for Brexit.[20] To the British prime minister (and her speechwriters), it also signified the "opportunity to reassert our belief in a confident, sovereign and global Britain."[21]

For the reviving nationalist, these declarations of will in the United States and Britain were not only "part of a global revolution"[22] but the "start of a new world order,"[23] with many established parties in free societies losing ground, or splitting, under the stress of conflicts over national identity, economy, inequality, and migration. "The genie will not go back in the bottle," declared the leader of the Dutch right,[24] while the Hungarian prime minister, applauding the victory of Donald Trump, saw in it the "fall of liberal non-democracy."[25] However, to shouting demonstrators in New York City and Chicago in November 2016, Trump was "Not My President!" and flags were burned; women's organizations, students, immigrants, and others protested from Los Angeles to Philadelphia; and in February 2017 the words "Democracy Dies in Darkness" were placed beneath the *Washington Post*'s website masthead. To Henry Kissinger, more obscurely, Trump's victory was "in large part a reaction of Middle America to attacks on its values by intellectual and academic communities,"[26] while to others the new president's politics were simply "neo-fascist."[27]

But as the world's balance of power shifts against the United States, Trump's calls to "make America great again" were more rhetoric than substance, while the "national self-determination" to which Eurosceptics aspire cannot in itself reverse a free society's dissolution. Meanwhile, most manifestations of discontent are still inchoate, with millions standing on the sidelines and watching in despair as their social orders unravel at the hands of market interest on the one hand and the libertarian's right to choose on the other. At the same time, "moralists" who remain "convinced of the advantages of virtue," as Edward Gibbon put it,[28] fight their rearguard actions against the growing disorder.

For concepts of Virtue sit uneasily with Madam Bubble. According to her value system, that of the market stall—here shared by a Trump—the environmental protectionist is the dupe of false theories of climate change while the advocate of social justice is a closet "Marxist." For their parts, most "progressive" libertarians see religious faith as little better than bigotry, tradition as a dead weight, and the upholder of nation as (again) a crypto-fascist. The "conventional" family is also regarded as old hat. Or as a liberal British politician declared in December 2011, "we should not take a particular version of the family institution, such as the 1950s model of the suit-wearing, bread-winning dad and aproned home-making mother, and try to preserve it in aspic."[29] Nevertheless, the desire in some (or many) for the "re-moralization" of the free society as its disintegration proceeds, and their hope that marginalized or discarded norms of personal and social behavior—including those of citizen obligation—might see a revival, are clear enough.

In Britain, calls to lower the age of consent and to legalize "assisted dying" have thus been rejected, in the latter case by a large majority in the House of Commons,[30] and President Trump quickly nominated to the US Supreme Court a justice known for his earlier objections to euthanasia. Similarly, some American state legislatures, against objections by civil libertarians, have introduced restrictions on abortion and curbs on private clinics performing them, while Trump appointed the former head of Americans United for Life to a senior position in the US Department of Health and Human Services.[31] He also permitted states to deny federal funding to abortion providers, and in January 2018 set up a federal office to "protect" those who refused on "moral or religious grounds" to participate in assisted suicides or to carry out abortions.[32] The right to "life, liberty and the pursuit of happiness" under the Constitution was "for all Americans, including the unborn," Trump's vice president declared.[33] "Pro-life," often Christian fundamentalist, has challenged "pro-choice"—including by vigils and protests outside US abortion clinics, and even by gun and arson attacks on them—while sexual freedom is held to be sexual promiscuity by others.

Similarly, scientific discovery and technical innovation bring new possibilities and "products" to the market which are welcomed by many as tokens of progress, but are seen by others as threats to the natural order. Indeed, public authority itself tries intermittently to prevent their advance. Thus, a ban was imposed by the European

Court of Justice on the patenting of stem-cell techniques which use human embryos for research and profit,[34] and the US Food and Drug Administration similarly announced a "crackdown" on "unscrupulous" or "rogue" clinics "marketing stem-cell products which could put patients at risk."[35] The "marketing" of gene-altered pigs whose manure had been made "environmentally friendly" was also halted.[36]

Efforts have likewise been made to curb "surrogacy tourism" by gay couples in order to stop "rent-a-womb exploitation,"[37] and in December 2012 a British medical review committee sought restrictions on the "aggressive marketing techniques" of the "cosmetic surgery industry," in which breast operations were described as being "sold like double-glazing."[38] Even Google glasses, whose use has been held to invade the privacy of the observed, were prohibited in a Seattle café and a San Francisco bar.[39] However, in the disordered free society, where objection to the sovereignty of choice and the concept of the "misdeed" is perceived as essentially authoritarian, the very word *conduct* holds an unspoken threat. But in some the "hope of Virtue" remains alive.

To the latter, it may dictate the need to "crack down" on executive pay, with some 60 percent of British Petroleum shareholders in April 2016 voting against the £14 million pay award to its chief executive,[40] and similar revolts at Unilever and Lloyds;[41] or to cut the welfare benefits of unemployed drug users and alcoholics if they refuse to accept treatment;[42] or to argue that drivers who kill while on a mobile phone should get life sentences;[43] or, as in Arizona, to reject the legalization of "recreational" marijuana[44] and in The Hague to ban the smoking of cannabis in the city center.[45]

The "judgmentalist" also scrutinizes—even with lie-detector tests—the ailments of the disabled and the incapacitated for work, and finds widespread abuses of welfare provision. This is an old story, with the nineteenth-century social observer Thomas Wright, cited earlier, distinguishing long ago between "the worthy and the unworthy poor." "The latter," he wrote in 1873—before "political correctness" exerted its grip—"are generally artists in their way. They are thoroughly conversant with the formalities of application, and the nature and extent of their rights. Their tales of woe are at the same time wondrously well-fitted to the requirements of the rules and regulations bearing upon them."[46]

Undaunted, hope of Virtue expels or re-houses "nuisance neighbors,"[47] threatens parents with a custodial sentence if their children are found bullying others,[48] seeks to prohibit term-time holidays—with police at a Bavarian airport making checks on traveling school-age children[49]—orders students to hand in their cell phones at the start of the school day,[50] or in France bans them from schools altogether.[51] Nuns were even enjoined by the Pope not to be distracted from the contemplative life by "noises, news and words."[52] Expressing itself in different ways, Reaction also introduces curricular changes in school education to emphasize legacies of history and to recall lost beliefs; it opposes school and university courses "designed primarily for pupils of a particular ethnic group," as overemphasis upon "diversity" speeds the dissolution of the social order;[53] and in some Texas districts[54] more severe Reaction has permitted the corporal punishment of disruptive children.

Facing rising levels of gun crime and gun death in the United States, public authority in various states has also attempted to restrict access to assault weapons and higher-capacity ammunition-magazines, a former Supreme Court justice called for the repeal of the Second Amendment which notionally permits the private citizen to bear arms,[55] while Facebook agreed to delete posts from gun users illegally advertising weapons.[56] Likewise, following the "mass shooting" in a Florida school in February 2018, Walmart—which had already stopped selling semiautomatics at its stores[57]—decided, with other market "outlets," to prevent under-21s from purchasing arms,[58] and Seattle passed a law that would fine gun owners for failing to lock up their weapons and for letting minors get access to them.[59]

In the immediate aftermath of the Florida killings, President Trump similarly directed the Department of Justice to consider a ban on rapid-fire "bump-stocks," declared himself in favor of strengthened background checks for gun buyers,[60] and thought that there should be federal restrictions on access by under-21s to assault rifles.[61] However, he also described the gun lobby's National Rifle Association (NRA) as "Great American Patriots,"[62] backed away from raising the minimum age for buying a rifle,[63] declared that the Second Amendment "will never be repealed"[64]—"there's no bigger fan of the Second Amendment than me," he told a meeting of state governors at the White House[65]—and in Dallas in May 2018 told the crowd that their "Second Amendment rights" would "never be under siege as long as I'm your president."[66] Moreover, in August 2017 he had also lifted a ban on the use by local police departments of surplus military equipment, such as armored vehicles and large-caliber weapons,[67] as if with the control of street warfare in mind.

Thus confusion reigns in the search for remedy for the free society's disorders, while hope of Virtue continues to battle powerful market interest and the free-chooser's habits. Alcohol is therefore subjected to minimum pricing, and an opioid tax—resisted by pharmaceutical companies—is attempted to be imposed on prescription painkillers.[68] Similarly, as obesity advances, hope of Virtue tries to curtail the sale by Madam Bubble of harm-doing foods and drinks. "Heart-clogging trans-fats" are proscribed, and "soda taxes" on sugary drinks are imposed upon—and resisted by—the "food and beverage industry";[69] in the United States, it has expended millions of dollars in an effort to deny the link between consumption of its "products" and ill-health.

Attempts are similarly made to restrain the TV advertising of fats, salt, and sugar-saturated junk food to children, and to stop the sale of self-harm in school vending machines. Fast-food concessions have even been closed on some military bases.[70] But a legislative proposal in Mississippi to ban restaurants from serving food to the obese was rejected on the grounds that it was "too oppressive for government to require a restaurant-owner to police another for their indiscretion."[71]

Hope of Virtue can also turn to, or attempt, personal sanction. Parents have been arrested for allowing their offspring to become "dangerously overweight,"[72] a pot smoker in Colorado temporarily lost custody of his children,[73] doctors in Britain were told to "report" patients observed to be putting on weight,[74] and proposals have been made that welfare claimants should be sent to slimming clubs if their weight prevents them from getting a job.[75] Penalizing the unhealthy—often victims of forces none can control or contain—fire-fighters in New Zealand similarly decided to limit the number of callouts to help the obese,[76] restrictions are imposed on their hip and knee operations, and over-heavy air travelers may be surcharged or even turned away.[77] Invoking "safety rules," Eurostar in November 2013 also stopped a "clinically obese" passenger weighing 230 kilos, or over five hundred pounds, from boarding one of its trains.[78]

Against the tobacco "industry's" resistance, hope of Virtue similarly restricts the open display of "tobacco products," images of diseased lungs are carried on its packets, and "generic packaging" shorn of brand names is imposed by law, the way led by Australia.[79] But with industry-funded scientists aiding the corporate counterattack,[80] objection in the United States holds that such restraints are in breach of free-speech protections even as the marketing of ill-health takes its increasing toll and healthcare costs for smokers in the United States are said to run to some $170 billion a year.[81] Meanwhile, on this battlefield, family members of those killed by smoking file actions for punitive damages against cigarette companies, while smokers themselves sometimes suffer medical sanctions and refusals of treatment. Even in vitro fertilization has been denied to smokers.[82]

To the libertarian, all of this is again an unwarranted intrusion by "moralizers" in matters of free choice. The "judgmentalist" disagrees, arguing that the costs of ill health are borne by the community in raised insurance premiums paid by the healthy, or in the burden of taxes needed to fund a democracy's health provision. Alternatively, where personal sanction fails, hope of Virtue turns to bribes. It may give rewards to truant children in return for their attendance at school, while some corporate entrepreneurs and public institutions offer their employees cash incentives to follow health advice and lose weight.

Moral polemic has also accompanied each step in the advance of gay rights. This has been the case, above all, in the refusal to accept the legitimacy of same-sex marriage, on the grounds that the union of male and female stands at the heart of the social and moral order. Such refusal, seen by libertarians and others as mere prejudice, has deep roots. Scorn—and worse—for homosexuals is an ancient theme; in the second century CE, the Roman satirist Juvenal wrote of the "execrable conduct" and "unnatural lust" of male "effeminates," and described homosexuality as a "plague."[83] Today, Reaction similarly declares that "I don't want to hear talk of 'parent one' and 'parent two.' In a family there's a mother and a father."[84]

With less ardor but in similar reaction to what is seen by some (or many) as "against nature," Pope Benedict XVI pronounced *ex cathedra* in January 2010 that "laws which undermine the difference between the sexes" were "threats to Creation."[85] To legalize it "in defiance of public opinion" was described as "totalitarian" by the Catholic Archbishop of Westminster,[86] while the future Catholic archbishop of San Francisco warned in 2011 that the "social experiment" of same-sex marriage would have "dire consequences";[87] an Italian priest was more specific, declaring that earthquakes were divine punishment for gay civil unions.[88] "The question of the family" was also the "question of what it means to be a man, and what it is necessary to do to be a true man," Pope Benedict added in December 2012.[89] Similarly, the Irish referendum result in May 2015 in favor of the legalization of gay marriage was called a "defeat for humanity" by the Vatican Secretary of State Cardinal Parolin.[90]

Likewise Patriarch Kirill, head of the Russian Orthodox Church, described the legalization of gay marriage as "at odds with the moral nature of human beings,"[91] and there was near-schism in the Anglican Church over the matter, with "repentance" urged by some clergy upon "gays who have sex,"[92] while an American Episcopalian bishop, describing same-sex relationships as "sinful," saw "Satan" at work in "bringing division into the church" on the subject.[93] Orthodox rabbis, as gay pride parades attracted tens of thousands of marchers in Jerusalem and Tel Aviv "waving rainbow flags emblazoned with the Star of David," likewise called LGBT groups "deviants,"[94] pronounced homosexuality to be a "cult of abomination,"[95] and judged liberals to hold "dangerous and poisonous views" on the subject.[96] Despite internal divisions, the Mormon Church similarly declared that gay unions offended "the Creator's plans,"[97] held gay marriage to be a "sin" meriting expulsion, in November 2015 banned baptisms of children living with gay parents until they have reached the age of eighteen,[98] and in September 2017 reaffirmed its positions.[99] A senior American Baptist had a different view, recalling that of Sinclair Lewis's realtor Babbitt on the subject of Sunday schools quoted in an earlier chapter. "De-emphasizing homosexuality," thought the former, would serve to "attract more members" to his church in "a free market system," adding (in nonjudgmental fashion) that "when all of society has moved in a certain direction you just have to be silent,"[100] while fears of an "economic backlash" and lost markets deterred some US state legislatures from curtailing LGBT rights.

Other responses to the US Supreme Court's decision in June 2015 that same-sex couples had a "constitutional right" to marry were less pragmatic and more concerned with Virtue. According to a former governor of Arkansas, who bluntly asserted that there was no right to same-sex marriage in the US Constitution, the decision was that of an "imperial court" and was "profoundly immoral" in pretending to "repeal the laws of nature and nature's God,"[101] the language of America's Founding Fathers. To dissenting Supreme Court Justice Antonin Scalia, the majority ruling was also a "threat to American democracy," and "had nothing to do with the law."[102] In Alabama, its chief justice Roy Moore, who had ordered the state's probate judges to refuse applications for same-sex marriage licenses[103] and was suspended for "abusing his authority,"[104] likewise asserted that the US Supreme Court had "destroyed the sacred institution of marriage."[105]

As gay rights campaigners cried "Love Must Win!" "Do Your Job!" and "Obey the Law!"[106] a Kentucky county clerk—Kim Davis, an apostolic Christian—similarly refused to issue marriage licenses to gays, on the grounds that "God's moral law" forbade it. Describing her refusal as a "heaven or hell decision,"[107] she was briefly jailed for contempt, her supporters protesting that her freedom had been infringed. Accused of "promoting her own religious convictions at the expense of others"[108] and of placing herself above the newly proclaimed law, she was released after undertaking not to prevent her deputies from issuing marriage licenses to gay couples.[109] She was then sued by a same-sex couple whose marriage license she had denied, and their suit succeeded, the state having to meet the costs of the legal action.[110] Her arguments had earlier been described by the government of Kentucky as a "meritless assault on the rule of law,"[111] while local civil libertarians declared her resistance to gay marriage to be a mere "blip on the radar of civil rights,"[112] and in November 2018 she lost her bid for reelection as county clerk.[113]

Nevertheless, battles for Gibbon's Virtue have persisted in the free society as gay rights have advanced. Thousands have marched in France, Italy, Mexico, and other countries not only objecting to gay marriage— its legalization was reversed in Bermuda[114]—but also opposing surrogacy by gay couples, and again invoking the "right of a child to have a mother and father."[115] Likewise, the contention that gay unions mark an historic step forward in human emancipation has encountered the fixed objection of some, or many, that "it still does not seem right for a woman to be able to marry a woman, and a male to marry a male."[116]

Thus Pentecostals, before the Supreme Court decision on gay marriage, expelled a student from a Christian college when she returned with her same-sex partner from their honeymoon in Las Vegas;[117] a Catholic teacher in California was fired after photographs of his wedding to a gay partner were published in a local newspaper;[118] and, despite the Supreme Court decision, a campus Evangelical group, the Intervarsity Christian Fellowship, sought the removal of supporters of same-sex relationships from college staffs,[119] while in Florida another Catholic teacher lost her job in February 2018 after marrying her female partner,[120] and in Texas a lesbian teacher who showed her elementary-school class a photo of her "future wife" was put on leave by her school district.[121] Similarly, the Supreme Court decision has not deterred numbers of state legislatures in the United States—Kansas and Oklahoma, for example—from passing laws protecting faith-based organizations which refuse to place children with gay parents, and the leader of the Liberal Democrats in Britain resigned from his position in June 2017 on the grounds that his party's support for gay marriage was incompatible with his Christian beliefs.[122]

In the non-Western world, affected at a distance by the breaking of bounds in disintegrating free societies, resistance to gay entitlement has taken more drastic forms. "If you do not stop this dirty act," a Shi'ite militia statement circulated in Baghdad warned, "the punishment of God will fall on you at the hands of the Mujahedeen."[123] It has brought executions in Iran and elsewhere in the Muslim world; in Egypt the arrests of homosexuals for "debauchery" and "sexual deviance,"[124] and in Turkey Gay Pride marchers—permitted in Lebanon in 2017—were met with tear gas and rubber bullets.[125] In the West, too, the voice of Islam on the subject has generally been unyielding. With over half of Muslims polled in Britain in 2016 believing that homosexuality itself should be "unlawful,"[126] a Shia Muslim scholar told his audience at the University of Michigan that "Death is the sentence. Out of compassion, let's get rid of them,"[127] while the father of the Muslim assailant in the June 2016 massacre at a gay club in Orlando declared that his son had earlier "seen two men kissing each other and got very angry."[128]

In Africa, where homosexuality has been declared "illegal" in more than three dozen countries, gays suffer lashings in some countries and death in others, in Mauritania by stoning. Uganda in June 2012 expelled a British theater director from the country for putting on a "gay play";[129] the Mombasa high court in June 2015 upheld the use of anal examination to determine a suspect's sexual orientation;[130] same-sex public affection is banned in Nigeria;[131] and in November 2016 fifty-four countries in the "Africa Group" rejected the notion that "sexual orientation and gender identity" are human rights issues.[132] In Malaysia, similarly, four male transsexuals who had undergone hormone therapy and found work as bridal make-up assistants argued before a court that they had a right to wear women's clothes, but they lost their case;[133] even a children's book stocked in Singapore's public libraries telling the tale of two male penguins raising a chick was ordered to be destroyed as a "challenge to existing norms";[134] and in Malaysia a lesbian couple found guilty in August 2018 of "attempting to have sexual intercourse" was ordered to be caned.[135]

In Eastern Europe, too—for example in Croatia, Hungary, Poland, and Slovakia—resistance to the advance of gay rights has sometimes been vicious even as gay rights advocates have grown bolder. Clashes between gay marchers and street gangs composed of skinheads and "ultra-nationalists" have turned to riot, with the kneeling religious praying on the pavement for delivery from "evil," and with gay parades described by Moscow's mayor as "satanic."[136] "Euthanasia for Gays, Concentration Camps for Lesbians," shouted members of the youth wing of the League of Polish Families during a gay march in Warsaw in 2007,[137] while the arrival in Poland's parliament of its first openly gay deputy was greeted by a Catholic priest with the comment that "the sodomites are coming."[138]

As gay rights in the free society moved forward, Russia's President Putin also objected in 2013 to the "fruitless so-called tolerance" which "makes no distinction between good and evil."[139] A federal law had already been unanimously passed by Russia's parliament outlawing "homosexual propaganda" and "non-traditional sexual relations";[140] a similar law was enacted in Ukraine in order to "preserve the moral, spiritual and physical health of the nation,"[141] while same-sex marriages were said in June 2018 to have "no real chance of being legalized under Poland's conservative government,"[142] although Polish police used tear gas and water cannons in October 2018 against opponents of a gay rights march in Lublin.[143] But in Moscow, gay pride marches were placed under a legal ban in 2012 "for the next hundred years,"[144] while fans of St. Petersburg's football team Zenit demanded that there be no gays in their squad, on the grounds that they were "unworthy of our great city."[145] And in June 2015, as the

US Supreme Court declared gay marriage to be a constitutional right, a new Russian road-safety law classed transsexuals and transvestites as "disabled" and banned them from driving.[146]

In Western democracies too, deep Reaction has stirred with the widening of moral choice and the breaking of taboo. Members of the Westboro Baptist Church in Kansas, carrying anti-gay placards reading "God Hates You," celebrated the deaths of US troops as punishment for American tolerance of "fags,"[147] while in North Carolina a man was "beaten and choked" by fellow members of his Evangelical church in order to expel his "homosexual demons,"[148] and an explosive was lobbed onto the porch of a "safe haven" home for transgender residents in Philadelphia.[149] But for the most part, Reaction in the free society to claims of new sexual rights of choice has been more measured. Before the Supreme Court decision of June 2015, American "family defense" organizations—denoted "socially conservative" by the free-chooser—thus sought approval by means of ballots and referenda for the entrenchment of marriage under state laws as a uniquely heterosexual institution, while various states of the union denied recognition to same-sex relationships on "public policy" grounds until the Supreme Court judgment undermined such position.

Nevertheless, even after June 2015, public and private authorities in various Western countries continued to resist claims that married welfare benefits, inheritance entitlements, and adoption rights be extended to same-sex partners; in Mississippi, a law was passed in April 2016 protecting the rights both of private individuals and local government employees to discriminate against LGBT people on religious grounds;[150] and the Missouri senate in March 2017 rejected a proposal to ban discrimination based on "gender identity and sexual orientation" in matters of employment and housing.[151]

Reaction sought to strike further blows for Gibbon's Virtue on President Trump's assumption of office. In February 2017,[152] he attempted to rescind the right of access by students to "bathrooms" which correspond to the individual's "chosen gender identity" rather than his or her birth-certificate gender, a right established by the

Obama administration.[153] At Trump's direction, the Department of Justice similarly instructed federal agencies to "do as much as possible to accommodate" those with religious objections to the conceding of rights to LGBT individuals,[154] in effect permitting Virtue to assert itself against what it perceives as Vice. Likewise, the Trump administration tried to halt recruitment to the US military of the transgendered, ignoring civil libertarian protest that such ban was an "unconstitutional violation of their rights."[155] The newly elected President Trump also removed the pages about LGBT rights from the White House website,[156] while the United States early in his presidency voted against a UN resolution condemning the death penalty for gay sex,[157] and in October 2018 the Trump administration was said to be considering a definition of gender as "a biological, immutable condition determined by genitalia at birth."[158]

On other fronts of Virtue's battle with new forms of sexual right, the right to choose one's gender among them, a Canadian judge ordered a mother to stop dressing her four-year-old son in girl's clothes in public, with the father blaming his wife for the child's "confusion";[159] a "Christian family" in Britain removed their son from primary school after a male classmate was allowed to come to school wearing a dress;[160] and a male-to-female "transgender teen" was asked to leave a Christian private school in New Hampshire and to consider "home-schooling or counseling" instead.[161] Likewise, a French appeal court refused to recognize the term "neutral gender" sought by an "intersex plaintiff";[162] a British court upheld the UK government's refusal to issue "gender-neutral" passports;[163] and an Ohio district judge refused to allow transgender teens to change their first names.[164] Similarly in Greece, church bells were rung in mourning after a law was passed making it easier to change one's gender on official documents,[165] and an elementary-school teacher in Florida was "transferred to adult education" after asking that children use "gender-neutral pronouns" in class.[166]

Reaction has also led newspapers to refuse to publish the marriage notices of gay couples[167] while, less moderately, some hotels and guest houses in Britain have turned them away or insisted that they have single beds, and been ordered to pay damages for doing so.[168] Similarly, some photographers, bakers, and florists in a number of free societies have been unwilling to service same-sex nuptials. A bakery in Northern Ireland refused to provide a cake decorated with a message supporting same-sex marriage, on the grounds that it "conflicted with their Christian beliefs," was vindicated in a unanimous decision by the British Supreme Court,[169] and saw its profits rise to over £1.5 million;[170] a Colorado baker similarly refused on religious grounds to bake cakes both for a gay wedding and a gender-transition celebration;[171] while a Pennsylvania bridal store declined to sell a wedding dress to a lesbian spouse, on the grounds that it would "break God's law."[172]

However, in a free market of wants, needs, and desires, the claim to a share of its liberties is hard to oppose, whatever previous moral convention and Gibbon's Virtue prescribe. A mayor of Venice may ban a gay pride parade, calling it the "height of kitsch";[173] rainbow flags are cut down outside a Swedish city hall;[174] a Mississippi opponent of a gay march in her town protests that "God made Adam and Eve";[175] and gay pride revelers are stabbed in a Jerusalem street.[176] But in a moral and market free-for-all, gay and lesbian claims can be made out to be as reasonable as any. Indeed, the entitlement to act upon one's choices, and to be free of intrusion and interference in doing so, is for many proof that society is "in touch with the twenty-first century,"[177] even if it is "Alice in Wonderland territory"[178] for others.

Such claims to entitlement are also shared by the incoming migrant and provide further ground upon which Reaction can stand. But with market interest demanding the free movement of goods, capital, and labor in a "global market" on the one hand, and with millions and tens of millions in flight from war and poverty in search of safety, sustenance, and work on the other, the tide flows on; and while the well-meaning in disordered democracies seek to maintain their countries' traditions of asylum, hostility toward migrants has been growing as their numbers have risen, and as the jihad has claimed more Western victims.

The incomer is thus seen by some (or many) as a further cause of disorder, with already deep confusions over national identity—confusions which owe relatively little to migration—increasingly blamed on the migrant. Moreover, as influxes swell in number and as cultural norms come under further siege, "progressives," recoiling from the nostalgia for nation, leave deeper Reaction, including in its most primitive and racist forms, to command the argument. "It's disgusting what's happening to our country. They're all over the place,"[179] is merely one expression of it, and a subject to which I will return.

The widespread sense in Western democracies of national and civic loss has thus opened the way further to a politics of protest, whose appeal is increasingly cross-class, and whose objections to the existing order are wide-ranging and often random. Crossing old boundaries between "left" and "right," they variously seek to address the concerns of "ordinary people"—as earlier mentioned—promise more "freedoms" of this or that kind in democracies collapsing from their excess, in pseudo-socialist fashion espouse the cause of the disadvantaged, or favor more market license rather than less, or all of them together. Such politics of protest may also seek to arouse nationalist and even secessionist impulses—in Britain, Catalonia, Corsica, and Italy's Lombardy and Veneto regions, for example—or make its main cause that of limiting immigration, whether from rational or xenophobic motives. "We're getting the bad dudes out" and "throwing them the hell out of our country," is merely one expression of it.[180]

The advance of Reaction is further assisted by the libertarian mind-set itself, and whether it be that of the market or the moral free-chooser. Careless of balance or restraint, it is oblivious that a polity and social order require bounds of many kinds if they are not to dissolve; Reason demands bounds, especially in a democracy, while Unreason recognizes no limits to individual interest and will. Moreover, since "progressives" also lack such sense of bounds, the way opens wider to the very Reaction the anti-fascist fears, in particular in relation to immigration. Aiding Reaction's cause is that many (or most) in the free societies' urban wildernesses are already strangers to one another

and citizenship has lost its meaning, with Reaction singling out some
as stranger than others whether by faith, language, or color.

Anxieties over civil society's dissolution, on which Reaction
feeds, are again hardly new. Turgot, Louis XVI's finance minister at
the time when France's troubles were deepening before the Revolution, described his nation as an "aggregate of different and incompatible social groups whose members have so few links between
themselves that everyone thinks of his own interests alone."[181] Similarly, with some 2.5 million "undocumented" immigrants in California,[182] perhaps 1 million and more "illegal" migrants in Britain,[183]
and with an eighth of Germany's 82 million population born outside
the country[184]—swelled by the hundreds of thousands, mainly from
Syria, Afghanistan, and Iraq, who surged into Western Europe through
the Balkans in 2015 and thereafter, also bringing 50,000 to Greece
in a single week[185]—today's democracies need more than a belief in
individual liberty if they are to cohere and survive.

In Britain, the foreign-born population has quadrupled in the last
six decades,[186] with almost one-third of births in 2017—reaching 60
percent in London—to mothers born outside Britain,[187] and with
more Romanians than Irish in the United Kingdom.[188] English is not
the first language of a majority of the pupils in one in nine schools
in England, and in two hundred schools 90 percent and more do not
have English as their first language;[189] the city of Manchester was said
in 2012 to "boast a population that speaks at least 153 languages,"[190]
with 91 languages allegedly spoken in Bristol,[191] and three-quarters
of a million in England said to "speak hardly any or no English."[192]
Today, many millions in presumptive Western democracies also lack
knowledge of, or much interest in, the histories, faiths, and customs of
their newfound lands; the conversion to Christianity at a Berlin evangelical church of "hundreds" of "mostly Iranian and Afghan" refugees
in 2015[193] was arguably more directed to the granting of asylum than
the gaining of a heavenly reward.

At the same time, flight from democracy's cities by the "indigenous"
is accelerating and is to some degree the expression of a xenophobic

desire for distance from the urban scene; the number of privately policed and barricaded communities is also growing in the United States.[194] Moreover, incomers' separatist claims to cultural and (in Islam's case) legal privileges for their own ways and values are accelerating the dissolution of the old civic and social order. Yet at the same time belief in the principle of separatist entitlement steadily gains ground, with objection to such entitlement remaining a taboo in libertarian eyes.

Meanwhile, ever-larger proportions of democracy's populations are not citizens or are citizens only in name, a negation of democracy itself, and with incomers' natural rates of increase generally outpacing those of the rest of the population, as in the United States, Reaction finds it easy to stir the pot. Bristling for a fight in Britain, it counts the numbers of migrants on the dole, blames increasing unemployment on rising immigration, and sees in every young Muslim male a jihadi plotting harm. In the United States, with its almost 11 million "illegal migrants,"[195] Reaction resists the setting up of shelters to house the now tens of thousands of unaccompanied children who have crossed its borders,[196] or, as under President Trump, imprisons arriving children after separating them from their parents[197]—since US law forbids the jailing of parents and children together—and threatens to deny citizenship to children born in the United States to unauthorized migrant parents, hitherto a constitutional right.[198]

Brandishing the Stars and Stripes—and in Saxony shouting "We are the people!" and "Go home!"[199]—Reaction also blocks buses transporting migrants to nearby towns, especially where unemployment is high,[200] and turns away children "without legal status" from local schools,[201] while "losing trace" of many unaccompanied children after placing them in the homes of "sponsors."[202] In Bulgaria, similar Reaction has deported lone children to their homelands "under duress";[203] in France it convicted a farmer for illegally helping migrants cross the border;[204] and in Italy it placed the mayor of a southern town under house arrest for "abetting" illegal migration.[205]

For his part, President Trump on entering office quickly sought to curb entry to the United States from a number of predominantly Muslim countries, a ban narrowly upheld by the US Supreme Court.[206] He also attempted to withhold federal funding from "sanctuary cities" which limit cooperation with the immigration authorities and seek to protect the immigrants themselves;[207] to deny asylum to migrants who illegally cross the US-Mexico border;[208] and to cut the numbers of migrants whom the United States would accept to 45,000 in 2018 and 30,000 in 2019[209]—President Obama had raised it in 2017 to 110, 000. Chancellor Merkel similarly agreed to a "cap" of 200,000 migrants a year in her effort to build a government coalition with her opponents;[210] Hungary, declaring its unwillingness to repeat Western Europe's "failed experiments in multiculturalism"[211] and its desire to "keep Europe Christian,"[212] proclaimed a state of emergency in March 2016 and attempted to shut its borders to the migrant influx; and Italy, calling for "international centres" in "transit countries,"[213] prevented migrants from disembarking at its ports.[214]

Expressions of opposition to migration and to the migrant have varied in degree but not in kind. "We cannot allow all of these people to invade our country," declared the US president,[215] and it would not become a "migrant camp."[216] The Italian interior minister, promising to expel thousands and "send them home,"[217] likewise announced that the "free ride" was "over" for illegal migrants;[218] the Italian prime minister called migration a "business";[219] Hungary proposed to levy a tax on NGOs supporting migration,[220] and the Bavarian prime minister described it as "asylum tourism."[221] "We will not accept migrants from the Middle East and North Africa in Poland," said the Polish prime minister in January 2018,[222] while anti-migrant protesters, blocking an Alpine pass on the French-Italian border, carried banners reading "You will not make Europe your home. Back to your homeland!"[223] and Australia banned access by asylum seekers arriving by boat and sent them to Papua New Guinea.[224]

Racism in democracy's disintegrating *polis* above all looks to color, counting white heads, brown heads, and black. "Fewer than half of people in London are white," says one source;[225] "white pupils are in a minority in state schools in the US," says a second;[226] "whites will no longer make up a majority of Americans by 2043," estimates a third;[227] and "white Britons are expected to be a minority by 2070," predicts a fourth.[228] Moreover, as the numbers of illegal and clandestine migrants, bogus students, and false asylum seekers increase by the day, Reaction is further incited by the arguments used by rights activists in pleading their case. "If they want citizenship, people should be able to choose it," thus declared the Coalition for Humane Immigration Rights of Los Angeles in 2013,[229] a principle—or antiprinciple—again incompatible with a true civic order.

In disintegrating Western free societies, access to their goods and entitlements is also available at the market's price. Human trafficking and document forging are therefore lucrative trades, with the passport a "product" like any other and with citizenship again stripped of its meaning. Recovering some of the lost ground on which a sense of it once stood ought to have been Reason's task, since the ethics of the market and of the free-chooser are insufficient to hold a society together, whatever its composition. But with moral and civic principles frowned upon by many as intrusions upon personal freedom, Reaction not Reason is left to come to the social order's defense.

It stands itching for the fray—sometimes with cudgel in hand—as economic migrants lay claim to political asylum, and as false asylum seekers vanish into the burrows of the decaying inner city. In Germany in 2016, the authorities admitted that they did not know the whereabouts of some 130,000 "asylum seekers,"[230] and both Italy and Greece were accused by the Dutch government of failing to register "about two-thirds" of the migrants arriving at their borders.[231] In the US, almost half of illegal entrants across the Mexican border are not caught,[232] while in a single year 700,000 foreigners who were supposed to have left the country at the end of their visa period overstayed.[233] Likewise in Britain, with the Home Office having "lost track" between 2015 and 2017 of "more than six hundred thousand" foreigners whose periods of stay had elapsed,[234] unknown totals of foreign nationals are living in the country illegally, wanted criminals included, with deportation orders not enforced or the intended deportees classified as "missing" and their cases "closed."[235] In March 2013, the UK Border Agency was itself held responsible for the chaos. It was abolished, leaving migrant figures "little better than a best guess," in the words of a parliamentary committee.[236] Moreover, "asylum" applications numbering in many tens of thousands are made in Britain by mere "over-stayers,"[237] passports are inadequately checked,[238] the authorities in the United States "mistakenly" give citizenship to migrants using false names,[239] and in Britain a private-sector company searches for the missing and is "paid by results."[240]

But the market's need for "growth" makes its own demands. Such need prompts retrospective "amnesties" in the United States for certain categories of clandestine entrants, the "regularization" of illegality, the granting of work permits and—again in the United States—the provision of a "pathway" to citizen status. With market interest upheld by the cause of human rights and with mainstream political parties deferring to the vote banks of incomers, civic debate upon the consequences for the social order also remains stifled by false scruple, again inviting Reaction, including in its extremer forms, to intervene.

However, it is not mere Reaction alone that counts the costs of the public provision of healthcare, education, and housing to its incomers, with over a million migrants in social housing in Britain.[241] Nor is it Reaction alone that notes the need in Britain to provide multilingual information for non-English speakers about the state's bounties—in seventy languages in one London borough alone[242]—while the translation service costs tens of millions of pounds a year. But Madam Bubble continues to weigh on her market scales the profits that cheap migrant labor brings, with public authority also calculating the tax benefits gained from incomers' legal employment and their contributions to the social security system, against the welfare costs of immigrant unemployment and family support.

Other responses are also based on cost-benefit analyses. Public authority thus dabbles with restrictive work permits and quotas, allocations of guest-worker status, and points systems for entry that privilege the qualified and the skilled. But when the cost-benefit analysis is negative, with local opposition intense, public authority carries out workplace raids, arrests workers, and penalizes employers of illegal and clandestine migrants—as in Minnesota, Nebraska, Ohio, and rural Tennessee[243]—and in some US cities punishes landlords who rent to them. Or it gives development aid to foreign emigrant regions in the hope of creating local employment, and of stemming the rate of departures from them.

Meanwhile, the expense of US "immigration enforcement programs" amounts to billions of dollars each year, with hundreds of thousands of migrants arrested annually at its borders, and asylum seekers, true or false, turned away without their claims being heard.[244] Other hundreds of thousands are "removed" each year, sometimes after commission of a minor crime or infraction. In 2016 almost a quarter of a million "illegal" immigrants to the United States, over half with criminal convictions, were deported;[245] in Italy, "asylum seekers" lost the right to appeal against expulsion orders;[246] in Germany, limits were imposed on migrants' rights to bring relatives to the country;[247] and President Trump sought to cancel the amnesty which permitted children who were illegally in the country to study and to work.[248]

In the chaos of it, would-be migrants have besieged the port of Calais and the Eurotunnel to England, tried to storm the Spanish enclave of Ceuta and Melilla in Tunisia, and even biked into Norway from its Arctic border.[249] Other porous land borders have been strengthened and policed, including with the aid of infrared sensors and watchtowers; on the US-Mexico border with Predator drones; and on the Hungarian border by the construction of a new army base, the deployment of troops, and the use of an electrified fence, razor wire, tear gas, and water cannons.[250] Similarly, Greek and Bulgarian troops were sent to the Turkish frontier; Bosnian police to the Serbian border; and Austrian troops to the Italian,[251] while drones and radar were offered by Italy to Libya for the surveillance of its desert borders.[252]

The seas are also patrolled and boats carrying asylum seekers are attempted to be turned back, as by Italy in 2018, with a rising body count of those who do not survive the effort to cross the Mediterranean or America's southern deserts. And as a last resort are walls; a 4-meter barrier wall in Calais to deter cross-Channel migrants, a 110-mile fence built by prisoners on the Hungarian-Serbian border, and President Trump's proposed "great, great wall"[253] on the US-Mexican border, some 2,000 miles long and at an estimated cost of $12–$15 billion.

Yet all the while Madam Bubble regards migrants as potential "human capital," trade unions hope to boost their shrinking ranks by recruiting them, and market interest continues to welcome and employ them, "legal" or "illegal." In some states in the United States—with former vice president Biden declaring immigrants to be "crucial to American innovation,"[254] and the entrepreneurial Donald Trump having employed them[255]—"illegals" may be provided with driving licenses to help them get to work. But too often they have their vulnerabilities exploited in construction, agriculture, and other sectors under near forced-labor conditions, conditions that the indigenous themselves refuse.

At the same time, temporary detention camps—using shipping containers on Hungary's southern borders[256]—are set up for the unwelcome, while in some Swiss and German towns[257] asylum seekers have been barred from use of the public library, the swimming pool, and the school playground; in Essen migrants were refused access to its food banks,[258] and Cottbus in Brandenburg sought to ban refugees from the city entirely.[259] Authority may also conduct random identity checks—denounced as racial profiling by human rights lobbies—in order to ascertain the immigration status of passers-by; in Cardiff, asylum seekers were given colored wristbands,[260] and in the English city of Middlesbrough their doors were painted red.[261] Moreover, Germany was said in March 2017 to be planning to "test software that can automatically recognize a person's dialect" in order to determine whether migrants' claims about their provenance are true.[262]

Worse, and sometimes in response to sexual assaults on women as in Germany, Finland, and Sweden, there have been street attacks by local vigilantes—and in Hungary by border police[263]—with asylum seekers' reception centers, shelters, and hostels firebombed and swastikas daubed on walls. Migrants sleeping rough have similarly had their tents torn down or been blasted by police water cannons, as in Rome.[264] Severity has also been shown in Europe to travelers, whose makeshift camps may be attacked by locals and dismantled, or "cleared out,"[265] by public authority itself. Regarded even by market interest as surplus to its requirements, and with Italy's interior minister calling for a "census" of them and describing them as "parasitic,"[266] their expulsion is roundly approved by Reaction, which wills it for other "aliens" too, while an American presidential candidate's call for a "total and complete shutdown"[267] on Muslim entry into the United States, earlier mentioned, arguably helped him to win the election. So, too, his readiness in November 2018 to dispatch active-duty troops to the Mexican border in order to prevent a "caravan" of thousands of Central American migrants entering the United States was said to have "animated Republican base voters"[268]—and others—in the midterm elections to Congress.

But despite the obstacles that Reaction places in their paths, many migrants, whether "legal" or "illegal," find their Promised Lands and prosper, their children also making their way. Others arrive with, or develop, a separatist sense of identity hostile to their adoptive homes. Thus in Italy, with nostalgia for the fascist past increasing, a Moroccan described as having a "militant attitude towards Italian institutions," to be concerned only with securing "welfare-support for himself and his family," and to have "no real interest in integrating into society," was issued with an expulsion order.[269]

In the face of such separatism and with Reaction closely watching the scene, a decomposing free society is at ever-greater loss, not least because nonjudgmentalism and "political correctness" have inhibited the enforcement of the obligations upon which any civic order—in particular a democratic civic order—depends. Worse, the contempt of some incomers for the free society's value system is sometimes just, their citizenship decreasingly prized save for the practical benefits it brings. There is again no true commonwealth in this.

Nevertheless, Western liberal societies have attempted to engage incomers, Muslims included, in a process of acculturation. In Norway, a "course manual" declares that "whatever a person's faith, the rules and laws must nevertheless be followed";[270] Bavaria has attempted to give lessons on "freedom of opinion, separation of religion and state, and the equality of men and women,"[271] and Denmark to instruct immigrant children in "democracy, Danish traditions and Christian holidays" with sanctions for non-enrollment.[272] For their part, the Dutch believe that all schoolchildren should see Rembrandt's *The Night Watch* and learn the national anthem;[273] and in September 2016 the French set up a "flagship" center in the Loire valley for the "de-radicalization of Islamists" which closed down ten months later for lack of attendees.[274]

Indeed, with such efforts generally a failure, sanction has increasingly been employed against culturally separatist Muslim ways, despite libertarian and human rights objections. In June 2008, France's Council of State refused citizenship, on grounds of "insufficient assimilation," to a niqab-wearing Moroccan woman described as being in "total submission to her husband," and who was said to have "no idea about the secular state."[275] Socrates would have understood the decision. "If an individual remains here while seeing how we administer justice and our public affairs," he declared of the Athenian *polis*, "then we can say that such a person has implicitly agreed to observe our laws."[276] In the name of such principle have also come bans on Muslim women's face-coverings in public places, a small number of prosecutions for female genital mutilation—with most Western feminists keeping silent on the subject—and prohibitions or annulments of child marriage and forced marriage.

On grounds of "failure to assimilate into French society," public authority similarly denied citizenship to a Moroccan man who had a "discriminatory attitude towards women," and who had "refused to shake the hand of a female official,"[277] and to a Muslim woman who refused to shake hands with male officials at the citizenship ceremony itself,[278] while in Switzerland a Muslim family's citizenship application was "put on hold" after two teenage sons also refused to shake hands with their female teachers.[279] But Swedish public authority dissented, in August 2018 ordering an employer to pay compensation to a female Muslim job applicant rejected for refusing to shake hands with her male interviewer.[280]

In the spirit not of Reaction but of the Enlightenment, French citizenship was also refused to a Muslim who was said to have called his wife an "inferior being" and to have "imposed the separation of men and women in his own home." "He has no place in our country," the prime minister of the time, François Fillon, declared.[281] Australia's citizenship test was likewise changed in April 2017 to establish whether an applicant had "inappropriate attitudes to women,"[282] the British citizenship of members of a mainly Muslim gang found guilty of "grooming" young girls for sex was revoked—the decision was appealed on the grounds of the defendants' "right to family life"[283]— and the Indian government in September 2018 approved an ordinance banning the Muslim practice of instant divorce, in which it is sufficient for a Muslim male to pronounce the word *talaq* three times to his wife—including by telephone, text-message, or social media post—to end their marriage.[284]

Or on lesser scale in Basel, the school system made mixed-gender swimming classes mandatory despite Muslim objection, a decision unexpectedly upheld by the European Court of Human Rights[285] as also by the German Constitutional Court in a separate case.[286] Similarly, in the name of "respect for the republican order" and for its secularism, French state schools were ordered in May 2018 to send home Muslim girls wearing the "clothes of religious observance," or who refused to take part in mixed sports lessons.[287] "You have to explain and punish if necessary," the French minister of education declared. Again, in Massachusetts a hotel canceled a booking for a men-only Eid celebration;[288] a halal supermarket in a Paris suburb was told to sell alcohol and pork or be shut down; mayors in four southern French towns made it illegal to smoke hookahs in public;[289] Bavaria ordered crucifixes to be placed at the entrances to all state administrative buildings;[290] while Reaction similarly erected a sign at a town entrance in the Italian province of Brescia declaring it to be "a place of Western culture and deep Christian tradition. Those who don't intend to respect them are invited to leave."[291]

Thus, as Muslim numbers and self-confidence in their diasporas grow, with over 25 million Muslims—half under the age of thirty—in Europe in mid-2016, a total that could more than double by 2050,[292] and Mohammed the most common name given to newborn males in London, Yorkshire, and the West Midlands,[293] Reaction responds in various ways. Permissions are refused for Muslim cemeteries as in the Texan town of Farmersville;[294] objections are made to the building of mosques—in Italy's Veneto region it was decreed that they be removed from city centers and confined to suburban areas, a decision upheld by the Constitutional Court[295]—or limits are introduced to restrict their size. In London in December 2012, and under the pressure of "fierce local opposition" to the project, planning permission for the building of a "megamosque" with a capacity for almost 10,000 worshippers—it would have been "three times the size of St. Paul's"—was denied;[296] Scottish Presbyterians held prayer vigils against the building of a mosque on an island in the Outer Hebrides;[297] and a ban on the foreign funding of mosques was introduced in Austria, with Turkish-funded imams expelled.[298] The measures were described by Turkey's president as "leading the world toward a war between the cross and the crescent."[299]

Past societies faced issues of the same kind. In ancient Rome, Tertullian tells us, the "introduction of a foreign cult"—a term which has been used of Islam in political debate in the United States[300]—required the Senate's authorization.[301] In such spirit, the building of minarets has come under ban in Switzerland, where campaigning politicians described them in May 2007 as "symbols of power,"[302] while the muezzin's call to prayer was forbidden in a German town.[303] In Italy imams have been asked, and even told, to preach to the faithful in Italian;[304] in Germany, the Federal Administrative Court ruled in November 2011 that Muslim pupils did not have the right to a prayer room in school;[305] and street prayer outside mosques was prohibited in Paris in September 2011 on the grounds that it "violated the principles of secularism."[306] "We could go as far as force," the French minister added. But Islam has stood its ground, aided by Western democracy's libertarians even when the principles of free thought are under challenge. Against such current, however, Iceland in July 2015 made blasphemy—which is to say free speech on matters of religion—legal.[307]

The free society has thus been set complex tasks by Islam's presence. They range from dealing with trivia—as when two fourteen-year-olds were excluded from class in Britain for refusing to shave off their beards[308]—to facing ethical problems of a different order. Thus an imam accused in France of "encouraging violent jihad, making anti-Semitic remarks, and justifying the use of corporal punishment of women, including whipping-to-death for adultery" was expelled from the country;[309] a Jordanian immigrant was sentenced to death in Texas for the "honor killing" of his daughter's American husband;[310] and almost one hundred applications were made to courts in Britain in a single year for protection orders against genital mutilation.[311] At a more mundane level, the xenophobe looks askance at a headscarf in the street, a Bible is thrown through the windows of an Islamic Center in Colorado,[312] and the carcass of a wild hog is dumped in a mosque parking lot in Oklahoma.[313] But there are also arson and other attacks on mosques from Manchester to Minnesota, and an imam is shot in Queens, New York;[314] an Austrian chancellor declares that "parallel societies have no place in our country";[315] and marchers in Germany carry the slogan *Kein Islam in Deutschland* ("No Islam in Germany").[316]

Meanwhile, the democrat in the free society objects to the wearing of a full face veil revealing only the eyes when swearing a citizenship oath, signing official documents, serving on a jury, appearing as a plaintiff, giving evidence as a witness, or standing trial, with bans upon them in government buildings, educational institutions, and on public transport introduced in Austria, Belgium, Denmark, France, Germany, the Netherlands, and elsewhere. In Britain, some hospitals have also prohibited the wearing of veils by "front-line staff" to ensure "face-to-face contact" with patients,[317] while a Paris Opera cast refused to continue a performance of *La Traviata* until a member of the audience in the front row removed her veil. She demurred and left the theater, and the opera continued.[318]

The struggle with Islam's advance in the free society has also led certain states in the United States to introduce resolutions, bills, and laws to prevent courts from using Islamic sharia law as a basis for decision, as in divorce cases or property disputes involving Muslims. Greece made the same decision in January 2018.[319] In Britain, a young Muslim convert was ordered by an Old Bailey judge to cease his "public campaigning" for a "sharia state,"[320] while "Marches Against Sharia" have taken place in numbers of US cities.[321] In fear of the jihadi, public authority has also increased its surveillance powers— as under the 2016 Investigatory Powers Act in Britain—infiltrated mosques, Muslim neighborhoods, and Muslim student groups, and monitored or taken down radical Muslim websites. "Comprehensive background checks" have even been carried out by New York City's police department on "those whose names sound Arabic or who might be from Muslim countries."[322]

Furthermore, the "targeting of radicals" and of "terror suspects" has led to intercepts of communications, curfews, and the use of electronic tags, seen by some as a breach of human rights; orders to report regularly to the police; and preemptive arrests and imprisonments of those thought to be planning to leave the country for weapons training or to "join the jihad." There have also been raids on mosques; extraditions and deportations of jihad recruiters and proselytizing imams; the withdrawal of passports from, and expulsions of, those thought to be readying themselves for combat; and revocations of the citizenship of those who have gone to join the battles in which Islam is engaged. In the wake of Islamic terrorist attacks, armed marshals and even troops travel on trains and patrol railway stations; the Los Angeles subway installed body scanners to screen passengers for weapons and explosives;[323] armed police are put on the streets on occasions of public festivity; and barriers of concrete and steel are erected to impede the jihadi truck driver. A state of emergency can also be declared, as in France after the November 2015 attacks in Paris, with schools and the metro closed and soccer matches canceled, and with the number of applicants to join the army rising.[324]

At the same time, disdain for the free society's moral disorders is growing among many Muslims themselves, their strength of faith and their numbers in Western democracies sustaining an increasing indifference to non-Muslim judgments of Islam. Aided by well-meaning defenders of Muslim rights, and by the silences of the "politically correct," this strength is for the most part benignly expressed. But resistance to the politics of the "crackdown" against "extremism"— whether such "crackdown" be imposed by the law or by Reaction in the streets—also becomes more stubborn, with some mosque preachers adding fuel to the flame. At worst come murders of cartoonists for mockery of Islam's prophet, and further suicide attacks in the name of the jihad.

Again in the dialectic of things, Reaction, occupying the void created by old socialist and old conservative failure, beats its chest in organized response, with hostility to the incomer beckoning the patriot and the racist alike, and with the politician quick to express it. The French Front National thus called for "a halt to immigration" and the "revision" of France's citizenship law";[325] the German AfD for the prohibition of the Muslim call to prayer;[326] the Dutch PVV for the "de-Islamization" of the Netherlands by the closing of mosques and Islamic schools and the "banning" of the Qur'an;[327] while the leader of Italy's La Lega described Islam as "incompatible" with the country's constitution.[328] Out of fear that "unchecked immigration threatens our civilization,"[329] xenophobia can also display posters— in a Swiss election—of a white sheep being driven by a black sheep from a national flag[330] and attack veiled women in the street; in Athens black-shirted heralds of a "Golden Dawn," describing Hitler as a "great personality,"[331] demanded a "Greece only for the Greeks" and a "one-race nation";[332] and an Australian senator called for a "final solution to the immigration problem."[333]

In these spreading lower depths, the targets for odium multiply and mutate, with Islam merely one among them. The mob invokes "white power"; gays are targeted for physical attack; "traitors," "Marxists," and "bankers" are excoriated; and a deranged Norwegian crusader slaughters innocents in the name of the Knights Templar. Migrant strengths and the strengths of Reaction, the latter still largely hidden, also increase together in the dialectic which binds them. As frustration grows, the desire to restore the sense of nation, a desire which helped bring President Trump to office and Britain to opt to leave the European Union, summons the frightened and the angered to "take back the country" by rougher methods. Shaven-headed and beer-swilling members of Defence Leagues thus rally to the "counter-jihadist" cause, and in Britain "Johnny Foreigner" faces harder times.

The advance of deepest Reaction in free societies is still in its early phases but continues to make its way. The killer of a British member of parliament gave his name in court as "Death to Traitors, Freedom for Britain" and had Nazi regalia at home;[334] in the 2017 French election Marine le Pen—"looking to the future"—attacked "money and media power" in the name of "the French people," and challenged those who "no longer believe in France";[335] and in Hungary the "Force and Determination" movement, claiming Europe to be "unlivable," has "ethnic self-defense" as its cause.[336]

In Reaction's political progress in Europe, "nation-first," anti-"globalist," anti-"establishment" and anti-migrant parties—dismissed by the French president as "nationalist demagogues"[337]—have therefore gained office, come close to it, or moved forward in many countries from Scandinavia to the Balkans. In Austria the Freedom Party, founded in 1956 by a former SS officer, entered government in December 2017 as a coalition partner; in Germany, the "far-right" AfD won almost one hundred seats in the German federal parliament in the September 2017 national election; and in Hungary the anti-migrant Fidesz and its leader Viktor Orban gained a third term by a "landslide" in April 2018.[338] In Italy the anti-migrant, "Italy first" and Eurosceptic Lega, joining hands in government in 2018 with the "populist" Five-Star movement, promised not only migrant deporta-tion—its effects already noted—but also cuts to parliamentary sala-ries and pensions, a "citizen wage," and the restoration of the Italians' "identity,"[339] with the leader of the Lega describing his movement as the "true defenders of European values"[340] and with President Trump's former adviser declaring that the "new elite" of Europe were its "patriots."[341]

"Anti-globalists" of the "alternative right," or "alt-right," in the United States—KKK members and neo-Nazis among them—had for their part hailed Donald Trump's victory and stood ready to fight restrictions on guns[342] and to "take America back,"[343] while in Charlottesville, Virginia, in August 2017 "white nationalists" and other marchers, who had allegedly come there from "at least thirty-five states,"[344] reawakened the conflicts of the American Civil War. "White nationalism" thus provoked the smashing or removal of Con-federate monuments across the United States,[345] and even of statues of Columbus in Baltimore and New York,[346] with "Black Lives Matter," "Muslims Welcome," and "Nazi Scum" among the slogans carried in the streets,[347] while in October 2017 "Columbus Day" became "Indigenous Peoples' Day" in a number of US cities,[348] and Columbus, Ohio, canceled its own "Columbus Day" celebrations.[349]

At the same time, the Spirit of Demolition continues to play its dangerous games with the free society's better surviving customs and necessary institutions. Simultaneously, the marketplace greeds of Madam Bubble's most ardent followers grow more rampant as inequality deepens, their defense of market interest as a condition of prosperity at almost any social cost inviting the further reprisals of Reaction. Today, there are many potential scapegoats for the free society's ills, with Jews, traditional scapegoats, once more among them. "Again and again in every report, every talk, Jewish Bolshe-vism, Jewish plutocracy, Jewish influence in the White House, etc etc etc," Victor Klemperer noted in his diary,[350] referring to Nazi broad-casts in Germany in 1943 as the camps filled with fascism's victims. Such obsession has long fastened upon the "Jewish lobby" for its supposedly conspiratorial (or "occult") powers over governments, civil society, and even the fate of nations.

Thus the "alt-right" marchers in Virginia in August 2017 cried "Jews will not replace us!,"[351] a new edition of *Mein Kampf* became a German bestseller in 2016—taking its publisher "by surprise"[352]—and the Holocaust is denied, while assault and abuse increase.[353] The campaign to "boycott, divest from, and sanction" Israel for its malfeasance also has echoes of the anti-Jewish boycotts of the 1930s, with some capable of seeing even the Islamic State as an "Israeli creation."[354] At the same time, thinly coded references by a Trump to "global financial firms,"[355] by British Labour's Jeremy Corbyn to "greedy bankers" and "crooked financiers,"[356] and by UKIP's Nigel Farage to "all these dreadful people hand-in-glove with Goldman Sachs"[357] pointed in a familiar direction.

Here, the involvement of Jews—proportionately few as may be—in banking and business malfeasance, including the $65 billion Madoff "Ponzi scheme," has served anti-Semitism's ancient fixations all too well. So, too, has the unconscionable defense by a Milton Friedman of market interest as a condition of prosperity at almost any social or moral cost. He explained even the origins of language in free-market terms. "How did language develop?" Friedman asks. "In much the same way," he answers, "as an economic order develops through the market—out of the voluntary interaction of individuals, in this case seeking to trade ideas or information or gossip."[358] Medical ethics is interpreted in similar fashion. "Competition for patients was fierce," he writes of ancient Greece, "and, not surprisingly, a concerted movement apparently developed to rationalize the discipline [of medicine] in order to eliminate "unfair competition." Accordingly, the medical people constructed a code of conduct [and] named it the Hippocratic Oath." He even calls it a "nice market-sharing agreement."[359]

But hymns are sung to the "free market" by every ethnicity and faith. Moreover, ethical and economic misdeed knows no racial bounds, while abuses of position, power, and wealth by democracy's political elite are the hallmarks of the failing free society itself. Such misconduct has added to public anger and dismay, while the Bad Faith of those who deny the very facts of the free society's true condition has obstructed reform, undermined Reason, and aided Reaction. First, the politicians.

CHAPTER 8

THE POLITICAL CLASS

As Western democracy's social and moral orders unravel, contempt for the political class is widespread. It is unsurprising. The political life has been reduced for most politicians to a career like any other, with party candidates increasingly drawn from backroom coteries of insiders who have little knowledge of other worlds. At the dawning of the United States, James Madison warned of the "diminution of attachment" which "steals into the hearts of the people towards a political system" when it displays "marks of infirmity and disappoints so many of their hopes."[1] "Infirmity" and "disappointment" understate the case in the United States, Britain, and other free societies today.

With the legitimacy of established parties declining—fifty new parties were registered with Britain's Electoral Commission in 2017 alone[2]—and weary distrust of the status quo reaching "unprecedented" levels,[3] objections to the "metropolitan elite,"[4] the Washington "swamp,"[5] and the "cesspit that is career politics"[6] have gained ground. "At some point," declared Tony Blair in March 2016, "the political class as a whole has got to get up and stand up for itself."[7] But as the turmoil in free societies intensifies and the professional politician's stock falls—Italy, for example, has had sixty governments since 1945—voices can be heard calling for a "global revolution"[8] and even a "Christian reformation."[9] Almost one-half of Americans polled in 2016 expressed "hardly any confidence" in Congress,[10] and in February 2018 no less than 85 percent disapproved of the job Congress was doing.[11] Some 63 million voted for Donald Trump, an outsider without previous political experience, while the more than 17 million Britons who chose departure from the European Union were said by the leader of the United Kingdom Independence Party to have expressed a desire to be "in charge of their own lives."[12] "There's a lot of anger in this country," Trump rightly declared, describing himself as "just a messenger" of it.[13]

The pressures underlying these turns of event are again hardly new. Objections to the absence of principle in a politician, and of a sense of direction in a party, are constants of public judgment. The early-Victorian British Conservative Party was criticized for having "neither genius nor doctrine," and the prime minister Robert Peel for speaking "frequently of conservatism" but having "no idea of what he wanted to conserve."[14] Similarly the modern Tory Party, divided over Europe, has lurched to and fro between espousal of the imperatives of the free market and policies of attempted social and economic intervention, while the Labour Party has been split asunder by personal animus and militant faction. Indeed, a lack of "genius" and "doctrine" are evident in most of democracy's leading figures. Unable to command the internal and external forces bringing the free society down—an impotence which provides the stimulus to Reaction— today's weak political class, laying claim to a high sense of public duty but with its policies for the most part a practical failure, often lacks elementary personal abilities, too; both Britain and the United States have been saddled in the last decades with prime ministers and presidents of little distinction.

Moreover, as democracies founder, "populist" challengers for office can be equally unfit for the tasks they assume. With falsehoods stated to be facts and facts declared to be false, Donald Trump thus expressed concern for the "American worker" while seeking to limit health-provision, and denied climate change while claiming that his "movement" was "about common sense, about doing the right thing,"[15] and even asserted that he had a "natural instinct for science."[16] Too often the pronouncements of the established political class are also without meaning. "We need to roll forward the frontiers of society," a leader of the Conservative Party could therefore declare;[17] and "to remain one nation it is essential that we should all have the chance to climb the ladder, but to do so with a sense of togetherness," a Tory Party statement urged,[18] as the metaphysical ladder collapsed before our eyes.

"Those with power need intelligence," says Menelaus in Euripides's drama *Iphigenia in Aulis*.[19] But it is possible now for a British prime minister not even to know the meaning of the words *Magna Carta*,[20] for a Tory member of parliament to call Jane Austen "one of our greatest living authors,"[21] and for a US presidential candidate to ask, during the siege and bombing of Aleppo in Syria, "What is Aleppo?"[22] Similarly, the tweeting Trump, asserting that the "silent majority" was frustrated by governments run by "stupid people,"[23] described himself as "honered " to serve as the president of the United States,[24] claimed that his campaign funds had "played no roll" in the payoff to a porn star,[25] and complained that "fake news likes to pour over my tweets looking for a mistake."[26] There is again little that is new in this. "We too often see men have great wealth, high titles, and boundless power heaped upon them who can hardly write two lines together correctly," William Cobbett declared in 1830,[27] while objection to "fake news" is an old one. "There are more direct falsehoods circulated by the American newspapers than by all the others in the world," wrote an observer of the United States in 1832.[28]

Observation of mediocrity in the democratic politician is an old theme too. "In the United States, I was surprised to find so much distinguished talent among the citizens and so little among the heads of the government. The ablest men in the United States are rarely placed at the head of affairs," de Tocqueville commented long ago, adding that "universal suffrage is by no means a guarantee of the wisdom of the popular choice."[29] Indeed, contempts for those who rule are historic constants. Or as Castiglione wrote in the early sixteenth century, "from not knowing how to govern there come so many woes. Yet some princes who are ignorant of government are not ashamed to attempt it."[30]

Modern democracy also provides no guarantee of scruple or care in decision on fateful matters. Thus, Tony Blair—with his "sofa style of government" which "kept ministers in the dark"[31]—was found by an official inquiry to have failed to establish "clear ministerial oversight of UK planning and preparation" for the Iraq war in 2003, and to have omitted to "discuss military options" or even to raise in cabinet "the Attorney-General's views on the legality of the war."[32] Likewise, the Brexit referendum of June 2016 was inadequately prepared for by the Tory government of the day, with insufficient assessment of the implications of withdrawal from the European Union provided to the British public before it voted, and with wild impulse governing many of the Trump administration's decisions.

Uncertainties of policy in response to the challenges that government faces are also of no new kind. "Weak counsels and weak actings undo all," declared Oliver Cromwell in September 1643.[33] In the free society today, it is a weakness often dictated by the ideal of liberty itself, which prevents determined action lest liberty be thought to be compromised by it. Hasty policy improvisations as public anxieties deepen are likewise nothing new, and for a political class to reveal its inadequacies—as the problems facing it grow—is a commonplace. Thus, members of the court and nobility in pre-revolutionary eighteenth-century France were described as "vacillating hopelessly at a time when clarity and resolution were the primary needs."[34] Today, the quickening speed at which the free society's dysfunctions increase, and its external foes advance, leaves democracy's politicians ever less certain of the direction they should take, as in the West's relations with Russia.

"What is to be done?" is an old political question, perhaps the oldest. It is a question which most free-society politicians, uncertain of immediate purpose but also without wider perspective, cannot now answer. Unable to stand up to the combined interests of the free-marketeer and the rights activist, the corporate mogul and the moral free-chooser, the weaknesses of the political class in Western democracies can again be understood. In the confusion some politicians, aspiring to halt the free society's disintegration, urge greater "control" of this or that activity and behavior. Others, running with the tide, seek an ever-greater "freeing-up" of possibility and widening of "choice." Others, again, wander in circles, buffeted to and fro as mavericks assail them. Together, their uncertainties and internal conflicts now make public policy a farrago of contradictions, discrediting the political class itself.

But the practical need to satisfy the free society's dominant interests has limited the scope of true political choice, and has driven most established politicians to converge upon the "center ground." It is ground upon which dominant interests can be met, while token deference is paid to civic interest and the national good. This ambivalence in turn invites hostility from the anti-establishment or "populist" newcomer, and from the would-be revolutionary of "right" or "left." Moreover, thought and principle weigh less on the "center ground" than a carefully managed media presence; and with arbitrary political ideas often adopted for merely demonstrative ends, both the defense of a position and resistance to it are decreasingly bound by party philosophy, tradition, or ethic, or are not bound by them at all.

It is therefore hard for ostensibly democratic politicians to establish in the public mind what their true beliefs and purposes really are. Or as Britain's Tory leader expressed it, "I have always said that politics shouldn't be about trying to be distinctive, politics should be about trying to be right. The parties are closer together than they have been in the past,"[35] precisely the objection of those who want no more of it. All the while the real center ground, the ground or foundation upon which the true commonwealth rests, lies elsewhere.

The present times are also hailed as "post-ideological," as if standing—or attempting to stand—on the supposed "center ground" was not an ideological position itself. Here, despite public posturing at times of election, much of it theater, differences of substance have largely dissolved, with the prevailing conceptions of liberty in foundering Western democracies considered to be the only rational ones. It is therefore held to be irrational to oppose or obstruct them, even if the policies based on them are increasingly helpless in face of the free society's disorders.

In Britain, political Tweedledum and political Tweedledee, turn and turn-about, have nevertheless continued to promise policies of "fairness," "toughness," or "compassion," and to offer the electorate inclusion, hope, empowerment, opportunity, or aspiration. Most of it is a masquerade, a play of words alone. Irreconcilable notions are also conjoined, as when "green politics" is made compatible with "growth," or when privatization and the ethos of public service are promoted together. Similarly, in the "center-ground" mêlée, the advocate of the free market can criticize "markets without morality, and capitalism without a conscience,"[36] and the erstwhile "socialist"— "what is socialism?" "I do not know"—can promise to "work very closely on the side of business."[37]

There has again been nothing new in such political cross-dressing when it suits party interest, as the career of Benjamin Disraeli demonstrated. But today most establishment politicians gyrate about one another crying out for "change," yet unable to do much or anything to amend the failing free society's condition, while born-again "socialists"—a Jeremy Corbyn, a Bernie Sanders, and others to come—wait in the wings with their old left primers in their hands. At the same time, this or that politician undertakes to create a "good society," to "confront the challenges of the global age," or to prepare this or that nation for a "new world." The maverick, too, can learn to speak this language, and with the help of wordsmiths its rhetoric becomes more Orwellian. Weak establishment politicians and militant newcomers alike may even speak of the "revolution" which they propose in this or that matter of state. But the only revolution is that of the free society, spinning about its own axis and with the political class spinning around with it.

Meanwhile, politicians increasingly shy away from the dilemmas— moral dilemmas in particular—posed by the free society's condition. Many merely weigh the totals and origins of incomers in their constituencies, and calculate what degree of deference to them is required if their political careers are to proceed and prosper. On such ground, again the "center ground," principle is an encumbrance and such issues as that of liberty's limits are sidestepped, even as social break-down deepens.

In this pantomime, the inability of the political class to arrest Western democracy's downward motion can even be in part excused. Appetite in the free society cannot be restrained if "growth" is to continue, while attempt must be made to satisfy material expectations if elections are to be won. At the same time, the liberties which are tearing the fabric of civil society apart must be upheld if the market is to prosper. Moreover, the sanctions necessary to protect the free society are for the most part incompatible with the free society's own ethic, and are by reflex perceived as repressive.

America's Founding Fathers thought differently. As Alexander Hamilton wrote in 1787, "It is essential to the idea of a law that it be attended with a sanction; or, in other words, a penalty or punishment for disobedience. If there be no penalty attached to disobedience"— the very word a taboo to today's libertarian—"the resolutions or commands which pretend to be laws will, in fact, amount to nothing more than advice or recommendation."[38]

But today many in the political class stare in confusion at the symptoms of social disintegration, and look away. "Leaving well alone" also greets many arguments for political intervention as social and ethical disorders mount. In the face of crime, some clench their platform-fists and bristle with words alone, while others deny the facts of it, a subject to which I will return. Alternatively, after a gun massacre in the United States, severity may for a while rule the scene of debate until gun-lobby powers regain control over the political class. Or concern for the public good may be driven from the polit-ical field by arguments that this or that measure of restraint will curb "choice," and once more impair liberty itself.

Behind such stasis there often lie hidden but rigid divisions, including on the supposed "center ground," which practical neces-sity cannot overcome. A national health service is therefore seen as little better than communism in disguise by some in the American political class, but as the precondition of a truly civil society by others.

Concern for the poor and needy is similarly matched, or blocked, by arguments over the costs of its provision; and, as families break down, the political class cannot decide whether the "stable home" is or is not a societal lynch-pin. In matters of migration, likewise, some politicians celebrate "diversity"—often for electoral calculation—while others harden their hearts or bury their heads. Economy and welfare, crime and family, education and population go to the heart of any social order's stability, and its prospects for long-term survival. Yet few in the political class possess the qualities of mind to command public attention on such subjects for long, or at all.

Moreover, it became possible for "Yes, We Can" to be the leading slogan of a successful US presidential campaign,[39] and "I alone can fix it" the claim of another.[40] "Fine words," believed Longinus, "are the very light of thought,"[41] while Plutarch held that "dignity and grandeur in speech" were "necessary to a politician" but that he "must be eloquent himself so that he has no need of another's voice" to speak for him.[42] Instead, speechwriters today provide many of democracy's political leaders with their seeming beliefs; and in the United States, until President Trump's accession to office, they also supply them with transcendental purple prose. Barack Obama thus attributed his first presidential victory to electors who had chosen to "put their hands on the arc of history and bend it once more to the hope of a better day,"[43] vacuity inflated to the Hollywood heavens. "In the United States," asserted de Tocqueville—long before a Trump described the alleged theft by the Chinese of a US drone as an "unpresidented act"[44] and was accused of being "semi-literate" and "dyslexic"[45]—"the individuals who conduct government are frequently unskilful."[46] But today, in all free societies, teams of consultants are at hand to invest politicians with qualities they do not possess, even as the difficulties of doing so mount, with President Trump described as "impetuous, adversarial, petty and ineffective" by an anonymous "senior official" in his administration,[47] and by others as "morally unfit to be president,"[48] a "charlatan,"[49] a "borderline psychotic narcissist,"[50] and "mentally declined."[51]

At the same time, diminishing light shines in the deeper reaches of the political process. Party membership and organization have lost much of their significance, while private interests insulated from the citizen body rule ostensible democracies undisturbed. In this penumbra, the invisible and the unaccountable make policy, and parliamentary sovereignty is mocked. Even senior ministers can be junior to a favored special adviser, and spin doctors with good media contacts command more influence in government than the elected representatives of the people. With decisions already taken, the charade of much congressional and parliamentary debate nevertheless continues, its voices of diminishing significance or unheard.

Some of this is again not new. "Night after night," wrote Charles Dickens of debates in the House of Commons—recalling his youthful experiences as a parliamentary reporter—"I record predictions that never come to pass, professions that are never fulfilled, explanations that are only meant to mystify. I am sufficiently behind the scenes to know the worth of political life."[52] The distance between media sham and true public debate is also no new theme; in 1930, Winston Churchill was already comparing "real political democracy" with a situation in which the "fluid mass of the public" is "distracted by newspapers."[53] But there is no historical precedent for the means now available in electronic limbo to disseminate falsehood, as well as to market the politician's media-ready nostrums to the millions for whom the term "civil society" has no meaning.

The practical failure of such nostrums also appears to leave many, or most, of the political class indifferent. The reason is not far to seek. For even though they are unable to command public respect, or to establish what their real beliefs are, increasing numbers of the political servants of market interest have the consoling prospect of a future in Madam Bubble's arms. Indeed, as free societies disintegrate, the unprincipled representatives of the people invite purchase and corruption spreads, with parliamentarians seeking compensation in personal profit for the lack of esteem in which they are held, while in Italy, for example, those ostensibly fighting corruption are often corrupt themselves.

Cicero thought that honesty was "the most powerful virtue in winning the confidence of mankind."[54] But patronage and sleaze have been features of the political world from ancient times to these. The Roman historian Sallust tells how he found "not decency, uprightness and ability" in public life, but "impudence, bribery and greed,"[55] while Petronius has a character in the *Satyricon* object that "public officials are in league with bankers." "You serve me and I'll serve you" is how he sums up the relation.[56] As the encrypted documents of a Panamanian law firm leaked in August 2015 revealed,[57] the representatives of the people in Western democracies—relatives of the Chinese president and members of his politburo also—now hide their wealth in offshore tax havens, while Sallust would have recognized modern Italy's Silvio Berlusconi. Elected prime minister in 1994, 2001, 2005, and 2008, he was at different times accused of abuse of office, corruption, sex with minors, tax fraud, and links to the mafia, with cases dropped and lapsed, one sentence served and other convictions overturned.

For its part, if on a lesser scale, the Clinton Foundation was alleged to have received large donations from corporate institutions, bankers, and others for access to government decision and similar favors,[58] and "that makes me smart" was Trump's response to accusations of tax avoidance.[59] Indeed, both Hillary Clinton and Trump were seen as "dishonest" by a majority of voters in the 2016 presidential election,[60] with Trump's associates variously pleading guilty to campaign-finance violations, bank fraud, and lying to the FBI about their relations with Russian political and economic interests.[61] "May none but honest and wise men ever rule under this roof," wrote John Adams, the first occupant of the White House in November 1800,[62] and in other times than these. In Britain the Mother of Parliaments, like other Western democratic assemblies, has also been raddled by corrupt practice and is called "Wasteminster" by some.[63] As standards of debate and even of elementary expressiveness fall, its callow members have been found out using base devices for gain, exploiting their positions to seek financial reward from those wanting favor and access, and most are unembarrassed when exposed.

Nearly one in five also have second jobs and incomes as directors of companies, consultants, and advisers.[64] Peers likewise claim daily allowances amounting in total to millions of pounds a year for attending the House of Lords—with more than 800 members it is the second-largest legislative chamber in the world after the National People's Congress of China[65] and has been described as "the best day-care center for the elderly in London"[66]—but often take no part in its debates and committee hearings, nor ask a single written question.[67] Furthermore, one in five British MPs has been found to employ family members—wives, husbands, and others—in their offices at public cost,[68] now a commonplace of the democratic parliamentary life. They have also filled their pockets by making false or unwarranted expense claims, disclosed in the British press in 2009 and followed by disciplinary action, resignations, and criminal charges.[69] They included claims for nonexistent mortgages and homes, for pornographic films, spa holidays and Christmas-tree decorations, and even for a toilet brush, a dog dish, and an ornamental duck house. Moreover, despite the exposures, subsequent expense claims are said to have run at an even higher rate.[70]

There is again nothing new in this type of fraud; in ancient Athens, a crippling fine of 6,000 drachmas was imposed on a certain Konon for claiming the city's festival attendance allowance for his son when the latter was in fact abroad.[71] Once, in Britain, a Cromwell could denounce and overturn a parliament whose members, in his stern judgment, were "self-serving," led "scandalous lives," and were guilty of profiting "themselves and their friends."[72] "These things," the Protector declared in November 1652, "do give much ground for people to open their mouths against them and dislike them," as they do now. Similarly, the eighteenth-century British parliamentary system with its jobbery, restricted franchise, and "rotten boroughs" had the grossest defects, while Cobbett wrote of the "loan-mongers and stock-jobbers" who "get fortunes in a few days" and become "honourable gentlemen" thereafter.[73]

But today's forms of political spoliation are taking place despite universal suffrage and in the teeth of it. Now, politicians bypass and abuse the democratic system itself, and in Britain old socialist class warriors become knights and peers of the realm. At the same time, orders of chivalry are awarded to the rock star, the cyclist, and the news reader; party donors are honored for public service; and a prime minister's wife's hairdresser has received the Order of the British Empire.[74]

Meanwhile, corporate interests and "campaign groups" fund or invest in would-be presidents, legislators, and other representatives of the people. On this terrain market interest is in its element, the "fund-raising binges"[75] of an American presidential election making Dickens's Eatanswill seem small beer. Recoil from it is again an old story. "Elections here," wrote the Earl of Chesterfield of an election in Northampton in 1768, "have been carried to a degree of frenzy hitherto unheard of," with the "contending parties" spending "at least thirty thousand pounds a side."[76] But the scale of it in the corrupted modern democracy is of a different order.

With "big business shoveling more money than ever into US political campaigns"[77] and with "poorly funded" candidates having little chance of success in ostensibly democratic contests whether at national or congressional district level, a billion dollars each was spent in their 2012 presidential contest by Barack Obama and Mitt Romney, above all on advertising and with large costs incurred in the organization of fund-raising itself. In its final stages, with spending running at a "furious pace," it had amounted to between two and three million dollars a day. Contributions from the "financial sector" were said to have reached "over $500 million,"[78] with the "cloak of anonymity" shielding "billionaire donors."[79]

In the 2016 US presidential primaries, the failed Republican candidate Jeb Bush likewise spent some $130 million in seven months before dropping out, including $33 million on airfare, $10 million on consultants, $84 million on advertising, and $4,837 on pizzas.[80] Again, the "socialist" candidate for the Democratic nomination, Bernie Sanders, complaining that "we can no longer continue to have a corrupt campaign finance-system,"[81] was raising over $40 million a month[82] in the concluding phase of his primary run, while Hillary Clinton had a "nearly 900-strong payroll" and raised almost $600 million in campaign funds,[83] including from the "securities and investment industry."[84]

She also spent tens of millions on TV advertisements[85]—or "buying time in TV markets"[86]—and invited "superstar" rockers and rappers to her free pre-election concerts;[87] a pair of seats at the top table of her fund-raising dinner in San Francisco, held in democracy's name, cost over $350,000.[88] As for the somewhat less expensive but victorious Trump bandwagon, it raised around $340 million, including "$66 million from his own pocket,"[89] spent $700,000 on "campaign shirts, mugs and stickers"—and over $200,000 on giveaway hats[90]—paid $7 million for a two-minute closing commercial,[91] and spent more than $100 million on his inauguration.[92]

Moreover, the "nation's relaxed campaign finance-system"[93] saw more than $1 billion spent in total on Senate races in 2012[94] and $850 million on state-level political broadcasts and TV advertising in 2014,[95] while Chicago's mayor was said in 2015 to have had $17 million available in his "push for a second term."[96] Indeed, the US Supreme Court has since 2010 loosened many restrictions on campaign financing, on the grounds of "the right in our democracy to participate in electing our political leaders."[97] Thus, the 2018 midterm elections—in a bitterly divided country which saw the Democrats take the House of Representatives and the Republicans maintain their hold on the Senate—were described in the *New York Times* as a "$5 billion debate,"[98] $2 billion was spent in 2018 on campaigns even for state governorships, state legislatures, and other state offices,[99] and $66 million was lavished on Montana's senate race at a rate of $85 for each potential voter.[100]

On these battlefields, "big money" "dwarfs" all others.[101] Defended as making for "more competitive elections,"[102] it includes contributions from "shadowy" and "unknown" sources, among them "non-profits that do not have to disclose their donors' names."[103] The Trump presidential campaign was thus said to have received large donations from beneficiaries of offshore "tax shelters,"[104] and in July 2018 the Trump administration further eased the donor-disclosure requirements, making it possible for more "dark money," including from foreign sources, to enter the political arena; in the 2018 midterms, even some of Britain's biggest companies with interests in the United States in the "defence, tobacco, pharmaceutical and finance sectors" were said to have made "contributions" of "tens of millions of dollars."[105]

But when the purse rules the politician and the elector alike, democracy pays the suicidal price. In particular, the millions spent by market interest on its favorites—often hedging its bets by backing both Tweedledum and Tweedledee—provide the open sesame to influence and gain, with corporations even described as "invest[ing] in politicians as a way of building their brand and raising their stock-price."[106] Moreover, in the United States, politicians themselves can speak of their candidacies in banking terms. After spending $5 million of "family money" on her unsuccessful campaign for the 2008 US presidential nomination, Hillary Clinton declared that the early favorable results had justified her "investment."[107]

Those who have held political office in a free society, as earlier mentioned, can also command high market prices from continuing access to power, public and private, and from the "celebrity" which the media creates and rewards. Thus, former president Obama was paid a fee of $400, 000 for a single speech to clients of an "asset management company"[108] and to a conference on healthcare,[109] and Hillary Clinton $475,000 for addressing the Deutsche Bank.[110] In Britain, Labour's Tony Blair after leaving office became adviser to a merchant-bank, a Gulf potentate, and a Central Asian despot, could command large sums in speaking fees—"as much as £200,000 for a single engagement"[111]—and acquired a "property portfolio" worth millions.[112]

Similarly, the former Tory chancellor George Osborne, while continuing to take his salary as a sitting member of parliament (for a constituency almost two hundred miles from London), became a consultant to a Wall Street bank, working four days a month for £650,000 a year,[113] editor of London's *Evening Standard* at a salary of more than £200,000,[114] adviser to an Italian company which owns the Juventus soccer club,[115] and a visiting fellow at Stanford, at the same time earning large sums for speeches to financial institutions, including JPMorgan.[116] "I hope," said Cromwell in December 1644, "that we have such zealous affection towards the general weal of our Mother Country as no Member of either House will scruple to deny their own private interests for the public good."[117] Cromwell's hope is a forlorn one today. Market interests have closed in on democracy's administrative system, while movement between the public and private "sectors" has become routine.

In addition, the free society's politicians must increasingly defer to the media's powers to make or break them, with the TV presenter and the chat-show host now political figures in their own right. "Look, if you're in a situation where these guys, particularly if they hunt in a pack, can literally take out any ministers and make your government rock," Blair declared in September 2011, "you've got no option but to work hard and try to bring them round."[118] Moreover, the transfer of political debate to the stage-managed television studio, and the need to keep the camera lens trained on the politician's wares, have made the political process itself a form of show business.

It has also made for a politics of "personality" in which sound bites, sales-pitches, and a Trump's tweets take the place of considered policy. Non-selling political ideas, images, and "brands" are quickly repudiated, while to catch the eye of the customer in democracy's marketplace is more urgent than to hold a national assembly's attention. In the marketing mind, a logo therefore counts more than a logic and a photo-op more than genuine political belief.

Thus, Nicolas Sarkozy spent £26,000 on makeup and "face and hair make-overs"[119] in the French presidential campaign of 2007, and his defeated rival Ségolène Royal "52,000 euros for make-up and hairdressing";[120] former President François Hollande, accused of "shampoo socialism," paid his hairdresser almost £100, 000 a year;[121] and President Emmanuel Macron is said to have spent €26,000 on makeup in his first three months in office.[122] Likewise, in the American contest for the Republican vice presidential nomination in 2008, Sarah Palin spent $290,000 on her "clothes, hair and cosmetics,"[123] while Hillary Clinton in her New York primary victory speech in 2016 was dressed in an Armani jacket—priced at from $7,497 to $12,495—as she set out the "bold progressive goals," including that of "reducing inequality," of her presidential campaign.[124]

Indeed, since the rules of the political marketplace make for standardization, mainstream politicians have become increasingly indistinct from one another, a uniformity which invests the unconventional outsider with seeming special merit. But large numbers in notional democracies continue to take no part in the political process; some 12 million people abstained or spoiled their ballots in the 2017 French presidential election.[125] British MPs and members of Congress also suffer abuse and threat,[126] most party memberships shrink, and the suffrage is decreasingly seen as a valued democratic right or civic duty, once more inviting Reaction to occupy the void.

"The spirit of faction is a natural attendant on civil liberty," as David Hume put it.[127] But today, beneath Western democracy's surface, a plague is wished by many upon the houses of the entire established political class. In the United States, a "throw the bums out mentality" was said in April 2006 to be "on the upswing," with "more and more" Americans wishing a "pox on both the Republican and Democratic parties."[128] Similarly, large majorities in the polls before the 2016 US presidential election held unfavorable views of the "honesty" and "trustworthiness" both of Trump and Clinton.[129] In what was called an "unpopularity contest,"[130] as many as 80 percent also declared that they would "feel afraid" whichever of them was elected,[131] with some of Trump's supporters warning of "conflict"—even "another Revolutionary War"[132]—were he to lose, while pipe bombs were sent to leading critics of his presidency in October 2018.[133]

Deeper sentiments are different. Opinion polls have thus found that "moral values" are a "defining issue" for voters, with "honesty," once more, by far the most popular single trait in the politician,[134] signifying the hope of many that integrity might one day rule the public domain. The ideal of the Athenian was also a political assembly "incorruptible by wealth, worthy of respect, inflexible of mind, and a vigilant sentinel of the land in defense of those who sleep."[135] But the US Congress and the British House of Commons bear little resemblance to such ideal.

Instead, as the weak political class of the free society veers this way and that, and outsiders come to the fore, the aggrieved and the anxious become more various, with different axes to grind. Moreover, poll findings in the US regularly find that majorities believe the country to be "headed in the wrong direction,"[136] a view which did not change after President Trump had taken office;[137] indeed, talk of his possible impeachment by invoking the Twenty-Fifth Amendment came early in his administration.[138]

Madison's warning in the earliest days of the United States against "loss of attachment" to its political system was thus prescient. But to remedy it has not been a priority for democracy's governing class. This is owed in large part to falsehoods and evasions about the free society's true condition. To this Bad Faith I now turn.

CHAPTER 9

BAD FAITH

A s the ills of the free society increase, unwillingness to recognize its real conditions becomes more entrenched in many, again the dialectic. To hold unwelcome truths at a distance is a natural impulse and to hope for the best is a virtue. But to evade, gloss over, or deny the known facts of Western democracy's disorders is Bad Faith and a further form of self-harm.

Some escapist wishful thinking, as when the worse is believed to be the better, is again Orwellian. "We live in the best of times,"[1] "capitalism has been a triumph,"[2] "family life is the best it's been for a thousand years,"[3] and "this is a golden age for the world,"[4] the voices declare. In equally Orwellian fashion, Bad Faith can claim that "there has never been a better time to be alive in Britain than today, no generation more blessed, never such opportunity for so many. And things are getting better all the time, horizons widening, education spiraling, everyone living longer, healthier, safer lives."[5]

Indeed, the larger the disorder which afflicts the free society, the more elaborate, ambiguous, or dishonest are the denials of it. Elementary questions go unasked or, if asked, self-censorship stops the answers and effects are untraced to their causes. Moreover, the advocates to "right" and "left" of this or that interest are quick to deny the harms to civil society that their special interests often bring. At the same time "realism" in a "new era," or "change" fitting for the "modern world," will be invoked in justification of policies that damage the entire social order. Statistical manipulations of the facts are also brought to Bad Faith's aid, in particular upon the growing extent in the free society of crime and educational failure.

Often leading the way in the exercise of Bad Faith is market interest, which largely keeps silent about Western democracy's deepening inequalities and injustices, since their potential outcome bodes ill for business. Indeed, since self-restraint in a market order is no virtue and the pursuit of self-interest no vice, this form of Bad Faith cannot acknowledge that many of our societies' profoundest ills are the outcomes of market interest's own value system. Hence, Western democracy's "food banks" and the dependency of millions of American children on "food stamps" are best not spoken of too much—or at all—by Bad Faith in its free-market dress, nor the differentials in child mortality rates and adult life expectancies between the free society's rich and poor.

Market-driven Bad Faith, two-faced, may acknowledge that HIV, with its 30 million worldwide deaths, its tens of millions living with AIDS and many unaware that they have it, its 1.5 million annual deaths and almost 2 million new infections per year[6]—a small decline, but there are now immune-resistant mutations of the disease[7]—has taken a toll comparable with that of Europe's fourteenth-century Black Death. But Bad Faith could not address the fact, earlier referred to, that the free society's corporate pharmaceutical giants, armed with their licensing and royalty policies, long resisted the technological transfer required to manufacture cheaper versions of the life-saving patents they owned. With a market made even of mercy and care, they put treatment with their "branded" drugs beyond the reach of uncounted numbers of the sick in the "developing" world. Moral pressure was to bring greater availability of treatment and the prospect of eventual cure, perhaps with "super-engineered antibodies,"[8] but half the infected are said still to lack access to treatment,[9] while there have been large increases in other sexually transmitted diseases in Britain and the United States.[10]

Market interests also avert their gaze from the industrial-scale ravaging of the environment, or dispute the facts of it and their co-responsibility for it. The findings of reputable scientists about the negative impact of human activities upon the natural order,[11] increasingly outpacing the planet's ability to absorb the damage, are thus dismissed. With "global warming" held by the US president to be "bullshit"[12]—or, varying his position, that the climate would "change back again"[13]—the Trump administration rejected the 175-nation Paris climate accord of 2011 to limit greenhouse-gas emissions,[14] and license was given in March 2017 to boost the use of fossil fuels in US energy production,[15] with a former coal-industry lobbyist chosen as acting head of the US government's Environmental Protection Agency in July 2018.[16] Cast aside was the judgment of Reason, which holds it to be "extremely likely" that "human influence has been the dominant cause of the observed warming since the mid-20th century."[17]

As temperatures climb[18] and the risk grows of irreversible "hothouse Earth conditions,"[19] Arctic and Antarctic sea ice melts—a "trillion-ton" iceberg "twice the size of Luxemburg" broke away from an Antarctic ice shelf in July 2017[20]—the permafrost thaws, and sea levels rise, threatening coastal cities from Charleston, Miami, and New Orleans to Shanghai. Hurricanes intensify, wildfires increase, and a combination of warming waters, falling oxygen levels,[21] and acidification destroy the oceans' flora and fauna.[22] Meanwhile, mass migration into already-disordered free societies, overwhelming democracy itself, is driven forward by climate change, drought, crop failure, and hunger, among other factors. Yet persisting Bad Faith, often prompted by Madam Bubble, can declare that "the game is up for climate-change believers,"[23] even as the facts and consequences of global warming become more evident with each passing season.

Despite this, advocacy groups, "conservative" think tanks, and industry associations in Western democracies continue to engage in large-scale funding of "climate-change denial," assisted by those who argue that "climate-change activism" is dictated by "left-wing anticapitalists" hostile to "business" and "growth."[24] Alternatively, the same market interests can hold that environmental harm is the necessary price to be paid for the goods and services provided by "the market" to the "consumer"; a Milton Friedman could even argue that "we must weigh the gains from reducing pollution against the costs" of doing so.[25]

The degrading of the earth and of the heavens now knows few bounds, and is again not a new concern. For example, the diarist John Evelyn complained in 1661 of the "infernal Smoake" and "stink" of London, and of how "a dismall Cloud of Sea Coal" "obscures our Churches," "fouls our Clothes," and "corrupts the Waters."[26] "Is there under Heaven such Coughing and Snuffing to be heard as in the London Churches and Assemblies of People?" Evelyn asked, describing "the Barking and the Spitting" as "incessant," with even visitors to London "find[ing] a universal alteration in their Bodies." However, the annual dumping of millions of tons of plastic trash in the world's seas[27]—found on ice floes in the Arctic and in the stomach of a beached whale[28]—and the accelerating extinction (or "biological annihilation"[29]) of species from primates to birds and insects were yet to come.[30] So, too, the warnings by the astrophysicist Steven Hawking that time is running out for the earth, and that humans will need to establish colonies on Mars or the moon, taking plants and animals with them, in order to create a new world.[31]

But equal Bad Faith on the "left" stifles debate upon issues to which taboos are attached by the self-censorship which nonjudgmentalism and "political correctness" demand. Thus, most of today's "progressives" betray their supposed beliefs in secularism, freedom of thought, and the equality of the sexes by offering little or no criticism of diaspora Islam's closures of mind. They remain largely mute on the Islamic world's persecution of Christians, its subordination of women, and other excesses—Saudi Arabia carried out forty-eight executions by beheading in the first four months of 2018 alone[32]—but are quick to condemn those who draw attention to Islamic fundamentalism as bigots. Some are bigots; others are doing Reason's work.

Meanwhile, most Western "progressives" appear unmoved by the hanging of gays, the stoning of adulterous women, and the selling of female captives taken in battle in distant lands; similarly with the plundering and destruction of the architectural sites, shrines, artefacts, and written records of pre-Islamic and non-Islamic cultures and beliefs, on a scale to make small beer of the *Kristallnacht* of the 1930s.

Indeed, the fear of being thought an "Islamophobe" is more potent than the will to stand by those principles of Reason which the "progressive" claims to espouse. In consequence, senior Labour politicians in Britain have seen fit to attend segregated political rallies[33] and most Western feminists ignore the plight of their sisters in the next street or next door. The excision of the clitoris of Muslim girls is not Enlightenment's work, yet "progressives" have not turned out in their thousands in Trafalgar Square or Times Square to protest it.

There are deeper reasons for these abstentions than mere cowardice, political or intellectual, although cowardice plays its part. They are derived, at least in part, from what George Orwell called the left's "transferred nationalism."[34] Once attached to the Soviet Union, this "transferred" or vicarious sympathy has now attached itself to Islam's battles with Western powers and to the Palestinians' battle with Israel; and with the old "socialist project" defeated—"What is socialism?" "I do not know"—has provided some (or many) rootless "progressives" with a sense of direction. It has also led to the revival of earlier forms of myopia. The "war on terror" has therefore been held to be a means to impose US-led "neo-liberalism" upon the world,[35] with even Islamic State (IS) described in 2014 as a "modern revolutionary movement" "dedicated to building a new society from scratch,"[36] as were the state-socialist utopias.

Fascistic assertions by the "progressive's" would-be partners-in-arms are also ignored. It has therefore been possible for some on the "left" to sidestep the propositions which the Hamas Covenant of August 1988 contains, an evasion again made possible by Bad Faith. For in this document[37] "Freemasons and Rotary Clubs" are called "Zionist organizations"; the Jews are said to "control the world media, publishing houses and broadcasting stations"; and, all-powerful, they are attributed not only with being "behind the French Revolution and the Communist revolution" but also "behind World War One and World War Two." The Covenant further declares that the "Zionist plan" was "embodied in the Protocols of the Elders of Zion," an early twentieth-century Russian fabrication distributed in Germany's classrooms in the 1930s by the Nazi party.

With anti-Zionism and anti-Semitism increasingly hard to distinguish—the French president described the first as the "reinvented
form of the second"[38]—and with "Islamophobia," held in Bad Faith
to be a greater sin than "Judeophobia," prominent British Labour
Party members could also claim that Hitler was a supporter of
Zionism, describe the creation of Israel as a "great catastrophe," and
call for the "re-location" of Israel in the United States.[39] Indeed,
with "far left" sometimes indistinguishable from "far right," and with
anti-Semitic "hate-crimes" increasing both in the United States and
United Kingdom,[40] a British parliamentary committee had asserted
by October 2016 that the Labour Party had "created a safe space for
those with vile attitudes towards Jewish people";[41] it resisted acceptance for many months of an internationally recognized definition
of what anti-Semitism is;[42] anti-Semitism was described as "the one
acceptable prejudice in the Labour Party" by a Labour member of
parliament;[43] and its leader Jeremy Corbyn was praised by David
Duke, the former KKK Grand Wizard.[44]

Thus Bad Faith, whether on "right" or "left" in the free society
and whether in relation to distant or domestic matters, knows few
bounds in its selective silences, its service of its own interests real or
imagined, its evasions of truths which infringe its taboos, and its plain
falsehoods. Narrow the focus from geopolitics to, say, the seemingly
lesser but serious issue of obesity, and one finds similar reflexes of self-
deception, Bad Faith again playing its part.

Here, corporate interest and the nonjudgmentalism of the "progressive" sometimes coincide, their belief in the value of "choice"
in the market and in moral decision a shared one. With tens of millions in Western democracies now clinically obese, policy which seeks
to deal with the consequences of it can thus be seen by the free-
marketeer, on the one hand, as an "anti-capitalist" intrusion upon the
"consumer" for the purpose of extending the authority of the state.[45]
"Fat or thin, it's not the state's business," Madam Bubble declares[46]
as the public costs of obesity soar. On the other hand, "progressive"
voices in Bad Faith denounce "preoccupation with obesity" as "fat

phobia,""fat oppression," and "fatism."[47] The latter has even been held
to be a form of "class prejudice."[48]

For its part, the American Center for Corporate Freedom—a
group with ties to the restaurant and food industry—insisted in June
2005 that "the public" had been "misled about the scope of the obesity
problem,"[49] even as its extent was breaking new bounds. Alternatively,
Bad Faith can regard obesity as a function of social progress, seize
upon the alibi of a "fatness gene,"[50] or describe obesity as an "epidemic,"[51] with its symptoms "caught as easily as a common cold."[52]
Other voices in equal self-delusion can dismiss obesity as a "myth"
and an "obsession" or, with the "progressive's" seeming erudition, as a
"construct built by culture."[53]

In the battle with Western democracy's rising crime rates, Bad
Faith is again on the scene. It contests the evidence of crime's extent,
masks the true figures of it, and hails an again Orwellian "progress"
amid the regress. Crime in the battered civic order can even be
declared to be "in long-term decline,"[54] with libertarians and self-
interested government ministers and officials joining hands to find
the crime rate falling. In 2014, for example, crime in Britain was
claimed to be "at its lowest level in 33 years," the decline allegedly
driven by a fall in violent offenses.[55] But on the same day, using different sources, violent crime was said to be "heading for a record
rise,"[56] three months later to be "surging,"[57] and in 2015 to have risen
by a further 23 percent.[58] Yet in June 2018, as the trends accelerated,
"levels of violent crime" were said by a commentator to be "stable."[59]

The truth is more telling: that crime is rising in all free societies.
Its staple lies in street robbery, drug offenses, sexual assault, and other
physical violence, with increasing resort to guns, "bladed weapons,"
acid, and other "noxious substances";[60] there were more than 40,000
knife-crimes in England and Wales in the year to March 2018, for
example.[61] With the murder rate rising in London, as also "gun-crime
with discharges,"[62] there were six stabbings in ninety minutes in its
streets on an April day in 2018,[63] and London saw more than 22,000
street crimes in 2017–2018, around sixty a day—committed mainly

by youths, often riding on mopeds and robbing passers-by of watches, iPhones, jewelry, and money[64]—and 69,000 young people in Britain under the age of fifteen themselves suffered injury from a stabbing or "other violent incident" in the twelve months to May 2018.[65]

Moreover, as the civic order loses control of the street in no true commonwealth, the number of attacks on women and the elderly, and of random assaults on strangers, also grow, with three homeless people beaten to death in Los Angeles in a single week.[66] At the same time, in many free societies, police numbers are reduced; by more than 20,000 in England and Wales since 2009, a reduction of some 16 percent,[67] and with over 600 police stations closed, about 100 of them in London,[68] while more than 7,000 neighborhood police officers—or "bobbies on the beat"—were "assigned to other duties" or "left the force."[69] Almost 10,000 police in England and Wales were also said to have second jobs, including cab driving and plumbing, in order to bolster their pay.[70]

Bad Faith has had two sources in Britain by which to bolster its again Orwellian case about static or falling crime rates. One resort is the flawed police record of crime. The other has been provided by asking a sample of the adult public whether it has suffered from a crime in a given period. From these slender sources, conclusions have been drawn about the scale of crime. But at the heart of the wishful thinking on the subject of crime, as when it is claimed in extremis that Britain is relatively crime-free,[71] stands the long history of police "mis-classification," or falsification, of crime statistics. At the same time, the Orwellian attributes any rises in these statistics to "improvements" in "police crime-reporting practices,"[72] and thus evades the significance of the actual increases in crime rates in Britain, including in rural areas where violent crime and robbery are also increasing, and organized drug gangs use young people as "mules" and dealers.[73]

Meanwhile, the "manipulation" and "massaging" by the police themselves of "official" crime figures in Britain, and in other failing civic orders, has been described by a criminologist as "cynical" and "a game";[74] even a former chief inspector of constabulary called it "dishonesty" and "fiddling."[75] In Britain and the United States, a competitive "performance culture" between police forces—akin to that of the wider market—also sets "targets" for "detection rates." It thus places a premium on the under-recording of, or falsehoods about, a locality's actual scale of crime in order to reflect the better on the efficiency of its police.

A "culture" said by a Metropolitan Police chief superintendent to "take its toll," the police "can only afford to have X numbers of burglaries per day," as he told a committee of the House of Commons.[76] Similarly in Kent, an official investigation found that crimes were pursued "on the basis of how easy they are to solve rather than on their severity or their impact on victims."[77] False claims of police success in Britain have even reached the point of arrests of police officers for corruptly rigging the figures, and of similar charges against members of the New York Police Department.[78]

On such basis come annual claims in Britain and in other free societies of "falls in crime." At the same time, the again Orwellian expectation that the police will continue to "cut crime" helps produce the outcome that libertarian Bad Faith wills. An outcome aided by the rarity of independent audits, it has nevertheless been discovered in the last decade that each year tens of thousands of crimes reported to the police, including violent assaults, domestic abuse, and public order offenses, go unrecorded.[79] In some police areas in Britain, as many as one-half of reported crimes—including robberies, domestic burglaries, and sexual attacks—have gone uninvestigated, or have been designated as "no crime" and as "not for action," a procedure said to be routine for "lack of evidence."[80] Such "editing," "screening out," and "capping"[81] is called "no criming" in the false-statistical trade.

In this fashion, as Britain's chief inspector of constabulary himself conceded, many hundreds of thousands of offenses each year, including one-third of all violent crime, are in effect ignored[82] "even after a suspect has been identified."[83] It is a phenomenon of such scale that in February 2018 the British Supreme Court held that the police can be made legally liable to victims for failing to bring serious offenders to justice.[84] In the case of the Thames Valley police, for example, more than 70 percent of total crimes recorded in its area were "screened out" in a single year, including more than 50,000 crimes of violence.[85] Likewise, in October 2017, the Metropolitan Police announced that on cost-saving grounds it would cease investigating many "lower level" crimes, including burglary—90 percent of burglaries in Britain go unsolved[86]—theft, and assault;[87] and in June 2018, in order not to "criminalise young people," it began "deferring" prosecutions of them for "minor offences."[88]

In the United States and under similar departmental pressures to "keep crime statistics low"[89] as proof of policing success, felonies are typically downgraded to misdemeanors, with 14,000 "serious offenses" recorded as "minor" by the Los Angeles Police Department in an eight-year period.[90] Moreover, in what has been called the "newest evolution in the numbers game"—again a game of the competitive market—many crimes in New York, as in Britain, are not recorded at all.[91]

Adding further to the unknown real crime rates are the numbers of crimes in the free society's false commonwealths of which the police are not informed, while many victims are said to give up on emergency calls which go unanswered, or which are cut off.[92] More than a quarter of crime in Britain's rural areas, for example, is similarly estimated not to be reported.[93] Driven by the often well-founded belief that they will not be followed up, more than half of violent crimes in the United States, especially cases of rape and sexual assault, have also been estimated by the FBI to go unreported,[94] while reported sexual assaults have been found not to be properly investigated by the New York police department.[95]

Likewise, the police in Britain have been said to investigate rape complaints less often than any other type of crime,[96] rape being for the most part a "no crime" in general police estimation. With pressure additionally placed on victims to "drop rape claims,"[97] women's organizations have alleged in the past that "some 80 percent of rapes" were not reported.[98] Despite this, over 40,000 rapes were recorded by the police in Britain in 2016–2017,[99] perhaps as the result of a greater willingness by victims to report the offense. But this is no true commonwealth once more.

In addition, when police investigation of perhaps a minority of the crimes committed is pursued, detection and clear-up rates are low. In the year to June 2017, for example, of 4.5 million recorded crimes in England and Wales almost one-half had no identified suspect,[100] while in the twelve months to June 2018, less than 10 percent of crimes resulted in a charge.[101] Similarly, the police had almost 1,600 unsolved homicides on their books in 2016,[102] in London alone some 300 murders between 2000 and 2012 went unsolved,[103] and of more than 50,000 homicides in the United States between 2011 and 2017 over half did not result in an arrest.[104] At the same time, large numbers of solved crimes, as in London, result only in cautions, including for crimes of violence, drug trafficking, and (again) rape and sexual assault.[105]

Of most of these salient facts Bad Faith, preferring to celebrate declines in crime, does not speak. In the meantime, the sense of criminal impunity grows and the risk of detection falls, despite the "routine use of violence"[106] from which Bad Faith again averts its gaze. Indeed, the chances of getting away scot-free in Britain and the United States with a robbery, a burglary, a rape, or a serious wounding are high, and in general increasing. However, this is not in itself a new complaint, an earlier-cited woman observer of America writing in 1832 that "trespass, assault, robbery, nay even murder, are often committed without the slightest attempt at legal interference."[107] But in a free society a sense of impunity is a perilous thing. Or as Thomas Hobbes declares, "presumption of impunity by force is a Root from whence springeth a contempt of all Lawes."[108]

But Bad Faith continues to look away as the currents of violent crime, especially in democracy's metropolises, run ever more strongly. Thus, 168 teenagers were murdered in London in the decade to February 2015.[109] Similarly, street-gangs in the United States, aided by a "culture" of ghetto intimidation "to keep potential witnesses silent,"[110] have made the inner city increasingly sovereign territory for crime. This is despite the arrests of many thousands of gang members in the last years for murder, extortion, and other offenses; in April 2016, for example, more than one hundred members and associates of two rival New York street gangs were arrested for crimes including drug trafficking, robbery, and homicide, with helicopters and armored trucks used in the early-morning raids.[111]

In Britain too—where over 10,000 weapons, including guns and almost 4,000 knives, were seized at the doors of, or inside, courts in Britain in a single year[112]—an anonymous senior police inspector admitted in 2013 that in many places in Britain "criminals now rule the streets," especially at night. Unarmed police, he declared, were "heavily outnumbered" by gangs against whom they stood "no chance."[113] But Bad Faith again closes its ears to such voices, and shuts its eyes.

With its lax gun laws and some 13,000 gun murders and manslaughters in the United States each year,[114] the fact that no shooting has occurred in New York or Chicago in a 24-hour period or during a weekend becomes worthy of a headline, or is described as a "statistical anomaly."[115] A decrease to "only"[116] some 300 homicides a year in New York—where there were 15,000 killings between 1965 and 2014[117]—or to a mere one per day in Detroit[118] is considered to be a mark of civic progress. Amid the gunfire, Bad Faith continues to fight its own battles on falsehood's behalf, generally locating the "peak" of violent crime in the past, and aided by the rigging of the record by the police. Meanwhile, falling homicide rates are celebrated in one US city but declared to be "soaring" in another, with Los Angeles seeing more than a thousand "shooting victims," dead and wounded, in a single year.[119]

Despite variations and fluctuations, the national toll of gun deaths in the United States has continued to increase, including at the hands of the police—who themselves lose more than sixty to gunfire in a typical year[120]—and with rising numbers of black suspects, both armed and unarmed, shot down.[121] In all there were more than 38,000 gun deaths by homicide, suicide, or accident in 2016 alone,[122] and 3,000 more Americans murdered in 2017 than in 2013.[123] Not even Bad Faith has been able to hide its dimensions. With gang and gun violence in Chicago's streets called "fratricidal," again no true common-wealth this, gang members were described by its police department in 2014 as believing that "the only way to resolve a conflict is to get a gun and go shoot to kill."[124]

In a city where the Department of Justice found that the police themselves "expect to use force and not be questioned about it"[125]—and where market minds even proposed a local "bullet tax" on the sale of ammunition as a deterrent to gun crime[126]—there was a tally in Chicago of almost 2,800 shootings and 650 homicides in 2017.[127] Hailed as an improvement on the previous year's battlefield scene, when there were over 3,500 shootings and almost 800 homicides,[128] 45 people were victims of gunfire at Easter in 2017,[129] and about 70 in an August weekend in 2018, 44 of them on Sunday, with the shoot-ings described by the mayor as "fueled by gang conflicts."[130] Simi-larly, in 2016, some 60 people were shot during the Memorial Day weekend,[131] 43 in celebration of Labor Day,[132] and over two dozen at Christmas,[133] while around 100 people were the victims of Chicago gun violence during the July 4 weekend in 2017.[134] As for America's capital, Washington, DC—where over 100 people were "slain" in the first nine months of 2015, for example[135]—a temporarily falling rate of fatalities from street warfare was in part attributed to "improved access to blood-transfusion services."[136]

Meanwhile, resilient Bad Faith in the United States continues to pretend that there are long-term downward trends in violence. The "great crime decline in nearly every major American city over the last 25 years" was hailed in November 2017,[137] as Baltimore, for example, registered the highest number of homicides ever recorded.[138] The numbers also increase of multiple or "mass" shootings with assault rifles in a workplace, a school, a college, a church, a synagogue, a movie theater, or other public place, as at a country-music festival in Las Vegas in October 2017, when twenty-three firearms were found in the shooter's room.[139] But after a period of media-exploited shock, political attitudinizing, familial grief, and community prayer, the dis-solving social order continues on its path. In a suicidal democracy, armed to the teeth, firearms sales rise after each new attack, and pleas for gun restrictions continue to be widely resisted.

Thus, before his election to the presidency and with about 30 percent of American adults owning a gun,[140] Donald Trump at a meeting of the National Rifle Association called such restrictions "heartless," describing the right to arm oneself as "the most basic human right of all."[141] Moreover, after his election, despite the restrictions in some states earlier referred to, gun rights were extended by Congress itself, and it was made easier to carry concealed weapons across state lines,[142] while Republican-controlled states permit hidden guns on college campuses in Georgia and Kansas, in bus stations and on buses in Tennessee, and even in the State Capitol in Iowa.[143] Similarly, Mississippi introduced a law to permit "designated" individuals to carry guns in churches,[144] and in Alabama a democracy's electors can bring guns to the polling station when they vote.[145] In many states it also remains possible for an eighteen-year-old to buy a semi-automatic, despite demands for the restriction of access to weaponry of such kind by teenagers, and even a home-printed 3D gun is now within the "customer's" reach.[146]

In arguments in the United States about the citizen's supposed gun rights, Bad Faith has long been active. For the American "gun lobby" rests its case for such rights, in the land of the free, on the US Constitution's Second Amendment, passed in 1791 in an early phase of development of the nascent nation's civil institutions. It states that "a well-regulated militia, being necessary to the security of a free state, the right of the people to keep and bear arms shall not be infringed." But given the existence today of a "well-regulated militia" in the form of armed, and even heavily armed, police forces and the National Guard, the claim that the private citizen possesses the reserve right to carry a gun for self-defense is strained and false. It requires Bad Faith, once more in freedom's name, to sustain it, with gun lobbyists even declaring that an "integral part of being an American" is the "choice" (once more) of "whether or not to carry a gun."[147]

Hobbes was wiser, and would have seen through the "gun lobby's" case. For he argued that it is only in an unprotected and pre-social state of nature that "private men" need to defend themselves by their "own strength."[148] However, Bad Faith and the "gun lobby" will have none of it, undoing the commonwealth—and democracy itself—at the cost of heaps of dead. In a notional civil society, gun-toting individuals thus shoot down fellow citizens and noncitizens alike, whether in criminal aggression or personal self-defense, while the NRA offers "murder insurance" to people who commit a shooting.[149]

In the generally unsuccessful attempts, minor in the scale of things, to restrict the supposed "right" of the US citizen to carry arms, action is taken to try to keep guns out of the hands of individuals with "mental-health problems" and those previously convicted of domestic violence, while a Colorado resident who objected to a prohibition on carrying a concealed gun when picking up his mail at the local post office had his claim of a "right" to do so rejected by the courts.[150] But Bad Faith dressed in the uniform of the armed libertarian—with almost 400 million guns in the United States, and with Americans buying some 14 million new firearms each year[151]—continues to claim that national well-being and individual safety depend upon such "right." Instead, such claim is incompatible with the ethic of a true commonwealth and a further cause of its dissolution.

Meanwhile, prison populations in Western democracies are continuously on the rise, doubling in Britain in two decades, with most jails filled to capacity and beyond, even as large numbers of offenders escape detection entirely, while tens of thousands of individuals on UK police databases wanted for crimes including murder, rape, and terror offenses were on the loose, unfound, in 2017.[152] At the same time, in the United States and other failing free societies, millions in total are behind bars, with almost 10 percent of American inmates serving life sentences.[153] More millions are on probation or parole, near overwhelming those tasked with their supervision. As crime rates rise, so severe is the pressure on prison capacity, despite the scale of "no-criming" in Britain and elsewhere—and with thousands of violent-crime suspects "routinely" released by the police without further action[154]—that judges are themselves under pressure not to imprison convicted sex offenders, burglars, and drug dealers, some third to a half of whom in Britain avoid a custodial sentence.[155]

To relieve the overcrowding in jails, early releases are also resorted to, again as in Britain,[156] while drug treatment, community service, tagging, curfews, and fines are increasingly seen as more appropriate punishments than "mass incarceration."[157] Nevertheless, in the United States in 2016 and described as the "fastest growing incarcerated population" in America,[158] there were almost twenty times more women in jail—over 100,000, a large percentage drug-addicted[159]—than there were in 1970.[160]

As the free society's dissolution quickens, about one-half of the imprisoned in Britain re-offend within a year of release, committing some half a million known crimes between them, violent crimes included;[161] the number of serious offenses committed by individuals on probation rises also;[162] and over half of all defendants sentenced to imprisonment in a given year had at least fifteen previous convictions or cautions.[163] Meanwhile, violence between prisoners, attacks on prison staff, self-harm, and prison suicides increase in Britain,[164] while drug use is rife, with more than 200 kilos of drugs found in prisons in England and Wales in 2016.[165] At the same time, over three hundred prison officers were dismissed between 2015 and 2017 for smuggling drugs, weapons, and mobile phones into jails.[166] Moreover, supervised community service, increasingly in the hands of Madam Bubble's private "providers"—or "community rehabilitation companies"—and described as a "mess,"[167] has become merely a low-order alternative to jail. Its meaning as an act of ethical reparation for harm-doing has been lost from sight amid the civic dereliction, and from which Bad Faith again turns away.

Although an informed citizenry is one of democracy's preconditions, education has also suffered as the free society's disorders have deepened. Decreasingly seen as essential to individual and collective well-being, Bad Faith nevertheless again finds progress as standards fall. Educational disciplines—the latter word anathema to the "progressive" libertarian—are scoffed at by the Spirit of Demolition and literacy and numeracy necessarily decline. Moreover, in the free society, other qualities than those which education can provide are required for street credibility, celebrity, and fortune. In addition, old pedagogical methods have been displaced by methods which often fail, including in the imparting of basic skills. They are failures which Bad Faith once more denies.

The disinclination to judge the unable, or even to distinguish between achievement and failure, also grows in some educational administrators and teachers. It is as if to make a negative judgment is to do the student a wrong. Instead, educational market choice is widened, method is tailored to wants and whims, and the "stresses" of study are tempered. But as the worse increasingly takes the place of the better in teacher and pupil alike, Bad Faith, aided by the Spirit of Demolition, claims a compensatory success in making school education more appetizing to the taste, with the young treated as the customers they will become.

Meanwhile, behind the back of Bad Faith, fee-paying schools in Britain flourish, with independent-school pupils said to be on average two years ahead of state-school children by the time they are sixteen.[168] Similarly, enrollments at American "charter schools," again operating independently of the often "low-performing" state system, have risen to more than three million.[169] The extent of homeschooling in the United States and Britain is also increasing, while in addition there is growing resort in Britain to private tutors, or "supplemental service-providers." In consequence, some two million children in the United States are homeschooled,[170] and almost half of 11-to-16-year-olds in London were said in 2017 to have received private tuition.[171]

Such developments reveal a truth that Bad Faith would rather conceal: the increasing need of parents to make good, for payment, "poor learning environments," bad teaching, and "negative peer pressures" in public education, the latter in part the consequence of the familial and domestic breakdown earlier referred to. All the while, the Spirit of Demolition gives the name of "rote-learning" to the learning of basic rules, seeking to depose from their didactic places the teaching of number, spelling, and grammar upon which a confident literacy and numeracy rest. Instead of "pressing times-tables onto children," a teachers' leader in Britain therefore recommended that they "use the computing ability on their mobile phones";[172] the philosophy that "whatever knowledge you do not solidly lay the foundation of before you are eighteen you will never be master of while you live"[173] is now largely discounted.

In the spiral of regression, decreasingly well-educated teachers—in Britain there are also 24,000 teachers unqualified to teach their subjects[174]—pass on their inadequate levels of knowledge to pupils and students. In the United States, fraudulent practice has been found in the teacher-certification process itself, with aspirant teachers in Arkansas, Mississippi, Tennessee, and elsewhere paying stand-ins to take the certification tests for them.[175] In England, a high school had to hire proofreaders to "catch teachers' spelling errors" in their reports to parents,[176] and teachers increasingly give "inappropriate assistance to candidates" during examinations;[177] some nine hundred teachers were penalized in 2017 for helping students to cheat.[178] Examination scrutineers have also been found unfit to judge standards, and 1,200 school inspectors were dismissed in Britain in June 2015, including for "lacking skill in writing reports" on the schools they had inspected.[179]

Bad Faith would place all this beyond the critic's reach, or pretend that such matters are exceptions. But as the state education system in Britain proceeds from success to success in Bad Faith's eyes—with "more primary pupils than ever" meeting the standards "needed for secondary school,"[180] or declared to have attained the highest levels of literacy "for a generation"[181]—basic skills in reading and writing fail to be acquired by large numbers of the young; one-fifth to one-quarter of children in Britain have been said to be "unable to read and understand books, newspapers and websites" by the time they leave primary school.[182] However, were it to turn out to be true that a "post-text future" beckons, that "video and audio" are "ascendant," and that "writing is being left behind,"[183] to be semiliterate will cease to be the handicap it was.

Meanwhile, tens of thousands of stressed teachers in Britain abandon the profession each year[184]—some one-quarter of those qualified since 2011 had ceased teaching by 2016,[185] in inner London over one-quarter recruited in 2015 had left by 2017,[186] while one-third of head teachers leave the profession within three years of taking up the post[187]—and the numbers of applicants for teacher training fall.[188] Similarly in the United States, teacher shortages were reported in 2017 in twenty-eight states, including in 80 percent of school districts in California,[189] while one in five US teachers have a second job.[190] Moreover, the struggle to teach basic skills to the recalcitrant and inattentive is now so hard in some schools that time must be taken from other syllabus subjects in order to make the attempt. In the effort to impart the means of study to the unwilling, some of whom return to domestic wildernesses at the school day's end, the substance of what is learned by the able and the willing thins out too.

A Cicero might argue that "to be ignorant of what occurred before we were born is to remain a child for life."[191] But in such schools—from which Bad Faith retreats—the teaching of history and geography, for example, shrinks in dimension, elementary facts of time and place become decreasingly known, and school libraries close.[192] If some excuse can be found for the insane George III's confusing the Mississippi with the Ganges,[193] there is less for British teenagers who think gravity was discovered by Christopher Columbus or that Horatio Nelson was a French soccer player of the 1960s.[194] In 2007, 72 percent of a sample of 29,000 American eighth-grade school students was even found unable to explain the purpose of the Declaration of Independence,[195] while in Britain almost one-third of a sample of 11-to-18-year-olds did not know that Shakespeare was a playwright.[196]

Intermittent efforts are made to reform early school education. Many such efforts in Britain have been blocked by the teaching unions themselves, while the grip of unsuccessful teaching methods, sustained by Bad Faith, remains tenacious. As failure, wearing the mask of success, makes its way from primary to secondary education, "lenient marks" and the "alteration of grades" are alleged to be "routine."[197] Moreover, although there has been some increase since 2014 in pupils taking "difficult subjects"—including the sciences[198]— and fewer studying "media and film" or "leisure and tourism,"[199] there have been sharp falls in the United Kingdom in the study of languages in the last decades,[200] with physical education more popular than French,[201] and with growing pressures for examinations to be replaced by easygoing assessments and multiple-choice tests, again in order to "improve" results.

At the same time, copying from the internet is increasingly overlooked or is impossible to monitor, with proposals made in Britain to ban pupils from wearing smartwatches (disguised as wristwatches) when taking exams,[202] but with the head of a major British school-examination board arguing in favor of the use of Google in examinations.[203] Meanwhile, Bad Faith continues to adjust and inflate examination grades until almost all pass and an extravagant proportion excels, with "grade-thresholds" in Britain lowered in order to "avert a dramatic fall in results."[204] Likewise, after final school examinations had been made "harder" to meet criticism of falling standards, grading was in compensation made more lenient to ensure that students were "not at a disadvantage."[205]

In the United States and also under Bad Faith's supervision, the national high-school graduation rate at "83.2 percent" was thus at an "all-time high" in 2017.[206] Similarly, the overall pass rate in the British "Advanced Level" school examinations "fell" in 2018 to 97.6 percent from 97.9 percent in the previous year, with genuine attainment harder to distinguish and the concept of failure objectionable to the libertarian. Long ago, Demosthenes asked himself and us what incentive there is to "improve, let alone excel" if no difference is made between "those who win and those who lose."[207] In today's disordered free society, the difference is ebbing away.

Furthermore, with Madam Bubble's private education companies competing in Britain for public education authority contracts in the fashioning of syllabuses, in the inspection of schools, and in the setting of examinations, the more irresistible becomes the incentive to depress standards and falsify results. For the higher the pass rate, the greater the claim of this or that company to a "bigger share of the market."[208] In the United States, school administrators and harried teachers are likewise pressured to deliver high test scores and exam grades in order to obtain federal funds or to avoid closure. "From Atlanta to Philadelphia, and Washington to Los Angeles"[209] charges have been brought against teachers for providing students with answers to the tests that they are to face, and some have been imprisoned for it,[210] while again in Philadelphia a teacher was fired for taking bribes from students in exchange for better grades.[211]

But Bad Faith remains tenacious. It therefore accuses those who criticize educational theory and practice in free societies of wishing to hold young people back or, as we saw earlier, of espousing a culture of "elitism." Bad faith also charges critics of being out of step with changed times, times of adaptation of means and methods to new ends and demands. Meanwhile, students good and bad, prepared or unprepared—but with the same certificates and diplomas in hand—proceed upon their academic journeys, Bad Faith accompanying them as they go.

The pedagogical triumph of it is less than it seems. Many colleges and universities have been driven to reduce their entry requirements (and standards) to meet those of incoming students, some of whom, despite their certifications, require remedial teaching in order to pursue their studies. In the United States, over 60 percent of high-school seniors failed in 2016 to meet college entrance standards in reading, English, math, and science,[212] while almost half of university teachers in Britain believe that incoming students are inadequately prepared, with many handicapped by poor English skills, habituation to plagiarism, and even "lack of attention-span and focus."[213] Moreover, almost 10 percent of applicants to British universities have been found to make fraudulent claims about themselves, inflating their school exam results, submitting false documents, and even adopting identities that are not their own.[214]

In March 2007, the time was already said to be "right" in Britain for an "honest and open debate on the qualities we expect from

those entering university."[215] Instead, fierce market competition
between universities in Britain to attract students has lowered the
threshold for entry to many courses, with the number of unconditional places offered regardless of school exam results rising sharply
in recent years, from less than 3,000 in 2013–2014 to some 58,000
in 2018,[216] or almost one-quarter of all applicants. In universities—
or degree-mills—with an increasingly corporate ethos, the competition to attract high-fee-paying foreign students has also become more
intense. The meeting of customer demand with appropriate supply
is therefore hailed as "progress," with institutions which fail Madam
Bubble's tests at risk of being driven to the wall.

Furthermore, in "traditional" areas of study in the humanities
enrollments have fallen[217] and significant numbers of university facul-
ties and departments in Britain have shrunk or even closed, some of
them declared in market terms to be no longer cost-effective. Meanwhile, as standards fall—and with teenagers from "disadvantaged
backgrounds" being admitted to some British universities with lower
grades than "middle-class" pupils[218]—the "easy degree," and even a
"culture of entitlement" to it,[219] continue to attract the ill-prepared.
In addition, "grade inflation" hands out an increasing proportion of
first-class degrees,[220] and at eleven universities in Britain in 2017 the
entire student body passed its final examinations.[221] A further thirty-
two universities awarded degrees to "99 percent or more" of their
students.[222]

Internet plagiarism, including for theses and dissertations, has
also spread. Tens of thousands of students in Britain[223] are said to buy
online custom-written essays, research papers, and even £7000 doc-
toral theses,[224] an "industry" said to be "worth over £100 million."[225]
One such "provider" in the United States, with "2,000 verified
writers," declares itself "ready to work on any kind of assignment"
and to provide a "high-quality unique paper for $5 a page." Another
offers an "assistant for any academic task," and can provide a "term
paper or an essay within three to four hours" and a research disser-
tation "within three weeks." The fee is payable "by Visa, Mastercard

or PayPal." In May 2014, even Harvard was driven to introduce an "honor code" in the hope of stopping cheating,[226] "record numbers" have been "caught cheating" at Oxford,[227] and there were thousands of cases of similar "academic misconduct" at British universities in 2017.[228]

But if Bad Faith has prevented an "honest and open debate" on the "inadequate" student, it has also prevented criticism of the dead weight of scholasticism which has simultaneously disabled so many university intellectuals from shedding light upon the free society's increasing travails during the last decades. Instead, much of today's un-illuminating "academic" writing obfuscates truth with its artifices and jargon, wastes our time, and is itself a form of Bad Faith. It is again an old theme. In 1640, Francis Bacon compared the study by "intellectualists" of "matters of no use or moment"—calling it "degenerate learning"—with that of the spider who "workes his Webbe" and "brings forth Cobwebs of learning of no substance,"[229] while William Godwin poured scorn on those who "deliver their oracles in obscure phraseology" and "consider themselves profound,"[230] as they do today.

There are neither brass tacks nor practical experience at work in most of it, and little or nothing of Thomas Paine's "common sense." Rather, its intellectual pretenses and elaborate lingo—most prevalent in the "social sciences"—insult the need to understand the forces that are bringing our societies down. Moreover, restrictions on free thought imposed by "political correctness" not only disable truth telling but place a premium on the obscurantism which gives no offense. The ancients again had a clear sense of the vacuum which the idler forms of scholarship inhabit. In his essay *On the Brevity of Life*, Seneca describes the "empty study of the superfluous" as an "affliction."[231] For Seneca knew that Rome was burning, as is the free society today, and was objecting to the same kind of trivia mongering which now occupies so much academic attention. Hobbes, too, had harsh words for the pedants around him, "conversing of matters incomprehensible" and "fluttering over their bookes."[232]

They were the forerunners of today's scribbler on the "nodes of public discourse," the "formal internal conventions of genre," and the "conjunction of historical transition with cultural practice and production."[233] Activity described by Hobbes as "a sort of Madnesse," contemporary scholarship continues to be plagued by what he called "frivolous Distinctions, barbarous Terms and obscure Language."[234] In the arts, Bad Faith similarly invests the meaningless with meaning. Here, order and form have been increasingly overtaken by disorder and deformation, the emperor is unclothed or dressed in dross, and an unmade bed, a pickled shark, or a pile of bricks are invested with a significance they do not possess. Noise likewise masquerades as music, and with the art of fiction drowning in a welter of industrial-scale over-production for Madam Bubble's market, there are more than seven hundred college courses in the United States in "creative writing."[235]

Meanwhile, the free society continues to provide some with high levels of expertise and others with a rounded knowledge for life. But increasing millions are left with neither. Among them are early school-leavers, college and apprenticeship dropouts—their numbers rising in Britain[236]—and poorly educated degree-holders. Both in Britain and the United States, surveys have also found consistently low and even declining standards of numeracy among teenagers and young adults. They have also shown them to be less well-educated than their predecessor generation, with American 18-to-24-year-olds, for example, having the "lowest numeracy skills" in the two dozen countries of an OECD survey.[237] Complaint has also been made on Madam Bubble's behalf that there are too few qualified American technicians with the ability to "turn basic science into marketable products."[238] Even US national security has been said to be "at risk if its schools do not improve."[239]

Diminishing "functional skill" and limited knowledge are now manifested in the free society in many different ways; British construction firms are driven to hire bricklayers in Bulgaria and plumbers in Poland, while the need to "dumb down" the plays on offer in London theaters has been blamed on reduced attention spans and falling levels of audience education.[240] Age-old as such type of complaint is, surveys have also found that one in four Americans are unaware that the earth revolves around the sun[241] and a third of British adults think Everest is in Europe.[242] With the teaching of history on the wane, long-lost too is the common sense of a William Cobbett that "for want of a thorough knowledge of what has been we are in many cases at a loss to account for what is, and still more at a loss to show what ought to be,"[243] or of a Chesterfield that "the more a young man is informed of what is past the better he will know how to conduct himself in future."[244]

As for the lack of verbal skills in the ostensibly educated, whether politicians or commentators on public affairs, criticism of it is again not new. A "widespread powerlessness in the use of words" was noted by Longinus in the first century CE,[245] while Cobbett, once more, complained of "university-educated scholars unable to write English with any tolerable degree of correctness."[246] Particularly low levels of expression, poor grammar, and semiliterate spelling are now found in much of Britain's press also. Even "by" and "buy," and "won" and "one," can be confused. But such impoverishment is not confined to the press. In January 2016, the UK Home Office website announced a "new English langauge [sic] test for migrants,"[247] while atrophied vocabularies and poor analytical skills have become broadcasting commonplaces, including in the BBC.

In the British "quality" press, true and false news, necessary information, ephemeral pontification, and continuous trivia-mongering make for an uneasy combination. "Is Melania Trump taking a more relaxed approach to her hair?," "How will Brexit affect our Euro-vision chances?," "Save us from the hell of motorway sandwiches," and "Ten things you need to know about vaginas" have thus been the subjects of articles in the Telegraph, Times, and Guardian.[248] The symptoms of educational failure are also a constant presence, whether in a photo caption reading "rural life in the countryside,"[249] or in references to "delectable delights"[250] and to an "isolated isle."[251] In print and internet editions, the Times can now give you "Napolean" (February 23, 2012) and "Maddona" (October 17, 2001), "Brittania" (November 20, 2012) and "Gibralter" (May 17, 2012); the Telegraph "Greek" (October 5, 2009) and "Old Etonion" (January 28, 2017);

and the *Guardian* "Egyption" (December 30, 2014), "Engles" (October 20, 2006), and so on.

Standard words of the political vocabulary can also be wrongly spelled. From "govenment" in a *Times* headline (August 30, 2009) or "idealogues" in the *Sunday Times* (February 17, 2008) to the *Telegraph*'s "conservativism" (August 22, 2009) and "terrist" (March 27, 2008), these are more than slips of the keyboard finger. New "legalization" is now pushed through parliament (*Times*, June 23, 2009), couples walk down the "isle" (*Telegraph*, February 21, 2007), "correspondants" file their reports (*Times*, February 24, 2008), and schools are judged to have "breeched" minimum standards (*Telegraph*, March 28, 2010), while the suggestion that the Elgin marbles be restored to the "Pantheon" was made by the *Times* on March 12, 2014.

"Aboration" (for *aberration*), "acheivement," "adaption," "all though" (for *although*), "alludes" (for *eludes*), "approched," "artic," "assent" (for "*ascent*"), "assignation" (for *assassination*), "athiest," "barron" (for *barren*), "baton down" (for *batten down*), "bequeaved," "bouquests," "breaks" (for *brakes*), "cemetary," "coat-tales," "collission," "conciliation" (for *consolation*), "deep-routed" (for *deep-rooted*), "defacate," "difinitive," "discrete" (for *discreet*), "duel" (for *dual*), "dying" (for *dyeing*), "earings" (for *earrings*), "embullience," "emmulate," "escourted," "exagerate," "excrutiating," "exited" (for *excited*), "facism" (for *fascism*), "femaile," "fiesty" (for *feisty*), "forth" (for *fourth*), "fued" (for *feud*), "granmother," "guage," and "hudge" (for *huge*) have all appeared in the online *Telegraph*, the least literate of the British "quality" press.

The same paper has presented its readers with "insolvable," "in vein," "loose" (for *lose*), "lossed" (for *lost*), "mesmirising," "occassion," "passed" (for *past*), "lottory," "perpatrators," "phased" (for *fazed*), "phenomenons," "plooms" (for *plumes*), "pouring over" (for *poring over*), "preemt" (for *preempt*), "professer," "propoganda," "punative," "pursuade," "reciept," "roll" (for *role*), "sabatuer," "satelittes," "seperation," "sewn" (for *sown*), "skelton" (for *skeleton*), "sucide," "thrown" (for *throne*), "vacinity," "venemous" and "vetinary." Yet in August 2017, under Madam Bubble's direction, it launched a "new brand campaign"—with the slogan "Words are powerful: Choose them well"—to encourage access to the paper's "award-winning writers."[252] Similarly, "ancester," "casualities," "complements" (for *compliments*), "devisive," "dietry," "dimise" (for *demise*), "dingeys" (for dinghies), "plebian," "prevelant," "rascism," "supress," "warrents," and "wierd" have been seen beneath the masthead of the *Times*, while the *Daily Mail* wrote in August 2017 of a "male masseuse."[253]

Some measure of the decline in literacy which such errors reveal—despite the counter-claims made by Bad Faith—was provided at the time of the closure of Rupert Murdoch's *News of the World* in the wake of a "hacking" scandal. Its final edition of July 10, 2011, included a facsimile of the newspaper's first editorial on October 1, 1843. Entitled "The State of the Nation," among the nouns used in it were "animation," "demesne," "exertion," "gradation," "patronage," "providence," "torpidity," and "utility." The verbs included "ameliorate," "apprise," "behove," "congeal," "precipitate," "prorogue," and "suborn," while among the adjectives were "attendant," "infamous," "manifest," "obnoxious," "respective," and "synonymous."

By the time of the paper's closure more than a century and a half later, monosyllabic nouns such as "babe," "boss," "cheat," "cop," "crook," "dad," "drug," "shame," "shock," and "star" (as well as "agony" and "fury," "love-rat" and "hooker," "shoot-out," and "terror"), together with verbs such as "axe," "bed," "blast," "dump," "flog," "grab," "quit," "romp," and "smash," and adjectives such as "big," "fat," "hot," and "top" (as well as "explosive," "secret," and "sentimental") had become a large part of the newspaper's stock-in-trade of expression.

But despite the atrophy of sensibility and skill that such verbiage represents, Bad Faith continues to argue that school success and college attainment are reaching unprecedented levels, while denials of it are held to have little or no warrant. "The current generation will be the best educated in history," a British minister for "school standards" could therefore proclaim;[254] "there is no evidence that exams have been 'dumbed down'" asserted a "quality- press" editorial;[255] and "rising standards in education" were declared to be "undeniable" by another senior Labour politician[256] as Bad Faith held its ground.

Yet in April 2011 some British government ministers were themselves reported to be "refusing to sign frankly illiterate correspondence put before them by officials."[257] Nevertheless, rejection of the claim that educational standards are rising continues to invite reproach, with critics of educational failure accused by "progressives" of wanting to "restore exclusivity," or even of seeking to "stop the masses getting above their station."[258] The Spirit of Demolition is also at work in arguments that "to make teenagers study languages" is "sheer snobbery" and that "consumer preferences"—market terms have few bounds—"should prevail."[259]

To "spell correctly" can likewise be declared by Bad Faith to be a "caste mark," the "last bastion of nanny knows best," and even as the "last fig-leaf of empire."[260] As elementary knowledge of the sciences declines, the Spirit of Demolition adds for good measure that science "should be a specialism for the interested few."[261] Worse, populist stances of this kind can be adopted, in supreme Bad Faith, by individuals who are educationally privileged, scoffing at the very expertise that they themselves possess while the ranks of the skill-less, unable to find a place in the "job market," swell.

In such fashion, the Orwellian displacement of unwelcome truths about the free society's self-degradation continues, as when crime rates are claimed to be falling when they are rising, and educational standards to be rising when they are falling, with the illusion-monger continuing to declare in Bad Faith that these are the best of times. "The young have never had it so good," says one;[262] "despite everything, life keeps getting better," asserts another;[263] "the world is easily in the best place it's ever been," pronounces a third.[264] We are likewise told that "this is the best time to be alive ever. This is a golden age,"[265] and "why 2017 was the best year in human history" is explained to us in a newspaper column.[266]

But large forces are at work in the world to dash such wishful thinking. They are forces beyond the reach of falsehood and taboo.

CHAPTER 10

THE DEMIURGE OF CAPITAL

Among the forces bestriding, building, and breaking down the civic order of free societies is one that Karl Marx came nearest to understanding. Like it or not—and market interest does not like it—he grasped, as none before, the nature of the Demiurge, the life force of "capital," and comprehended how it makes, remakes, and unmakes the world, driving it to great heights of technical innovation and depths of self-destruction, as today. He also saw this Demiurge as itself driven by the constant need to "magnify and increase itself" in an "endless process" of expansion.[1] It was an impetus that "gives capital no rest," Marx wrote in 1847, but "continually whispers in its ear 'Go on! Go on!'"[2]

This unrelenting pressure upon capital to increase has brought us the "world market," the "globalization" of production at the Demiurge's dictation, immense cash reserves in the hands of great corporations, and the assumption that continuous "growth" is synonymous with "progress." The same compulsion has generated new prospects and old hardships, recurrent economic crises, and gigantism which is often without redeeming content. It has also struck increasingly heavy ethical and cultural blows at the deformed social orders over which the Demiurge presides, and at the populations that comprise them. "In democracies," thought de Tocqueville, observing the United States in the 1830s, "nothing is greater or more brilliant than commerce."[3] Marx in the following decade was arguably sager. "There can be too much industry, too much commerce," he warned.[4]

For, in Marx's judgment, the Demiurge was an "unconscionable"[5]

force, allowing for few or no moral bounds and with its drive dependent on unrestraint. Culturally and ethically unanchored, it is nevertheless served in today's Western democracies by most of the political
class, and it has the near-totalitarian power, exercised in freedom's
name, to discredit and disallow alternatives to itself with relative ease.
Roaring on in its cosmos of mobile capital, rapid technology transfer
and "flexible" labor, the Demiurge's ideal is the "free-selling and
buying"[6] of everything under the sun at a global Vanity Fair, with "all
nature explored in order to discover new useful qualities in things,"[7]
including now in the melting Arctic.

Recoil from such type of material ambition is again an ancient
theme, and as old as moral thought itself. "There is nothing so harmful
as money. It wins cities, chases men from their homes, and turns the
minds of the honest to ill-doing," Creon declares in Sophocles's *Antigone*.[8] A similar type of criticism is implicit in de Tocqueville's description of the "spirit of gain" in the America of his day—with its puritan
ethos already on the wane—as "always eager."[9] Indeed, the "love of
wealth" was exaggeratedly claimed by him to be "at the bottom of all
that the Americans do."[10] Another mid-nineteenth-century observer
was still harsher, describing Americans as "tyrannized over" by a "very
exacting and spirit-grinding ruler, Mammon."[11]

But Marx's Demiurge of "capital" is a much grander force than that
which drives mere cupidity. Striving to "tear down every barrier,"[12] to
"conquer the whole earth for its market,"[13] and to "create a world after
its own image,"[14] it belongs everywhere and nowhere. Without respect
for nation, civic institutions, and social customs, and without regard for
local place or particular "workforce," it builds pyramids of wealth while
at the same time—the dialectic—digging pits beneath our feet. Following Karl Marx's pointing finger, we behold "globalization's" shining
cities rise but also the redundant human beings, discarded values, and
other waste products of its herculean creative efforts.

Today's world of "capital," with its speculative profits and sovereign debts, its scale of tax evasion, its widening gap between rich and
poor, and its privatization of public assets matches and sometimes

exceeds Marx's prognostications. He would also have found vindication, and a perverse satisfaction, in the cyclical crashes of the Demiurge's fortunes, the summoning of "rescue funds" to its aid in order to prevent wider failure, and the placating of "the markets" until its onward march resumes.

In the "bailing out" of economies and in the "recapitalization" of debt-exposed banks during periods of crisis, the Demiurge is now sustained both by private and public resources. Quick to do its bidding from fear of further contagion, governments of ostensible democracies are ready to cut welfare provision at civil society's expense in order to gain the favor of international creditors or bond holders, and to help rescue the over-reaching Demiurge from itself. Under the Demiurge's rule, profit can also be made by some from the purchase and sale of the growing debts of others, or from investment in the prospect of others' loss. And when balance has been temporarily restored, the whispering in the Demiurge's ear of "Go on! Go on!" resumes, and with it the promise of restored plenty, further "growth," and even wider "choice."

Thus the deity proceeds, seeking to make a "business" of all endeavor, and conflating the multiplicity of humankind into an aggregation of "consumers" and "money-spenders," as Marx wrote long ago.[15] Indeed, the Demiurge shapes perception itself. Hillary Clinton could therefore be seen by a commentator as a "stable option" for the US presidency "in market terms,"[16] while Donald Trump described the European Union as having been "created to beat the US when it comes to making money."[17] A British foreign secretary likewise called Trump "one of the great global brands,"[18] while the politics of a Trump is the politics of corporate business.

Marx also saw that the "discovery, creation and satisfaction of new needs"[19] is essential to the Demiurge's "self-magnification." Moreover, "as the mass of products grows," he wrote in 1857, "the demands made on consumption"—that is, the pressures on us to "consume" such "products"—also rise.[20] Under such pressures, imposed by the Demiurge, free societies have come to be ruled less by real "choice" than by market-driven compulsions in personal conduct. It is also no surprise that the Demiurge's most ardent followers have made "greed" a "good," even as the obese embodiments of Marx's "over-consumption" increase in girth and number.

Despite the harms done to the social order, the Demiurge drives on. In pursuit of ever-higher returns on its investments, it must seek an always greater distribution and turnover of its "products" in the "mass market," while Madam Bubble fingers all values—moral values included—in the search for a profitable line and a commanding "market share." In the resulting "epidemic of over-production," as Marx described it,[21] "success" is measured by numbers of sales, with even books called "consumer products" and Nobel prizes awarded in 1971 and 1987 for studies of "growth."

Ranging the earth for the most favorable "investment climate," the Demiurge, enlarged to a scale predicted by Marx, finds it easy to secure the subordination of public policy to its needs and demands, and strikes market bargains with nominally sovereign states from strength. In free societies it does so without genuine democratic con-sultation or sanction, and gains easy exemption, open and covert, from law, from tax regulation, and even from ethical restraint. For all its size, it is also swift in its movements, acting speedily to cash in on advantageous changes of government or of regime, while there was no "draining" of "the swamp," no cleaning out of the Augean stables, when President Trump took office.

Moreover, Marx's Demiurge, to the insistent cry of "Go on! Go on!" not only gives a "cosmopolitan character" to the market in every country but undermines local manufacture and the "national ground on which it stood,"[22] whatever the objections of the protectionist and the anti-globalizer. Indeed, long before the facts of it had become as manifest as they are today, Marx had seen coming the "entangle-ment of all peoples" in a "world market."[23] Similarly, long before the creation of such corporate entities as the European Union, or "single market," with its "principles" of the "free movement of goods, capital, services and people,"[24] Marx had anticipated the "lumping together" of "separate interests, laws and governments" into "one nation, one government, one code of laws and one frontier."[25]

Today, as the process accelerates—and with attempts to keep a distance from it having divided Britain—the subordination of the national to the global is regarded by market interest as a necessity of "progress" itself, whatever the negative effects on local sovereignty, democracy, and local employment. Delegates to the World Economic Forum thus assemble each year as "stakeholders in the world economy" in order to "shape the global agenda."[26] In times when "markets slide" after North Korea fires a missile over Japan[27] and when "strong Chinese manufacturing data lift the FTSE,"[28] heads of state, central bankers, international bureaucrats, corporate chiefs, "tech titans," and the mass media's ringmasters gather in Davos.

In the belief, or hope, that a world order can be built upon the market's foundations, ministers of agriculture, development, economy, energy, enterprise, finance, foreign affairs, industry, security, and trade—from Albania and Bangladesh to the Ukraine and the United States—are in attendance in a typical year. At Davos in 2017 even the Chinese president described his country's "integration into the global economy" as an "historical trend," and declared that China needed to have the "courage to swim in the vast ocean of the global market" if its own economy was to "grow."[29] Before his appearance at the World Economic Forum, Xi Jinping had also objected to the blocking by the United States of Chinese acquisitions of American technology companies as interference with "pure market behavior";[30] in October 2017, a resolution of the Chinese Communist Party's central committee spoke approvingly of "giving play to the decisive role of market forces in resource allocation";[31] and in June 2018 the Chinese foreign minister declared that "We're not doing nineteenth-century trade. Goods flow from one country to another along the globalized industrial value chains."[32] They are the very chains which the Demiurge has fastened around the earth.

To Marx, such "entanglement of all peoples" in a "world economy," dwarfing Madam Bubble's local market stall, represented a gross over-reaching of the Demiurge's ambition. Vital and all-conquering as such ambition might appear, he believed that it was mortal, doomed. According to Marx's scenario, the Demiurge's nemesis and agent of its downfall would be the "international proletariat," its massed ranks united in class solidarity for the final round of a cosmic class struggle and for the coming of a new dawn. But the "workers of the world" were to fail in their allotted role as "gravediggers" of the "bourgeoisie."[33] "Capital" proved too powerful for "labor," the classless utopia dreamed of in Marx's heaven turned out to be an illusion, while objection to "globalism" became Reaction's cause.

Moreover, for all that "socialism" is still alive in some hearts as an ideal, state socialism created a nightmare world. The voices from it return, in Budapest telling me that the "notion of the citizen" had been "destroyed" by "proletarian dictatorship,"[34] and describing Romania as an "atomistic society where social morality has been forgotten."[35] Here, said the Czech school teacher sacked for calling for civil rights in his country, "people daren't demand their rights and are even frightened of their duties."[36] "What kind of moral state do you dream of?" I asked him. "A state where there is the possibility of being decent in a normal way," he replied.

For his part, a former leading member of the Czech apparatus, expelled for his dissent, blamed the "disasters of communism" on the "negative example of what capitalism does to its peoples." But "real life," he added, "is more complex than theories."[37] Despite this truth, and capitalism's "negative example," absolutist market-thought has displaced Marxist thought in promising humanity "progress." Or as Ayn Rand has one of her manufacturer heroes say, "It is we who move the world."[38] But it is at ever-greater cost and risk—including that of provoking extreme Reaction—as the globe's inhabitants-turned-customers are increasingly liberated from ties of family, place, faith, and nation. Marx anticipated it. Under "capital's command," he wrote in 1848, "all that is solid melts into air" and "all that is holy is profaned."[39] But his foresight also failed him. His hope of the world's redemption at the hands of the "proletariat" was a form of idealistic self-deception. He has his counterparts today, including the deluded for whom the Western free society is history's culmination, and who cannot read the writing on its walls.

CHAPTER 11

QUESTIONS OF BELIEF

We have thus seen that delusions in market societies about their moral strengths and long-term staying powers are comparable in their self-deception with those in the old state-socialist utopias. With the Demiurge of capital in command of many of the free society's ostensible liberties, the "sovereignty of the people" is also mocked by the extent of democracy's inequalities and injustices. Nevertheless, even as other forces advance at quickening pace, the health of the free society continues to be measured by the scale and variety of its material enlargement. But no stable social order can rest upon the principle of "growth" alone.

Moreover, Western democracies depend for such "growth" upon the very freedoms, both real and apparent, which cause them greatest harm. At the same time, the lost sense of the true "commonwealth"— which is not the same as the collective consumption of the goods and services "the market" provides—has left the free society floundering in an ethical void. The most potent alternative belief systems of its past, whether socialist or Judeo-Christian, are now shadows of their former selves.

Softened up by overindulgence, confused by its swirl of rights and choices, and weakened by misguided forms of toleration and educational failure, the United States in particular is unable, despite its armories, to hold its position in the world. A Samson among free societies, it is disabled by the wrong judgments of its political class, and even the Demiurge is losing its American accent. Ever less certain of its step as its imperium wanes—and evading the truth about itself—

its bewilderments and strategic errors in diplomatic arenas and on foreign battlefields have increased. It has armed its enemies in the vain hope of gaining their favor, preached the virtues of liberal democracy to despots, and combined iron-fisted toughness in the face of "terror" with denials that the latter is faith-inspired. Meanwhile, the campaigning politician on the electoral stump in the US continues to declare that "the world needs American leadership,"[1] or promises to "make America great again." But the world order is changing.

Western democracies, with the United States and Britain leading the way, are above all uncomprehending of the reviving strengths of Islam. An apocalyptic belief system which is both religious and social, private and public, pacific and violent, it also possesses a potent counter-ethic to the tawdriness of market-thought and the self-harm of free moral choice. Aided by Western naïvetés about Islam's nature, texts, and doctrine, Islam is confident of its future as other faiths wane, while being assured by divinity that it will rule the globe in the fullness of time.

The world's fastest-growing religion and destined to become the largest during the course of the twenty-first century[2]—"make not three but five children because you are the future of Europe," President Erdogan told his fellow Turks in 2017[3]—Islam's tribunes make no bones about its ambition. "We are on the path that leads to the rule of Islam worldwide," declared the commander of Iran's Revolutionary Guards,[4] and "a day will come when the Muslim will walk everywhere as master" promised Caliph Abu Bakr al-Baghdadi of the too-soon-written-off Islamic State.[5]

This confidence is largely justified. For Islam tells its burgeoning millions an old tale, a tale now little heard in free societies clinging to the apron-strings of Madam Bubble and which have lost their moral way. Ignorant of the history of Islam's previous upsurges— such as that which brought the Ottomans to the gates of Vienna in 1683—disordered free societies are unable to recognize the appeal of its certitudes, or the sense of belonging that it provides to the faithful. Moreover, the spirit of the Enlightenment and its belief in free speech are easily betrayed by "progressives" fearful of being thought

"Islamophobic," even as the principles which "progressives" espouse are flouted and offended by fundamentalist Islamic theory and practice. Francis Bacon was less inclined to mince his words, in 1639 calling the Turks a "Cruell People,"[6] while in 1830 the US president John Quincy Adams described the "precept of the Koran" as that of "perpetual war against all who deny that Mahomet is the prophet of God."[7] Also forgotten is the sage advice of the past that "fear, instead of avoiding danger, invites it."[8]

Others of the "free," today riffling among their moral and material choices, are out of their depths in dealing with such an unfamiliar foe. In a universe of goods and options, there can be no real grasp of a mind-set which deals in stern distinctions between right and wrong conduct. They are distinctions of a kind from which the free-choosing libertarian recoils, but without which, to a Muslim, there can be no morality at all. Moreover, to make a virtue of armed combat for a religious cause, as does the jihadi, is not in today's Western order of things. The "imperialist" world also has little sense of culpability for the sins with which it is charged, nor knows that the securing of the "infidel's" submission to Islam is the latter's ultimate aim.

Meanwhile, naive Western wishful thinkers saw the harbingers of a democratic dawn in the revolts against a handful of despots during the "Arab Spring," ignoring the warning of ninety religious scholars from many parts of the Muslim world that to "allow the people to have the final say in full democracies" would permit them to "vote for things that are prohibited in Islam."[9] A Jordanian Salafi leader, Abu Muhammad al-Tahawi, similarly declared that "God's law" was "contradicted" by "the ruling of the people by the people,"[10] while the "spiritual head" of Algeria's Salafist movement, Shaikh Abdul Malek Ramdani, objected that "during unrest, men and women are mixed, and this is illicit in our religion."[11]

Nevertheless, timidity in the non-Muslim world continues to hope for the best, or the best as Western ethics defines it. "Spring turns to Summer," a *Times* editorial thus pronounced on the upheaval in Egypt in June 2012, describing the election of a Muslim Brotherhood president as the "first step on Egypt's journey from dictatorship to democracy."[12] The Muslim Brotherhood's beliefs and purposes— "the Qur'an is our law, jihad is our way"[13] is its slogan—were once more sidestepped by wishful thinking, with inquiry into them held presumptively to be "Islamophobic."

But as radical militias battled for control of the streets in the "Arab Spring" after the overthrow of a number of authoritarian regimes, others saw an "Islamic awakening"[14] in the uprisings. The revolts were even described as a "prelude to the battle for Jerusalem,"[15] while Osama bin Laden shortly before his death declared that "the sun of revolution has risen from the Maghreb."[16] Moreover, the belief that "liberal" reform of the clan-dominated and faith-driven polities of the Islamic world is at hand, or is possible, is itself a liberal illusion; on his visit in January 2013 to what he described as the "new Libya" after the fall of Muammar Gaddafi, the British prime minister was greeted by trainee police officers—under the "new" dispensation— with chants of "Allahu Akhbar!"[17]

Recoil from such cries is misplaced. For although the open mind of the freethinker retreats from any creed that would "shut the whole world up in a cage,"[18] the governing ideas of the market society are as limited as Islam's beliefs are held to be. Islam also has a signal advantage. In whatever form it takes, the jihad knows no limits of time, while Islam's belief in its invincibility surpasses that of the most ardent servant of the free market.

The essentials of the faith are also comprehensible to the least lettered, with its adherents schooled early in a sense of duty to defend it from scorn or attack; the bounty offered by Iran for Salman Rushdie's assassination was raised in 2016.[19] Or as Thomas Carlyle put it, "no Christian since the early ages, or only perhaps the English Puritans, have stood by their Faith as Moslems do by theirs."[20] The physical armory of the free society can have little permanent impact on such true battlefield strengths, notwithstanding the assertions of a de Tocqueville that Islam is a "form of decadence,"[21] or of a Winston Churchill that it "paralyses the social development of those who follow it."[22]

Indeed, Muslims have gained only two Nobel prizes in the sciences in over a century, despite constituting some 20 percent and more of the world's population; Jews, a mere 0.2 percent of humanity, have been awarded over 140 Nobels in physiology, medicine, chemistry, and physics. With a ban announced in July 2017 on the teaching of Darwin's theory of evolution in Turkey's schools[23]—and even chess described by Saudi Arabia's grand mufti as "the work of Satan"[24]—Islam's "disengagement from science and the process of creating new knowledge"[25] has harmed it less than might have been anticipated. Bought-in technology, joint ventures, oil sales, and foreign assistance have largely sufficed.

Moreover, the claims of Reason rank low in Islam today against the upsurge of its faith, whose prescriptions and fatwas are seen as the path to true well-being. From such certitude free thought backs away in distaste. But distaste for Islam is not an arm against it, while the torpor of Arab lands, for example, is an old and hackneyed theme. "There is a lack of vigor in its tenor of life, its nature that of sloth," Lucan wrote of Libya in the first century CE, "and, unconscious amid its unmoving sands, so the year passes."[26] Today, however, it is Islam, fully aware of its prospects, that is in movement, while the Occident makes incoherent responses to its advance.

On the "right," some therefore persist in thinking that the values of the free society, even as it disintegrates, can vanquish the moral absolutism of the "fanatic." Similarly obtuse, "progressives" can hold that the retreat of Western "imperialism" from its various battlefields would bring the jihad against the "infidel" to an end. Meanwhile, anxious jihad-watchers in their electronic limbos monitor the progress of Islam's frontline fighters, thus helping to build the sense of the latter's momentum by recording their every act. The free society's media, cashing in on public alarm, similarly invest heinous crimes—including jihadi attacks in Barcelona, Berlin, Boston, and Brussels; in London, Manchester, and Munich; in Nice and Stockholm; in Saint Petersburg and San Bernardino—with an indecent glamor. "Risk appetite" in "the market" was even said in May 2011 to have got a "boost" from Osama bin Laden's death.[27]

Above all, it is clear that democracy's political and military class is at a loss in face of Islam's challenge. Alive, bin Laden was dismissed by a US presidential candidate as "more symbolism than anything else";[28] dead, his killing became a "momentous achievement."[29] Neither assertion was true. The first was a minimization of his significance, the second an exaggeration of it. In similar confusion, al-Qaeda was said in January 2013 by then president Barack Obama to have been "decapacitated [sic]"[30] but ten months later the FBI's director declared that al-Qaeda had become "hydra-headed."[31]

Nevertheless, most policymakers in Western democracies still appear to believe that the Muslim faith at its most aggressive can ultimately be brought to heel by force, while simultaneously professing—or pretending—that Islam is a "religion of peace," an old illusion. Or as the philosopher Anthony Collins, a friend of John Locke, wrote in the early eighteenth century, "Let any Man look into the History and State of the Turks, and he will see the influences which their tolerating Principles and Temper have on the Peace of their Empire. The Peace of the Turkish Empire is so perfect by virtue of the Charity and Toleration which prevail among them."[32] The Armenians have a different view.

Moreover, the word *Islam* does not mean "peace"—despite assertions both by Muslims and non-Muslims that it does—but "submission." Derived from the root *s-l-m*, it signifies "surrender"; the *Muslim* is "one who surrenders" to the deity's commands, whether they be belligerent or pacific. Despite this, a chorus of voices has continued to declare Islam to be a pacific creed not merely by doctrine but as if by definition, whatever the contrary evidence may be.

When Muslims proclaim it, some do so in good faith. "Islam means peace," declared Malala Yousafzai,[33] the young Pakistani activist for female education who survived a Taliban assassination attempt in October 2012. Other Muslims do so in formulaic repetition of received wisdom, and yet others from guile and dissimulation—that is, to bamboozle the credulous "infidel"—for which the Qur'an, naming it *taqiyya*, gives license.[34] Or as an imam in the southern Italian town of Sarno expressed it after the November 2015 attacks in Paris, "we preach love, only and exclusively love. In our credo, we do not speak of violence, death and destruction."[35] Likewise, the Muslim Council of Britain described the Paris massacre as "outside the boundaries of our faith,"[36] while London's mayor Sadiq Khan—who in earlier days had called moderate Muslims "Uncle Toms"[37]—condemned terrorist violence as having "no place in Islam."[38]

"Radical" Muslims have a different view, and do not hesitate to express it. "You can't say that Islam is a religion of peace. Because Islam does not mean peace. Islam means submission. And there is a place for violence in Islam,"[39] pronounced Anjem Choudhary, a British-educated Muslim "activist" and lawyer who was jailed in September 2016 for encouraging support for IS. Indeed, Islam's aspiration, unconcealed in its texts, is to "prevail over all religions,"[40] with migration, or *hijra*, also seen as a means of advance.[41] Nevertheless, with the Qur'an and its commentaries generally unread, the number of non-Muslims in high places declaring Islam to be a "religion of peace" has grown, even as the reverses at its hands and attacks in its name have increased, and as the free societies' confusions in the face of them have mounted. It is as if there were an unspoken international accord to avert the gaze, once again, from truths impossible or unwise to tell, whether from fear or diplomacy or both.

"All of us recognize that this great religion cannot justify violence," thus declared an American president;[42] "the real face of Islam is a peaceful religion," asserted his secretary of state;[43] while an English high court judge told two Muslim defendants accused of killing a soldier in a London street that their crime was a "betrayal of Islam." "That's a lie," one of them with some justice shouted back, "you don't know what Islam is."[44] In similar fashion, jihadis fighting in Syria were dismissed as mere "extremists,"[45] their "warped narratives" and "maverick form of Islam"[46] a betrayal of their faith. Likewise, a British home secretary—later to become prime minister—and an American secretary of state concurred in declaring that the Paris attacks in November 2015 had "nothing to do with Islam,"[47] while another

English high court judge, sentencing a bomber of the London Under-
ground to jail, told him that he would have "plenty of time to study
the Koran in prison in the years to come," and would "understand
that the Koran is a book of peace."[48]

With fighters in their tens of thousands from "more than one
hundred member-states" of the United Nations reported in May
2015[49] as having joined the ranks of IS and other jihadi groups, to
a British shadow home secretary the "perverted ideology" of IS and
its caliphate again bore "no relation to Islam";[50] to a British prime
minister the Kenyan mall jihadis similarly did "not represent Islam
or Muslims anywhere in the world";[51] and to François Hollande,
then French president, the *Charlie Hebdo* assailants had "nothing to
do with the Muslim faith."[52] Likewise to an American president,
IS represented "no faith, least of all the Muslim faith" and was "not
Islamic";[53] to a CIA director, al-Qaeda had "distorted the teachings of
Mohammed";[54] to Hillary Clinton, after the Paris attacks, "Muslims"
had "nothing whatsoever to do with terrorism";[55] and to John Kerry,
IS was an "ugly insult to the peaceful religion they violate every day."[56]

But Muhammad Bayoudh al-Tamimi, a Jordanian politician, had
a different view. It is a view anathema to apologists, whether Muslim
or non-Muslim. "There is no such thing as 'IS ideology,' it's Islam,"
al-Tamimi declared in August 2014, asserting that its "doctrine and
conduct" were those of "the Qur'an and the Sunna."[57] America's
Homeland Security secretary could nevertheless call the Boston mar-
athon attack in April 2013 "senseless,"[58] while a "hunt" was carried on
to discover a "motive" for it.[59] To have seen the "sense" in the attack
was too large a step to take.

Such evasions, whether from delusion or varieties of calculation,
have been continuous in Western political responses to the twenty-
first century's jihad, and from "right" and "left" alike. "Islamist terrorism" was therefore again a "perversion of a great faith" in a British
Tory prime minister's opinion,[60] while the jihadi's was a "warped
interpretation" of Islam according to Rex Tillerson, President Trump's
then secretary of state.[61] Similarly, a Manchester bomber was "a ter-

rorist not a Muslim" in the view of the city's Labour mayor,[62] and to the Labour Party leader the attack was "not Islam at all."[63]

Newly elected President Trump (and his speechwriters) took a different position. Declaring in his inaugural address that "we will unite the civilized world against radical Islamic terrorism and eradicate it completely from the face of the Earth"[64]—an impossible project—he went on to tell Muslim leaders in Riyadh in May 2017 to purge their societies of the "foot-soldiers of evil" and to "drive them out of your places of worship."[65] "Barbarism," he added, "will deliver you no glory."

But as the challenge to the non-Muslim world deepens, self-censoring "progressives" in particular have continued to avoid the truths of it. At the same time, they have recast Islam as a David struggling with a maleficent Goliath and in battle with the new "Crusaders" in Muslim lands. The Western anti-"colonialist" can thus call the United States an "imperialist power in the most sinister sense of the term,"[66] while Labour's Jeremy Corbyn described the beheading by IS of a British aid worker as the "price of war, intervention and jingoism."[67] Some (or many) on the nonjudgmental "left" are also capable of sidestepping Islam's hostilities to their own libertarian ideals. Thus, most gays have remained silent on Islam's punishments of homosexuals, and Western feminists can argue that to protest against the maltreatment of women and girls in the Muslim world—a woman's worth is only half that of a man, the Qur'an declares[68]—is a form of "imperialism" itself.[69] Moreover, to ban the burqa, the niqab, or the burkini in Western societies signifies the "undressing" of Muslim women, denies them their "empowerment," and is another act of "imperial subjugation."[70]

Others invest Islam with qualities it does not possess or which are contrary to its expressed beliefs. In his speech in Cairo in June 2009 at al-Azhar University, then president Obama declared that "America and Islam share common principles of justice and progress, tolerance, and the dignity of all human beings."[71] But this is contradicted by such Qur'anic assertions as that "infidels" are the "most vile of created beings,"[72] or that Jews are the "descendants of apes and swine."[73] He also told his Cairo audience that Islam had "paved the way for Europe's Enlightenment" and had "always been a part of America's story,"[74] even as its ardors cast an increasing shadow upon Western freedom of thought and speech, and its ambition builds the strengths of its worldwide *umma*, or global community of the faithful. But the former president had no doubts. Islam, he declared at a Baltimore mosque in February 2016, was a "source of peace,"[75] terrorists had "perverted Islam,"[76] and faith could "unite us under the banners of fellowship and love."[77]

At the same time, and in accord with the free societies' norms, many diaspora Muslims peaceably avail themselves of the rights which floundering Western democracies provide. But they also make the choices which serve their individual interests and the interests of their faith, while for the most part remaining silent about the "extremists" in their ranks.[78] And as British Islam's least-restrained followers—a minority— shout "Democracy, go to Hell!"[79] on its streets, well-wishing libertarians stand aside to give anti-libertarians free passage, and in June 2018 even the director of the Uffizi Gallery expressed the hope that there would one day be a "great Mosque with a splendid golden dome" in Florence, adding, in Arabic, "Inshallah" or "God willing."[80]

Meanwhile, the bomb attacks on churches in the wider Muslim world, the deaths of Christians, and the assertion that nine of the ten nations in which Christians suffer "extreme persecution" are Muslim[81] are minimized or even ignored. Likewise, the denial in some Muslim countries of religious rights to other faiths goes largely unprotested. Saudi Arabia does not provide legal protection for freedom of religion; Somalia and Brunei ban Christmas celebrations;[82] in Iran non-Muslim women must wear the headscarf; and El Al is not permitted to over-fly, let alone land in, most Muslim countries.[83] Even the Saudi grand mufti's call in March 2014 for the "destruction of all churches"[84] in the Arabian Peninsula caused little stir in the Christian world, while in his Christmas addresses in 2010 and 2011 Pope Benedict XV1 described violence against Christians committed by Muslims in

Nigeria, Pakistan, and the Philippines, among other places, as merely "absurd."[85] His successor similarly diminished the significance of the massacre of over 140 Kenyan Christian students in April 2015 by calling the killings "senseless."[86]

Thus, in clerical high places a mixture of good intentions, wishful thinking, vacillation, and occlusion of the truth have greeted the Islamic advance. In October 2012, over two hundred Catholic prelates called for "intensified outreach to Muslims";[87] in November 2013, an "Apostolic Exhortation of the Holy Father Francis" described "authentic Islam" as "opposed to every form of violence";[88] and in January 2016, the secretary general to the Catholic synod of bishops pronounced that "the Muslim faith preaches non-violence in the name of God."[89]

But in August 2014, changing tack, the massacres of Christians and others in Iraq were said by the Vatican to have "shamed humanity";[90] the pope in May 2016 described the "idea of conquest" as "inherent in the soul of Islam";[91] and in May 2017, after the murders of Copts in Egypt, he declared that there were "more Christian martyrs today than in ancient times."[92] Other Catholic voices have been even more forthright. "Islamism," said an Egyptian Jesuit theologian in September 2017, "is Islam unveiled in all its logic and rigor."[93] It was a rigor, he asserted, "present in Islam like the chicken in the egg" and "the cause of the barbarisms committed in its name."

Meanwhile, religious and lay traditions in non-Muslim countries can be modified or set aside—whether from courtesy or anxiety, or both— lest they give offense to Islam, even when they do not. In February 2008, an Archbishop of Canterbury in a discourse on "Civil and Religious Law in England"[94] thus recommended a "constructive accommodation with some aspects of Muslim law," or sharia, in order to meet Muslim requirements; he did so without reference, in a notional democracy, to the general will. The archbishop also described sharia as "governed by revealed texts,"[95] implying assent by the highest of Anglican prelates to the claim that the Islamic belief system is of divine origin.

Thomas Hobbes had a different and brisker view of such matters. "If a man cometh from the Indies hither," he wrote in *Leviathan*, and "teach anything that tendeth to disobedience of the Lawes of this Country, though he be never so well perswaded of the truth of what he teacheth, he commits a Crime."[96] But today, as the Christian faith weakens in once-Christian lands, a Muslim prayer service giving "thanks to Allah" was ecumenically held in a central London Anglican church,[97] an imam recited the Islamic call to prayer in Blackburn Cathedral,[98] and a former Bishop of Oxford argued that readings from the Qur'an should form part of the coronation service for British monarchs.[99] Indeed, deference to Islamic susceptibility and scruples, real or imagined, has gone far. "Rude statues" were therefore covered at the Capitoline Museums in Rome during the Iranian president's visit "in order not to offend,"[100] and the Bishop of London applauded clergymen in areas of the city with large Muslim populations for growing beards in an effort to "reach out" to the local "culture."[101]

Yet Islam's own texts counsel the faithful to have "no intimates other than your own folk" and to be "merciful to one another but ruthless to unbelievers," while the infidel's "unbelief" is described as a form of "defiance." Islam, while acknowledging Jews and Christians to be "people of the Book," also holds essential features of the Christian story to be untrue. It denies that Christ was crucified, that "Mary's son" was "the Messiah," that "God is one of three," and that Christ was "the son of God."[102] Today's Christian ecumenism, in turning the other cheek, is at least true to itself, however neglectful it may be of the plight of Christians in many Muslim lands.

Indeed, both innocence and ignorance have helped to disable non-Muslim responses to the challenges posed by Islam, a wide swath of whose texts openly proclaim it to be a warrior faith. As evidence of Islam's nonbelligerent nature, and adding to the confusion, the well-meaning Muslim may cite Qur'anic statements such as "he that kills a man is like killing the whole of humanity,"[103] and "let there be no compulsion in religion."[104] But Muslim scholars themselves consider the Qur'an's milder early injunctions to have been "abrogated," or superseded, by the more severe. Objective commentary therefore has no choice but to note the violences counseled to the Muslim—as proofs of faith—in the Qur'an, and in its associated scriptural texts, as well as the punishments decreed in this life and promised in the next for apostasy from it.

As Islam advances, such texts give "radicals" more warrant for their actions than they give those who claim that its nature is essentially pacific. The jihadi can, and therefore does, point to Qur'anic verses that command the faithful to "strike terror into the hearts of unbelievers" until they "submit to your religion"; to "expel them from lands from which they expelled you"; to "strike at the necks" of "infidels"; and to "slaughter" those who take up arms against Islam, but with some captives given the possibility of "paying ransom" for the sparing of their lives. Moreover, the "humiliation" of the "infidel" is said to "heal the hearts of believers" and to "remove their rage," while paradise is promised to those who kill, or who are killed, for their faith.[105] License can perhaps also be found in the Qur'an, if one looks, for the surprise attack on the Twin Towers in September 2011. "How many sinful townships have we destroyed so that they be in ruins, and how many a lofty tower!"[106] may have set the example to those who brought down the World Trade Center.

There are hundreds of millions of "moderate" Muslims, and some have protested at the deeds done in their names. But the protesters are a small minority. In Milan and Rome, cities each with Muslim populations of many tens of thousands, only a few hundred turned out to demonstrate their opposition to the November 2015 Paris attacks,[107] while in Paris itself there were "about one hundred."[108] For the truth is that Islam—when its texts and teachings, belligerent and benign, are weighed in a just balance without "Islamophobia" on the one hand or wishful thinking on the other—is not a "moderate" faith. Moreover, despite the pacific and mystical currents in the profounder reaches of Islamic thought, the number of its injunctions to do battle with the "unbeliever" potentially make foes of much of the rest of humankind.

Indeed, Islam sees the world as divided between the "infidel" domain, denoted the *dar al-harb*—the realm of warfare—and the *dar al-islam*, the realm of those who have "surrendered" to Islam's dictates.

They are perceived in Muslim teachings as two separate mental and moral spheres; in Marx's words, a "simple and convenient distinction" which "reduces the geography and ethnography of the various people to two nations and two countries."[109] It also implied, he believed, "a state of permanent hostility between the Mussulman and the unbeliever."

The judgment was too sweeping. For Islam also offers the non-Muslim the options of conversion to the faith or submission to its rule, whether achieved by violence, by the exaction of tribute, or by acquiescence to it, willing or resigned. Across the span of the centuries, all of these have come to pass. They are once more coming to pass by dint of battle, cultural attrition, and force of numbers as well as by moral example, the last being set to an increasingly degraded non-Muslim world. Moreover, unconditional and permanent toleration of the "infidel" is contrary to Islam's belief system, whatever the naïve non-Muslim may think or hope. It is similarly naïve for the credulous Muslim, or ex-Muslim, to call for Islam to be "reformed" and for its "core concepts" to be brought "into the modern age."[110]

They cannot be, and the reason is plain: the securing of victory over the "infidel" in the *dar al-harb*, the realm of warfare, by jihad or "struggle" (both with the self and with the "unbeliever") is not an option. It is an obligation of faith. In the words of the Muslim historian Ibn Khaldun (1332–1406), to "convert everybody to Islam either by persuasion or force" and to "gain power over other nations" is a "religious duty."[111] With many Muslims looking on in passive silence while other Muslims seek to fulfill such "duty" by various means, it is bringing with it not only a clash of arms and wills, but of rival world-views and opposed ethical systems.

The ethical battle is one which the morally disordered free society is increasingly unfit to wage. This is so even in face of the challenge to Reason that the *dar al-islam* promises the "infidel" world. Moreover, whether primed for a martyr's self-immolation or preaching disdain (and worse) from the pulpit, Islam's avatars easily find the words to condemn the free society's delinquencies and defects. They thus proclaim Western democracy a failure, and call on the non-Muslim world to "liberate" itself from the "deception, shackles and attrition of the capitalist system."[112] Just as the "Islamophobe" sees the promise of a long night of the soul in the advance of Islam, so one president of Iran could denote the present times "under Western dominance" as an "era of darkness,"[113] while another asserted that in the United States "morality has no place."[114]

Easily dismissed as such rhetoric may be, to scoff at an ayatollah's description of "today's world" as "full of thieves and plunderers of human honor, dignity and morality"[115]—three terms which are passing from usage in free-society debate—is misplaced. Some expressions of Islam's growing confidence are cruder, as in the call to Muslims by a spokesman of IS to reject "democracy, secularism, nationalism and other garbage from the West."[116] But societies ruled by market interest and by the anti-ethic of free moral choice can no longer vaunt a monopoly of truth in matters of right government. They are also no longer in command of the world's fortunes, the Demiurge has insatiable needs for the Muslim world's oil, and Saudi Arabia has twice as many warplanes in its armory as the Royal Air Force.[117]

Moreover, the free society is ruled by the shallow belief that the rest of humanity, whatever its separate faiths, traditions and values, aspires to have the same material, moral and political choices as those which the free society has on its stall. This is also a time when historical knowledge has never been more needed if right judgments are to be made of Western democracy's lost direction. But in its citizen-bodies, or aggregates of consumers, such knowledge—as earlier mentioned—is now at a low ebb, especially in the United States and Britain. "How can we hope to understand the world of affairs around us, if we do not know how they came to be what they are?" asks the historian.[118] Or, as Hobbes put it, "ignorance of remote causes disposeth men to attribute all events to the causes immediate, for these are all the causes they perceive."[119]

Islam has been spared this degree of disconnection between past and present. Indeed, Gibbon saw in Islam's "long memory" a guarantee of its "perpetuity" as an "independent" faith. Knowledge of its own history, he thought, "animated succeeding generations" of Muslims to "maintain their inheritance,"[120] and for good or ill such knowledge still does so. Thus, in recall of the defeat suffered by Islam's invading military forces at Tours in France in the eighth century, a Muslim commentator, citing the name of a "martyr" who fell in combat there, could pray in 2007 that "Allah sends us another such as he in order to finish what he started in Europe."[121] But if the free society now has shrinking memory of its own past, it has even less knowledge of the past of others.

Awareness of Islam's previous upsurges is therefore largely absent from contemporary public debate. Moreover, even those who possess such knowledge remain reticent on the subject, their fear of being thought "Islamophobes" again playing its part. De Tocqueville had no such hesitation, describing Islam as having in the past "overrun the whole world with its apostles, militants and martyrs."[122] Montesquieu, lacking today's self-censoring restraint, similarly asserted that "the Mahometan religion speaks only by the sword"—an exaggeration—and "acts upon men with that destructive spirit with which it was founded."[123]

Harsh as such type of judgment may be, within a century of Mohammed's presumed death in 632 CE, Armenia, Persia, Syria, Egypt, Iraq, Jerusalem, north Africa, Cyprus, Sicily, and Spain had fallen to Islamic conquest. By 732 CE, with half of France taken, Arab legions had also reached the Loire, to be routed at Tours by the armies of the Frankish general Charles Martel. Had Islam's forces not been defeated on that occasion, speculated Gibbon (in a once-familiar passage), "perhaps the interpretation of the Koran would now be taught in the schools of Oxford and her pulpits might demonstrate to a circumcised people the sanctity and truth of the revelation of Mohammed."[124] In Islam's new renaissance, the same "revelation" is today ranging an increasingly frontier-less world.

Islam's previous upsurges were sometimes halted and reversed, as at Tours. Likewise, the defeat of the Turkish fleet in 1571 at Lepanto in the Gulf of Corinth—a battle in which Cervantes lost an arm—dealt a severe blow to Muslim sea power in the Mediterranean. But Islam's warrior energies, the "religion of peace" notwithstanding, have rarely been in abeyance for long. Despite intermittent periods of torpor and quiescence, in successive centuries they were to bring Islam, whether by subjugation or settlement or both, to Anatolia and the Balkans; to the Crimea and southern Russia; to Afghanistan; to central Asia; and to India, where the toll of Hindu deaths ran to tens of millions; to Sinkiang, and further into China; to southeast Asia; to the Horn of Africa, West Africa, the east African coast, and beyond; and today to the Americas, and once again to Europe.

Moral zeal and self-belief, physical courage and a readiness to take life, together with successful organization, shrewd calculation, and peaceful proselytization, have been—and are again—Islam's arms. With weapons old and new, it is well-girded today for its conflicts with the confused "infidel" world, whose mixture of market freedoms and unmanned drones cannot douse Islam's renewed ardors, military and moral. Mid-ninth-century jihadis sacked churches in Rome; "Rome will be conquered," a likeminded successor declares, preaching from a Western pulpit.[125]

In its third worldwide uprising, and as the dissolution of the free society from many causes accelerates, Islam is now the Church Militant that Christianity once was. In comparison with Islam's renewed momentum and increasing numbers—there could be more than 50 million Muslims in Europe by 2050,[126] as earlier mentioned—much of the Christian world is beset by shrinking totals of practicants, while the delinquencies of some of its clergy have taken their own toll. Or as Hobbes expressed it, "the fayling of Virtue in the Pastors maketh Faith faile in the people."[127] But as churches "consolidate" or close—for example, over three hundred Evangelical churches closed in Germany between 1990 and 2010,[128] and more than one hundred Anglican churches in Wales in the last decade[129]—new mosques open in non-Muslim lands,[130] and the numbers of "active Muslims" rise.[131]

Conversely, surveys indicate that less than half of the British population now identifies itself as Christian, with as few as 2 percent of young adults and only one in seven of the population as a whole—a "record low," down from 31 percent in 2002—saying they belong to the Church of England,[132] while "typical Sunday attendances" in England have more than halved in the last four decades[133] to less than 1.5 percent of the population.[134] In addition, despite some increase in 2018 in applicants for the Anglican priesthood,[135] one-quarter of the Anglican clergy is aged over sixty-five,[136] with "part-time" priests who have "other weekday jobs" being pressed into service.[137] As the decline accelerates, some 2,000 rural parishes had "fewer than ten regular worshippers" in 2015;[138] only one in three people in Britain marry in church;[139] less than a third of funerals are conducted by the Church of England;[140] and "hundreds" of "forlorn" Methodist communities now have less than twenty members.[141]

Indeed, a former Archbishop of Canterbury himself described England as a "post-Christian" country,[142] while a public commission called in 2015 for a "new settlement in religion and belief in the United Kingdom" in order to ensure that the "pluralist character of modern society is reflected,"[143] signifying the abandonment of the Church of England's claim to be the national church. Nevertheless, market-thought has tried to come to its rescue. "If the Church of England is to return to growth," the Archbishops of Canterbury and York declared in January 2015, "there is a compelling need to re-align resources and to ensure that scarce funds are used to best effect."[144]

In the United States, as the numbers of Presbyterians, Lutherans, and Southern Baptists fall, Protestants now constitute a minority for the first time in America's history,[145] and in recent years there have been no Protestants among the justices of the Supreme Court. Furthermore, over 50 million Americans, including an increasing percentage of young adults, declare themselves to be of "no particular religion,"[146] while Catholic church attendance in the United States has been in decline since the 1950s. Even in Catholic Boston only about one in eight attend mass,[147] and the Catholic faith has waned among Hispanic Americans also, with many tens of thousands said to have converted to Islam.[148] In contrast, on Easter Sunday in 2014, about 80,000 people attended the "biggest marijuana rally in history" in Denver, with a "thick fog of cannabis fumes" rising over its civic center.[149]

Elsewhere in the Catholic world, there have been sharp falls in attendance at mass in Ireland also,[150] where two-thirds voted for repeal of the constitutional ban on abortion in a referendum in May 2018, and where gay marriage has been legal since 2015; a reduction by almost one-half in donations to the Church in Italy between 2014 and 2017;[151] and a similar drop in the number of Catholic pilgrims to Fatima and Lourdes.[152] There has also been a continuous decline in vocations and ordinations. Reduced to two monks—the rules of their order stipulated the need for three—the Augustan monastery at Gela in Sicily, founded in 1438, closed its doors;[153] the Ursuline Sisters, their numbers fallen, sold their conventicle on Long Island;[154] and in England and Wales, only two dozen novices—compared with over 150 in 1985—entered training for the priesthood in 2016,[155] and the ordination of married men began to be considered by the Church.[156] The Church of England has gone much further; in December 2017, a woman was appointed the 133rd Bishop of London.[157] Such an event was anticipated in the early sixteenth century by Erasmus, but only as satire. "If you do not mend your manners," an abbot is warned, "learned Women may come to take Possession of your Pulpits and your Mitres,"[158] and so it has come to pass.

Above all, the Catholic Church has been riven by internal conflicts on contraception, divorce, abortion, and gay unions, from the last of which Islam recoils. It has also been shamed by the extent of sexual abuse committed by its priests in Australia,[159] Chile,[160] Germany,[161] the Netherlands,[162] Poland,[163] the United States, and elsewhere. In 2011 and 2012 alone, some four hundred were defrocked by Pope Benedict XVI for pedophilia,[164] and eight hundred expelled between 2004 and 2013.[165] In 2017, the archdiocese of Los Angeles made a $660 million settlement with over five hundred victims;[166] the archdiocese of New York was forced in 2017 to seek a $100 million mortgage on its Manhattan property in order to fund compensation for those sexually abused by its priests;[167] "more than one thousand children"—"and possibly many more"—were found by a grand jury to have been sexually molested by more than three hundred "predator priests" in six Pennsylvania dioceses "over a period of decades,"[168] with complaints covered up to "avoid scandal,"[169] information concealed, and the priests transferred out of sight; and the diocese of Montreal banned its clergy from being alone with children in order to "preserve the integrity, security and good reputation of God's people."[170]

In December 2014, the Church had been warned by Pope Francis in an address to the Curia that its "moral edifice" could fall "like a house of cards" from the multitude of its ills; among them he included "spiritual Alzheimer's," "narcissism," and the "pathology of power."[171] But after condemning in May 2018 a "culture of abuse and cover-up" in the Church,[172] he was himself accused by a senior prelate of having not only known about the sexual abuses committed by a former US cardinal but also to have "repealed the sanctions" imposed on him by the previous pope,[173] accusations described as "blasphemous" by a Canadian cardinal,[174] and attributed by Pope Francis to the devil.[175] Likewise, there are thousands of case files dating back to the 1950s of sexual abuse in the Church of England,[176] with "collusion and cover-up" again found to be rife,[177] while the Episcopal church in the United States has acknowledged similar abuse by its clergy.[178]

The discovery that "the Holinesse of the Professors of Religion is decayed and full of Scandal" is again nothing new.[179] But Christian failures in free societies have come at a time of wider moral impoverishment at liberty's hands. This was true of the 1930s too, when Robert Musil wrote that "the Church no longer stands a chance against the moral ruin of the present age."[180] Moreover, the betrayal of Hebraism's ethics of justice—and of the laws of war—in defense of Israel's threatened existence has given its own hostages to fortune in times when fierce counter-emotions, some of them pre-fascist, are astir both on the anti-Semitic "right" and the anti-Semitic "left."

With "progressivism" espousing the cause of the embattled Palestinians, the Western "left" thus held its tongue as "the Jews" were declared by a Palestinian preacher to be the "enemies of all the nations,"[181] when Fidel Castro attributed the creation of IS to Israel's Mossad,[182] and when the "Arab Spring" was described as the "work of Zionism" by a prime minister of Algeria.[183] A "progressive" silence also reigned at the call by an Iranian military chief of staff for the "full annihilation of Israel,"[184] at the description of it as an "insult to all humanity"[185] and as a "rabid dog,"[186] and at the judgment by a Malaysian "religious scholar" that "Hitler may have been right."[187] There was a "progressive" silence, too, including from the United Nations, when Iran test-fired two ballistic missiles in March 2016 with the words "Israel must be wiped out" branded upon them;[188] when an adviser to the Iranian Revolutionary Guards' Al-Quds Force declared that "with the equipment at our disposal we will raze the Zionist regime in less than eight minutes";[189] and when Ayatollah Khamenei in February 2017 described the creation of Israel as "one of the dirty chapters of history that will be closed, with the grace of God."[190]

In the silence which greets this type of declaration Islam is more able to make its way, its fundamentalism generally unremarked even by the freest of supposed freethinkers. At the same time, amid the free society's confusions, combat with Islam is offered in faraway theaters of conflict—with advance today and retreat tomorrow—while compromise bows to its claims at home. But both tolerance and intolerance can be made to serve Islam's advancing cause: tolerance grants Islam a growing range of rights, while intolerance justifies Islam's claims that it suffers wrong. Indeed, the more violent the stances of Reaction in Western democracies, the greater the justification for jihadi reprisal. "You could take out their holy sites," suggested an American legislator in July 2005;[191] or "America, acting alone and with overwhelming force, must destroy the Iranian Islamic state now. Iran must go," a follower of Ayn Rand declared in 2006[192] in the manner later adopted by President Trump.

Historic parallels with the free society's dilemmas in face of today's Islamic revival can be found in pagan Rome's responses to early Christianity's rising strengths. In search of compromise with it but in hope of quelling the Christian advance, the emperor Galerius in 309 CE permitted Christians, in Gibbon's words, to "profess their private opinions" and to "assemble in their conventicles"—churches once, mosques now—provided that they showed "due respect to the established laws and government"[193] of Rome. It is a demand which today's libertarian opposes, and which the frightened democrat hesitates to make.

There is even more to be learned from the criticisms by Demosthenes in the fourth century BCE of the Athenians' wishful thinking, as Philip II of Macedon and his armies moved forward against them, referred to in an earlier chapter. They had been too slow, he declared, and now found themselves "besieged" by "democracy's irreconcilable foe."[194] Out of a refusal to believe that the Macedonian meant them harm, "you show yourselves ready to be deceived" and "are anxious only to be pleasing," Demosthenes told them. "Only here is it permitted to speak with impunity in favor of a foe," he added. But he did not know the modern free society's even greater propensity to self-harm. Moreover, Demosthenes understood something that we do not: "the larger the sphere of influence we leave to him"—Philip II of Macedon—"the greater will be his hostility to us."[195]

Time and again, Demosthenes appealed to the Athenians to rouse themselves, objecting that their "indifference," "negligence," and "inertia" outweighed their "concern for the future."[196] "You are always lagging behind events," he protested, "and when you arrive on the scene, late, you halt."[197] "We are like those who have taken mandrake or some other narcotic,"[198] he observed, speaking to our times as well as to his own.

But the free society's confusions at Islam's revival run deeper. Some (or many) are inhibited by their own benevolence, both real and imagined, from acting upon the fears of Islam that they repress. Others, no longer fully social beings, are too lost in their private electronic limbos to be aroused at all. At the same time, as earlier mentioned, many "progressives" harbor a desire to see their own societies brought down for the harms they have committed in the past, or continue to commit now. With racist Reaction also occupying part of the democratic ground, there can be no commonality of purpose— on this or other matters—without a shared ethic to defend or to promote: mere belief in "freedom" cannot provide it. The warnings of Demosthenes proved in vain, too, and Athens fell.

In exchanges early in 2013 with John Kerry, the US secretary of state, I told him that "the combination of fear of giving offence to Islam, ignorance of it, belligerence against it and feeble compromise with it" was "the worst of all combinations."[199] I also recommended that his aides should "look at the Qur'an";[200] if they did not, "the history of our age may one day be written under a Caliphate's supervision."[201] "I agree with a great deal of what you've said," Kerry replied.[202] To Hobbes—for whom the "businesse of a Commonwealth" included the defense of the people "against forraign Invasion"—the "fit counsellour" of government needed, and still needs, "more than ordinary study" to be worthy of his position.[203]

Instead, it is an irony of history that today the United States, including at the highest levels of government of whatever political persuasion, appears to have as little understanding of its Islamic opponents as Britain had during its losing eighteenth-century struggle with the American colonial rebellion. "What woeful variety of schemes have been adopted," Edmund Burke declared in 1774 of British policy, "what enforcing and what repealing; what bullying and what submitting; what doing and undoing; what troops sent out to quell resistance, and on meeting that resistance, recalled; what shiftings and changings and jumblings of all kinds of men at home."[204] Britain was also burdened by a radical Trojan Horse which supported the cause of American independence, while today's "progressives" sympathize with those fighting "neo-colonialism" in the Middle East and elsewhere.[205]

Moreover, just as the free-marketeer and the moral free-chooser cannot understand a faith-driven adversary who has a copy of the Qur'an in hand—"we can only destroy IS when we destroy the attractiveness of its brand," declared US general John Allen, in market-speak, in December 2014[206]—so most of the British establishment did not understand the moral zeal and ambition of the settlers in the New World, and were defeated. But at least Burke was aware that much of the strength of the colonists derived from their refusal to make "submissions of the mind"[207] to the British. Puritan Islam, with its contempt for the free society's "entire doctrinal and moral system,"[208] similarly refuses such submission to the weakened non-Muslim world today.

Indeed, a Western democracy is now little more than the sum of its disjoined parts. It is less a civil society than a political space in which the lost individual must make his or her own way, step-by-step proceeding deeper into a private desert. With faith reduced (for many) to belief in the sanctity of choice and right, and with little held to be of intrinsic worth unless a price can be put upon it, the Judeo-Christian inheritance has been squandered. The worshippers who once gathered at its altars have been largely displaced by false fraternities of free-choosers. Yet these are times when a public ethic, the ethic of a commonwealth, has never been more needed.

Despite this, and in the name of protecting the United States from a religion of state, libertarian and atheist plaintiffs—their cases variously upheld and rejected by American courts[209]—have sought to forbid the taking by young people at their school assemblies of the Pledge of Allegiance to their country on the grounds that it is "unconstitutional." In the pledge, America is denoted "one nation under God," a minimal statement of common belonging; instead, an Atlanta charter school decided in August 2018 to cease reciting it "in an effort to begin our day as a fully inclusive and connected community,"[210] the intended sense of the pledge itself.

Objection to it has rested upon the Constitution's First Amendment, which stipulates only that "Congress shall make no law respecting an establishment of religion": the United States, therefore, is not in terms a "Christian nation"; it possesses no religion of state, and public authority cannot impose a particular faith upon the people. But excessive libertarian scruple, turning puritan zeal on its head, seeks to prohibit—in liberty's name—not only the "endorsement of monotheism"[211] but all publicly sanctioned reference to "God." To do so flies in the face of the very beliefs that inspired America's founders. Most of them were deists who rejected revealed religion, yet acknowledged the existence of God. Indeed, the Declaration of Independence claims for Americans the "separate and equal station to which the laws of Nature and of Nature's God entitle them," while George Washington in his Farewell Address of 1796 wrote that, without "religious principle," "national morality" could not be expected to "prevail."[212]

Nevertheless, recoil in today's United States from a publicly stated ethic—other than that of belief in market- and moral-choice—now runs deep. This is despite the fact, again, that George Washington called for America's first Thanksgiving Day in November 1789 to be dedicated not to the anti-principles of an Ayn Rand but to the "service" of "that great and glorious Being who is the beneficent author of all that is, that was, or that will be."[213] Washington also called on "the people" to "unite in rendering unto Him our sincere and humble thanks for his kind care and protection of the people of this country previous to their becoming a nation."[214] But even "nation" is a term from which many of today's "progressives" recoil.

John Adams, America's president from 1796 to 1800, went further. During a hard period of conflict for the nascent United States, he declared (in Philadelphia in March 1798) that the "safety and prosperity of nations"—again that word so feared today—"ultimately depend on the protection and blessing of Almighty God." Invoking the "Father of Mercies," he also urged upon his fellow Americans the "duty of imploring the benediction of heaven,"[215] a public statement of faith that most of today's libertarians would disallow. Calling for "a day of solemn humiliation, fasting and prayer" on April 25, 1799, Adams similarly recommended that "citizens"—a term largely displaced by "consumers"—"devote the time to the sacred duties of religion in public and in private."[216] But the language of "duties" is overshadowed now by the language of "rights."

Moreover, in March 1805 even the freethinking Thomas Jefferson in his inaugural address invoked the "Being" to whom Washington had appealed. Jefferson described this "Being" as having led America's first settlers to the New World; and "as Israel of old"—a comparison that cannot be made today for the odium Israel's name arouses in many—"planted them in a country flowing with all the necessities and comforts of life."[217] James Madison, president in 1808 and 1812, likewise lauded the "Almighty Hand" which had been "so frequently and signally extended to our relief in the critical stages of the revolution" against British rule. He also called it a "transcendental law" that the "safety and happiness of society"—in his day seen as more than the sum of its fragmented parts—should be "the objects at which all political institutions aim."[218]

Handicapped by the lack of knowledge of America's past, those who today object to such conceptions can detect the denial of "liberty"—and even "discrimination" against atheists—in mere formality's mention of "God," as indicated earlier. Violations of the American Constitution and the wrongful "establishment of religion" can therefore be found in a school prayer, a prayer before a town meeting, or a Christian blessing at a presidential inauguration, even as the revived faith of Islam advances in the world. Misapplied rule and further misjudgment can turn a Gospel citation by public authority, the display of the Decalogue's text, a war memorial cross on public land, or a Bible club on campus into breaches of the First Amendment. By implication it holds them to be offenses against the common good. A prime minister's description of Britain as a "Christian country"[219] was similarly condemned by fifty-five public figures, a prominent Muslim among them, as "fostering alienation and division."[220]

Equally, many lay civic principles, whether ethical, social, or jurisprudential—the principle of duty among them—receive treatment as rough as that meted out in the United States to the most modest echoes of its founders' deist beliefs. This is despite the fact that such principles could have served to keep the democratic free society's dissolution at bay. Some have been undermined by the Spirit of Demolition and others have fallen under varieties of taboo, with fundamental truths dismissed to "left" and "right" as bigotry, pronounced oppressive, or rejected as "socialistic."

At the same time, incoherent deference is paid to stronger moralities than the free society's own. On the one hand, objection is made by atheists to mention of God in the Pledge of Allegiance; on the other, publicly funded Muslim charter schools and community colleges in the United States teach Islam's credo to their students, while "Trojan Horse" schools in Britain have imposed it upon Muslim and non-Muslim pupils alike. In fear of being thought discriminatory, the United States also sets aside time and place for Muslim prayer in government institutions—in a Texas high school, too[221]—and has in general turned a deaf ear to the preaching of jihad from mosque pulpits in its towns and cities, while libertarians who seek "freedom from religion" shrink from the words "In God We Trust" on the nation's dollar bills and coins.

The deist Founding Fathers of the United States were wiser. George Washington was wiser than Rand's John Galt, while Mohammed could turn out to have been wiser than Milton Friedman.

CHAPTER 12

THE TRUE COMMONWEALTH

Personal well-being is dependent in large part upon the maintenance of a coherent civic and moral order, but rights-bearing isolates in free societies are not real citizens at all. Moreover, their entitlements are often without substance, or cannot be exercised for lack of the resources to do so. Democratic politics is also increasingly helpless in face of the free society's confusions, with the social and other costs of free moral and market choices a growing one. Indeed, in today's liberal democracies, the very sense that there is a social order has largely evaporated, citizenship is no longer a badge of belonging, and too many public institutions have been dispersed into private hands.

Despite this, the supremacy of a libertarian ethic of individual entitlement and of dutiless right is little challenged, and the "free play of market forces" rides roughshod equally over community and nation. At the same time, even modest notions of social justice raise fears, in some, of "socialism" or even of "Marxism." Others regard it as offensive to the spirit of liberty to insist that a democracy cannot survive without the fulfillment of obligations to it. But if duties without rights make the individual a slave, rights without duties make us strangers to one another and the commonwealth dissolves.

Alexis de Tocqueville was perceptive: the "individualism" of a democratic society, he wrote of America, "at first only saps the virtues of public life. But in the long run it attacks and destroys all others."[1] Such moral and economic "individualism" has ultimately brought with it lost sense of place, community and belonging, as well as dismissiveness and unawareness of the lessons of the past. Meanwhile, the Demiurge plunders and wastes the earth's resources, the proto-fascist stirs, and the Spirit of Demolition—a notionally free spirit—hovers over the moral principles and human ties that bind us. It is a spirit capable of describing the very idea of "personal responsibility" as "dubious."[2]

America's settlers were wiser, hoping for "security beyond the law and above the law" through the performance of "all the duties" which members of a community "owe to each other and to society."[3] For these were times before a US Supreme Court Justice, no less, could hold that "you don't have the duty to rescue someone in danger. The blind man is walking in front of a car and you don't have a duty to stop him, absent some relation between you."[4] Common membership of civil society was by implication insufficient.

Nor can there be a true commonwealth where the degree of inequality is so great, as in today's free societies, that "the Rich cannot long or safely continue such" in the words of the seventeenth-century English jurist Matthew Hale;[5] where the healthcare of a people, as in the United States, is met by half measures in the name of "small government"; and where tradition and inheritance are sought to be canceled, as in the attempt in 2017 by Harvard's "Presidential Task Force on Inclusion and Belonging" to erase reference to the university's Puritan past.[6] Nor can there be a true commonwealth where "honesty" is seen merely as a means to "make you happier,"[7] a winning lottery ticket purchased in the now-misnamed Commonwealth of Massachusetts brings in over $750 million,[8] and the vulgar opulence of a Trump Tower mocks America's Founding Fathers.

Today's "liberty" is also not the freedom fought for in the French and American revolutions. Rather, it is the liberty of "customers" promised "more of their own money," of the moral free-chooser for whom self-realization is the highest good, and of those for whom the slogan "live and let live" is the sum of their ethics. The awareness that liberty is a civic and social construct has been displaced by the belief that it is a birthright for which nothing is owed. Indeed, the very understanding that we live in a shared commonwealth, however disordered, has (for many) receded over the horizon. This absent sense has left the free society on its knees, but to no god or redeeming secular faith. Again, the moral principles by which to live are not to be found in the nexus between supply and demand, producer and consumer, and buyer and seller. Even the elementary notion—a commonplace in all times except these—that there can be no liberty without order is seen as a threat to freedom. To some, attempts by sanction to prevent liberty's worst abuses appear more perilous than the abuses themselves, while the abuse of liberty is held by many to be a mark of liberty itself.

Our false certitudes are of a long-standing kind. By the first century BCE, Polybius had already challenged artless assumptions about what a democracy is, asserting that "one ought not to call a "democracy" a system in which the mass of the people merely has the power to do all that it wants and has in mind to do";[9] and two and a half thousand years ago Aristotle thought that the "freedom to do as one likes" ignored the "element of badness that exists in all of us."[10] "Who is ever free?" the Roman poet Horace also inquired.[11] It is a question more searching than modern libertarians are accustomed to ask.

Today, despite the steady dissolution of the social order, "free choice" is exercised with increasing sense of right, conduct often more fitting to a pre-social state of nature. Moreover, the principles of the true commonwealth—or "civill communitie" resting upon "affections truly bent upon the common good," as America's first settlers expressed it[12]—are not to be found in a Milton Friedman's dismissiveness of the "so-called general interest,"[13] nor in the refusal by a John Galt to "sacrifice" his "intellectual integrity" to "the greatest good of the greatest number."[14] Long-lost, too, is the judgment of the "free market's" philosopher of philosophers, Adam Smith himself, that government by a "company of merchants" is "perhaps the worst of all governments for any country whatever."[15]

Forgotten also is that George Washington in January 1795 called upon "all Americans" to "beseech the Great Ruler of Nations"—again the deist's God—to "preserve us from the arrogance of prosperity."[16] It is a call no president of the United States could or would make now.

Indeed, the sense of the old American "commonwealth" has been so largely eclipsed by market forces that an "innovation adviser" to Hillary Clinton when she was secretary of state could proclaim that only "the most open societies"—defined by him as those in which "religious and cultural norms" were "not set by central authorities"— would see "trillions of dollars of wealth-creation" in future.[17] For "norms" of such kind are perceived by market-thought as obstacles to "progress."

Nor again can there be a true commonwealth where concealed guns are carried, or where the human face is covered from sight; where millions, as in Britain, are said to suffer "alarming levels of loneliness" and to have "no close friends";[18] and where "social media" have displaced other forms of human interaction. Nor, on a larger scale, can there be a true commonwealth where a nation's sovereignty has been surrendered to unaccountable extraterritorial powers. But today the very concept of nation, deformed by past and present nationalists, is held by many to be redundant as a source of identity and recidivist as a place of belonging, while its defense, described in other times as "saving the vineyard of the commonwealth" from the "wild boar,"[19] is considered to be Reaction's cause alone. At the same time, "globalism"—at the Demiurge's command—makes a false virtue of a transnational or supranational "citizenship of the world." But such "citizenship" is a contradiction in terms.

Moreover, despite the fact that a majority of Americans lamented in a 2017 poll that the US was "losing its identity,"[20] the celebration of "diversity" gains ground even as the civic bond weakens. "There is no core identity, no mainstream in Canada," its prime minister can therefore proclaim as if with pride, calling his country the "first postnational state."[21] "National borders are becoming irrelevant," similarly declared a leading figure in the Trotskyized British Labour Party,[22] while an Italian president, in the wake of Britain's decision to leave the European Union, described attempts to "recover national sovereignty" as both "myopic and presumptuous."[23] But to refuse subordination to extraterritorial legislative and legal powers—most derived from political cultures different from, and often at odds with, Britain's own—was neither myopic nor presumptuous, whatever other view be taken of the decision.

In the politics of a Donald Trump on the issue of "the nation," there has been a combination of Reason and Reaction. It has been rational to argue that "there is no such thing as a global flag"[24] and "no global anthem,"[25] and also rational to hold that "a nation without borders is not a nation at all."[26] Furthermore, it is a just cause to make the protection of the "safety"[27] of the citizenry a political duty. But to put America "first,"[28] to promote the cause of "Americanism,"[29] and to seek to shelter behind tariffs and high walls in order to do so cannot overcome America's travails. For when inequalities grow and educational standards fall, when violence increases and the political class is unworthy of its charge, when "political correctness" seals the lips and taboo replaces truth, only a false commonwealth remains.

Nor can there be a true commonwealth when looters, sometimes armed, arrive at the scene of hurricanes, earthquakes, and floods in Texas, in central Italy, in northern England, or in the Caribbean;[30] when stores in Britain sell knives to teenagers as knife crimes increase;[31] when firemen, as in Sicily, start fires to earn callout income;[32] when navigation buoys off the Maine coast are stolen, putting other mariners at risk;[33] or when hoax calls to an ambulance service, their number doubling in Scotland between 2012 and 2017, "threaten people in urgent need."[34]

There is again no true commonwealth when nearly half the population has seen no police officer on patrol in twelve months, as in Britain;[35] when a heavily pregnant woman is robbed in the street at gunpoint, as in Annapolis, Maryland, after going into labor;[36] when members of the public cheer as an armed man in London escapes from the police;[37] or when a "group of teens" in Florida, "laughing the whole time," can film the dying moments of a drowning disabled man[38] and suffer no sanction under the law.[39] There is also no true commonwealth when pressures mount for those convicted of serious crimes to retain their voting rights, including while in jail;[40] when a prison inmate serving a life sentence for murder can run for a US Senate seat in Minnesota;[41] or when a Californian city pays a monthly stipend of $1,000 to those considered "at risk of committing a violent crime" if they stay out of trouble.[42] Moreover, the spirit of the true commonwealth was again absent when "access to literacy" and to a "minimally adequate education" was held by a federal judge in Michigan in June 2018 not to be a fundamental constitutional right.[43]

There can also be no true commonwealth when citizenship itself is seen as little more than a means of access to material benefit rather than a place of belonging; no true commonwealth where the noncitizen gains citizen rights to vote and even to serve on a jury; no true commonwealth where a migrant defendant charged with domestic violence can escape prosecution, as in New Hampshire, on the grounds that he "lacked the cultural competency to participate in the American justice system";[44] and no true commonwealth when Seattle's Office for Civil Rights can recommend that the word *citizen* not be used by its administrators lest it cause the noncitizen "offense,"[45] or when public authority challenges the proposal that US Census respondents be asked about their citizenship status on the ground that the question would create "fear and distrust."[46]

Nor can there be a true commonwealth when significant numbers of its nominal citizens, enclosed in their own worlds, feel themselves bound by laws not merely distinct from, but opposed to, those of the polity they have joined. For if a civil society is to cohere, we must be citizens before we are Christians, Muslims, or Jews. Instead, concession is made in freedom's name to values other than, and again often opposed to, those that previously upheld the social order, flawed as the latter might be. At the same time, there has come a degree of multicultural separatism to split such order asunder. In particular, Islam's potent ethic, as well as its own spirit of community and deep-rooted traditions, furnish the ground for an autonomous existence in the free society's moral wilderness.

Yet Islam's texts and customs, as in holding men and women—and Muslims and non-Muslims—to be unequal, deny the very principles upon which Western democracy has rested. Nevertheless, Islam's confident monoculture has gained increasing space in multicultural-ism's name, and in matters large and small. They have been relatively small, as when a German district court in Wuppertal held that "sharia police-patrols" which had told locals to stop drinking infringed no law;[47] but much larger when Muslim-run schools in Britain, as earlier mentioned, were found to be openly hostile to secularism,[48] to have narrowed the curriculum on grounds of faith to exclude the teaching of art and music,[49] and to have discriminated between Muslim and non-Muslim teachers and pupils.[50] Moreover, children "forced to follow a multicultural timetable" in the London borough of Lambeth were said to be unable to "see themselves or their lives reflected in it";[51] now unknown the warning of a Francis Bacon that the "altera-tion of Laws and Customes," especially in deference to "strangers," is among "the Causes of Seditions."[52] Today, it is one of the causes of the advance of Reaction.

The values of the true commonwealth are further lost from sight when multiculturalist scruple—too often a cover for moral cow-ardice—prefers self-deception to the facing of unwelcome truth. A determined researcher into child abuse, committed on large scale in a British city mainly by Muslim men against non-Muslim girls and children, could therefore be sent on an "ethnicity and diversity course" as she came under pressure to change her views about what she was finding.[53] In similar breach of the freedom of speech, an apostate critic of Islam and advocate of Muslim women's rights was denied an honorary degree by a leading American academic institu-tion, on the grounds that "certain" of her past statements—"we are at war with Islam itself"[54] was among them—were "inconsistent" with the university's "core values."[55]

False scruple can also be seen at work in some legal decisions in Britain. After a young Muslim desecrated a war memorial, daubing it with the words "Islam will dominate the world," the accused—who was said to have shown "no remorse"—was ordered in June 2014 to pay £500 in compensation and was conditionally discharged.[56] But in the same month, a young girl who had attached bacon to the door handle of a mosque, and thrown strips of it into the building, was sent to jail for twelve months for her "religiously aggravated attack." "It hurt my feelings," declared a Muslim witness, "it is against our culture and religion." "It does not seem to me that there is any way to deal with this case other than by custody," pronounced the Edinburgh judge.[57] However, imprisonment for an adolescent jape was also an act of deference to Islam in a non-Muslim land; the daubing of a memorial to the dead, many lost in an earlier battle with un-Reason, had a more lenient outcome. Nor does such false scruple diminish; in December 2017, a Florida man who similarly left bacon at a mosque front door and smashed its windows was jailed for fifteen years.[58]

Meanwhile, numbers of Muslim citizens of the free society leave to join the jihad against the non-Muslim world to which they notionally belong. In doing so, they challenge the spirit of the true commonwealth to the point of committing treason against it. At the same time, enemy combatants in Guantanamo seek to sue the government for their wrongful detention, an army cadet selling poppies in Manchester city center is attacked on Remembrance Sunday,[59] the jihadist's flag flutters over a housing estate in London,[60] and more than a quarter of British Muslims expressed "some sympathy" for the motives behind the *Charlie Hebdo* attacks in Paris.[61] But self-deception again backs away, with the Spirit of Demolition joining the fray. "If Britons want to join IS, let them!" the Spirit cries in a newspaper column, describing such decision as a "family matter" and merely the outcome of a "teenager's wayward dreams."[62]

The same Spirit of Demolition is at work when American civil libertarians describe as "ludicrous"[63] the withholding of voting rights from those who cannot prove that they are citizens; when a California governor's veto of a proposal to allow noncitizens to serve as jurors is diagnosed as a "sign of prejudice";[64] and when objection is made to the exclusion from university platforms of extremist preachers of violent jihad.[65] At the same time, necessary surveillance in the interests of public safety raises the reflex libertarian presumption that it is the work (again) of a "police state," while those who imperil the commonwealth by the disclosure of state secrets are acclaimed by some as heroes.

Nevertheless, and again in the necessary dialectic of things, such self-harm arouses—or revives—awareness in others of the need to defend the civic order. Thus, just as early settlers in New England made a "covenant" among themselves at Plymouth in November 1620 to create a "civill body politike for our better ordering and preservation" with "laws and Ordinances" for "the generall good of the Colony,"[66] the same need today creates the urge to find, if necessary by a new social contract, a truer balance between the rights and duties of those who belong to it, or who seek to belong to it, in the interests of democracy itself.

In consequence, as earlier indicated, a desire for such contract in the name of "civic integration"[67] has led public authority in Britain, Italy, the Netherlands, and Norway, among other European nations, to get commitments from migrants to learn the local language, to acknowledge the equality of men and women, to report attempts to commit terrorist acts, and to respect the religious symbols of faiths other than their own. These commitments, often wanting in the outcome or merely pretended, have been made preconditions of citizenship or residency, and of access to welfare and the other benefits which the free society provides.[68]

A belated awareness of what a true commonwealth requires, and again in attempted fulfillment of the duty of "Political Power" to "make Laws and annex such Penalties to them as may tend to the preservation of the whole" in John Locke's words,[69] has also brought legislation in a number of states in the US formally banning application of sharia principles and rules in judicial decision. In Britain, it likewise led an Old Bailey judge to reject a Muslim's claim that his religion prohibited jury service;[70] and in Italy, a local Salafist Muslim leader who declined to swear an oath on the Italian constitution before taking up citizenship, on the grounds that his beliefs were incompatible with its provisions, was repatriated.[71] The same awareness was manifest in the arrest in the

United States of a citizen for avoiding jury duty,[72] and in the requirement that Arizona students pass a test in civics—including questions on America's Founding Fathers—before they can graduate.[73]

In Britain this civic counter-force, timid and random as may be, has likewise brought the suspension of welfare payments to the jobless for failing to do enough to find work, for turning down job offers, and for missing appointments.[74] It has also seen the prosecution of taxi drivers for refusing on "religious" grounds—but in breach of elementary civic and moral obligation—to transport the blind and their guide dogs.[75] Against libertarian opposition, the same counter-force may seek (as in Germany) to restrict unemployed migrants' rights to welfare,[76] or in Britain propose to withhold tax-exempt status from so-called "faith charities" which promote "hatred and violence."[77]

Overcoming previous hesitations on a subject referred to in an earlier chapter, the civic counter-force also led the European Court of Human Rights to uphold the 2010 French ban on the wearing of a full-face veil in public places, a ban in accord with the republican heritage of France. In a momentous but again elementary verdict, the Court held that "the face" plays a "significant role in social interaction," that the "possibility of open interpersonal relationships" is an "indispensable element of community life"—or life in a true commonwealth—and that there is a "right to interact with someone by looking them in the face."[78] Equally indispensable, especially in a free society, is the right to speak openly and with knowledge on the subject of Islam, a right which has been blocked by a combination of false scruple and fear, and again to the true commonwealth's harm.

Moreover, despite the awakening of the counter-force of Reason, the evolution of Western political thought has come to a near-standstill in the academy's hands, while public discourse is increasingly dominated by the shallow columnist and swamped by the blogger and the tweeter. This combination has aided the belief in some that the era of "ideology" is over, even as Western democracies lose their way in a free-for-all of their own creating, and with the best aspects of their inheritance increasingly unknown.

This inheritance, although marred by past injustices, still has much to teach. Thus, patriotism was perceived in ancient Athens as a virtue not a vice, and greed not as a "good" but as a form of self-abasement,[79] while citizenship could be lost for serious crime and ethical default. In Athens, the very word citizen, *politès*, meant "person of the citadel," one who keeps watch over the city's safety.[80] It implied a moral duty and social role of which market-thought and the "consumer" know little or nothing today.

The "good" and "useful" citizen was also held to be a citizen sufficiently educated to take part in the life of the city[81] and to offer mature judgment in its councils;[82] the laws of Athens were required to be taught in its schools;[83] the "just" citizen was one who conformed with local custom and usage;[84] and the well-being of the polity was held to be dependent on "like-mindedness" in the citizen body.[85] But multiculturalism and its values have dictated otherwise, and disaggregation has followed.

Of all the ills that could beset the Athenian city-state, it was anarchy that was most feared. Its sixth-century BCE lawgivers would have recognized the various forms of it in our free societies, if they had returned. "When tradition is strong and when there survive habits of reverence for the gods, care for parents, respect for the aged and obedience to the law, and where in such communities majority opinion prevails, such polity can be termed a democracy," wrote Polybius.[86] His is a voice from the grave. Moreover, to today's libertarian, a would-be citizen of the world, such preconditions for democracy denote unacceptable restraints upon free agency and moral choice.

As for the Roman civic bond, it was one of "fidelity of the citizens to each other" in Edward Gibbon's words,[87] a bond which has little parallel in these times of lost identities and absence of belonging, while to declare oneself a *civis Romanus*, a Roman citizen, was a badge of pride of a kind again rare today. In addition, Rome was in possession of a truth about the "public" and the "private" which the modern world has forgotten, or never knew. For the Latin adjective *publicus* signified that which "belongs to the people," and is accessible and available to them, while the adjective *privatus* was derived from the verb *privare*, to take away or deprive. The "private" thus meant, in essence, that which had been removed from the public sphere, taken from it.

This etymology points to a profound Roman insight: that private subtractions from the public domain represent a public loss. Indeed, many of today's "privatizations" or transfers to the "private sector"—considered by the Demiurge of capital to be to the benefit of all—have withdrawn from the citizen body public properties which had been funded for decades from public resources. The Romans would also not have understood calls by market interest to "open up" the public domain to the "private sector," since by their definition the first was already open and the second by definition closed.

Now unknown, too, is that Adam Smith—the supposed avatar of the free market—himself argued that "erecting and maintaining those public institutions and those public works which may be in the highest degree advantageous to a great society" was a "duty,"[88] a notion anathema to a Milton Friedman. The latter objected, for example, to a "postal monopoly" in the state's hands—as mentioned in an earlier chapter—while Adam Smith singled out "the post office" as one of the "public institutions" which there was a "duty" to "maintain."[89] Moreover, without the provision of public goods by public authority the very sense of a civil society, and in particular one that is democratic, loses much of its meaning and substance, as earlier argued. Indeed, the common good may be said to depend in large part upon the protection of a society's common possessions, its "commonwealth" in the most literal sense. This fundamental truth America's first settlers also knew.

But, as already indicated, unawareness of the beliefs of early America is widespread. Not only is the deist faith of its Founding Fathers an unfamiliar matter today, but their qualified notions of freedom are equally unknown. Indeed, Alexander Hamilton counseled the nascent United States against a "zeal for liberty more ardent than enlightened,"[90] while James Madison was even more far-seeing. For he declared not only that "liberty may be endangered by the abuses of liberty as well as by the abuses of power," but that it was abuses of liberty which were "most to be apprehended by the United States."[91]

Moreover, to Madison, the "most wild of all projects" was that of "rending us in pieces to preserve our liberties,"[92] as some contemporary American "conservatives" would do. John Jay even thought that surrender by "the people" of "some of their natural rights," a surrender abhorrent to the unthinking libertarian, was necessary if government was to be "vested with requisite powers."[93] Likewise, it was "greater energy of government"—not individual moral autonomy or abasement to "market forces"—that to Alexander Hamilton was "essential to the welfare and prosperity of the community."[94] They were ends which could only be secured by "civil power, properly organized and exerted."

Hamilton was even opposed to the inclusion of a bill of rights in the US Constitution on the grounds that it would "afford a pretext to claim more [rights] than were granted."[95] He further held that "if individuals enter into a state of society, the law of that society must be the supreme regulator of their conduct,"[96] an almost Hobbesian proposition; or, as Hobbes himself expressed it, "to say that all the people of a commonwealth have liberty in any case whatsoever is to say that, in such case, there hath been no law made."[97] Hence, to Hamilton, the legislature's task was not merely to "command the purse" but to "prescribe the rules by which the duties"—placed first—"and rights of every citizen are to be regulated."[98]

In this there is little of our "freedom to choose," while today's Wiki-Leaking of state secrets is unlikely to have found favor with John Jay, who believed that "the most useful intelligence may be obtained if the persons possessing it can be relieved from apprehension of discovery."[99] Instead, now, a former US intelligence officer found guilty of leaking nearly three-quarters of a million classified and unclassified government and military documents, and who was sentenced to thirty-six years' imprisonment by court-martial in July 2013, received clemency from a latter-day US president, and was released in January 2017.[100] In January 2018—transgendered from male to female—she announced that she would run for the Senate,[101] and in a Democratic primary in Maryland failed to secure the nomination but gained over 32,000 votes.[102] However, the world of America's Founding Fathers was not that of today's free-choosers, anti-statists, free-marketeers, and self-interested legislators. Instead, it was the world of a nation's creators as they sought to establish the ground rules by which their new commonwealth might be governed, in the hope of its preservation. Moreover, when Hamilton referred to "all the obligations that form the bounds of society"[103]—obligations undermined today by hostility to the placing of curbs upon personal interest and individual will—he was speaking to the very ethic which America's first settlers brought with them to the New World.

Yet today's American courts, as mentioned earlier, have sought to forbid public display of a crucial part of this patrimony. To place the words of the Decalogue outside a state capitol building or a city hall, in a public park, outside a police station, in a courthouse or a courthouse precinct, has been held to be unconstitutional and an offense to civil liberty, even as civic bonds unravel, and despite the fact that a depiction of the Ten Commandments can be found on a frieze in the US Supreme Court building itself.

"Houses are built by rule, and commonwealths," wrote the seventeenth-century poet George Herbert.[104] But in a number of mistaken judgments, the Decalogue has been perceived as an instrument of religion or a "religious statement," and even to contain an "inherently sectarian message."[105] The intention of the American Constitution has further been held to be that of removing "faith" from the public square, despite the fact that such intention cannot be attributed to America's first settlers or to its founders. For them, individual preferences and choices were insufficient to compose a public morality upon which their commonwealth—or "new Jerusalem" in a Promised Land—could rest. They knew better. The New World's seventeenth-century colonists thus drew upon the Decalogue, among other ethical teachings, as a source for the right ordering of their communities. These teachings were not seen as a matter of "religion" narrowly understood. They again knew better.

Instead, the Decalogue's prescriptions[106] are an abbreviated set of socio-ethical rules of this-worldly provenance. They were derived from practical experience, and plainly had as their object that of preventing a community's disintegration from avoidable causes. It is also evident that the community, or commonwealth, to which the rules of the Decalogue were addressed was a settled one. Hence, its fourth "commandment"—more correctly translated as "statement"—is directed among others to the "stranger within thy gates." They are the gates of settled habitation.

Similarly, the tenth "commandment" or statement enjoins the members of the community not to covet a "neighbor's house." It is a further indication that these rules had a more mundane, or this-worldly, source than that of divine revelation to homeless itinerants in a trackless desert. Rather, the attribution of these rules of communal life to an ethereal hand was clearly intended—by the jurists and sages who composed them—to give the rules an extra-legal authority beyond lay challenge. Even the four statements which specifically refer to "God" have a general social and political purpose. It is that of the well-being of the community's members in this life, not the next.

The first statement of the ten, although couched in "religious" terms in prescribing that the community should have a single deity only, makes one sovereign source of legitimacy and a shared belief system prerequisites for the commonwealth's survival. The second statement forbids the service of graven images or idols, a practice implicitly held to be irrational and self-demeaning, and which therefore harms the moral condition of the community as a whole. The third statement is a warning against "taking the name of the Lord in vain." This rule is directed against the oath-breaker who has invoked "God" in a false pledge, and is plain counsel to keep one's word to fellow-members of the community as a matter of ethical principle, again in the interests of all. The first three statements thus enjoin a common value system, admonish debasement to unreason, and disapprove of pretended commitment to others.

The fourth "commandment," or statement, calls on the community to work for six days and to rest on the seventh. It is again a socio-ethical rule. A rational bound is being set upon labor, and repose urged upon all for their own good; and although the "sabbath" is described as a hallowed day, no mention is made of particular ceremony or "sectarian" rite by which it should be celebrated. For it is again less a "religious" statement, reductively understood, than a rule of measure by which the commonwealth is being instructed to work and to live.

Its impact on early nineteenth-century American life, before the Demiurge swept such bounds away, was well observed by de Tocqueville. "In the United States on the seventh day of every week," he wrote, "the trading and working life of the nation seems suspended; all noises cease; a deep tranquility succeeds the turmoil of the week."[107] Such sense of measure was dictated to the ancient Hebraic commonwealth—whose rules the American colonists brought with them—not by a deity but by Reason. Or as Roman Seneca declares of his times, too, "legislators established holidays so that people might be brought by a community precept to have their pleasures and moderate their labors, as they need to do."[108]

It again took no divine fiat from a mountaintop to commend, in the Decalogue's fifth statement, that "honor" be shown to parents. The sages who were its authors also make clear that to pay such honor is more than a private or personal obligation. It is a means by which the commonwealth might endure, or—as the text of the rule has it—so that "thy days may be long upon the land." This phrase makes evident the nature and purpose of the Decalogue as a whole: that it is a text of public ethics directed not only to a community's right government but to its very survival. Yet today's moral and legal misjudgments would hide its words from a self-harming America's view lest the libertarian be offended.

In this fifth statement, then, there is made out to be a connection between the maintenance of the familial bond and the long-term tenacity, or holding power, of civil society as a whole. It is also noteworthy that the statement refers to the honoring of parents, and not to love of them. It treats the filial relation not as a matter of sentiment but of duty, the fulfillment of which is once more for the common good. This is again not "religion," whether "sectarian" or any other. Instead, it looks to the safeguarding of the community from the normlessness which would harm it, as our free societies are being harmed and undone today.

Recoil from humankind's capacity to inflict mortal wounds upon itself, and upon its fragile social constructs, is the elemental subject of the sixth pronouncement against murder. It thus takes its place in the Decalogue alongside injunctions to espouse a common system of belief, to avoid intellectual delusion, to maintain trust in words, to find a rational balance between work and repose, and to fulfill familial obligation.

The seventh statement disapproves of adultery, and again has nothing to do with God's fiat, nor is it stated to be a "sin." For this is not a pietistic sermon, but a prudential and jurisprudential text. As with the fifth injunction to honor parents, the seventh thus makes the moral condition of the household a matter of public concern. Moreover, just as the first statement of the Decalogue commended a single deity rather than "other gods" to the community's devotion, as did America's Founding Fathers, the seventh similarly commends a single loyalty in marital relations.

The injunction of the eighth, not to steal, is also no divine command. It is directed to the dishonest depredation which, in a commonwealth, strikes at the security and well-being of all. Theft is also a breach of faith, but the faith that is broken is not faith in God. It is faith in one's fellows. In the ninth statement, a settled community's lawmakers similarly warned its members not to "bear false witness" against a "neighbor." It is a socio-ethical rule, once more, which is neither divinely inspired nor "religious." Instead, it looks to the need in a commonwealth—not in a nomads' temporary encampment—for trust, truth-telling, and public peace.

It is therefore in congruence with the purpose of the Decalogue as a whole: that of collective self-preservation. Moreover, an injunction against false witness points to circumstances in which a dispute has become a public matter, with honest testimony a prerequisite for just judgment between the parties. It is therefore again a juridical and this-worldly, not a sacral and otherworldly, concern. The tenth and last statement—in which greed, once more, is not held to be "good"—is a moral admonition against avidity for a "neighbor's" possessions, and is therefore directed to those who live in proximity to one another in the commonwealth they share. The ninth, on false witness, counsels good faith among its members; the tenth warns against too close pre-occupation with what others own. It is a just balance.

Grounded in human reason and derived from human experience, the Decalogue contains in concentrated form a social code directed to the protection of the always-precarious community from self-inflicted and self-destroying harms. They were harms the New World's settlers were right to fear. That latter-day American jurists, in forbidding the placing of the Decalogue's text in stone or on mural in the public square, should have misinterpreted it as a work not of Reason but of "religion"—and even held it, absurdly, to be an obstacle to "free thought" in the "marketplace of ideas,"[109] the view of Madam Bubble in Justice's robes—signifies the extent to which the principles of America's founders, puritan or deist, have been betrayed.

But retreat from the prescriptions of the Decalogue is easily understood. Addressing every member of the commonwealth in the second-person singular, their governing assumption is that each is co-responsible for the fate of all, and is constrained by duty to others. But where "choice" is sovereign, a "moral commandment" can be described (amorally) by Rand's John Galt as a "contradiction in terms." "The moral is the chosen not the forced," she has him declare,[110] while it is falsely asserted in the same work that the "moral premise" of America's foundation was that "man is an end in himself."[111] Milton Friedman could equally untruthfully call the United States the "first nation in history established on the principle that every person is entitled to pursue his own values,"[112] a notion alien to America's old commonwealth spirit.

The early settlers were again wiser. Liberty of "choice" did not define what freedom is, while the contingent nature of individual freedom was well understood by America's founders. License had not yet been given to what John Winthrop, the seventeenth-century governor of Massachusetts, called "natural corrupt liberties and what is good in your own eyes."[113] Instead America's colonists—who knew that "when every man exercises his natural freedom, no man is free"[114]—sought and found liberty in self-chosen compacts governed by laws and ethical principles which were directed to their collective well-being.

Or, as de Tocqueville put it, an "alliance" had been "contracted" between "politics and religion," with "many of the customs, manners and opinions that contribute most to the success of a republic" "bequeathed" by the first settlers to their descendants. "I think I see the destiny of America embodied in the first Puritan who landed on these shores," he added.[115] It was to turn out to be an over-optimistic judgment, with much of the "bequest" squandered in freedom's name, while America's first colonists would not have concurred with today's court judgments that the display of the Decalogue in public places is improper.

On the contrary, the early laws of the settlers, as in Massachusetts, were in part derived from it. Their societies were seen as resting upon a "covenant" with God. Massachusetts' first selectmen and judges consulted Old Testament laws good and bad, while the Decalogue, together with the alphabet and the Lord's Prayer, was included in elementary-school primers. Remote from today's insistence on the absolute separation of church and state, the Massachusetts Constitution also invested its legislature with the right to "require" the towns of the Commonwealth to "make suitable provision for the public worship of God,"[116] and even "required" "every corporate town and other public body politic to be constantly provided with a public Protestant teacher of piety, religion and morality," with fines stipulated for the "delinquency" of failing to do so.[117] Today's libertarians, whether of "left" or "right," and whether moral free-choosers or market free-loaders, would again have none of it.

For "our right to live as we see fit"[118] had not yet taken hold as the defining quality of freedom itself. Instead, the settlers' liberties derived from their duties; loyalty was pledged by inhabitants to their township for their own well-being; obligation was expected of its members and of those who sought to join it; and its material goods and moral principles were equally carefully guarded, while those in need were supported from communal resources. It was a politics of the kind which will have to be rediscovered if the free society is to survive.

For the townships of New England belonged to active and participant citizen-populations. Each town's inhabitants were declared by the laws of Massachusetts to constitute "a body politic and corporate,"[119] "formed by a social compact,"[120] and "empowered" to make rules "for the common good."[121] With the "township system" described by de Tocqueville as "deeply rooted in the habits of the English,"[122] he saw that "the doctrine of the sovereignty of the people came out of the townships" where "the people" were the "source of power," a principle which was the "law of laws."[123]

Today, as popular sovereignty in the free society wanes in the face of unelected and unaccountable forces, and with wide areas of social and ethical concern beyond public reach and sanction, it is democracy itself which is at stake. The early American settlers were again wiser, having brought with them to New England what de Tocqueville called the "best elements of order and morality,"[124] two words from which today's libertarian again recoils. Instead, in seventeenth-century Watertown, Massachusetts, and in other democratic townships, no one could settle without the express permission of its freemen;[125] here there were no grants of civic rights to incomers living an autonomous life within their own social and ethical enclaves. Similarly in Marlborough and in Sudbury, Massachusetts, grants of land were confined to those who lived in the town, served the community, and paid its taxes.[126]

With each township seeking an orderly life for its inhabitants' well-being—as had the authors of the Decalogue—personal misconduct was held to be a public matter. For the Athenians, too, "having an eye to the virtue and vice of the citizens," in Aristotle's words,[127] was held essential to the existence of the social order. Or as Hobbes expressed it, "the skill of making and maintaining commonwealths consisteth in certain rules."[128] They are rules from which today's moral free-chooser again retreats, even as modern community life is undone by their absence and the free society founders, its democracy with it.

Some of the townships' rules of "order and morality" were petty or too severe, others well-judged. But each had the "general welfare," a term derided by Milton Friedman,[129] as its object. They included the sanction in Marlborough of forfeiture of "all interest" in the township for those who failed to "perfect their house-lot,"[130] and in Watertown of the "return to the Town" of land neglected by the owner;[131] the power throughout Massachusetts to prosecute for "Injuries to Public Buildings";[132] and the duty of constables to report those who "profanely curse or swear in their hearing." This was said to be "inconsistent with the dignity and rational cultivation of the human mind" and to "loosen the bonds of civil society."[133] Likewise, the "names of all persons reputed to be common drunkards misspending their time and estate" might be "posted up"[134] in the township and their fellow citizens prohibited from supplying them with liquor, as de Tocqueville noted.[135] They even ran the risk of disenfranchisement.[136]

The distant echoes of this ethic can still be heard in today's United States, despite the scorn it arouses in the free-booter. Thus in Aurora, Illinois, its councilors in August 2015 approved the keeping of a list of "habitual drunkards" who would be prevented from purchasing liquor in the city in the interests of "public safety,"[137] and in June 2012 a town meeting in Middleborough, Massachusetts, voted by a large majority to impose a fine for swearing in public.[138] Equally resonant, an Ohio court in April 2014 ordered a man convicted of harassing a neighbor, including with a racist slur, to stand on a street corner in South Euclid carrying the sign "I am a bully";[139] and in Liberty Township, again in Ohio, a defendant was similarly offered the option in March 2016 of either wearing a sign saying "I am a thief" for ten days outside a store from which he had stolen or thirty days in jail. He chose the former.[140]

To the early settlers of America, the harms, large or small, caused by such type of misconduct were seen as threats to the civil society they were seeking to create, and their prevention an expression of that "sovereignty of the people" which de Tocqueville found in the microcosm of the early township. This sovereignty, a democratic sovereignty, expressed itself more largely in the township's careful regulation of land use, in the taxes imposed on its members for the common good, and in the help given to the township's needy. For the time had not yet arrived in which welfare provision would be seen as "taking money from our pockets that we could use to buy goods and services to meet our separate needs,"[141] while the proposition that in education "the parent and the child are the consumers, the teacher and the school administrator the producers"[142] had not yet been uttered.

Instead, in the early American commonwealths, as in Athens, education was held to be a "public responsibility not a private affair," in Aristotle's words.[143] The Massachusetts legislature therefore imposed on each township not merely the "duty" of providing schooling,[144] but the formal obligation to "impress upon the minds of children and youth" the "virtues which are the ornament of human society and the basis upon which the republican constitution is structured."[145] They were virtues which included "justice," "benevolence," "moderation," and the "love of country." For public interest had not yet been held synonymous with the free pursuit of private ends, while the freedom to "take our own risks and to bear our own losses, to earn our profits and to make our own fortunes," in the words once more of Rand's John Galt,[146] had not yet been identified with liberty itself. Or, as de Tocqueville wrote of the first settlers in the New World, "they did not cross the Atlantic to improve their wealth. Their object was the triumph of an idea."[147]

Their notion of what a true civil society is had not yet been assailed by the bracing disciplines of the "private sector." An ever-wider "market" in public properties, services, and institutions had not yet become a measure of "progress," and the aspirations of America's first colonists to create a true commonwealth had not yet been undermined by modern libertarians. "The civilization of New England has been like a beacon upon a hill," wrote de Tocqueville in 1835,[148] whereas the mountain refuge of Rand's corporate moguls in *Atlas Shrugged* was crowned by "a dollar sign made of solid gold" which "hung in space above the town as its coat-of-arms."[149]

Today, in suicidal Western democracies feebly led, market interests and claims of individual right have gained mastery over them, while neither socialist nor libertarian prescriptions can deal with the civic order's disintegration. For a free society, equitable and just, to survive at all, its citizens old and new must fulfill their obligations to the would-be commonwealths to which they belong if extreme Reaction, and even civil war, are to be held at bay.

Meanwhile, the number of optimists about our condition is shrinking, and the sense that "darkness" threatens to "cover the earth"[150] is growing. In today's free societies, most do not feel that they are living in a "summer dawn of time," as Charles Dickens described the perspective (of some) in 1850.[151] For if hope springs eternal, despair is a constant too; the sense that the world is going to the devil is an old one. "Every vice has reached its climax. There will be nothing more that posterity can add to our ways," thought the Roman poet Juvenal of his own times,[152] and even in the mid-fifth century BCE complaint could be heard that "men no longer compete with one another to serve the common good."[153] But the ancient belief that there is "a cycle in human affairs" which "in its turning does not allow any people to find permanent good fortune,"[154] and that "in every polity there is a natural growth, a crowning moment, and then a decline,"[155] was tempered by the efforts of Greek and Roman thinkers to find curatives for the harms from which their societies, like ours, suffered.

"Though nothing can be immortal which mortals make," wrote Hobbes in similar vein, "their commonwealths might be secured from perishing by internal diseases."[156] But Athens, Hebraic Jerusalem, and Rome, weakened within and assaulted from without, all fell. We have not yet come to terms with the possibility or prospect of the free society's own fall, as its internal disorders mount and external pressures increase. "Where are you headed, Europe?" Poland's prime minister demanded to know, after a terrorist attack in Manchester in May 2017. "Rise from your knees," she declared, "or you will be crying for your children every day."[157] The distress of it was again an historic one, often expressed in such fashion. "Can this be England, can this be my country, that country which has hitherto been eminent above all others for the blessings of social order?" Harriet Martineau similarly asked, after witnessing riots in the streets of the same Manchester in 1826.[158]

Today, as the modern democratic social order dissolves, it is clear that liberty alone, however "progressive" it may be held to be, will not restore it, for "we have turned, every one, to his own way."[159] Old socialism—"What is socialism?" "I do not know"—is also spent as a counter-force, while the Demiurge of capital, leading Madam Bubble by the hand, is not subject to the dictates of Reason. Moreover, "in the Youth of a State, Armes do flourish; in the Middle Age of a State, Learning; in the Declining Age of a State . . . Merchandize," as the prescient Francis Bacon warned.[160]

Gibbon, writing of another decline and fall, believed that the "sense of misfortune," our sense now, could be "diverted by the labour of thought."[161] But we do not need diversion, and mere thought is not enough. For without the practical renewal of the politics and ethics of the civic commonwealth, resting upon a social contract of reciprocal rights and duties, supported by sanction and upheld by a political class that can hear the bell tolling, our "rending in pieces," in Madison's words, will continue to its bitter end.

NOTES

CHAPTER 1: AS OTHER POWERS ADVANCE

1. UN Dept. of Economic and Social Affairs, Population Division, 2017 Revision, New York, June 21, 2017.

2. Federal Aviation Administration, Hartsfield-Jackson Atlanta International Airport, February 21, 2018.

3. *Financial Times*, February 24, 2017.

4. Traffic Volume Trends, Federal Highway Administration, US Dept. of Transport, qu. A.P., February 22, 2016.

5. UN Department of Economic and Social Affairs, qu. A.P., December 19, 2017.

6. A. Tajani, president of the European Parliament, qu. *Il Messaggero*, July 7, 2017.

7. *Essayes or Counsels, Civill and Morall*, London, 1639, no. 58, p. 337.

8. e.g., S. Baker, *Guardian*, October 2008; S. Kriss, Vice News, April 7, 10, 2017; opendemocracy.net, June 24, 2017.

9. *The End of History and The Last Man*, London, 1992.

10. *Democracy in America* (1835), London, 1998, p. 7.

11. *The History of the Decline and Fall of the Roman Empire* (1776–1789), 8 vols., London, 1908, vol. 1, p. 177.

12. *De Tranquillitate Animi (On Peace of Mind)*, 11:9.

13. op. cit., vol. 4, p. 406.

14. A. Bloom, *The Closing of the American Mind*, NY and London, 1988, p. 382.

15. State of the Union Address, qu. *New York Times*, January 31, 2018.

16. US Department. of State, qu. A.P., January 19, 2017.

17. M. Pompeo, qu. A.P., May 2, 2018.

18. D. Trump, at Nashville, Tenn., qu. Reuters, May 30, 2018.

19. E.P. Nieto@EPN, May 30, 2018.

20. qu. A.P., September 25, 2018.

21. *New York Times*, January 12, 2016.

22. US 173rd Airborne Brigade report, qu. *Times*, September 4, 2017.

23. A.P., September 27, 2018.

24. spacedaily.com, June 20, 2018; Reuters, August 9, 2018.

25. Senator J. McCain and Rep. M. Thornberry, qu. Government Executive, Defense, February 8, 2018.

26. V. Putin, Address to Federal Assembly, Moscow, qu. Reuters, March 1, 2018.

27. A.P., December 6, 2016.

28. Major-General A. Batschelet, US Army Recruitment Command, qu. *Wall Street Journal*, June 27, 2014.

29. Lewin Group, Qualified Military Available (QMA), Final Technical Report, October 10, 2013.

30. Maj. Gen. D. Laich, Army Times, July 27, 2018.

31. A.P., September 21, 2018.

32. D. Laich, loc. cit.

33. qu. *New York Times*, May 2, 2011.

34. S. Rice, qu. A.P., June 29, 2013.

35. N. Wolf, *Guardian*, August 24, 2007.

36. *Oeuvres*, Paris, 1913–23, vol. 5, p. 539.

37. qu. Huffington Post, January 13, 2016.

38. *Telegraph*, April 14, 2018.

39. J. Lewis, chair, House of Commons Defence Select Committee, qu. *Guardian*, November 21, 2016.

40. Gen. Sir R. Barrons, to Defence Select Committee, qu. *Guardian*, November 14, 2017.

41. Gen. Lord Houghton of Richmond, qu. *Times*, June 26, 2018.

42. National Audit Office, qu. *Guardian*, April 18, 2018.

43. Herodotus, *Histories*, bk. 1:207,2.

44. *Times*, May 5, 2018; A.P., June 28, 2018; A.P., July 15, 2018; and Y. D. S. Poblete, US Asst. Sec. of State for Arms Control, Verification and Compliance, qu. Reuters, August 14, 2018.

45. H. R. McMaster, former US National Security Adviser, qu. *Washington Post*, April 4, 2018.

46. A.P., August 20, 2018; also A.P., April 12, 2017.

47. S. Lavrov, United Nations General Assembly, qu. A.P., September 29, 2018.

48. R.T. Erdogan, qu. Reuters, October 31, 2018.

49. R.T. Erdogan, qu. *Sunday Times*, July 16, 2017.

50. qu. A.P., August 11, 2018.

51. R.T. Erdogan, in Trabzon, qu. *Times*, August 13, 2018.

52. R.T. Erdogan, at Sarajevo, qu. aljazeera.com, May 20, 2018.

53. Letter from the President to the Speaker of the House of Representatives and the President of the Senate, www.whitehouse.gov, August 6, 2018.

54. cf. *Times*, July 2, 2018.

55. M. Fitzpatrick, "Iran and North Korea: The Proliferation Nexus," Survival, Institute for Strategic Studies, vol. 48, no. 1 (2006), pp. 61–80.

56. *New York Times*, June 5, 2018; A.P., June 28, 2018; Reuters, July 18, 2018; A. A. Salehi, Atomic Energy Organisation of Iran, Teheran, qu. A.P., September 11, 2018.

57. Pres. H. Rouhani, qu. al-jazeera.com, April 24, 2018.

58. M. J. Zarif, *Face the Nation*, CBS, qu. A.P., April 22, 2018.

59. Maj-Gen. M. Bagheri, qu. Reuters, May 23, 2018.

60. Pres. H. Rouhani, qu. Reuters, August 6, 2018.

61. A. Motahari, qu. Reuters, July 31, 2018.

62. Gen, Q. Soleimani, qu. Press TV, July 26, 2018; *Washington Post*, July 26, 2018.

63. H. Rouhani, qu. A.P., September 27, 2018.

64. US Defense Intelligence Agency, qu. *Washington Post*, August 8, 2017; Cho Myoung-gyon, South Korean Unification Minister, qu. A.P., October 2, 2018.

65. Kim Jong-un, qu. *Times*, September 11, 2017.

66. Kim Jong-un, qu. KCNA, November 14, 2017.

67. Ri Il-bae, commander, North Korean Red Guards, qu. KCNA, September 24, 2017.

68. Ri Yong-ho, North Korean foreign minister, qu. bbc.com/ news/Asia, September 21, 2017.

69. Donald J. Trump, @realDonaldTrump, June 13, 2018.

70. qu. A.P., April 24, 2018.

71. qu. *Washington Post*, June 12, 2018.

72. CNN Politics, June 1, 2018.

73. *Washington Post*, June 30, 2018, July 2, 2018; UN Security Council Sanctions Committee on North Korea, Reuters, August 3, 2018; Report by Director-General, International Atomic Energy Authority (IAEA), August 20, 2018, pp. 1–6.

74. F. V. Fabian, 38 North (Stimson Centre), June 26, 2018.

75. e.g., *Washington Post*, July 30, 2018; *New York Times*, November 12, 2018; nknews .org, November 15, 2018.

76. J. Bermudez and others, Center for Strategic and International Studies (CSIS), Washington DC, November 12, 2018.

77. qu. *New York Times*, July 17, 2018.

78. Agence France-Presse, September 19, 2018.

79. A.P., November 3, 2018.

80. *The Old Regime and the French Revolution* (1856), tr. S. Gilbert, New York, 2010, p. 157.

81. *The Wealth of Nations* (1776), Books IV-V, London, 1999, p. 197.

82. *Letters from England*, London, 1807, p. 180.

83. *Past and Present* (1843), Berkeley and London, 2005, p. 188.

84. M. Friedman and R. Friedman, *Free to Choose: A Personal Statement*, NY and London, 1980, p. 41.

85. demographia.com, qu. *Telegraph*, September 3, 2017.

86. Xinhua, qu. Reuters, June 16, 2018.

87. chinadaily.com, October 21, 2018.

88. Centre for Economics and Business Research, qu. *Times*, December 26, 2015.

89. US Treasury Data, February 2016, qu. CNN, Money (US), May 10, 2016.

90. e.g., CNBC, May 2, 2018; Reuters, May 19, 2018.

91. Gen. Wei Fenghe, Chinese defense minister, at International Security Conference, Moscow, qu. Tass, April 3, 2018.

92. A.P., August 3, 2017.

93. e.g., A.P., June 20, 2018.

94. The Diplomat, May 24, 2016; *New York Times*, July 28, 2018.

95. chinamil.com.cn, April 17, 2018.

96. A.P., May 24, 2017; R. Zhong, *New York Times*, May 3, 2018.

97. *Guardian*, October 20, 2015; *Sunday Times*, July 8, 2018.

98. National Counterintelligence and Security Center report, A.P., July 26, 2018; A.P., October 31, 2018.

99. *Times*, November 17, 2018.

100. *Global Times*—owned by the Chinese Communist Party's *People's Daily*—qu. A.P., March 2, 2015.

101. Zhou Qiang, qu. *South China Morning Post*, February 26, 2015.

102. *People's Daily*, July 10, 2009; *Financial Times*, July 26, 2018.

103. *People's Daily*, July 25, 2017.

104. chinadaily.com.cn, October 25, 2017.

105. *New York Times*, August 20, 2017.

106. State Council policy statement, qu. *New York Times*, July 20, 2017.

107. Li Guoping, China National Space Administration, qu. Ecns.ca, September 19, 2018.

108. Speech to World Economic Forum, Davos, qu. Xinhua, Beijing, January 19, 2017.

109. New Year's Eve address, qu. A.P., December 31, 2016.

110. qu. *New York Times*, October 17, 2017.

111. Final Address, 19th Party Congress, Great Hall of the People, Beijing, qu. *Guardian*, October 24, 2017.

112. Address to Thirteenth National People's Congress, Great Hall of the People, Beijing, qu. A.P., March 20, 2018.

113. *Atlas Shrugged* (1957), New York, 1992, p. 967.

114. op. cit., 970–71.

115. *India Today*, August 29, 2018.

116. op. cit., pp. 964, 970.

117. *Global Times*, qu. *Guardian*, June 18, 2014.

118. Pew Research Center, qu. A.P., April 2, 2015.

119. *Select Works*, ed. E. J. Payne, Oxford, 1885, vol. 1, p. 233.

120. Suleiman al-Omar, Almajd TV, June 13, 2004.

121. R. T. Erdogan, qu. RT, April 11, 2017.

122. B. Assad, qu. *Sunday Times*, November 6, 2016.

123. H. Rouhani, Pres.ir, March 9, 2015.

124. e.g., Estado de S. Paulo, April 12, 2018.

125. e.g., Major-Gen. M. Hicks, US special ops commander, Africa, qu. A.P., April 13, 2018.

126. M. Badie, almasry-alyoum.com, January 10, 2012.

127. M. Badie, qu. *Wall Street Journal*, February 15, 2011.

128. *New York Times*, May 19, 2005.

129. A. Larijani, Press TV, July 5, 2012.

130. A.P., March 12, 2015.

131. qu. *Guardian*, September 12, 2002.

132. The Global Islamic Civilization, January 20, 2013.

133. J. Hussain, RT, June 16, 2014; IS video, *Telegraph*, February 18, 2015.

134. D. Cameron, Al-Arabiya, October 29, 2013.

135. K. Livingstone, qu. *Telegraph*, March 19, 2012.

CHAPTER 2: RICH AND POOR

1. *The Politics*, 1279b 26.

2. 2016 Global Nutrition Report, qu. *Guardian*, June 14, 2016.

3. *Guardian*, June 17, 2017.

4. *Wall Street Journal*, July 24, 2018.

5. *New York Times*, June 1, 2017; A.P., May 2, 2018; China Labor Watch, A.P., June 27, 2018.

6. Hermes Investment Management, *Times*, January 17, 2018.

7. G. Chamberlain, *Guardian*, June 9, 2018.

8. M. M. Mekonnen and A.Y. Hockstra, *Science Advances*, vol. 2, no. 2, February 12, 2016, p. 1.

9. D. Beasley, UN World Food Program, qu. A.P., March 23, 2018.

10. Fred Hollows Foundation, qu. *Guardian*, July 15, 2017.

11. *Times*, April 27, 2008.

12. *Telegraph*, August 21, 2010.

13. "Man and Hunger—The Perspectives of History," address of January 9, 1963, to FAO World Food Congress, Washington DC, p. 4; MS. text in Helen C. Abell Coll., Univ. of Guelph, Ontario.

14. *Satires*, 5:93–6.

15. Food and Agriculture Organization (FAO), qu. *Telegraph*, January 2, 2018.

16. Worldwide Responsible Accredited Production (WRAP) Report, *Telegraph*, December 8, 2014; *Times*, January 10, 2017.

17. Office of National Statistics (ONS), qu. *Guardian*, November 7, 2013; Love Food Hate Waste, qu. *Guardian*, February 25, 2016 and *Times*, February 5, 2018.

18. Trussell Trust, qu. *Guardian*, April 25, 2017, June 29, 2017, May 28, 2018, August 3, 2018; Independent Food Aid Network (IFAN), *Guardian*, May 29, 2017, June 29, 2017.

19. Dept. of Health, qu. *Guardian*, November 25, 2016.

20. ONS, qu. Press Association, February 5, 2018.

21. US Dept. of Agriculture, Supplemental Nutrition Assistance Program (SNAP), November 2017, p. 1.

22. Oxfam and Credit Suisse "Global Wealth Report 2017," qu. CNBC, January 22, 2018.

23. Equality Trust report, May 6, 2017.

24. op. cit., p. 85.

25. *Satires*, 1: 112–114; 14:204.

26. *The Pilgrim's Progress* (1678), Harmondsworth, 1970, pp. 361–63.

27. op. cit., p. 384.

28. op. cit., p. 251.

29. op. cit., pp. 384–85, 880.

30. B. Johnson, Margaret Thatcher Lecture, Centre for Policy Studies, qu. *Guardian*, November 28, 2013.

31. *Telegraph*, October 28, 2006.

32. J. Daley, *Telegraph*, January 23, 2012.

33. qu. *Telegraph*, February 18, 2007.

34. *De Tranquillitate Animi (On Peace of Mind)*, 3:7.

35. *On the Sublime*, 44:6.

36. M. Friedman and R. Friedman, op. cit., p. 3.

37. qu. A.P., September 18, 2012.

38. op. cit., pp. 13, 127.

39. op. cit., p. 170.

40. M. Friedman and R. Friedman, op. cit., p. 117.

41. op. cit., p. 740.

42. *The Virtue of Selfishness*, New York, 1964.

43. op. cit., pp. 840–41.

44. *Philippics*, bk. 4, 39–42.

45. op. cit., p. 447.

46. op. cit., p. 1075.

47. e.g., Income and Poverty in the United States, US Census Bureau, September 13, 2016, and April 20, 2017.

48. S. Dickman and others, "Inequality and the Health Care System in the USA," *Lancet*, vol. 389, no. 10077, April 8, 2017, pp. 1431–1441.

49. Longevity Science Panel, qu. *Times*, February 15, 2018.

50. A.P., December 28, 2016; *Economist*, September 16, 2017; A.P., July 20, 2018.

51. Resolution Foundation, Living Standard Audit, July 24, 2018; H. Koball and Y. Jiang, *Basic Facts about Low Income Children*, National Center for Children in Poverty, New York, January 2018, pp. 1–8.

52. *Telegraph*, November 30, 2015.

53. Herodotus, op. cit., bk. 1, 32:5.

54. Poverty in Later Life, Age UK, April 2018, pp. 1–7; also Health and Social Care Information Centre, *Telegraph*, October 6, 2015.

55. Poverty and Social Exclusion in the United Kingdom (PSE), qu. *Guardian*, June 19, 2014; Shelter report, qu. *Guardian*, November 8, 2017; "Fuel Poverty Crisis," *Independent*, February 22, 2018; Ministry of Housing and Local Govt., English Housing Survey, July 12, 2018.

56. J. Rose, *The Intellectual Life of the British Working Classes*, New Haven, 2010, p. 53.

57. "Households Below Average Income," Dept. for Work and Pensions, June 28, 2016, pp. 1–13; Joseph Rowntree Foundation, Press Association, December 9, 2016; Trust for London, *Guardian*, October 9, 2017.

58. J. McTernan, *Times*, November 4, 2013.

59. Resolution Foundation, qu. *Guardian*, March 3, 2017.

60. Internal Revenue Service, A.P., September 10, 2013.

61. Income and Poverty in the United States, US Census Bureau, September 2016, p. 8.

62. The Chronicle of Philanthropy report, based on Internal Revenue data, A.P., October 6, 2014.

63. *Leviathan* (1651), Harmondsworth, 1981, part 2, chap. 27, p. 339.

64. *Satyricon*, 14:2.

65. Tax Justice Network USA, www.taxjustice.net, July 19, 2012.

66. *Telegraph*, May 11, 2018; *Der Spiegel*, May 11, 2018; *La Stampa*, July 5, 2018.

67. Chartered Institute of Personnel and Development (CIPD) and High Pay Centre, qu. *Independent*, August 15, 2018.

68. Ibid., also High Pay Centre, qu. *Independent*, January 5, 2016; Equality Trust, qu. *Guardian*, March 22, 2017; High Pay Centre, qu. *Guardian*, January 4, 2017, *Telegraph*, January 22, 2018, and *Independent*, August 15, 2018.

69. Equilar, qu. A.P., May 25, 2018.

70. A.P., May 25, 2016.

71. Equilar, qu. A.P., May 25, 2018.

72. *The Condition of England* (1909), London, 2009, p. 223.

73. *Forbes*, July 27, 2017.

74. A.P., June 13, 2017.

75. *Times*, November 25, 2017.

76. Institute for Policy Studies, qu. *Guardian*, March 12, 2014; T. Di Napoli, New York Comptroller, qu. A.P., March 26, 2018.

77. *Times*, March 16, 2018.

78. R. Cheung, Evelina Children's Hospital, London, qu. *Observer*, December 23, 2017; also Public Health Committee, British Medical Association, qu. *Telegraph*, July 3, 2013.

79. Poverty and Social Exclusion in the United Kingdom (PSE), qu. *Guardian*, June 19, 2014.

80. Joseph Rowntree Foundation, qu. *Guardian*, April 27, 2016.

81. Ministry of Justice data, qu. *Guardian*, February 11, 2016.

82. Resolution Foundation, qu. *Guardian*, August 2, 2016.

83. Resolution Foundation and ONS, qu. August 19, 2017.

84. Shelter report, qu. *Guardian*, July 23, 2018.

85. Dept. for Communities and Local Government (DCLG), Press Association, December 14, 2017; Freedom of Information Act disclosure, *Guardian*, December 25, 2017.

86. A.P., July 18, 2017, July 21, 2017.

87. The 2016 Annual Homeless Assessment Report to Congress, US Dept. of Housing and Urban Development, DC, November 2016, p. 8.

88. A.P., May 11, 2017.

89. *New York Times*, May 31, 2016, January 14, 2018.

90. Freedom of Information Act disclosure and Bureau of Investigative Journalism, *Guardian*, April 23, 2018.

91. Dept. of Homeless Services, NYC, *New York Times*, August 28, 2016, September 17, 2016, January 13, 2017.

92. *Los Angeles Times*, May 31, 2017.

93. A.P., June 25, 2013.

94. CBC News, May 17, 2018.

95. *Los Angeles Times*, November 19, 2015.

96. *New York Times*, February 3, 2007.

97. *Times*, July 26, 2017.

98. Freedom of Information Act disclosure, *Guardian*, May 20, 2018.

99. A.P., July 25, 2018.

100. A.P., December 4, 2014, January 30, 2015.

101. *Guardian*, June 26, 2014; *Telegraph*, December 27, 2014; *Telegraph*, March 19, 2015.

102. A.P., June 7, 2016, July 15, 2016, December 27, 2016.

103. *Dallas Morning News*, November 4, 2016.

104. E. Holder, qu. A.P., July 14, 2014.

105. A.P., April 11, 2016.

106. Economic Innovation Group, qu. A.P., July 5, 2016.

107. Centers for Disease Control and Prevention (CDC), Morbidity and Mortality Report, vol. 65, no. 25, July 1, 2016, p. 642; *Portland Press Herald*, March 3, 2018.

108. At Annual Convention of the American Farm Bureau Federation, Nashville, qu. *Tennessean*, January 8, 2018.

109. T. Vilsack, qu. A.P., December 8, 2012.

110. UN Habitat report, qu. A.P., May 18, 2016.

111. Public Health England, *Times*, January 17, 2018.

112. T. Evans of Padstow in Cornwall, qu. *Observer*, August 17, 2013.

113. op. cit., p. 8.

114. op. cit., p. 71.

CHAPTER 3: SOCIALISM'S DEFEAT

1. D. Selbourne, *Death of the Dark Hero: Eastern Europe, 1987–90*, London, 1990, pp. 49–51.

2. op. cit., p. 5.

3. op. cit., p. 170.

4. op. cit., pp. 3, 10, 60.

5. op. cit., pp. 19–20, 23.

6. op. cit., p. 81.

7. K. Howells, *Sunday Times*, September 15, 1996.

8. qu. *Guardian*, September 19, 1996.

9. qu. *Guardian*, September 10, 1997.

10. P. Mandelson, qu. *Guardian*, January 11, 2008.

11. qu. Politics Home, December 3, 2016.

12. Dept. for Business, Energy and Industrial Strategy, "Trade Union Membership in 2017," Statistical Bulletin, May 2018, p. 4.

13. Bureau of Labor Statistics, US Dept. of Labor, January 26, 2017.

14. BBC News, US and Canada, February 2, 2016; *Chicago Tribune*, March 15, 2016.

15. Portland, Oregon, qu. *USA Today*, March 26, 2016.

16. Pittsburgh, qu. A.P., March 31, 2016.

17. qu. *Guardian*, March 25, 2016.

18. A.P., May 21, 2016.

19. qu. *Guardian*, June 8, 2016.

20. A.P., July 21, 2018; www.dsusa.org/about_dsa.

21. Xi Jinping, Great Hall of the People, Beijing, qu. Xinhua, May 4, 2018.

22. Xinhua, October 4, 2017.

23. N. P. Trong, qu. *Guardian*, January 28, 2016.

24. *Guardian*, June 29, 2017; A.P., April 6, 2018.

25. A.P., April 6, 2018.

26. *Guardian*, October 5, 2016.

27. A.P. June 20, 2017.

28. Credit Suisse report, qu. A.P., October 9, 2013.

29. Panama Papers, qu. *Telegraph*, April 4, 2016.

30. Russian Statistical Service (Rosstat), *Moscow Times*, June 11, 2015, December 10, 2015; T. Golikova, Russian Audit Chamber, qu. Tass, Business and Economy, June 25, 2017.

31. Levada Center, qu. A.P., June 26, 2017.

32. A.P., November 7, 2017.

33. *Guardian*, July 17, 2017.

34. e.g., Supreme Court of the US: Epic Systems v. Lewis, www.supremecourt.gov/opinions, pp. 1–30, May 21, 2018.

35. Office of National Statistics (ONS), qu. *Times*, May 31, 2018.

36. A.P., August 6, 2017.

37. *Il Giorno*, May 9, 2017.

38. *Times*, May 3, 2017.

39. *Libération*, September 19, 2017.

40. L. di Maio, at Pomigliano d'Arco, qu. *La Stampa*, March 6, 2018.

41. B. Grillo, at Brindisi, qu. *La Repubblica*, January 18, 2013; L. di Maio, qu. *Il Giorno*, January 6, 2018, and internazionale.it, March 5, 2018.

42. qu. *Il Giorno*, April 11, 2017.

43. Tecnè Research Institute, qu. *Corriere della Sera*, April 21, 2018.

44. qu. *Guardian*, December 29, 2016.

45. qu. *Guardian*, April 20, 2017.

46. M. le Pen, at Hénin-Beaumont, qu. *La Voix du Nord*, April 24, 2017.

47. qu. *New York Times*, November 9, 2016.

48. qu. *Washington Post*, October 13, 2016.

49. D. Trump, at West Palm Beach, Florida, qu. vox.com, Oct 13, 2016.

50. D. Trump, at Atkinson, New Hampshire, qu. *New York Times*, November 5, 2016.

51. D. Trump, Inaugural Address, DC, qu. A.P., January 20, 2017.

52. D. Trump, at CPAC meeting, National Harbor, Maryland, qu. Time.com, February 24, 2017; *Times*, February 25, 2017.

53. e.g., Donald J. Trump, @realDonaldTrump, June 10, 2018.

54. J. Goldberg, National Review, September 5, 2015; A. Garfinkle, The American Interest, March 14, 2016.

55. qu. *Wall Street Journal*, May 1, 2017.

56. "Statement from the New Prime Minister, Theresa May," Prime Minister's Office, 10 Downing Street, July 13, 2016.

57. qu. *Telegraph*, January 19, 2017.

58. Conservative and Unionist Party Manifesto, 2017, p. 7.

59. qu. *Guardian*, July 13, 2016.

60. qu. *Times*, October 5, 2016.

61. *Babbitt* (1923), London, 1973, pp. 172–74.

62. pp. 721–22.

63. e.g., J. Sanderson and N. I. Silber, Huffington Post, April 29, 2013; A. Brown, *Washington Post*, January 6, 2016.

64. *Australian*, December 1, 2012.

65. CNN, July 26, 2012; *Times*, November 12, 2012; *Sunday Times*, July 29, 2012.

66. M. Thompson, CEO, *New York Times*, qu. cnbc.com, February 12, 2018.

67. *New York Times*, September 19, 2018.

68. *Times*, April 30, 2018.

69. A.P., July 13, 2018.

70. H. Rose, *Times*, May 24, 2018.

71. op. cit., p. 119.

72. T. Blair, Romanes Lecture, qu. Oxford Today, Hilary Issue, 2000, p. 2.

73. A. Haldenby, *Telegraph*, October 13, 2011.

74. J. Daley, *Telegraph*, October 9, 2011.

75. E. Badger, *New York Times*, December 8, 2016.

76. F. Hollande, qu. BBC World News, February 23, 2016.

77. S. Marsh, *Times*, August 29, 2012.

78. A. Reid, qu. *Telegraph*, June 23, 2005, and Reuters, June 26, 2017.

79. H. Vickers, *Telegraph*, July 9, 2011.

80. Speech at St. Andrew's Hall, Glasgow, October 11, 1906, in *Liberalism and the Social Problem*, London, 1909, pp. 79–81.

81. *Times*, November 8, 2016.

82. Cato the Censor, *De Praeda Militibus Dividenda*, 1:69.

83. National Audit Office, qu. *Times*, January 18, 2018.

84. *Guardian*, January 16, 2018; Report of the House of Commons Joint Select Committee, qu. *Times*, May 16, 2018.

85. qu. *Telegraph*, September 2, 2016.

86. National Audit Office, qu. *Times*, February 22, 2018.

87. Friedman, op. cit., pp. 154, 163.

88. cf. S. Sodha, "The Great Academy Schools Scandal," *Observer*, July 22, 2018.

89. *Guardian*, August 5, 2018.

90. Friedman, op. cit., p. 146.

91. F. Nelson, *Telegraph*, July 13, 2010.

92. *Times*, March 28, 2017.

93. *Guardian*, May 16, 2018.

94. e.g., *Times*, July 26, 2016, August 20, 2018.

95. Sainsbury Bank, qu. *Times*, January 3, 2017.

96. D. Cameron, qu. *Telegraph*, October 10, 2013.

97. op. cit., p. 297.

98. Annual Report, National Offender Management Service, July 31, 2017.

99. *Times*, August 20, 2018.

100. *Little Dorrit* (1855), Oxford, 1982, pp. 87, 101.

101. Freedom of Information Act disclosure, Health Service Journal, April 17, 2018; also NHS Protect: Reported Physical Assaults, March 2017, pp. 1–10.

102. Unison Scotland, qu. *Times*, October 21, 2017.

103. e.g., A.P., August 16, 2013.

104. e.g., *Daily Mail*, July 2, 2016; *Manchester Evening News*, October 12, 2017; metro .co.uk, October 26, 2017.

105. *Johnny Robinson*, London, 2 vols. 1868, vol. 2, p. 209.

106. *The Great Unwashed*, London, 1868, p. 2.

107. *Johnny Robinson*, vol. 2, p. 208.

108. *The Road to Wigan Pier*, London 1937, p. 170.

109. *Culture and Anarchy* (1869), Cambridge, 1971, pp. 34–35.

110. op. cit., pp. 74–75, 195.

CHAPTER 4: BREAKING THE BOUNDS

1. *Private Correspondence*, London, 1820, p. 286.

2. *Passages from the American Notebooks*, London, 1868, p. 193.

3. *Independent*, April 20, 2016.

4. *Telegraph*, July 26, 2016.

5. op. cit., part 2, chap. 30, p. 383.

6. *The Old Regime and the French Revolution* (1856), New York, 2010, p. 7.

7. History, bk. 1, 8:1.

8. *Democracy in America*, p. 203.

9. A. Rand, *Atlas Shrugged*, p. 976.

10. l. 1230–1.

11. Health and Social Care Information Centre, qu. *Telegraph*, July 9, 2014.

12. NHS Digital, Prescriptions Dispensed in the Community, 2006–2016, June 29, 2017; Freedom of Information Act disclosure, *Guardian*, August 10, 2018.

13. CDC, Press Release, June 7, 2018.

14. National Center for Health Statistics, qu. *Washington Post*, April 22, 2016.

15. *Times*, June 1, 2016; ONS, *Times*, September 4, 2018.

16. ONS, qu. *Times*, September 4, 2018.

17. *Charleston Gazette-Mail*, December 17, 2016.

18. US House of Representatives Energy and Commerce Committee, qu. A.P., May 8, 2018.

19. L. Mordecai and others, "Patterns of Opioid Prescription in England," *British Journal of General Practice*, February 12, 2018; ONS, qu. BBC News, England, March 15, 2018.

20. *New York Times*, June 1, 2018.

21. IMS Health, qu. A.P., December 15, 2016.

22. National Household Survey on Drug Use and Health, *New York Times*, June 30, 2017.

23. "Results from the 2017 National Survey on Drug Use and Health," Substance Abuse and Mental Health Services Administration (SAMHSA), US Department of Health and Human Services, September 2018, figures 21, 40; CDC, qu. A.P., September 14, 2018.

24. A.P., February 20, 2017.

25. The Center for Public Integrity, qu. A.P., September 18, 2016.

26. CDC, Prescription Opioid Overdose Data, August 1, 2017.

27. US Drug Enforcement Administration, qu. A.P., November 2, 2018.

28. Report, Centre for Social Justice, qu. *Telegraph*, February 9, 2015.

29. statnews.com, April 5, 2016; US Senate Permanent Committee on Investigations, qu. *New York Times*, January 25, 2018.

30. Report of Senate Homeland Security and Government Affairs Sub-Committee, Reuters, January 24, 2018.

31. A.P., May 24, 2017.

32. A.P., May 27, 2018.

33. A.P., July 9, 2017.

34. *Times*, September 3, 2015.

35. J. Hunt, Drug Enforcement Agency, qu. CBS New York, March 6, 2017.

36. *New York Times*, February 13, 2018.

37. UN Office on Drugs and Crime (UNODC), qu. *Guardian*, July 14, 2017.

38. European Monitoring Centre for Drugs and Drug Addiction, Drug Report 2017, Luxembourg, p. 47; *Guardian*, June 7, 2018.

39. *Times*, November 3, 2016, March 15, 2018.

40. Press Association, June 4, 2015; *Telegraph*, July 11, 2015.

41. *Independent*, October 23, 2017.

42. National Transportation Safety Board, qu. A.P., January 27, 2017.

43. A.P., July 17, 2017.

44. News Center, University of Buffalo, August 31, 2017.

45. Washington Department of Fish and Wildlife, qu. Kiro7.com, May 23, 2018.

46. CDC Report, A.P., March 6, 2018.

47. NHS Digital, qu. *Sunday Times*, April 8, 2018.

48. ONS, "Deaths Related to Drug Poisoning in England and Wales," August 2, 2017, p. 3; NHS Scotland, qu. *Telegraph*, June 12, 2018.

49. CDC report, qu. *Washington Post*, August 15, 2018.

50. *New York Times*, December 29, 2016.

51. DrugWise report, *Times*, February 7, 2017.

52. *Times*, November 1, 2016, A.P., July 6, 2017.

53. J. McCarthy, Gallup News, August 8, 2016.

54. A.P., January 2, 2017; *New York Times*, April 15, 2017.

55. A.P., January 29, 2017.

56. A.P., July 2, 2017.

57. A.P., January 2, 2017.

58. B. Gallant, premier of New Brunswick, Canada, qu. *Guardian*, April 10, 2017.

59. A.P., March 6, 2013.

60. A.P., December 25, 2017.

61. A.P., December 30, 2017.

62. A.P., July 30, 2018.

63. *Los Angeles Times*, July 13, 2017.

64. *Fortune*, August 4, 2017.

65. Oregon Office of Economic Analysis, qu. A.P., May 14, 2018.

66. City News Toronto, October 19, 2018.

67. E. B. Tapper and N. D. Parikh, "Mortality Due to Cirrhosis and Liver Cancer in the United States, 1999–2016," *British Medical Journal*, July 18, 2018.

68. Alcohol Health Alliance (AHA), qu. *Guardian*, October 6, 2016; ONS, "Alcohol-Specific Deaths in the UK," November 7, 2017, p. 2; House of Commons Library research, qu. *Independent*, September 13, 2018.

69. NHS Digital, Statistics on Alcohol, England, May 3, 2017, p. 7.

70. WHO report, qu. *Times*, September 26, 2018; *BMC Public Health*, qu. Press Association, October 10, 2018.

71. op. cit., vol. 2, bk. 2, chap. 15, p. 244.

72. CDC, qu. A.P., December 8, 2016.

73. CDC, qu. A.P., October 13, 2017.

74. *Our Old Home*, Edinburgh, 1865, p. 266.

75. OECD, qu. *Times*, November 10, 2017.

76. *Lancet*, qu. *Guardian*, May 29, 2014; Disease in Childhood, King's College, London, qu. *Telegraph*, January 30, 2015; Public Health England, qu. *Guardian*, November 30, 2015; NHS Digital, qu. *Telegraph*, June 25, 2017; Diabetes UK, *Guardian*, February 27, 2018.

77. National Child Measurement Programme, qu. *Times*, May 29, 2018; Public Health England, qu. *Guardian* July 24, 2018; National Child Measurement Programme, qu. *Guardian*, October 11, 2018.

78. Royal College of Paediatrics and Child Health (RCPCH), qu. *Guardian*, August 18, 2018.

79. UK Health Forum, qu. *Telegraph*, May 9, 2014; *Lancet*, qu. *Telegraph*, April 1, 2016.

80. A. Moses, Novis Nordisk Research and Development, at European Congress on Obesity, Vienna, qu. Agence France-Presse, May 23, 2018.

81. Z. J. Ward and others, "Simulation of Growth Trajectories of Childhood Obesity into Adulthood," *New England Journal of Medicine*, vol. 377, no. 22, November 30, 2017.

82. Public Health England, qu. *Telegraph*, September 28, 2017; *Times*, September 12, 2018.

83. Obesity Health Alliance, qu. *Guardian*, May 4, 2017; NHS Digital, qu. *Times*, November 8, 2018.

84. Institute for Health Metrics and Evaluation, Univ. of Washington, qu. *New York Times*, September 22, 2016.

85. Military Times, qu. *Times*, September 14, 2016.

86. *Advice to Young Men*, London, 1829, p. 277.

87. McKinsey Global Institute Report, *Telegraph*, November 20, 2014.

88. Institute for Health Metrics and Evaluation, Univ. of Washington, *New England Journal of Medicine*, June 12, 2017.

89. M. Moss, *New York Times*, February 20, 2013.

90. Public Health England, National Diet and Nutrition Survey, qu. *Telegraph*, November 22, 2016.

91. *Telegraph*, November 2, 2012.

92. A.P., October 23, 2012, November 9, 2012, December 18, 2012.

93. Anon, *A Helpe to Discourse*, London, 1635, p. 336.

94. *On the Nature of Things*, bk. 5, l. 1007–1008.

95. *The Art of Love*, bk. 3, l. 757–58.

96. *Dombey and Son* (1848), London, 2012, pp. 320 ff.

97. Suetonius, *Lives of the Caesars*, 4:50.

98. J. Keates, *Handel: The Man and His Music*, London, 2008, p. 307.

99. W. Oxberry, *Anecdotes of the Stage*, London, 1827, p. 44.

100. C. R. Chalmers and E. J. Chaloner, *Journal of the Royal Society of Medicine*, December 1, 2009, p. 514.

101. Centre for Diet and Activity Research (CEDAR), Univ. of Cambridge, qu. *Guardian*, July 25, 2017.

102. CDC, qu. A.P., October 3, 2018.

103. *USA Today*, February 12, 2013; Business Insider, November 23, 2017.

104. S. K. Boddhula and others, *British Medical Journal* Case Reports, April 9, 2018, pp. 1–2.

105. *New York Post*, April 3, 2017.

106. A.P., November 27, 2012.

107. Freedom of Information Act disclosure, *Times*, July 16, 2018.

108. American Academy of Orthopaedic Surgeons, qu., A.P., March 11, 2014; G. Erens and M. Crowley, Total Hip Arthroplasty, Up to Date, September 14, 2017, p. 1.

109. V. Philpot, British Dietetic Association, qu. *Observer*, April 16, 2009.

110. M. Waites, *The Age of Consent: Young People, Sexuality and Citizenship*, New York, 2005, pp. 135–36.

111. *Telegraph*, November 4, 2014.

112. *Telegraph*, September 25, 2014.

113. *Guardian*, June 20, 2015.

114. Obergefelt v. Hodges, qu. *New York Times*, June 26, 2015.

115. qu. A.P., June 26, 2015.

116. Ibid.

117. A.P., June 25, 2011.

118. A.P., November 18, 2012.

119. A.P., April 27, 2013; *Sydney Morning Herald*, April 28, 2013.

120. A.P., September 5, 2013.

121. Williams Institute, UCLA, qu. nwi.com, September 4, 2013.

122. A.P., February 3, 2016.

123. *Telegraph*, August 1, 2017.

124. *New York Times*, January 9, 2013.

125. *Guardian*, June 8, 2017.

126. A.P., November 12, 2018.

127. J. John, *Telegraph*, July 23, 2012.

128. C. Kenny, qu. *Guardian*, July 1, 2017.

129. A.P., July 10, 2017.

130. Amoris Laetitia [The Joy of Love], qu. *Guardian*, April 8, 2016.

131. *An Essay on Man*, London, 1733, 1, 284.

132. K. Yeung, Nuffield Council on Bioethics (NCB), qu. *Independent*, July 16, 2018.

133. J. Savulescu, University of Oxford, "It's Our Duty to Have Designer Babies," readersdigest.co.uk, August 2012, qu. *Telegraph*, August 16, 2012.

134. qu. *Guardian*, November 3, 2012.

135. *Telegraph*, January 13, 2016; *Times*, September 1, 2017.

136. *Guardian*, October 6, 2017.

137. A.P., January 8, 2014.

138. *Times*, June 9, 2017.

139. *Times*, September 10, 2018.

140. *Telegraph*, February 14, 2015.

141. *Telegraph*, March 7, 2015.

142. *Telegraph*, May 29, 2011.

143. *Times*, October 30, 2017.

144. *Sydney Morning Herald*, September 21, 2018.

145. UPI, March 16, 2006; cleveland.com, December 20, 2007.

146. e.g., *Washington Post*, October 2, 2014.

147. CNN.com, September 27, 2016; A.P., December 14, 2017; *Ottawa Citizen*, April 6, 2018.

148. A.P., May 18, 2015.

149. qu. *Le Monde*, July 6, 2007.

150. S. Canavero, Turin Advanced Neuromodulation Group, *Telegraph*, April 27, 2017.

151. *New Scientist*, February 25, 2015; *Times*, September 8, 2015.

152. *Times*, May 30, 2015.

153. *American Journal of Bioethics*, vol. 4, no. 3, September, 2004, qu. A.P., September 17, 2004.

154. K. Gutowski, qu. A.P., September 18, 2005.

155. *Telegraph*, August 19, 2015.

156. BBC News, Science and Environment, August 5, 2013.

157. *Science News*, October 11, 2018.

158. T. Hildebrandt and others, Nature Communications 9, no. 2589, July 4, 2018.

159. A. Regalado, MIT Technology Review, April 25, 2018.

160. D. Niu and others, "Inactivation of Porcine Endogenous Retrovirus in Pigs," *Science*, August 10, 2017, and *New York Times*, August 11, 2017; Y. Bogliotti and others, *Proceedings of the National Academy of Sciences* (PNAS), February 9, 2018.

161. M. Rees, *New Statesman*, December 5–11, 2014.

162. Xinhua, qu. *Guardian*, November 9, 2018.

163. A. Guadamuz, *The Author* (Journal of the Society of Authors), Summer 2018, p. 46.

164. e.g., N. Bostrom, "Existential Risk Prevention as Global Priority," Global Policy, vol. 4, issue 1, pp. 15–31.

165. Draft Report, European Parliament Committee on Legal Affairs, May 31, 2016, Intro., p. 4.

166. N. Bostrom, Future of Humanity Institute, Oxford, qu. BBC News, Business, March 2, 2014; S. Hawking, qu. *Telegraph*, December 3, 2014; S. Russell, qu. *Telegraph*, January 21, 2015.

167. Open Letter to International Joint Conference on Artificial Intelligence (IJCAI), Melbourne, August 2017, qu. *Business Insider*, August 21, 2017.

168. Z. Liu and others, "Cloning of Macaque Monkeys by Somatic Cell Nuclear Transfer," *Cell* 172, February 8, 2018, pp. 1–7.

169. At Salk Institute, La Jolla, California, *Guardian*, January 26, 2017.

170. F. Gage, Salk Institute, qu. statnews.com, November 6, 2017.

171. e.g., A. Van der Heide and others, "End of Life Decisions in the Netherlands over 25 Years," *New England Journal of Medicine*, vol. 377, no. 5, August 3, 2017, pp. 492–94.

CHAPTER 5: THE HOME FRONT

1. *Eudemian Ethics*, 1242b1.

2. op. cit., pp. 43, 436, 493, 896.

3. ONS, Families and Households: 2017, November 8, 2017, pp. 3–4.

4. US Census Bureau, qu. *New York Times*, May 26, 2011; K. Parker and R. Staples, Fact Tank, Pew Research Center, September 14, 2017; ONS, Population Estimates by Marital Status, 2002–2016, July 13, 2017, p. 7.

5. G. Livingston, Fact Tank, Pew Research Center, December 22, 2014.

6. Marriage Foundation, qu. *Times*, September 22, 2018.

7. ONS, October 18, 2017.

8. ONS, qu. *Telegraph*, September 26, 2018.

9. ONS, *Telegraph*, August 6, 2013, June 11, 2017.

10. *Times*, January 3, 2017.

11. *Times*, June 9, 2018, September 15, 2018.

12. Pew Research Center, qu. *New York Times*, July 14, 2017.

13. ONS, qu. *Times*, July 14, 2017.

14. Aviva report, qu. *Telegraph*, February 6, 2014.

15. ONS, qu. *Telegraph*, April 1, 2017.

16. European Foundation, qu. *Guardian*, March 24, 2014.

17. Pew Research Center, A.P., May 24, 2016; J. Vespa, The Changing Economics of Young Adulthood: 1975–2016, US Census Bureau, April 2017, p. 2.

18. Italian Statistical Service (Istat), qu. *Il Giorno*, May 18, 2017.

19. ONS, qu. *Independent*, November 8, 2017.

20. ONS, *Telegraph*, February 9, 2014.

21. Resolution Foundation, qu. *Observer*, April 28, 2018.

22. US Census Bureau, A.P., November 14, 2013.

23. Health Foundation, qu. *Times*, June 18, 2018.

24. A.P.-NORC Center for Public Affairs Research, A.P., October 14, 2016.

25. Aeschines, *Against Timarchus*, 1:24.

26. *Guardian*, February 26, 1998.

27. BBC News, Beijing, July 1, 2013.

28. Age UK, *Telegraph*, March 6, 2014, August 14, 2014.

29. *New York Times*, September 5, 2016.

30. Independent Age, *Guardian*, October 13, 2014.

31. ONS, *Telegraph*, December 10, 2013; UK Government Actuary's Department, qu. *Times*, January 10, 2018.

32. The State Pension Funding Gap: 2016, Pew Charitable Trusts, April 12, 2018.

33. Genworth Financial Report, qu. A.P., June 1, 2016.

34. Which? Policy Report, "Beyond Social Care: Keeping Later Life Positive," *Times*, August 20, 2018.

35. Resolution Foundation, qu. *Guardian*, January 16, 2017.

36. ONS, qu. *Telegraph*, August 13, 2018.

37. US Census Bureau, CB 18–41, March 13, 2018.

38. US Census Bureau, qu. A.P., June 22, 2017.

39. US Census Bureau, *New York Times*, May 7, 2014.

40. Statistics Canada, qu. A.P., May 3, 2017.

41. Internal Affairs and Communications Ministry, qu. *Japan Times*, September 17, 2018.

42. *Kyoto News*, September 14, 2018.

43. ONS and M. Marmot, Institute of Health Equity, University College, London, qu. *Guardian*, July 18, 2017; J.Y. Ho and A. S. Hendl, "Recent Trends in Life-Expectancy across High-Income Countries," *British Medical Journal*, August 15, 2018, pp. 1–14.

44. A. Albert, Carehome.co.uk, May 24, 2017; "Prospects for Public Health," *Lancet*, vol. 2, no. 5, May 2017.

45. Association of Directors of Adult Social Services, qu. *Times*, June 12, 2018.

46. Age UK, *Times*, July 9, 2018.

47. A.P., January 6, 2014, July 23, 2014; Age UK, *Times*, December 14, 2017.

48. CDC, qu. A.P., May 17, 2017.

49. ONS, qu. *Guardian*, March 18, 2017.

50. ONS, *Times*, March 27, 2018; CDC, qu. A.P., May 17, 2018, and *New York Times*, August 4, 2018.

51. ONS, qu. *Telegraph*, September 26, 2018.

52. ONS, qu. *Guardian*, March 15, 2018.

53. H. Levine, N. Jorgensen, and others, "Temporal Trends in Sperm-Count," *Human Reproduction Update*, Oxford Univ. Press, July 25, 2017, pp. 1–14.

54. CDC, National Vital Statistics, vol. 66, no. 1, January 5, 2017, p. 2; ONS, November 29, 2016.

55. Istat, qu. *Il Giornale*, November 29, 2016.

56. *New York Times*, October 24, 2018.

57. Guttmacher Institute, qu. A.P., January 17, 2017; ONS, qu. *Telegraph*, July 19, 2017; also CDC, qu. A.P., May 17, 2018.

58. CDC, "Teen Pregnancy in the United States," May 9, 2017; CDC, Youth Risk Behavior, 2007–2017, p. 9.

59. US Census Bureau, qu. *New York Times*, May 21, 2016.

60. A.P., February 16, 2016.

61. cf. J. L. Grossman, "The New Illegitimacy: Tying Parentage to Marital Status for Lesbian Co-Parents," *American University Journal of Gender Social Policy and Law* 20, no. 3 (2012), pp. 671–720.

62. Goodridge v. Department of Public Health, 798 N.E.2d 941 (Mass., 2003); *New York Times*, February 5, 2004.

63. *Times*, September 19, 2018.

64. *Times*, March 8, 2002.

65. *Times*, April 6, 2006.

66. A.P., May 12, 2004.

67. *Telegraph*, July 10, 2007; *Guardian*, August 6, 2007.

68. A.P., June 10, 2015.

69. Department of Education, "Children Looked after in England," November 15, 2018, pp. 4–5.

70. ONS, qu. *Telegraph*, May 8, 2014; ONS, qu. *Times*, November 28, 2017.

71. Centre for Social Justice, *Telegraph*, June 10, 2013.

72. National Centre for Social Research, *Telegraph*, November 20, 2013.

73. Centre for Economics and Business Research, *Telegraph*, January 22, 2015.

74. Gingerbread, *Guardian*, July 27, 2014.

75. Gingerbread, *Guardian*, March 11, 2015.

76. ONS, *Guardian*, September 1, 2016.

77. ONS, qu. *Guardian*, July 26, 2018.

78. Resolution Foundation, qu. *Times*, July 24, 2018.

79. Child Poverty Action Group, qu. *Guardian*, June 7, 2017; Joseph Rowntree Foundation, qu. *Times*, March 17, 2017; *Guardian*, May 7, 2018.

80. "Households Below Average Income," Dept. for Work and Pensions, March 16, 2017, p. 1.

81. UNICEF report, qu. *Guardian*, May 15, 2017.

82. All-Party Parliamentary Group, House of Commons, qu. *Guardian*, April 24, 2017.

83. National Center on Family Homelessness, A.P., November 17, 2014.

84. *New York Times*, October 31, 2018.

85. Dept. of Education, qu. *New York Times*, June 6, 2016; Independent Budget Office, qu. *New York Times*, October 11, 2016; Institute for Children, Poverty and Homelessness, *New York Times*, August 15, 2017; New York State Technical and Education Assistance Center, *New York Times*, October 10, 2017; *New York Times*, October 15, 2018.

86. *Guardian*, December 28, 2016.

87. Shelter, qu. *Guardian*, January 17, 2018.

88. Child Abuse and Neglect Fatalities, 2016, US Department of Health and Health Services, Children's Bureau, July 2018, pp. 1–8.

89. P. G. Schnitzer and others, "Advancing Public Health Surveillance to Estimate Child Maltreatment Fatalities," Child Welfare, 2013, 92 no. 2, pp. 77–98.

90. Centre for Social Justice, *Guardian*, August 2, 2014.

91. Reuters, December 7, 2015; *New York Times*, July 13, 2017; CDC report, qu. NBC News, October 9, 2017.

92. A.P., September 22, 2017.

93. Agence France-Presse, October 7, 2014.

94. A.P., January 8, 2016.

95. A.P., September 14, 2016.

96. CDC, qu. A.P., March 23, 2017.

97. A.P., September 14, 2016.

98. A.P., April 10, 2017.

99. A.P., December 10, 2016.

100. A.P., December 24, 2016.

101. *Times*, August 22, 2016.

102. S. C. Curtice and others, Drug Overdose Deaths among Adolescents Aged 15–19 in the US, 1999–2015, National Center for Health Statistics, Data Brief no. 282, August 2017.

103. Freedom of Information Act disclosure, bbc.com/news/health, May 3, 2018; *Times*, May 4, 2018.

104. NHS data, qu. *Guardian*, June 18, 2017; *Times*, July 21, 2018.

105. The Key, qu. *Telegraph*, May 9, 2016.

106. National Association of Head Teachers (NAHT), and Family and Childcare Trust, qu. *Telegraph*, September 6, 2017; A. Spielman, chief inspector, Ofsted, qu. Press Association, June 1, 2018.

107. M. Wilshaw, chief inspector, Ofsted qu. *Telegraph*, July 3, 2013; *Telegraph*, October 16, 2014; Enlightenment Foundation, BBC Education, March 27, 2015; D. Hinds, Secretary of State for Education, qu. *Guardian*, July 31, 2018.

108. qu. *Telegraph*, May 9, 2016.

109. Prison Reform Trust, qu. Press Association, May 23, 2016.

110. *Le Parisien*, September 30, 2017.

111. J. Bingham, *Telegraph*, March 22, 2016.

112. International Congress on Physical Activity and Public Health, qu. *Telegraph*, November 20, 2016.

113. Prince's Countryside Fund, qu. *Telegraph*, July 31, 2017.

114. Children's Society, qu. *Guardian*, November 29, 2016.

115. Royal College of Psychiatrists, *Telegraph*, June 3, 2015; Mental Health Trusts England, qu. *Independent*, May 4, 2017; NHS Digital, qu. *Guardian*, February 12, 2018.

116. *Guardian*, February 24, 2015.

117. S. Berelowitz, Deputy Children's Commissioner for England, qu. BBC News, UK, January 26, 2013.

118. NHS Digital, qu. *Guardian*, October 3, 2016.

119. NSPCC report, qu. *Guardian*, May 14, 2018.

120. Higher Education Statistics Agency (HESA), qu. *Guardian*, May 23, 2017.

121. Institute for Public Policy Research (IPPR), qu. *Times*, September 4, 2017.

122. Girls' Attitudes Survey, Girlguiding UK, London, 2015, pp. 5, 7.

123. ONS, Suicides in England and Wales (2014), qu. *Times*, October 7, 2015.

124. ONS, *Guardian*, February 4, 2016.

125. CDC, qu. A.P., November 21, 2017; CDC Youth Risk Behavior Survey, 2007–2017, p. 47.

126. Place2BE, *Times*, March 17, 2015.

127. C. Morgan and others, "Incidence, Clinical Management and Mortality Risk Following Self-Harm among Children and Adolescents," *British Medical Journal*, October 18 2017.

128. *Dombey and Son* (1848), London, 2012, p. 638.

129. C. Morgan and others, "Incidence, Clinical Management and Mortality Risk Following Self-Harm among Children and Adolescents," *British Medical Journal*, October 18, 2017; "Self-Harm and Self-Poisoning Admissions for Patients under 18 in England, 1997–98 to 2016–17," Secondary Care Analysis, NHS Digital, July 3, 2018; also Freedom of Information Act disclosure, *Times*, June 9, 2018.

130. NSPCC, qu. *Guardian*, December 9, 2016.

131. The Secondary Care Analysis Team, NHS Digital, qu. *Sunday Times*, July 23, 2017.

132. M. A. Monto and others, *American Journal of Public Health*, 108, no. 8, August 1, 2018, pp. 1042–48.

133. "A Sleep to Startle Us," *Household Words* (March 13, 1852), vol. 4, no. 103, p. 577.

134. T. Adorno, *Contro l'Antisemitismo*, Rome, 1994, pp. 47–48, 51.

135. Centre for Social Justice, *Telegraph*, June 10, 2013.

136. Irish National Teachers' Organization (INTO), qu. *Telegraph*, October 10, 2016.

137. Association of Teachers and Lecturers, qu. *Guardian*, June 11, 2016.

138. GMB survey, qu. *Guardian*, June 5, 2017.

139. Press Association, May 12, 2017.

140. *Sunday Times*, April 13, 2017.

141. A.P., April 14, 2017.

142. National Center for Education Statistics, qu. A.P., March 29, 2018.

143. A.P., December 15, 2016.

144. *Detroit News*, September 12, 2018.

145. *Milwaukee Journal Sentinel*, June 2, 2014, February 1, 2018.

146. *Times*, June 25, 2018.

147. *Times*, May 2, 2018.

148. *Times*, May 4, 2017.

149. Freedom of Information Act disclosure, BBC Panorama, qu. *Times*, October 9, 2017.

150. Department of Education, Exclusion Statistics, qu. *Guardian*, July 20, 2017.

151. *Times*, May 4, 2017.

152. *New York Times*, August 3, 2015; A.P., January 20, 2017; *Miami Herald*, January 27, 2018.

153. A.P., August 26, 2018.

154. A.P., February 23, 2018.

155. US Department of Education, qu. *U.S. News & World Report*, June 7, 2016.

156. A.P., June 17, 2018.

157. Department of Education, *Times Educational Supplement*, March 23, 2017.

158. National Children's Bureau, qu. *Times*, January 29, 2018.

159. Department of Education, *Guardian*, May 19, 2016, and *Telegraph*, October 19, 2017.

160. *Times*, May 10, 2018.

161. Department of Education, *Telegraph*, March 23, 2016.

162. *Telegraph*, August 22, 2016.

163. J. Platt, qu. *Guardian*, April 6, 2017.

164. Ministry of Justice, qu. *Guardian*, December 14, 2017.

165. NHS Digital, qu. *Sunday Times*, July 1, 2018; A. Brooks, trauma surgeon, Conference on Knife Crime, Royal Society of Medicine, London, July 31, 2018, qu. *Telegraph*, August 1, 2018.

166. K. Crossley, London Ambulance Service, loc. cit.

167. D. Bew, trauma surgeon, loc. cit.

168. Ministry of Justice, qu. *Times*, March 10, 2017.

169. ONS, Crime in England and Wales, 2010–2017, table F22, July 20, 2017.

170. everytownresearch.org/not an accident/4056/, September 17, 2018.

171. cleveland.com, December 23, 2016.

172. *Advocate*, November 15, 2016, September 17, 2018.

173. A.P., August 30, 2017.

174. A.P., July 9, 2018.

175. CBS Los Angeles, March 24, 2017.

176. *Washington Post*, April 18, 2018.

177. A.P., February 2, 2018.

178. *Indianapolis Star*, April 18, 2018.

179. *The Politics*, 1336b24.

180. A.P., June 27, 2011.

181. *New York Times*, October 31, 2010.

182. New York Police Dept., A.P., May 1, 2014.

183. *Germania*, 21:1.

184. J. Williams, qu. A.P., May 1, 2014.

185. *Prosecution of Aristogeiton*, 25:81.

186. *The Laws*, 9: 879.

187. *Tulsa World*, July 24, 2015, August 9, 2018.

188. *Telegraph*, May 7, 2015.

189. *Guardian*, November 4, 2013; *Times*, March 10, 2015.

190. First Philippic, iv:10.

191. op. cit., bk. 1, 137:2.

192. *The Laws*, 9:869a,b and 873b.

193. op. cit., part 2, chap. 27, p. 352.

194. Aristotle, *The Politics*, 1262a.

CHAPTER 6: IN LIMBO

1. Herodotus, op. cit., bk. 1, 207:2.

2. *Histories*, bk. 6, 51:4.

3. op. cit., pp. 170–71.

4. *Republic*, bk. 7, 514a2–517a7.

5. *Paradise Lost*, Oxford, 2008, 3:495.

6. Solving the Electronic Waste Problem (STEP), United Nations University, June 3, 2014, p. 4.

7. Facebook Mission Statement, February 4, 2004; M. Zuckerberg, Chicago, qu. *Forbes*, June 25, 2017.

8. A.P., April 6, 2018.

9. A.P.–NORC Center for Public Affairs Research, A.P., April 24, 2018.

10. Bureau of Labor Statistics, qu. *New York Times*, May 5, 2016.

11. J. Baker, loc. cit.

12. *Observer*, March 17, 2018; *New York Times*, April 5, 2018, April 8, 2018, October 12, 2018.

13. *Guardian*, July 11, 2018.

14. loc. cit.

15. Bloomberg, July 26, 2018, July 27, 2018.

16. *Telegraph*, October 30, 2018.

17. *New York Times*, July 28, 2018.

18. D. Trump, Charlotte, NC, October 14, 2016, qu. Reuters, October 15, 2016, etc.

19. wearesocial.com, January 30, 2018.

20. GSM Association, The Mobile Economy 2018, p. 2.

21. Ofcom, Communications Market 2018 Report: Summary, August 2, 2018.

22. Ofcom, qu. *Guardian*, August 3, 2017.

23. Aviva report, qu. *Times*, January 30, 2017; Centre for Time Use Research, University of Oxford, *Times*, December 22, 2017.

24. Ofcom, qu. *Times*, November 29, 2017.

25. Ofcom, Communications Market Report 2018, qu. *Telegraph*, August 2, 2018; Childwise, qu. *Telegraph*, October 4, 2018.

26. Aviva report, qu. *Sunday Times*, January 22, 2017.

27. Annenberg Center for the Digital Future, University of Southern California, 2017 Report, April 17, 2018, p. 5.

28. GfK and Common Sense Media, Teens' Use of Social Media in 2018, September 10, 2018.

29. *Fortune*, May 1, 2018.

30. CNN Money July 31, 2018; *New York Times*, August 2, 2018.

31. *Telegraph*, August 30, 2016.

32. *Telegraph*, October 4, 2017.

33. *New York Times*, June 27, 2017.

34. *New York Times*, July 18, 2018.

35. *History of the Peloponnesian War*, bk. 1, 71:3.

36. G. Storah, CEO, Hudson's Bay Co., qu. A.P., May 18, 2016.

37. Ofcom Report, BBC News, Technology, July 18, 2012.

38. A.P., July 22, 2016.

39. M. Zuckerberg, San Jose McEnery Convention Center, qu. *San Francisco Chronicle*, April 18, 2017.

40. T. Starner, qu. A.P., October 1, 2013.

41. e.g., C. K. Ra and others, "Association of Digital Media Use with Subsequent Attention-Deficit Hyperactivity Disorder Among Adolescents," *Journal of American Medical Association*, July 17, 2018, pp. 255–63.

42. H. Clinton, BBC News, February 17, 2011.

43. D. Casaleggio, Cinque Stelle, *Corriere della Sera*, May 11, 2018, May 19, 2018.

44. *Guardian*, October 22, 1997.

45. *Times*, May 16, 2018.

46. P. Bergen, cnn.com, September 26, 2013.

47. M. Reid, *The Child Wife: A Tale of the Two Worlds*, London, 1868, vol. 3, p. 183.

48. qu. A.P., January 23, 2014.

49. K. Mills, UCL Institute of Cognitive Neuroscience, qu. *Telegraph*, July 2, 2015; M. J. George and others, "Concurrent and Subsequent Associations between Daily Digital Technology Use and High-Risk Adolescents' Mental Health Problems," *Child Development*, May 3, 2017.

50. *The City in History* (1961), New York, 1989, p. 512.

51. Earl of Chesterfield, *Letters to His Son*, vol. 1, no. 143 (January 24, 1749), London, 1774, p. 391.

52. BBC News, Asia, December 18, 2013.

53. *Daily Mail*, January 20, 2017.

54. A.P., June 9, 2017.

55. *Times*, June 9, 2018.

56. *Telegraph*, June 14, 2015.

57. *Newsweek*, July 19, 2018.

58. Agence France-Presse, June 13, 2018.

59. *Quotidiano di Puglia*, April 8, 2018.

60. ONS, Internet Users in the UK: 2017, May 19, 2017.

61. House of Commons Science and Technology Committee, Press Association, June 13, 2016.

62. *New Hampshire Union Leader*, September 25, 2017, October 11, 2017.

63. M. M. Seforim, *The Nag* (1873), New York, 1955, p. 512.

64. A.P., December 26, 2013.

65. National Society for the Prevention of Cruelty to Children (NSPCC), qu. BBC News, August 11, 2013.

66. *Observer*, August 10, 2013.

67. NSPCC, Childline Study, qu. *Guardian*, November 14, 2016.

68. Parent Zone and Ipsos Mori, qu. *Telegraph*, June 28, 2018.

69. *Telegraph*, April 29, 2014.

70. *Telegraph*, April 6, 2018.

71. LBC, May 18, 2018.

72. T. Wolfe, *Hooking Up*, London, 2000, p. 215.

73. G. Reynolds, *Telegraph*, February 1, 2016.

74. A. Pearson, *Telegraph*, April 20, 2016.

75. *Telegraph*, January 22, 1996, March 6, 2015; cnn.com.world/Asia, November 9, 2013; *Telegraph*, May 22, 2013; *Telegraph*, September 7, 2017; *New York Times*, November 1, 2017; *Il Messaggero*, August 14, 2018.

76. *New York Times*, October 31, 2017.

77. Y. Clarke, qu. *Guardian*, March 10, 2011.

78. D. Smith and B. Jacobs, *Observer*, April 23, 2016.

79. A.P., December 22, 2012.

80. op. cit., vol. 1, chap. 1, p. 80.

81. C. Raven, *Guardian* January 22, 2002.

82. V. Bennett, September 24, 2004.

83. Z. Williams, July 4, 2007.

84. H. Baxter, *Guardian*, May 27, 2014.

85. Z. Mansell, July 3, 2015.

86. "Glosswitch," *New Statesman* online, December 9, 2014.

87. H. Davis, March 23, 2013.

88. E. Barnett, *Telegraph*, November 13, 2013.

89. D. Ross, October 8, 2015.

90. A. Liptrot, May 29, 2018.

91. R. Coslett, August 10, 2012.

92. B. Gordon, *Telegraph*, November 3, 2016.

93. D. Ross, *Times*, May 12, 2016.

94. L. Dodsworth, *Guardian*, May 23, 2017.

95. O. Smith, *Telegraph*, January 22, 2018; M. Hanson, *Guardian*, December 5, 2016.

96. M. Daubeny, *Telegraph*, July 8, 2016.

97. C. Newman, September 13, 2016.

98. M. Parris, *Times*, July 25, 2018.

99. P. Elan, *Guardian*, May 11, 2016.

100. L. Kynaston, *Telegraph*, June 3, 2016.

101. P. Connolly, *Guardian*, June 12, 2017.

102. *Guardian*, June 9, 2016, April 14, 2016.

103. A. Murphy, *Times*, October 8, 2016.

104. August 8, 2004.

105. May 1, 2000.

106. December 7, 2011.

107. *Guardian*, August 28, 2011.

108. J. Oliver, qu. *Guardian*, February 20, 2017.

109. D. Mitchell, January 6, 2013.

110. T. Garton Ash, April 10, 2008.

111. E. Morgan, *Guardian*, February 11, 2013.

112. C. Brooker, *Guardian*, September 28, 2009.

113. May 15, 2012.

114. S. Jeffries, *Guardian*, December 27, 2017.

115. V. Lewis-Smith, March 10, 2004.

116. *Times*, February 11, 2006.

117. June 13, 2004.

118. November 28, 2010.

119. February 11, 2005.

120. *Telegraph*, March 14, 2012.

121. *Telegraph*, July 25, 2012.

122. D. Judd, *Radical Joe* (1993), London, 2010, p. 203.

123. M. Parris, October 13, 2007.

124. I. Jack, *Guardian*, October 1, 2004.

125. A. Grayling, *Guardian*, October 31, 2012.

126. *Guardian*, October 18, 2013.

127. R. Dreyfuss, *Guardian*, July 24, 2016.

128. L. Mangan, *Guardian*, July 24, 2012.

129. C. Odone, *Telegraph*, January 4, 2013.

130. I. Dale, April 25, 2008.

131. T. Hardy, qu. *Guardian*, September 11, 2011.

132. J. Kirkup, *Telegraph*, September 25, 2015.

133. H. Rumbelow, "Coming Soon: Fab Females in Distress," *Times*, November 20, 2007.

134. T. Halpin, *Times*, January 19, 2005.

135. K. Maher, *Times*, October 17, 2016.

136. T. Young, *Telegraph*, October 10, 2013.

137. C. Leadbeater, August 22, 2016.

138. D. Finkelstein, July 18, 2012.

139. op. cit., bk. 3, 37:3.

140. J. Cooper, *Times*, August 12, 2016.

141. Z. Strimpel, *Telegraph*, December 31, 2017.

142. *La Prima Radice*, Milan, 1996, p. 53.

143. op. cit., 3:7.

144. D. Birkett, October 4, 2004.

145. P. Toynbee, *Guardian*, November 1, 2000.

146. E. Wiseman, *Guardian*, September 18, 2016.

147. C. Bennett, *Observer*, March 11, 2018.

148. S. Jenkins, June 2, 2000.

149. M. Linklater, *Times*, December 6, 2000.

150. *Telegraph*, January 30, 2008.

151. *Times*, July 5, 2010.

152. R. Liddle, *Spectator*, August 20, 2011.

153. A. Stone, *New York Times*, January 5, 2018.

154. L. Beisner, *Guardian*, August 15, 2012.

155. B. Gordon, *Guardian*, August 19, 2017.

156. K. Blundell, Mother and Baby, June 2010, qu. *Observer*, June 27, 2010.

157. *Times*, December 27, 2007.

158. T. Hodgkinson, *Telegraph*, February 16, 2008.

159. June 8, 2012.

160. April 1, 2010, July 27, 2010.

161. July 13, 2012.

162. V. Young, *Telegraph*, March 26, 2017.

163. T. Wallace, *Telegraph*, May 27, 2017.

164. *Sunday Times*, February 10, 2008.

165. O. Rickett, February 13, 2015.

166. R. Webb, *Telegraph*, August 30, 2017.

167. L. Mangan, *Telegraph*, April 26, 2016.

168. S. Heawood, *Guardian*, November 1, 2014.

169. S. Heritage, *Guardian*, January 3, 2014.

170. H. Rifkind, *Times*, November 14, 2017.

171. M. Woollacott, *Guardian*, July 13, 2001.

172. January 11, 2016.

173. BBC News, October 9, 2013.

174. M. Pemberton, *Telegraph*, March 20, 2010.

175. P. Lees, *Guardian*, September 16, 2015.

176. J. Harris, November 12, 2010.

177. *Telegraph*, February 28, 2008.

178. D. Hill, *Guardian*, April 4, 2008.

179. *Times*, September 14, 2009.

180. *Times*, February 7, 2008.

181. W. Hemingway, *Guardian*, March 22, 2012.

182. J. Warner, *Telegraph*, September 27, 2013.

183. I. Vince, *Guardian*, May 24, 2012.

184. G. Coren, *Times*, July 9, 2016.

185. M. Parris, *Times*, January 2, 2016.

186. S. Leith, *Telegraph*, March 31, 2007.

187. B. Macintyre, September 6, 2011.

188. C. Moore, *Telegraph*, November 23, 2013.

189. M. Parris, *Times*, July 18, 2015.

190. O. Kamm, *Times*, November 12, 2015.

191. M. Parris, December 25, 2011.

CHAPTER 7: REACTIONS

1. Canto 3:37–39.

2. op. cit., bk. 1, 91–97.

3. op. cit., 44:16.

4. op. cit., p. 51.

5. Donald J. Trump, @realDonaldTrump, January 20, 2017.

6. *Washington Post*, January 23, 2017.

7. qu. *New York Times*, February 7, 2018.

8. Acceptance speech, Republican National Convention, qu. *Washington Post*, July 22, 2016; speech to UN General Assembly, New York, qu. *New York Times*, September 25, 2018.

9. Speech to Congress, Federal News Service, qu. *New York Times*, February 28, 2017.

10. Speech to GOP Convention, Cleveland, qu. A.P., July 21, 2016.

11. Ibid.

12. Reuters, February 23, 2017.

13. qu. *Washington Post*, October 22, 2018.

14. e.g., N. Farage, United Kingdom Independence Party, qu. *Daily Express*, June 24, 2016.

15. YouGov poll, qu. *Guardian*, January 10, 2017.

16. T. May to D. Tusk, qu. *Telegraph*, March 29, 2017.

17. B. Johnson, in Munich, qu. Bloomberg Politics, February 17, 2017.

18. V. Bogdanor, BBC, June 24, 2016.

19. National Centre for Social Research, qu. *Guardian*, December 15, 2016.

20. ONS, qu. *Telegraph*, May 24, 2018.

21. T. May, Philadelphia, qu. *Financial Times*, January 26, 2017.

22. N. Farage, Washington DC, qu. *Telegraph*, January 10, 2017.

23. A. Banks, United Kingdom Independence Party, qu. *Times*, November 16, 2016.

24. G. Wilders, qu. *Guardian*, March 15, 2017.

25. V. Orban, qu. *Times*, November 11, 2016.

26. qu. *Washington Post*, November 21, 2016; and *Atlantic*, December 2016, pp. 50–57.

27. D. Pipes, *Philadelphia Inquirer*, April 7, 2016.

28. op. cit., vol. 1, chap. 6, p. 287.

29. N. Clegg, *Observer*, December 18, 2011.

30. *Guardian*, November 18, 2013; *Telegraph*, July 16, 2015.

31. A.P., April 29, 2017.

32. A.P., January 19, 2018.

33. M. Pence, March for Life Rally, DC, qu. A.P., January 27, 2017.

34. A.P., October 10, 2011.

35. Food and Drug Administration (FDA), qu. *New York Times*, August 28, 2017, May 10, 2018.

36. *New York Times*, April 4, 2012.

37. *Telegraph*, January 18, 2013.

38. *Telegraph*, December 31, 2012.

39. mynorthwest.com, March 8, 2013; *Telegraph*, April 22, 2014.

40. *Guardian*, April 14, 2016.

41. *Times*, May 3, 2018, May 18, 2018.

42. *Guardian*, July 28, 2017; A.P., July 17, 2018.

43. *Guardian*, October 14, 2017.

44. *Phoenix New Times*, November 10, 2016.

45. *Guardian*, April 16, 2018.

46. *Our New Masters*, London, 1873, p. 364.

47. ONTD Political, April 12, 2012.

48. A.P., October 9, 2017.

49. *Der Spiegel*, March 20, 2018.

50. *Telegraph*, August 30, 2017.

51. *Le Figaro*, December 10, 2017; AFP, May 7, 2018.

52. Cor Orans, chap. 3, Separation from the World, II, 168–171, vaticannews.va, April 1, 2018.

53. HB 2120, Arizona Legislature, January 2017, qu. *Guardian*, January 13, 2017.

54. A.P., September 26, 2012.

55. J. P. Stevens, *New York Times*, March 27, 2018.

56. *New York Times*, January 30, 2016.

57. A.P., August 26, 2015.

58. *New York Times*, February 28, 2018; A.P., March 1, 2018, March 2, 2018.

59. *Seattle Times*, October 19, 2018.

60. CNN Politics.com, February 21, 2018.

61. A.P., February 22, 2018; *New York Times*, March 1, 2018.

62. Donald J. Trump, @realDonaldTrump, February 22, 2018.

63. *New York Times*, March 12, 2018.

64. Donald J. Trump, @realDonaldTrump, March 28, 2018.

65. qu. Politico.com, February 27, 2018.

66. At NRA Annual Meeting, Dallas, Texas, qu. *Dallas Morning News*, May 5, 2018.

67. *New York Times*, August 27, 2017, August 28, 2017.

68. A.P., April 28, 2018.

69. *Times*, April 30, 2018; A.P., June 28, 2018, July 18, 2018.

70. *Times*, March 30, 2010.

71. *New York Times*, February 4, 2008.

72. *Telegraph*, June 6, 2014.

73. A.P., June 15, 2014.

74. *Telegraph*, December 25, 2014.

75. *Times*, December 6, 2016.

76. *New Zealand Herald*, September 24, 2017.

77. *Telegraph*, June 18, 2013; ABC News, May 3, 2012.

78. BBC News, Europe, November 20, 2015.

79. abc.net.au, 21; *Guardian*, May 20, 2016; Reuters, May 4, 2017.

80. *Telegraph*, August 28, 2015.

81. X. Xu, E. E. Bishop, and others, "Annual Healthcare Spending Attributable to Smoking," *American Journal of Preventive Medicine*, March 2015, pp. 326–33.

82. *Guardian*, June 21, 2008.

83. op. cit., 2, 46–48 ff.

84. M. Salvini, leader of Italian Liga and deputy prime minister, qu. *La Stampa*, June 1, 2018 (author's trans.).

85. qu. *New York Times*, January 11, 2010.

86. *Telegraph*, December 25, 2012.

87. S. Cordileone, *National Catholic Register*, February 14, 2011.

88. Radio Maria, qu. *Corriere della Sera*, November 5, 2016.

89. qu. *Telegraph*, December 21, 2012.

90. qu. *Guardian*, May 27, 2015.

91. qu. RT, November 21, 2016.

92. e.g., R. Thomas, bishop of Maidstone, qu. *Times*, June 7, 2018.

93. Revd. W. Love of Albany, New York, qu. *Times Union*, November 12, 2018.

94. *Ha'aretz*, July 28, 2018.

95. Former Chief Rabbi R. S. Amar, qu. *Israel Hayom*, November 18, 2016.

96. Rabbi J. Dweck, qu. *Guardian*, June 18, 2017.

97. *New York Times*, November 14, 2008.

98. A.P., November 13, 2015.

99. D. Oaks, Quorum of the Twelve Apostles, Salt Lake City, qu. A.P., September 30, 2017.

100. D. W. Key, director of Baptist Studies, Emory University, qu. A.P., January 31, 2013.

101. M. Huckabee, *USA Today*, June 26, 2015; Business Insider, June 26, 2015.

102. At Rhodes College, Memphis, Tenn., qu. A.P., September 23, 2015.

103. Reuters, January 6, 2016.

104. *New York Times*, May 6, 2016.

105. qu. A.P., April 27, 2017.

106. A.P., June 30, 2015, July 1, 2015, August 13, 2015.

107. A.P., September 2, 2015.

108. US District Judge D. L. Bunning, A.P., August 13, 2015.

109. BBC News, World, US and Canada, September 9, 2015.

110. *Courier-Journal*, May 2, 2017; wkyt.com, July 21, 2017.

111. A.P., October 1, 2015.

112. C. Hartman, Louisville Fairness Campaign, qu. A.P., September 3, 2015.

113. *Louisville Courier Journal,* November 6, 2018.

114. Reuters, February 7, 2018.

115. *Guardian,* January 31, 2016.

116. J. Sidell, *New York Times,* October 14, 2006.

117. A.P., July 15, 2014.

118. A.P., August 2, 2013.

119. A.P., October 7, 2016.

120. *Miami Herald,* February 9, 2018.

121. *Dallas Morning News,* March 27, 2018, May 8, 2018.

122. Reuters, June 14, 2017.

123. A.P., March 11, 2012.

124. *Times,* October 4, 2017.

125. Reuters, June 25, 2017.

126. ICM Research, qu. *Sunday Times,* April 10, 2016.

127. Farrokh Sekaleshfar, April 26, 2013, www.youtube.com/watch?v =URRsCtJLTQo.

128. S. Mateen, qu. NBC News, June 13, 2016.

129. *Guardian,* December 11, 2013.

130. A.P., June 16, 2016.

131. *Guardian,* June 20, 2012.

132. *Times,* November 7, 2016.

133. A.P., October 11, 2012.

134. A.P., July 12, 2014.

135. A.P., August 29, 2018.

136. Y. Luzhkov, qu. *Guardian,* January 30, 2007.

137. *Guardian,* March 20, 2007.

138. T. Rydzyk, qu. *Observer,* December 15, 2012.

139. qu. *Guardian,* December 12, 2013.

140. *Guardian,* June 12, 2013.

141. P. Ungurian, qu. A.P., June 23, 2013.

142. A.P., June 9, 2018.

143. A.P., October 13, 2018.

144. BBC News, Europe, August 17, 2012.

145. *Corriere della Sera,* December 10, 2012.

146. *Telegraph,* January 9, 2015.

147. *Guardian,* April 18, 2006.

148. A.P., June 1, 2017.

149. A.P., June 29, 2018.

150. *Washington Post,* April 5, 2016.

151. A.P., March 1, 2017.

152. *New York Times,* February 22, 2017.

153. US Dept. of Justice (Civil Rights Division) and US Dept. of Education (Office for Civil Rights), May 13, 2016, pp. 1–8.

154. Attorney General J. Sessions, qu. A.P., October 6, 2017.

155. *New York Times*, July 26, 2017; A.P., August 28, 2017, December 12, 2017, February 2, 2018, March 24, 2018.

156. *Washington Post*, January 20, 2017.

157. *Telegraph*, October 4, 2017.

158. *New York Times*, October 22, 2018.

159. *Guardian*, November 19, 2016.

160. *Telegraph*, September 10, 2017.

161. A.P., October 1, 2017.

162. *Guardian*, March 23, 2016.

163. *Guardian*, June 22, 2018.

164. WCPO Cincinnati, March 3, 2018.

165. A.P., October 15, 2017.

166. A.P., September 27, 2017.

167. *New York Times*, October 24, 2010.

168. BBC News, England, November 27, 2013.

169. *Guardian*, October 10, 2018.

170. *Belfast Telegraph*, May 8, 2017.

171. *New York Times*, June 4, 2018; A.P., August 15, 2018.

172. A.P., August 3, 2017.

173. *Guardian*, August 26, 2015.

174. A.P., July 26, 2016.

175. D. Isaac, qu. *Starkville Daily News*, February 21, 2018.

176. *Telegraph*, July 31, 2015.

177. B. Summerskill, Stonewall, qu. *Guardian*, February 6, 2013.

178. R. Gale, Ibid.

179. D. Trump, qu. A.P., September 15, 2015.

180. D. Trump, at Conservative Political Action Conference (CPAC), National Harbor, Md., qu. *Time*, February 24, 2017.

181. A. de Tocqueville, *The Old Regime and the French Revolution* (1856), New York, 2010, p. 107.

182. *Orange County Register*, January 8, 2016; "Undocumented Immigrants in California," Public Policy Institute of California, March 2017, p. 1; American Immigration Council, Fact Sheet, October 4, 2017.

183. R. Whiteman, former head of UK Border Agency, qu. *Times*, August 3, 2016; *Times*, June 16, 2017.

184. World Population Review, German Population 2018, June 16, 2018; also German Federal Statistics Office (Destatis), qu. dw.com July 1, 2017; *Der Spiegel* April 19, 2018.

185. *Telegraph*, October 23, 2015; *Times*, December 10, 2015; German Federal Statistics Office (Destatis), qu. dw.com, July 1, 2017.

186. ONS, *Telegraph*, December 17, 2013; OECD, International Migration Outlook, qu. *Times*, June 30, 2017.

187. ONS, Statistical Bulletin, "Births by Parents' Country of Birth," section 8, para. 1, August 24, 2017.

188. ONS, qu. *Guardian*, May 24, 2018.

189. *Telegraph*, March 24, 2014, September 2, 2017.

190. *Guardian*, December 16, 2012.

191. *Daily Express*, April 25, 2016.

192. S. Javid, Communities Secretary, UK Government, qu. *Guardian*, March 14, 2018.

193. A.P., September 4, 2015.

194. cf. E. J. Blakely and M. J. Snyder, *Fortress America: Gated Communities in the United States*, Brookings Institution, Washington, DC, 1997.

195. Center for Migration Studies, US Undocumented Population, table 2, February 22, 2018.

196. A.P., July 23, 2014.

197. A.P., June 15, 2018.

198. *Washington Post*, October 31, 2018.

199. A.P., February 19, 2016.

200. A.P., July 15, 2014.

201. Georgetown University Law Center, qu. A.P., April 11, 2016.

202. US Department of Health and Human Services, A.P., September 20, 2018.

203. *Times*, March 17, 2017.

204. A.P., August 8, 2017.

205. *Corriere della Sera*, October 2, 2018.

206. *New York Times*, June 26, 2018.

207. e.g., A.P., April 15, 2018, July 28, 2018, August 1, 2018.

208. A.P., November 9, 2018.

209. A.P., September 18, 2018.

210. *Guardian*, October 9, 2017.

211. *Telegraph*, September 26, 2015.

212. V. Orban, *Frankfurter Allgemeiner Zeitung*, September 3, 2015.

213. *La Stampa*, June 23, 2018.

214. *Il Messaggero*, June 11, 2018; *La Stampa*, July 12, 2018; *La Repubblica*, August 20, 2018.

215. Donald J. Trump, @realDonaldTrump, June 24, 2018.

216. D. Trump, White House, qu. BBC.com, US and Canada, June 19, 2018.

217. M. Salvini, at Sondrio, qu. *La Repubblica*, June 1, 2018.

218. At Vicenza, qu. *La Repubblica*, June 2, 2018.

219. G. Conte, address to Italian parliament, Rome, qu. *La Repubblica*, June 6, 2018.

220. Reuters, June 19, 2018.

221. M. Soder, qu. *Der Spiegel*, June 15, 2018.

222. M. Morawiecki, qu. uawire.org, January 3, 2018.

223. *Le Monde*, April 22, 2018.

224. *Australian*, July 19, 2013.

225. *Telegraph*, December 11, 2012.

226. US Dept. of Education, qu. BBC News, Education and Family, August 26, 2014.

227. US Census Bureau, A.P., December 12, 2012.

228. *Times*, May 2, 2013.

229. A.P., February 8, 2013.

230. Agence France-Presse, February 26, 2016.

231. *Times*, May 3, 2018.

232. Dept. of Homeland Security, qu. A.P., October 7, 2016.

233. Department of Homeland Security, A.P., August 7, 2018.

234. Report on Exit Checks, Inspector of Borders and Immigration, UK Government, qu. *Times*, March 29, 2018.

235. R. Whiteman, UK Border Agency, qu. *Telegraph*, September 29, 2012.

236. Public Administration Committee, House of Commons, qu. BBC News, UK, July 28, 2013.

237. Home Office, qu. *Telegraph*, August 14, 2016.

238. House of Commons Public Accounts Committee, *Times*, March 4, 2016.

239. Dept. of Homeland Security, A.P., September 19, 2016.

240. *Telegraph*, September 19, 2012.

241. National Census, qu. *Telegraph*, July 23, 2013.

242. *Guardian*, March 12, 2013.

243. A.P., May 14, 2018, June 5, 2018, June 20, 2018, August 9, 2018.

244. A.P., January 18, 2017.

245. Dept. of Homeland Security, A.P., December 30, 2016.

246. *Libero*, February 9, 2016.

247. *Deutsche Welle*, March 1, 2016.

248. *New York Times*, September 5, 2017.

249. A.P., August 31, 2015.

250. A.P., September 17, 2015, October 15, 2015, March 20, 2017; *Guardian*, June 4, 2018.

251. *Times*, August 18, 2017; *Guardian*, April 29, 2018; A.P., May 17, 2018.

252. *Times*, January 10, 2017.

253. Candidacy Announcement Speech, The American Presidency Project, June 16, 2015.

254. J. Biden, qu. A.P., May 4, 2014.

255. *New York Times*, February 25, 2016.

256. A.P., February 9, 2017.

257. e.g., A.P., January 15, 2016.

258. A.P., February 23, 2018.

259. *Die Zeit*, January 19, 2018.

260. *Guardian*, January 24, 2016.

261. *Guardian*, January 20, 2016.

262. A.P., March 17, 2017.

263. C. Stokes, Médecins Sans Frontières, qu. A.P., March 7, 2017.

264. *Times*, August 26, 2017.

265. A.P., August 27, 2015, referring to a camp on the outskirts of Paris; also A.P., May 24, 2018, May 30, 2018.

266. M. Salvini, qu. *Corriere della Sera*, June 19, 2018; *La Repubblica*, July 25, 2018.

267. D. Trump, qu. *New York Times*, December 7, 2015.

268. A.P.-NORC, "VoteCast" Survey, qu. A.P., November 11, 2018.

269. *Resto del Carlino*, November 8, 2017 (author's trans.).

270. *New York Times*, December 19, 2015.

271. A.P., January 12, 2016.

272. Reuters, June 28, 2018; *New York Times*, July 2, 2018.

273. Agence France-Presse, September 28, 2017.

274. *Times*, July 28, 2017.

275. *Telegraph*, July 9, 2010.

276. Plato, *Apology*, 51d–e.

277. Agence France-Presse, July 9, 2010.

278. *Times*, April 20, 2018.

279. *Guardian*, April 19, 2016.

280. SVT Nyheter, Stockholm, August 15, 2018.

281. *Christian Science Monitor*, February 3, 2010.

282. *Australian*, April 20, 2017.

283. *Telegraph*, August 8, 2018.

284. A.P., September 19, 2018.

285. A.P., January 10, 2017.

286. Reuters, December 7, 2016.

287. J. M. Blanquer, qu. *L'Express*, May 29, 2018; *Times*, May 31, 2018.

288. A.P., September 1, 2017.

289. *Times*, August 5, 2015.

290. *Die Zeit*, April 24, 2018.

291. *Il Giorno*, December 17, 2015.

292. Pew Research Center, Religion and Public Life, November 29, 2017.

293. ONS, qu. *Telegraph*, September 21, 2018.

294. *Houston Chronicle*, July 24, 2015; *Dallas Morning News*, August 29, 2018.

295. *Corriere della Sera*, April 8, 2017.

296. *Telegraph*, December 5, 2012; *Telegraph*, October 25, 2015; *Guardian*, February 7, 2018.

297. *Times*, April 9, 2018.

298. A.P., February 26, 2015; Reuters, June 8, 2018; Agence France-Presse, June 10, 2018.

299. R. T. Erdogan, qu. Agence France-Presse, June 10, 2018.

300. A.P., July 20, 2012.

301. *Apology*, 5:1, 13:3.

302. *New York Times*, May 25, 2007.

303. *Die Westfalenpost*, February 1, 2018.

304. *Corriere della Sera*, January 19, 2009.

305. A.P., November 30, 2011.

306. *Telegraph*, September 15, 2011.

307. BBC News, Europe, November 3, 2015.

308. *Guardian*, October 3, 2013.

309. Agence France-Presse, October 31, 2012; also *Pakistan Observer*, May 7, 2012.

310. *Houston Chronicle*, August 14, 2018.

311. Ministry of Justice, Family Court Statistics, England and Wales, December 15, 2016, p. 5.

312. A.P., March 26, 2017.

313. A.P., December 9, 2016.

314. *New York Times*, August 13, 2016.

315. S. Kurz, qu. Reuters, June 8, 2018.

316. A.P., May 27, 2018.

317. *Telegraph*, September 19, 2013.

318. *Telegraph*, October 21, 2014.

319. Agence France-Presse, January 9, 2018.

320. *Guardian*, February 15, 2014.

321. A.P., May 31, 2017, June 9, 2017.

322. *New York Post*, October 26, 2011.

323. A.P., August 15, 2018.

324. *Le Monde*, November 19, 2015; *New York Times*, November 27, 2015.

325. www.frontnational.com, July 26, 2016.

326. Reuters, May 1, 2016.

327. *Independent*, August 28, 2016, and A.P., August 26, 2016.

328. M. Salvini, at Umbertide, qu. *La Stampa*, February 8, 2018.

329. N. Sarkozy, qu. *Guardian*, March 12, 2012.

330. *Guardian*, December 13, 2007.

331. *Guardian*, April 16, 2014.

332. A.P., April 13, 2012, November 12, 2012.

333. F. Anning, qu. *Sydney Morning Herald*, August 14, 2018.

334. *Guardian*, June 17, 2016; *Telegraph*, June 18, 2016.

335. Speech in Nantes, qu. *Le Parisien*, February 26, 2017; speech at Paris rally, qu. France-Soir, April 18, 2017.

336. A.P., July 8, 2017.

337. E. Macron, in Helsinki, www.elysee.fr, August 31, 2018.

338. *Guardian*, April 8, 2018.

339. M. Salvini, in Strasbourg, qu. euobserver.com, March 13, 2018.

340. M. Salvini, at Isola Tiberina, Rome, qu. rai news.it, September 22, 2018.

341. S. Bannon, qu. A.P., September 22, 2018.

342. *Guardian*, June 20, 2016, October 18, 2016.

343. *Washington Post*, August 12, 2017; *New York Times*, August 12, 2017.

344. Anti-Defamation League, qu. A.P., October 9, 2017.

345. *New York Times*, August 28, 2017; *Los Angeles Times*, October 22, 2017; A.P., August 5, 2018; *New York Times*, August 21, 2018.

346. *Baltimore Sun*, August 21, 2017; *New York Daily News*, August 30, 2017.

347. e.g., *Boston Globe*, August 19, 2017.

348. *USA Today*, October 8, 2017.

349. A.P., October 7, 2018.

350. *Diaries* 1933–1945, London, 2000, p. 662.

351. *New York Times*, August 12, 2017.

352. *Guardian*, January 8, 2016; A.P., January 3, 2017.

353. Community Security Trust, Antisemitic Incidents Report, February 1, 2018; Anti-Defamation League, *New York Times*, February 27, 2018.

354. M. Freeman, Global Research, April 7, 2016.

355. At West Palm Beach, Florida, vox.com, October 13, 2016.

356. Election campaign speech, Manchester, qu. *Times*, May 9, 2017.

357. TalkRadio, qu. *Telegraph*, November 10, 2016.

358. op. cit., p. 25.

359. op. cit., pp. 230–31.

CHAPTER 8: THE POLITICAL CLASS

1. *The Federalist Papers*, ed. L. Goldman, Oxford, 2008, no. 62, p. 308.

2. *Times*, February 14, 2018.

3. L. Atkeson, Center for the Study of Voting, Elections and Democracy, qu. *Guardian*, October 21, 2016.

4. P. Nuttall, UKIP, qu. *Telegraph*, January 21, 2017.

5. D. Trump, at Green Bay, Wisconsin, qu. *Washington Post*, October 17, 2016; at Colorado Springs, qu. *Denver Post*, October 18, 2016, etc.

6. N. Farage, breitbart.com, November 22, 2016.

7. BBC Today, qu. *Guardian*, March 11, 2016.

8. N. Farage, Conservative Political Action Conference (CPAC), National Harbor, Md., qu. *Guardian*, February 24, 2017.

9. P. Swick, qu. *New York Times*, October 27, 2016.

10. A.P.-NORC Center for Public Affairs Research, A.P., May 28, 2016.

11. A.P.-NORC Center, A.P., February 26, 2018.

12. N. Farage, qu. *Telegraph*, November 9, 2016.

13. qu. *Guardian*, March 13, 2016.

14. A. Maurois, *Disraeli: A Picture of the Victorian Age*, London, 1927, p. 92.

15. At Nashville, Tenn., qu. Politico.com, August 29, 2016.

16. qu. A.P., October 17, 2018.

17. D. Cameron, qu. *Guardian*, November 2, 2006.

18. Breakdown Britain, Conservative Party, London, December 2006, p. 22.

19. l. 374.

20. D. Cameron in "Late Show with Letterman," *Times*, September 27, 2012.

21. A. Leadsom, leader of the House of Commons, qu. *Telegraph*, July 20, 2017.

22. G. Johnson, qu. *New York Times*, September 8, 2016.

23. qu. A.P., March 4, 2016.

24. Donald J. Trump, @realDonaldTrump, January 21, 2017.

25. Donald J. Trump, @realDonaldTrump, May 3, 2018.

26. Donald J. Trump, @realDonaldTrump, July 3, 2018.

27. *Advice to Young Men*, London, 1829, letter 1, sect. 44, p. 41.

28. F. Trollope, *Domestic Manners of the Americans*, London, 1832, p. 152.

29. op. cit., vol. 1, chap. 13, p. 83.

30. *The Book of the Courtier* (1528), New York, 1959, p. 292.

31. J. Sherman, qu. *Times*, July 7, 2016.

32. Statement by Sir John Chilcot, The Iraq Inquiry, July 6, 2016, p. 8.

33. *Letters and Speeches*, ed. T. Carlyle, London, 1850, vol. 1, p. 227.

34. S. Zweig, *Marie Antoinette: The Portrait of an Average Woman*, London, 1933, p. 214.

35. D. Cameron, qu. *Guardian*, October 13, 2007.

36. D. Cameron, World Economic Forum, Davos, *Guardian*, January 31, 2009.

37. G. Brown, National Council of Voluntary Organizations, September 3, 2007.

38. op. cit. (no. 15), p. 76.

39. B. Obama, qu. *New York Times*, January 8, 2008, etc.

40. D. Trump, Republican National convention, Cleveland, Ohio, *USA Today*, July 21, 2016.

41. *On the Sublime*, 30:1.

42. *Political Precepts*, 801d,f; 803b,e.

43. At Grant Park, Chicago, qu. *Time*, November 5, 2008.

44. Donald J. Trump, @realDonaldTrump, December 17, 2016.

45. M. Wolff, qu. *New Yorker*, January 4, 2018.

46. op. cit., vol. 1, chap. 14, p. 92.

47. Anon., "I Am Part of the Resistance inside the Trump Administration," *New York Times*, September 5, 2018.

48. J. B. Comey, qu. ABC News, April 15, 2018.

49. J. Ganz, *New York Times*, June 12, 2018.

50. T. Kushner, qu. A.P., June 11, 2018.

51. O. M. Newman, former White House official, NBC's *Meet the Press*, qu. Politico.com, August 12, 2018.

52. *David Copperfield*, Oxford, 1983, p. 512.

53. *My Early Life*, London, 1930, p. 357.

54. *On Duties*, bk. 2,24.

55. *Conspiracy of Catiline*, 3:2.

56. 44:13.

57. *Guardian*, April 3, 2016; *Hong Kong Free Press*, April 5, 2016.

58. *Wall Street Journal*, February 17, 2015; *New York Times*, April 19, 2015, etc.

59. First Presidential Debate, cnbc.com, September 26, 2016; *Washington Post*, September 27, 2016.

60. NYT/CBS News Poll, *New York Times*, November 3, 2016.

61. *New York Times*, December 1, 2017; *New York Post*, December 30, 2017, February 23, 2018, etc.

62. Founders Online, National Archives, http:/founders.archives.gov/documents/Adams/99-03-02-0784.

63. A. Seldon and D. Kavanagh, *The Blair Effect, 2001–5*, Cambridge, 2005, p. 33.

64. Committee on Standards in Public Life, MPs' Outside Interests, July 2018, p. 28.

65. *Times*, October 17, 2017.

66. P. Tyler, life-peer, qu. *Guardian*, February 21, 2017.

67. *Telegraph*, July 30, 2015; *Times*, August 6, 2016; *Sunday Times*, April 2, 2017.

68. *Telegraph*, June 29, 2015; *Guardian*, March 15, 2017.

69. "Full List of MPs Investigated," *Telegraph*, May 8, 2009.

70. M. Williams, *Parliament Ltd*, London, 2016, passim.

71. Hypereides, *Prosecution of Demosthenes*, 5:27.

72. B. Whitelocke, *Memorials of English Affairs* (1682), Ann Arbor and Oxford, 2007, p. 524.

73. op. cit., London, 1829, letter 1, 21, p. 9.

74. *Telegraph*, August 1, 2016.

75. A.P., June 8, 2012.

76. op. cit., vol. 2, no. 196 (April 12, 1768), p. 529.

77. A.P., November 27, 2007.

78. *Guardian*, January 19, 2015.

79. A.P., September 21, 2012; November 21, 2012.

80. *New York Times*, February 22, 2016.

81. qu. BBC News, US and Canada, February 2, 2016.

82. *New York Times*, March 1, 2016.

83. Federal Election Commission, qu. A.P., December 9, 2016.

84. OpenSecrets.org, qu. A.P., February 5, 2016.

85. A.P., May 6, 2016; *New York Times*, June 12, 2016.

86. A.P., August 16, 2015.

87. A.P., November 5, 2016.

88. *Times*, March 29, 2016.

89. Federal Election Commission, A.P., December 9, 2016.

90. K. Pierson, Trump spokesperson, qu. CNN Politics, June 21, 2016.

91. A.P., December 9, 2016.

92. *New York Times*, February 15, 2018; A.P., August 14, 2018.

93. A.P., December 7, 2012.

94. A.P., November 4, 2012.

95. A.P., December 19, 2015.

96. A.P., January 31, 2015.

97. Chief Justice J. Roberts, McCutcheon v. Federal Election Commission, no 12–536, qu. *New York Times*, April 2, 2014.

98. November 5, 2018.

99. National Institute for Money in Politics, A.P., November 1, 2018.

100. A.P., October 27, 2018.

101. D. Keating, Center for Competitive Politics, qu. A.P., August 3, 2015.

102. Ibid.

103. A.P., February 3, 2016.

104. Paradise Papers, qu. A.P., November 8, 2017.

105. *Times*, October 20, 2018.

106. T. Stanley, *Telegraph*, August 14, 2013.

107. *Times*, February 7, 2008.

108. *Times*, September 21, 2017.

109. *Guardian*, April 26, 2017.

110. A.P., February 6, 2016.

111. *Telegraph*, June 20, 2015.

112. *Guardian*, January 10, 2008; *Telegraph*, June 12, 2010; *Telegraph*, June 28, 2015.

113. *Times*, March 9, 2017.

114. *Times*, March 18, 2017.

115. *Times*, May 25, 2018.

116. *Guardian*, December 8, 2016; *Telegraph*, April 14, 2017.

117. op. cit., vol. 1, pp. 161–62.

118. *Telegraph*, September 30, 2011.

119. *Telegraph*, January 19, 2008.

120. loc. cit.

121. *Le Canard Enchainé*, July 13, 2016.

122. *Le Monde*, August 25, 2017.

123. *Telegraph*, December 6, 2008; Politico, October 21, 2008.

124. fashion.com, June 8, 2016; *New York Post*, June 5, 2016; CNBC, June 6, 2016.

125. *Le Soir*, May 7, 2017.

126. *Times*, July 13, 2017; US Federal Election Commission, qu. A.P., July 10, 2017.

127. *Private Correspondence*, May 15, 1761, London, 1820, p. 2.

128. A.P., April 12, 2006.

129. A.P.-GfK poll, A.P., April 12, 2016; NYT/CBS poll, May 13–17, 2016, pp. 16–18, qu. *New York Times*, May 19, 2016; *Washington Post*, May 21, 2016.

130. I. Stelzer, *Sunday Times*, June 12, 2016.

131. A.P., July 14, 2017.

132. J. Halbrook, qu. *New York Times*, October 27, 2016.

133. *New York Times*, October 25, 2018; *Miami Herald*, October 26, 2018.

134. *New York Times*, November 4, 2004; A.P., March 11, 2007.

135. Aeschylus, *Eumenides*, l.704–706.

136. e.g., A.P.-NORC Center for Public Affairs Research A.P., January 30, 2016; April 11, 2016; July 18, 2016.

137. A.P.-NORC Center for Public Affairs Research, qu. A.P., March 30, 2017; December 15, 2017; February 23, 2018; March 26, 2018; August 24, 2018; October 25, 2018; November 7, 2018.

138. e.g., M. Gold, "The Campaign to Impeach President Trump Has Begun," *Washington Post*, January 22, 2017; A. Green, "Calling for the Impeachment of the President," Congressional Record, US House of Representatives 63(85), pp. H. 4227–4228, May 17, 2017; also E. Holtzman, *The Case for Impeaching Trump*, New York, 2018.

CHAPTER 9: BAD FAITH

1. P. Collins, *Times*, December 23, 2016.

2. J. Browne, *Telegraph*, April 7, 2012.

3. G. Monbiot, *Guardian*, May 15, 2012.

4. F. Nelson, *Telegraph*, August 10, 2012.

5. P. Toynbee, *Guardian* December 30, 2005.

6. UNAIDS report, qu. *Guardian*, July 12, 2016, July 31, 2016.

7. Z. L. Brumme and others, "Extensive Host Immune Adaptations in a Concentrated North American HIV Epidemic," AIDS (International Aids Society), vol. 32, issue 14, September 10, 2018, pp. 1927–38.

8. L. G. Bekker, International Aids Society, qu. *Telegraph*, September 23, 2017.

9. Ban Ki-Moon, UN secretary-general, qu. A.P., July 18, 2016.

10. e.g., Public Health England, Sexually Transmitted Infections in England, 2017, Health Protection Report, vol. 12, no. 20, June 5, 2018, p. 1; CDC and California Department of Public Health, qu. A.P., May 15, 2018.

11. cf. G. Whiteman, C. Hope, and P. Wadhams, *Nature*, vol. 49, pp. 401–403, July 25, 2013.

12. Donald J. Trump, @realDonaldTrump, January 25, 2014, January 29, 2014.

13. qu. CBS *60 Minutes*, October 14, 2018.

14. *New York Times*, June 1, 2017.

15. Reuters, March 28, 2017.

16. A.P., July 6, 2018.

17. e.g., US Global Change Research Program, Washington, DC, Climate Science Special Report, November 2017, vol. 1, key finding 3; UN Intergovernmental Panel for Climate Change (IPCC), Special Report on Global Warming of 1.5° C, October 8, 2018, pp. 1–4.

18. Reports of World Meteorological Organization (WMO), NASA, UK Meteorological Office, National Oceanic and Atmospheric Administration (NOAA), and Goddard Institute for Space Studies.

19. W. Steffen and others, *Proceedings of the National Academy of Science* (PNAS), August 2018, qu. Science News, August 6, 2018.

20. *New York Times*, July 13, 2017; H. Konrad and others, "Net Retreat of Antarctic Glacier Grounding Lines," *Nature Geoscience*, qu. Science Daily, April 2, 2018.

21. D. Breitburg and others, *Science*, vol. 359, no. 6371, January 5, 2018.

22. cf. T. P. Hughes and others, "Global Warming Transforms Coral Reef Assemblages," *Nature*, April 18, 2018, pp. 1–16.

23. C. Moore, *Telegraph*, April 7, 2014.

24. A. Rudd, Energy and Climate-Change Secretary, UK Govt., qu. *Telegraph*, July 24, 2015.

25. op. cit., p. 215.

26. J. Evelyn ["J. E."], *Fumifugium*, London, 1661, pp. ii, 5–6, 9–10.

27. J. R. Jambeck and others, "Plastic Waste Inputs from Land into the Ocean," *Science*, vol.

347, issue 6223, February 11, 2015, pp. 768–71; Plastic Oceans, qu. *Times*, May 22, 2017; UK Government Office for Science, Future of the Sea, qu. *Times*, March 21, 2018, "Microplastics and Persistent Fluorinated Chemicals in the Antarctic," Greenpeace, June 2, 2018, p. 5.

    28. *Guardian*, September 24, 2017; A.P., February 3, 2017.

    29. G. Ceballos and others, *Proceedings of the National Academy of Sciences* (PNAS), July 10, 2017.

    30. World Wildlife Fund (WWF), Living Planet Report, 2018, pp. 7–10.

    31. Address to Starmus Festival, Trondheim, Norway, qu. *Telegraph*, June 20, 2017.

    32. Human Rights Watch, April 25, 2018.

    33. *Telegraph*, May 4, 2015; *Guardian*, December 1, 2015.

    34. "Notes on Nationalism" (1945), *Collected Essays*, London, 1961, pp. 273–74.

    35. cf. G. Lafer, "Neoliberalism by Other Means: The 'War on Terror' at Home and Abroad," *New Political Science*, vol. 26, 2004, issue 3, pp. 323–46.

    36. J. Gray, BBC News, Magazine, July 11, 2014; *Guardian*, August 20, 2014.

    37. The Covenant of the Islamic Resistance Movement, August 18, 1988, Articles 17, 22, and 32, http://avalon.law.yale.edu/20th_century/hamas.asp.

    38. E. Macron, qu. *L'Express*, July 16, 2017.

    39. K. Livingstone, former London mayor, Vanessa Feltz Show, BBC London, qu. *Telegraph*, April 28, 2016, and *Guardian*, March 30, 2017; K. Livingstone, Al Ghad Al Arabi TV, May 4, 2016; N. Shah, MP, Facebook, August 5, 2004, at 21:06.

    40. US Department of Justice, Hate Crime Statistics, 2017, Table 1 (Bias Motivation), Fall 2018, p. 2; Community Security Trust and Guardian, February 1, 2018.

    41. Report, Home Affairs Select Committee, qu. *Sunday Times*, October 16, 2016.

    42. e.g., *Guardian*, July 20, 2018; *Telegraph*, August 11, 2018.

    43. J. Mann, MP, chairman, All-Party Parliamentary Group Against Anti-Semitism, qu. *Evening Standard*, March 29, 2018.

    44. *Times*, August 3, 2018; *Telegraph*, August 24, 2018; also David Duke.com, September 14, 2015, and *Daily Stormer*, September 15, 2015.

    45. D. Hannan, *Telegraph*, October 22, 2007.

    46. *Telegraph*, January 2, 2008.

    47. e.g., K. Stryker, Huffington Post, May 5, 2014; A. W. Eaton in S. Irvin, ed., Body Aesthetics, Oxford, 2016, pp. 37–59.

    48. *Boston Globe*, September 17, 2007; *Telegraph*, January 2, 2008.

    49. A.P., June 3, 2005.

    50. *USA Today*, August 19, 2015; *Times*, June 1, 2018.

    51. N. Mitchell and others, "Obesity: Overview of an Epidemic," *Psychiatric Clinics of North America*, vol. 34, issue 4, December 2011, pp. 717–32; *Sunday Times*, April 15, 2018; *Telegraph*, June 22, 2018.

    52. *Telegraph*, January 26, 2009.

    53. cf. P. Campos, *The Obesity Myth*, New York, 2004; D. Kulick, *Fat: The Anthropology of an Obsession*, New York, 2005.

    54. *Guardian*, June 9, 2006; cf. S. Pinker, *The Better Angels of Our Nature: Why Violence Has Declined*, New York, 2011.

55. *Guardian*, April 24, 2014.

56. *Telegraph*, April 24, 2014.

57. *Telegraph*, July 17, 2014.

58. ONS, *Telegraph*, July 16, 2015, October 15, 2015.

59. R. Ford, *Times*, June 8, 2018.

60. Metropolitan Police report, qu. *Guardian*, July 7, 2017; NHS England, *Guardian*, August 31, 2017.

61. ONS, qu. *Guardian*, July 19, 2018.

62. Metropolitan Police report, qu. *Guardian*, May 15, 2018.

63. *Telegraph*, April 7, 2018.

64. Metropolitan Police statistics, qu. *Telegraph*, June 26, 2018.

65. J. Sebire, National Police Chiefs' Council, qu. *Times*, November 2, 2018.

66. UPI, September 21, 2018.

67. Police Workforce (England and Wales), Home Office, Statistical Bulletin, January 25, 2018, p. 7.

68. Freedom of Information Act disclosure, *Sunday Times*, September 2, 2018.

69. *Sunday Times*, August 26, 2018.

70. Police Federation of England and Wales, qu. *Guardian*, August 7, 2018.

71. P. Toynbee, *Guardian*, January 13, 2015.

72. *Guardian*, October 20, 2016, January 26, 2018.

73. *Sunday Times*, July 22, 2018; *Times*, September 22, 2018.

74. M. Fitzgerald, University of Kent, qu. *Guardian*, April 12, 2014.

75. T. Winsor, qu. *Guardian*, January 15, 2014.

76. P. Barron, qu. *Telegraph*, November 20, 2013.

77. Her Majesty's Inspectorate of Constabulary (HMIC), *Guardian*, June 17, 2013.

78. *Guardian*, November 15, 2012; A.P., July 17, 2015.

79. e.g., Her Majesty's Inspectorate of Constabulary (HMIC), qu. *Times*, July 17, 2018.

80. *Telegraph*, December 23, 2008, and November 20, 2013; Freedom of Information Act disclosure, *Times*, March 31, 2017.

81. S. Walby, University of London, qu. *Times*, June 9, 2015.

82. *Guardian*, May 1, 2014; November 18, 2014; Freedom of Information Act disclosure, *Times*, April 17, 2017.

83. *Sunday Times*, July 8, 2018.

84. Commissioner of Police of the Metropolis (Appellant) v. DSD and another (respondents) 2108, UKSC 11; BBC.com/news/UK, February 21, 2018.

85. Freedom of Information Act disclosure, *Times*, April 17, 2017.

86. ONS, qu. *Telegraph*, October 19, 2017.

87. M. Simmons, Deputy Assistant Commissioner, Metropolitan Police, qu. *Guardian*, October 16, 2017.

88. J. Stokley, Metropolitan Police, qu. *Guardian*, June 1, 2018.

89. *New York Times*, December 30, 2011.

90. *Los Angeles Times*, October 15, 2015.

91. *New York Times*, December 30, 2011.

92. Freedom of Information Act disclosure, *Times*, February 20, 2017; HMIC, qu. *Telegraph*, March 22, 2018.

93. National Rural Crime Network, *Times*, September 15, 2015.

94. A.P., October 24, 2013.

95. New York City Department of Investigation, A.P., March 27, 2018.

96. *Telegraph*, August 21, 2012.

97. Independent Police Complaints Commission, *Telegraph*, January 10, 2013, February 26, 2013.

98. *Telegraph*, March 12, 2012.

99. Home Office, Police Recorded Crime, 2016–2017, April 1, 2017, Table 1.

100. Home Office statistics, qu. *Times*, December 29, 2017.

101. ONS, qu. *Times*, October 18, 2018.

102. *Sunday Times*, August 7, 2016.

103. *Times*, January 11, 2012.

104. *Washington Post*, June 7, 2018.

105. *Guardian*, May 13, 2013; Freedom of Information Act disclosure, qu. *Independent*, May 7, 2017.

106. J. Grange, Assoc. of Chief Police Officers, qu. *Observer*, May 28, 2006.

107. F. Trollope, op. cit., p. 136.

108. op. cit., part 2, chap. 27, p. 347.

109. Citizens' Report, qu. *New Statesman*, January 9, 2015.

110. A.P., May 1, 2014.

111. A.P., April 27, 2016.

112. *Telegraph*, December 26, 2014.

113. "Inspector Gadget," qu. *Telegraph*, January 7, 2013.

114. Gun Violence Archive, qu. BBC News (US and Canada), January 5, 2016; Centers for Disease Control and Prevention, National Center for Injury Prevention and Control, February 19, 2017.

115. e.g., A.P., January 20, 2012; *New York Times*, November 23, 2012; *New York Times*, October 15, 2018.

116. A.P., January 4, 2017, December 21, 2017, January 6, 2018.

117. A.P., July 2, 2014.

118. A.P., January 2, 2014, January 3, 2014, March 31, 2015.

119. A.P., November 24, 2015.

120. A.P., December 30, 2016.

121. The Counted, qu. *Guardian*, July 7, 2016.

122. Centers for Disease Control and Prevention, qu. A.P., November 3, 2017.

123. FBI data, qu. *Guardian*, September 24, 2018.

124. R. Holt, Chicago Police Dept., qu. *Guardian*, April 21, 2014.

125. "Investigation of the Chicago Police Department," qu. *Chicago Tribune*, January 14, 2017.

126. A.P., October 18, 2012.

127. Chicago Police Dept., A.P., January 1, 2018.

128. A.P., January 27, 2017, December 21, 2017.

129. *Chicago Tribune*, April 17, 2017.

130. R. Emmanuel, qu. A.P., August 7, 2018.

131. A.P., May 31, 2016; *New York Times*, September 18, 2016.

132. A.P., September 6, 2016.

133. Reuters, December 27, 2016.

134. *USA Today*, July 6, 2017.

135. A.P., September 6, 2015.

136. A.P., July 25, 2012.

137. E. Badger, *New York Times*, November 9, 2017.

138. A.P., January 1, 2018.

139. Asst. Sheriff T. Fasulo, qu. A.P., October 3, 2017.

140. K. Parker and others, America's Complex Relationship with Guns, Pew Research Center, June 22, 2017, pp. 4–5.

141. In Louisville, Kentucky, qu. A.P., May 20, 2016, and *Washington Post*, May 20, 2016.

142. A.P., November 30, 2017, December 7, 2017.

143. A.P., April 12, 2017, July 1, 2017, July 17, 2017.

144. A.P., April 15, 2016, May 8, 2018.

145. A.P., July 9, 2014.

146. A.P., July 31, 2018, August 28, 2018.

147. B. Simpson, Georgiacarry.org, qu. *Telegraph*, July 7, 2014.

148. op. cit., part 2, chap. 22, p. 287; chap. 26, p. 335.

149. A.P., October 19, 2017.

150. A.P., March 21, 2016.

151. Small Arms Survey, qu. A.P., June 19, 2018.

152. HM Inspectorate of Constabulary (HMIC), qu. *Telegraph*, March 2, 2017.

153. US Department of Justice, Correctional Populations in the US, January 21, 2016, p. 1.

154. Freedom of Information Act disclosure, qu. *Guardian*, March 30, 2018; *Times*, August 22, 2018.

155. Ministry of Justice report, *Telegraph*, September 9, 2012, December 6, 2012.

156. Ministry of Justice report, qu. *Times*, June 22, 2018.

157. Report of Brennan Center for Justice, qu. *Guardian*, December 11, 2016.

158. *Guardian*, August 17, 2016.

159. loc. cit.

160. Bureau of Justice Statistics, qu. A.P., May 21, 2018.

161. *Telegraph*, October 25, 2012; Ministry of Justice and Prison Reform Trust, Summer 2016, p. 4; *Sunday Times*, January 14, 2018.

162. G. Stacey, chief inspector of probation, qu. *Times*, December 15, 2016, June 19, 2017.

163. Ministry of Justice, qu. *Telegraph*, August 14, 2015.

164. Ministry of Justice, qu. *Guardian*, October 19, 2016, January 26, 2017; qu. *Times*, April 28, 2017; qu. *Guardian*, July 27, 2017, October 26, 2017, October 11, 2018; Safety in Custody, Ministry of Justice, qu. *Times*, October 25, 2018.

165. HM Inspectorate of Prisons (HMIP), September 2016, qu. *Telegraph*, November 5, 2016; Ministry of Justice, qu. *Guardian*, July 9, 2017; HMIP, qu. *Guardian*, May 16, 2018.

166. Freedom of Information Act disclosure, Ministry of Justice, qu. *Observer*, September 1, 2018.

167. House of Commons Justice Committee, qu. *Independent*, June 22, 2018; *Guardian*, July 27, 2018.

168. Centre for Education and Monitoring, January 2016, pp. 19 ff.

169. National Alliance for Public Charter Schools, Estimated Enrollment, 2016–2017, p. 2.

170. M. Smith, Home School Legal Defense Association, qu. *Telegraph*, January 20, 2018; *Guardian*, November 3, 2018.

171. Sutton Trust, qu. *Evening Standard*, September 6, 2017.

172. C. Blower, general secretary, National Union of Teachers, qu. *Independent*, January 4, 2016.

173. Chesterfield, op. cit., no. 101, p. 243.

174. Dept. of Education, School Workforce Survey, qu. *Telegraph*, July 20, 2017; National Audit Office, qu. *Times*, July 29, 2017.

175. A.P., November 26, 2012, August 20, 2014.

176. *Telegraph*, November 21, 2012.

177. *Times*, December 11, 2015.

178. Office for Qualifications and Examinations Regulation (Ofqual), qu. *Telegraph*, January 5, 2018.

179. BBC News, Education and Family, June 14, 2015.

180. Dept. of Education statement, qu. BBC News, Education, August 30, 2015; also Dept. of Education, qu. *Guardian*, July 5, 2016, July 4, 2017.

181. Progress in International Reading Literacy Study (PIRLS), qu. *Telegraph*, December 4, 2017.

182. e.g., "Reading for a Fairer Future," Save the Children, qu. *Telegraph*, September 8, 2014; Dept. of Education, Statistical First Release, National Curriculum Assessment, 2014; K. Lawton and H. Warren, The Power of Reading, Save the Children, 2015, p. 1.

183. F. Manjoo, *New York Times*, February 9, 2018.

184. N. Gibb, British schools minister, qu. *Times*, October 25, 2016; National Foundation for Educational Research, qu. *Times*, May 17, 2017; Dept. for Education, *Guardian*, January 31, 2018.

185. *Guardian*, July 8, 2017, January 3, 2018.

186. Department of Education, Analysis of Teacher Supply, Retention and Mobility, September 2018, Table 7.3, p. 67.

187. Department of Education, qu. *Telegraph*, May 5, 2018.

188. *Times*, January 5, 2018.

189. D. Carver-Thomas and L. Darling-Hammond, Teacher Turnover, Learning Policy Institute, August 2017, pp. 1–60; *Guardian*, September 6, 2018.

190. Bureau of Labor Statistics, qu. A.P., July 21, 2018.

191. *Letters to Brutus*, 34:120.

192. *Times Educational Supplement*, April 6, 2016; *Times*, November 24, 2017.

193. H. Aptheker, *The Colonial Era*, London, 1960, p. 146n.

194. *Telegraph*, October 20, 2010.

195. National Assessment of Educational Progress, A.P., May 16, 2007.

196. OnePoll, qu. *Times*, October 19, 2018.

197. Dispatches, Channel Four, qu. *Telegraph*, June 15, 2015.

198. Ofqual, Entries for GCSE, AS and A Level, May 24, 2018, p. 3.

199. Department for Education, qu. *Telegraph*, August 1, 2018.

200. J. Swinney, Scottish Education Secretary, qu. *Sunday Times*, May 6, 2018; Joint Council for Qualifications (JCQ), *Times*, August 15, 2018.

201. JCQ, qu. *Times*, August 17, 2018.

202. JCQ, qu. *Times*, May 16, 2018.

203. *Telegraph*, April 30, 2015.

204. *Sunday Times*, August 13, 2017; *Times*, August 28, 2017.

205. D. Hinds, Secretary of State for Education, qu. *Telegraph*, August 22, 2018.

206. Education Week, May 8, 2017.

207. *To a Boy*, 61:52.

208. *Guardian*, December 8, 2011.

209. A.P., December 31, 2011.

210. A.P., April 2, 2015.

211. nbcphiladelphia.com, June 5, 2018.

212. A.P., August 24, 2016.

213. Teaching Survey for 2017, *Times Higher Education Supplement*, February 16, 2017.

214. Universities and Colleges Admissions Service (UCAS), *Times*, May 31, 2018, and *Times Higher Education Supplement*, May 31, 2018.

215. *Times Higher Educational Supplement*, March 29, 2007.

216. UCAS, qu. *Guardian*, July 26, 2018.

217. *Times*, September 25, 2018.

218. *Telegraph*, April 29, 2018.

219. W. Richardson, general-secretary, Headmasters' and Headmistresses' Conference, qu. *Telegraph*, July 30, 2015.

220. Higher Education Statistics Agency, *Telegraph*, July 20, 2017.

221. Freedom of Information Act disclosure, *Sunday Times*, January 7, 2018.

222. loc. cit.

223. Freedom of Information Act disclosure, *Times*, January 2, 2016; Lord Storey, co-chair, Liberal Democrat Committee on Education, Families and Young People, qu. *Telegraph*, January 13, 2017.

224. *Times*, February 21, 2017.

225. *Telegraph*, January 31, 2017.

226. *Harvard Magazine*, May 7, 2014; *Telegraph*, May 9, 2014.

227. *Times*, June 16, 2018.

228. Freedom of Information Act disclosure, *Guardian*, April 29, 2018.

229. *Of the Advancement and Proficiency of Learning*, Oxford, 1640, *To the Reader*, p. 3, and bk. 1, chap. 4, pp. 30–31.

230. *Thoughts on Man*, London, 1831, p. iv.

231. 13:1–3.

232. op. cit., part 1, chap. 4, p. 105; chap. 8, p. 146.

233. From a work on European history published by Stanford University Press in 2012, passim.

234. op. cit., part 1, chap. 8, p. 147; part 4, chap. 47, p. 708.

235. Association of Writers and Writing Programs (AWP), A.P., April 7, 2017.

236. Centre for Economic and Social Inclusion, *Telegraph*, February 2, 2015.

237. National Assessment of Educational progress, qu. *New York Times*, April 27, 2016, and A.P., October 27, 2016; Program for International Student Assessment (PISA) and OECD, qu. A.P., December 6, 2016; Trends in International Mathematics and Science Study, qu. A.P., December 29, 2016; Scottish Survey of Literacy and Numeracy (SSCN), qu. *Herald*, May 9, 2017.

238. A.P., October 8, 2006; *New York Times*, December 15, 2006.

239. US Council on Foreign Relations, A.P., March 20, 2012.

240. *Telegraph*, February 11, 2015, February 19, 2015.

241. National Science Foundation, *Telegraph*, February 15, 2014.

242. National Geographic survey, *Guardian*, November 14, 2007.

243. op. cit., letter 5, sect. 316.

244. op. cit., vol. 1, letter 14, p. 38.

245. op. cit., 44:1.

246. op. cit., letter 5, sect. 314.

247. *Guardian*, January 22, 2016.

248. *Telegraph*, June 20, 2017, April 28, 2017; *Times*, October 11, 2016; *Guardian*, September 24, 2016.

249. *Telegraph*, April 29, 2017.

250. *Telegraph*, December 21, 2017.

251. *Telegraph*, January 23, 2017.

252. *Telegraph*, August 25, 2017, August 29, 2017.

253. August 30, 2017.

254. D. Miliband, qu. *Guardian*, May 20, 2004.

255. *Observer*, August 12, 2007.

256. T. Jowell, qu. *Guardian*, May 16, 2010.

257. *Telegraph*, April 7, 2011.

258. P. Wilby, *Guardian*, August 19, 2006.

259. P. Wilby, *Guardian*, December 14, 2006.

260. S. Jenkins, *Guardian*, November 3, 2006.

261. S. Jenkins, *Guardian*, June 24, 2007.

262. J. Warner, *Telegraph*, January 7, 2004.

263. D. Hannan, *Telegraph*, December 27, 2013.

264. A. Heath, *Telegraph*, October 29, 2013.

265. T. Chivers, buzzfeed.com, January 14, 2015.

266. N. Kristof, *New York Times*, January 7, 2018.

CHAPTER 10: THE DEMIURGE OF CAPITAL

1. *Grundrisse* [Foundations of the Critique of Political Economy] (1857–1858), Harmondsworth, 1973, p. 270.

2. "Wage Labour and Capital" in *K. Marx: Selected Writings*, Oxford, 1978, p. 264.

3. op. cit., vol. 2, bk. 2, chap. 18, p. 250.

4. "Communist Manifesto," *Selected Writings*, p. 226.

5. op. cit., p. 223.

6. Ibid.

7. *Grundrisse*, p. 409.

8. l.295 ff.

9. op. cit., vol. 2, bk. 1, chap. 9, p. 188.

10. op. cit., vol. 2, bk. 3, chap. 16, p. 310.

11. E. S. Wortley, *Travels in the United States*, London, 1851, vol. 1, p. 13.

12. *Grundrisse*, p. 539.

13. Ibid.

14. *Selected Writings*, p. 225.

15. *Grundrisse*, pp. 419–20.

16. B. Henderson, *Telegraph*, November 7, 2016.

17. qu. *Business Standard*, April 24, 2016.

18. B. Johnson, Fox News, November 9, 2017.

19. op. cit., p. 409.

20. op. cit., p. 422.

21. *Grundrisse*, pp. 415–16.

22. *Selected Writings*, p. 224.

23. Capital, vol. 1 (1865), *Selected Writings*, p. 487.

24. G. Verhofstadt, European Parliament representative, qu. A.P., October 4, 2016.

25. *Selected Writings*, p. 225.

26. cf. "The Dawn of Collaborative Innovation," World Economic Forum, Davos, 2008, p. 4.

27. *Guardian*, August 29, 2017.

28. *Telegraph*, August 31, 2017.

29. Speech of President Xi Jinping, World Economic Forum, Davos, January 17, 2017.

30. qu. A.P., December 5, 2016.

31. Chinadaily.com.cn, October 25, 2017.

32. Wang Yi, in Singapore, qu. A.P., June 2, 2018.

33. *Selected Writings*, p. 231.

34. op. cit., p. 19.

35. op. cit., p. 60.

36. op. cit., p. 10.

37. op. cit., p. 79.

38. *Atlas Shrugged*, p. 88.

39. *Selected Writings*, p. 223.

CHAPTER 11: QUESTIONS OF BELIEF

1. G. Romney at Fairfax, Virginia, qu. A.P., September 13, 2012.

2. Pew Research Center, qu. *Telegraph*, March 1, 2017; *Guardian*, April 5, 2017.

3. Speech at Eskisehir, qu. A.P., March 17, 2017.

4. A. Jafari, qu. Tasnimnews.com, Iran, March 11, 2017.

5. Dabiq, no. 12, November 18, 2015, p. 2.

6. *The Essayes, or Counsels Civill and Morall*, London, 1639, no. 13, p. 67.

7. *The American Annual Register for the Years 1827–9*, New York, 1830, p. 274.

8. Chesterfield, op. cit., no. 94, p. 223.

9. Al-Arabiya, February 21, 2011.

10. ammonnews net, January 6, 2013.

11. qu. Reuters, March 16, 2011.

12. June 26, 2012.

13. cf. A. El-Awaisi, Jihad in Education and the Society of the Muslim Brotherhood, *Journal of Beliefs and Values*, vol. 21, no. 2, 2000, pp. 213 ff.

14. Ayatollah Ali Khamenei, Fars News Agency, March 1, 2011.

15. Omar al-Bashir, president of Sudan, qu., Agence France-Presse, March 6, 2011.

16. qu. *Guardian*, May 19, 2011.

17. *Telegraph*, January 31, 2013.

18. S. Zweig, *Erasmus of Rotterdam*, London, 1934, p. 109.

19. *Guardian*, February 22, 2016.

20. *On Heroes, Hero-Worship, and the Heroic in History* (1841), London, 1870, p. 70.

21. Letter to Arthur Gobineau (October 22, 1843), The Tocqueville Reader, London, 2002, p. 229.

22. *The River War*, London, 1899, vol. 2, p. 248.

23. Hurriyet, *Daily News*, July 27, 2017.

24. A. Al-Sheikh, qu. *New York Times*, January 21, 2016.

25. P. A. Hoodhboy, "Science and the Islamic World," *Physics Today*, August 2007, p. 1.

26. *Pharsalia*, bk. 9, 435.

27. A.P., May 2, 2011.

28. F. Thompson, qu. A.P., September 8, 2007.

29. George W. Bush, qu. *New York Times*, May 2, 2011.

30. Reuters, January 12, 2013.

31. J. Comey, qu. Press Trust of India, November 18, 2013.

32. *A Discourse of Free-Thinking*, London, 1713, p. 83.

33. qu. *Guardian*, May 8, 2014.

34. 3:28, 3:54, 8:30, 10:21.

35. L. Dernati, qu. *Il Mattino*, November 22, 2015 (author's trans.).

36. A.P., November 14, 2015.

37. Interview, Press TV, Iran (2009), youtube.com/watch?v=BPqHMcNUuPO, and *Independent*, May 4, 2016.

38. *Evening Standard,* June 5, 2017.

39. A. Choudhary, qu. CBN News, April 5, 2010.

40. e.g., Qur'an, 9:33.

41. Qur'an, 4:100.

42. B. Obama, Mumbai, qu. *Hindustan Times,* November 7, 2010.

43. J. Kerry, qu. Daily Caller, March 9, 2014.

44. *Telegraph,* February 26, 2014.

45. M. Rowley, London assistant police commissioner, qu. *Telegraph,* August 27, 2014.

46. K. Armstrong, *New Statesman,* November 21, 2014.

47. T. May, qu. *Spectator,* November 16, 2015; J. Kerry, "Remarks to the Staff and Families of the US Embassy, Paris," US Dept. of State, November 17, 2015.

48. Mr. Justice C. Haddon-Cave, qu. *Times,* March 24, 2018.

49. UN Security Council report, qu. *Guardian,* May 26, 2015.

50. Y. Cooper, qu. *Sunday Times,* August 24, 2014.

51. D. Cameron, qu. BBC, September 22, 2013.

52. BBC News, Europe, January 10, 2015.

53. B. Obama, Office of the Press Secretary, White House, February 18, 2015; qu. *Washington Post,* September 10, 2014.

54. J. Brennan, cnsnews.com, March 11, 2014.

55. November 19, 2015, qu. Town hall, November 20, 2015.

56. *National Journal,* August 20, 2014.

57. Arabic News Broadcast (ANBTV), August 31, 2014.

58. J. Napolitano, Department of Homeland Security Press Office, April 19, 2013.

59. A.P., April 20, 2013.

60. T. May, House of Commons, A.P., March 23, 2017.

61. R. Tillerson, qu. *New York Times,* March 22, 2017.

62. A. Burnham, LBC, May 24, 2017.

63. J. Corbyn, BBC One, May 26, 2017.

64. Remarks of President Donald J. Trump, Inaugural Address, January 20 2017, Washington, DC.

65. *Washington Post,* May 21, 2017.

66. G. Gilmore, Yale Daily News, October 11, 2002.

67. At Stop the War rally, qu. *Telegraph,* December 4, 2015.

68. 2:228, 2:282, 4:11.

69. A. Russo, *International Feminist Journal of Politics,* vol. 8, no. 4, December 2006, pp. 557 ff.

70. Letter entitled "Women's Liberation and the French Burkini Ban," signed by forty-five feminists, *Guardian,* September 2, 2016.

71. Remarks by the President on a New Beginning, Office of the Press Secretary, White House, June 4, 2009.

72. 98:6.

73. 5:60.

74. loc. cit.

75. At Masjid al Rahman, White House transcript, qu., *Baltimore Sun*, February 3, 2016.

76. At US Treasury, qu. *Washington Post*, June 14, 2016.

77. At Eid celebration, WhiteHouse.gov, September 12, 2016.

78. The "Prevent" Program, *Times*, December 26, 2015.

79. e.g., Regent's Park, London, April 5, 2015, http://www.liveleak.com/view?i=afe_1429533805.

80. E. Schmidt, qu. *Quotidiano Nazionale* (QN), June 23, 2018 (author's trans.).

81. MidEast Church News (MCN), March 13, 2012; *Catholic Herald*, March 16, 2012.

82. *Star* (Kenya), December 23, 2015; Ministry of Religious Affairs, Brunei, qu. *Sydney Morning Herald*, December 21, 2015.

83. cf. Reuters, March 6, 2018.

84. CBN News, March 17, 2014.

85. *Corriere della Sera*, December 27, 2010; A.P., December 26, 2011.

86. Pope Francis, qu. BBC World Service, Europe, April 4, 2015.

87. A.P., October 27, 2012.

88. Vatican.va, November 24, 2013.

89. Mgr. B. Forte, qu. *La Stampa*, January 5, 2016 (author's trans.).

90. Vatican Pontifical Council for Interreligious Dialogue, A.P., August 12, 2014.

91. *La Croix*, May 17, 2016.

92. w2.vatican.va, May 27, 2017.

93. H. Boulard, Tempi.it, September 7, 2017 (author's trans.).

94. R. Williams, qu. *Guardian*, February 7, 2008.

95. loc. cit.

96. op. cit., part 2, chap. 27, p. 338.

97. *Telegraph*, March 13, 2015.

98. *Times*, November 18, 2018.

99. Lord Harries of Pentregarth, qu. *Telegraph*, January 29, 2014.

100. *La Repubblica*, January 26, 2016.

101. R. Chartres, qu. *Church Times*, January 22, 2016.

102. Qur'an 3:118, 48:29, 3:28, 4:157, 5:72, 5:73, 9:30.

103. 2: 256.

104. 5:32.

105. 3:151, 8:60; 2:191; 8:12; 5:33; 47:4; 9:14–15; 9:111.

106. 22:45.

107. *Il Mattino*, November 22, 2015.

108. *Paris-Match*, November 13, 2015.

109. *New York Daily Tribune*, April 15, 1854.

110. S. Rushdie, *Times*, September 12, 2005.

111. *The Muqaddimah* (1377), Princeton, 1981, p. 183.

112. O. bin Laden, video-text, September 6, 2007, qu. *New York Times*, September 8, 2007.

113. M. Ahmadinejad, UN General Assembly, qu. *Telegraph*, September 26, 2013.

114. H. Rouhani, qu. A.P., October 23, 2016.

115. A. Khamenei, Fars News Agency, qu. *Daily Mail*, May 26, 2014.

116. Abu Muhammad al-Adnani al-Shami, "This Is the Promise of Allah," qu. BBC News, Middle East, June 30, 2014.

117. *Telegraph*, May 6, 2015.

118. A. L. Rowse, intro., M. Ashley, *Oliver Cromwell and the Puritan Revolution*, London, 1958, p. 7.

119. op. cit., part 1, chap. 11, p. 166.

120. op. cit., vol. 6, chap. 50, p. 203.

121. Faisal al-Baghdadi, qu. Ynet News, April 23, 2007.

122. *The Old Regime and the French Revolution* (1856), New York, 1955, p. 13.

123. *The Spirit of the Laws* (1748), Berkeley, 1977, p. 323.

124. op. cit., vol. 6, chap. 52, p. 387.

125. Imam S. S. Mady, Edmonton, February 16, 2016, www.youtube.com/watch?v=pN118To55wg.

126. Pew Research Center, Religion and Public Life, November 29, 2017.

127. op. cit., part 1, chap. 12, p. 182.

128. T. Begrich, head of finances, Evangelical Church of Germany (EKD), qu. *Der Spiegel*, February 13, 2013.

129. BBC News, Wales, September 24, 2017.

130. e.g., J. Kaleem, "Islam in America: Mosques See Dramatic Increase," Huffington Post, February 29, 2012.

131. e.g., "How Big Is the Muslim Congregation?" onreligion.co.uk, October 24, 2017.

132. National Centre for Social Research (NatCen), British Social Attitudes Survey, qu. *Guardian*, September 7, 2018; also S. Bullivant, "Europe's Young Adults and Religion," St. Mary's University, Twickenham, qu. *Guardian*, March 21, 2018.

133. *Telegraph*, January 12, 2016.

134. *Guardian*, December 22, 2016.

135. *Observer*, August 19, 2018.

136. Ibid.

137. *Times*, December 27, 2017.

138. Rt. Rev. J. Inge, report to Church of England Synod, qu. *Telegraph*, November 25, 2015.

139. *Telegraph*, July 21, 2015.

140. *Times*, October 29, 2016.

141. *Times*, October 4, 2017.

142. R. Williams, qu. Press Association, April 24, 2014.

143. "Living with Difference," Commission on Religion and Belief in Public Schools, *Guardian*, December 7, 2015.

144. qu., *Telegraph*, January 12, 2015.

145. A.P., June 7, 2016, June 9, 2016.

146. Pew Research Center, qu. A.P., May 12, 2015.

147. P. Daly, *National Catholic Reporter*, January 12, 2015.

148. G. Espinosa and others, "Latino Muslims in the United States: Reversions, Politics and Islamidad," *Journal of Race, Ethnicity and Religion*, vol. 8, issue 1, June 2017, p. 5; A. Arriaga, *Chicago Sun-Times*, June 30, 2018.

149. N. Allen, *Telegraph*, April 21, 2014.

150. C. O'Donovan, Towers Watson report to Archdiocese of Dublin, September 16, 2015, p. 20.

151. Conferenza Episcopale Italiana (CEI), *Il Giorno*, March 19, 2017.

152. Opera Italiana Pellegrinaggi, *Libero*, January 25, 2017.

153. *Resto del Carlino*, September 27, 2016.

154. A.P., May 1, 2017.

155. *Guardian*, April 29, 2017.

156. Pope Francis, interview, *Die Zeit*, March 9, 2017.

157. *Times*, December 18, 2017.

158. *Twenty Select Colloquies of Erasmus*, trans. R. L'Estrange, London, n.d., pp. 213–14.

159. *Sydney Morning Herald*, July 3, 2018; *Newcastle Herald*, August 14, 2018.

160. A.P., May 14, 2018, June 11, 2018, August 18, 2018.

161. A.P., September 13, 2018, September 25, 2018.

162. *NRC Handelsblad*, September 15, 2018; Agence France-Presse, September 16, 2018.

163. A.P., October 7, 2018.

164. A.P., January 17, 2014.

165. Archbishop S. Tomasi, evidence to UN Committee Against Torture, Geneva, qu. A.P., May 7, 2014.

166. *Los Angeles Times*, July 15, 2017.

167. Reuters, March 1, 2017; A.P., December 7, 2017.

168. A.P., August 15, 2018; *New York Times*, August 15, 2018.

169. A.P., August 3, 2018.

170. *Globe and Mail*, June 23, 2016.

171. qu. *New York Times*, December 29, 2014.

172. qu. *La Stampa*, May 31, 2018.

173. Testimony by His Excellency Carlo Maria Viganò, Rome, August 22, 2018, pp. 9–10; E. Pentin, *National Catholic Register*, August 25, 2018; A.P., September 28, 2018.

174. M. Ouellet, prefect of the Congregation of Bishops, qu. A.P., October 8, 2018.

175. qu. A.P., October 27, 2018.

176. Independent Inquiry into Child Sexual Abuse, qu. *Times*, March 22, 2018.

177. D. Greenwood, qu. *Guardian*, March 23, 2018.

178. A. Dietsche, "The Season of Listen Has Come," Episcopal Diocese of New York, September 12, 2018.

179. F. Bacon, *The Essayes or Counsels, Civill and Morall*, London, 1639, p. 333.

180. *The Man Without Qualities* (1930–1932), London, 1954, vol. 1, p. 359.

181. Bahsir al-'Ashi, Hamas TV, August 31, 2014.

182. Agence France-Presse, September 2, 2014.

183. Ahmed Ouyahia, qu. *Guardian*, May 9, 2012.

184. Maj.-Gen. H. Firouzabadi, Iranian chief of staff, qu. A.P., November 20, 2013.

185. Pres. Ahmadinejad of Iran, qu. A.P., August 17, 2012.

186. Ayatollah Khamenei, qu. A.P., November 20, 2013.

187. Mohammed Asri Zaimul Abidin, *Malaysia Today*, July 15, 2014.

188. Fars News Agency, March 9, 2016.

189. A. Karimpour, qu. Fars News Agency, May 19, 2016.

190. qu. A.P., February 21, 2017.

191. T. Tancredo, qu. *New York Times*, July 18, 2005.

192. J. Lewis, "No Substitute for Victory," *Objective Standard*, vol. 1, no. 4, Winter 2006–2007, pp. 39 ff.

193. op. cit., vol. 2, chap. 16, p. 279.

194. *Philippics*, 2:27, 3:13, 3:64, 4:15, 4:66.

195. op. cit., 4:26.

196. op. cit., 1:11, 2:27.

197. op. cit., 4:21.

198. op. cit., 4:6.

199. "Position Paper" (unpublished), January 17, 2013, p. 7.

200. D. Selbourne to J. Kerry, e-mail, January 4, 2013.

201. "Position Paper," loc. cit.

202. J. Kerry to D. Selbourne, e-mail, February 3, 2013.

203. op. cit., part 2, chap. 29, pp. 307–308.

204. Speech on American Taxation, House of Commons, April 19, 1774, *Select Works*, Oxford, 1885, vol. 1, p. 151.

205. e.g., D. Douglas-Bowers, "Neo-Colonialism, Imperialism and Resistance in the 21st Century," Global Research (Centre for Research on Globalization), January 3, 2011.

206. qu., *Der Spiegel*, December 31, 2014.

207. Speech to the House of Commons, March 22, 1775, op. cit., pp. 180–81.

208. Ayman al-Zawahiri, qu. *New York Times*, May 6, 2007.

209. cf. Newdow v. US Congress, 292 F 3rd 597, 9th Circ. 2002; Doe v. Acton-Boxborough Regional School District, SJC 1137, May 9, 2014.

210. *Atlanta Journal-Constitution*, August 8, 2018.

211. K. Greenawalt, *Religion and the Constitution*, Princeton, 2009, vol. 2, passim.

212. "Farewell Address, September 17, 1796, to the People of the United States," American Daily Advertiser, September 19, 1796, and Senate Document no. 106–21, 2000, p. 20.

213. J. Woolley and G. Peters, The American Presidency Project, http://www .presidency.ucsb.edu/ws/?pid=65502.

214. Ibid.

215. http://www.presidency.ucsb.edu/ws/?pid=65661.

216. http://www.presidency.ucsb.edu/ws/?pid=65675.

217. http://www.presidency.ucsb.edu/ws/?pid=25804.

218. op. cit., *The Federalist* (nos. 37, 43), pp. 179, 220–21.

219. D. Cameron, qu. *Guardian*, April 17, 2014.

220. *Telegraph*, April 20, 2014.

221. *Dallas Morning News*, March 17, 2017, March 22, 2017.

CHAPTER 12: THE TRUE COMMONWEALTH

1. op. cit., vol. 2, bk. 2, chap. 2, p. 205.

2. G. Younge, *Guardian*, December 1, 2014.

3. D. Webster, *A Discourse in Commemoration of the First Settlement of New England*, Boston, 1821, pp. 85, 90.

4. Justice A. Kennedy, Supreme Court Oral Arguments, Dept. of Health and Human Resources vs. Florida, March 27, 2012, 11–398, p. 31.

5. *A Discourse Touching Provision for the Poor*, London, 1683, p. iii.

6. A.P., April 8, 2017.

7. *New York Times*, Health Section, September 19, 2017.

8. A.P., August 24, 2017.

9. op. cit., bk. 6, 3:4–5.

10. *The Politics*, 1310a22.

11. *Satires*, 7:83.

12. Anon., *A Relation or Journall of the English Plantation Settled at Plimoth*, London, 1622, pp. xliv–xlv.

13. op. cit., p. 141.

14. op. cit., pp. 940, 947.

15. op. cit., p. 151.

16. The Papers of George Washington, Presidential Series, vol. 17, Charlottesville, 2013, p. 354.

17. A. Ross, at Hay Festival, qu. *Telegraph*, May 30, 2016; also A. Ross, *The Industries of the Future*, New York, 2016.

18. Relate, qu. *Telegraph*, August 12, 2014.

19. W. Allen, *Killing No Murder*, London, 1689, p. 20.

20. A.P.-NORC Center for Public Affairs Research, qu. A.P., March 5, 2017.

21. P. Trudeau, qu. *New York Times*, December 13, 2015.

22. J. McDonnell, qu. *Guardian*, February 1, 2016.

23. S. Mattarella, qu. *La Repubblica*, September 3, 2016.

24. D. Trump, Conservative Political Action Group (CPAC), National Harbor, Md., qu. *Time*, February 24, 2017.

25. D. Trump, Cincinnati, Ohio, qu. *Guardian*, February 2, 2016.

26. Donald J. Trump, @realDonaldTrump, September 17, 2016.

27. D. Trump, GOP Retreat, Philadelphia, January 26, 2017.

28. D. Trump, CPAC, National Harbor, Md., February 24, 2017, loc. cit.

29. D. Trump, speech to American Legion, qu. *Washington Examiner*, September 1, 2016.

30. *USA Today*, September 10, 2017; *Il Messaggero*, August 25, 2016; *Telegraph*, December 29 and 30, 2015, August 30, 2017; Reuters, September 11, 2017.

31. Local Government Association, qu. *Guardian*, July 29, 2017.

32. *Corriere della Sera*, August 7, 2017.

33. A.P., June 1, 2018.

34. Freedom of Information Act disclosure and A. Cole-Hamilton, qu. *Times,* December 27, 2017.

35. Report for H. M. Inspectorate of Constabulary, *Telegraph,* December 28, 2017.

36. *Baltimore Sun,* March 3, 2014.

37. *Telegraph,* August 18, 2018.

38. Y. Martinez, Cocoa Police Department, qu. *Florida Today,* July 21, 2017.

39. A.P., June 22, 2018.

40. e.g., C. Brettschneider, 'Why Prisoners Deserve the Right to Vote," Politico.com, June 21, 2016.

41. A.P., July 14, 2018.

42. *Richmond Standard,* July 27, 2015.

43. B. Gary and others v. R. Snyder and others, Case 2:16-cv-132932-SJM-A.P.P, June 29, 2018, p. 37.

44. *New Hampshire Union Leader,* July 8, 2017.

45. *Telegraph,* August 2, 2013.

46. E. Schneiderman, Attorney General of New York, qu. Reuters, March 27, 2018; also A.P., June 23, 2018.

47. *Deutsche Welle,* January 5, 2014.

48. P. Clarke, Report into Allegations concerning Birmingham Schools, qu. *Guardian,* July 17, 2014.

49. *Telegraph,* July 22, 2014.

50. Department of Education report, *Telegraph,* April 18, 2014.

51. *Telegraph,* June 27, 2014.

52. op. cit., no. 15, p. 82.

53. *Telegraph,* September 2, 2014.

54. Ayaan Hirsi Ali, qu. *Spectator,* November 28, 2017.

55. A.P., April 9, 2014.

56. *Telegraph,* July 1, 2014.

57. Sheriff A. Noble, qu. BBC News, Scotland, June 30, 2014.

58. *Florida Today,* December 5, 2017.

59. *Telegraph,* November 2, 2014.

60. *Guardian,* August 7, 2014.

61. *Telegraph,* February 25, 2015.

62. M. Dejevsky, *Guardian,* February 23, 2015.

63. A.P., October 8, 2013.

64. B. Wieckowski, qu. *New York Times,* October 7, 2013.

65. e.g., *Telegraph,* March 15, 2015.

66. Anon., *A Relation or Journall of the English Plantation Settled at Plimoth,* London, 1622, p. 3.

67. e.g., "Civic Integration in the Netherlands," Government.nl, December 2, 2015, pp. 1–2.

68. e.g., *Independent,* January 8, 2016; *Guardian,* April 2, 2016; ANSA, January 8, 2016; A.P., June 20, 2017.

69. *Two Treatises of Civil Government* (1690), *Second Treatise*, chap. xv, para. 171, London, 1962, p. 205.

70. *Telegraph*, May 11, 2015.

71. *Corriere della Sera*, September 8, 2016.

72. A.P., March 24, 2015.

73. A.P., January 16, 2015.

74. *Telegraph*, November 20, 2014, February 20, 2015.

75. Press Association, November 21, 2014.

76. BBC News, November 12, 2014.

77. Charity Commission, qu. *Guardian*, February 29, 2008.

78. *Guardian*, July 1, 2014.

79. Demosthenes, *Prosecution of Aristogeiton*, 35:25 ff.

80. A. E. Zimmern, *The Greek Commonwealth*, Oxford, 1911, p. 76 fn.

81. T. A. Sinclair, *A History of Greek Political Thought*, London, 1952, p. 199.

82. Xenophon, *Agesilaus*, 10:1.

83. E. Barker, *Greek Political Theory*, London and New York, 1960, p. 43.

84. K. J. Dover, *Greek Popular Morality in the Times of Plato and Aristotle*, Oxford, 1974, p. 186.

85. E. M. Wood and N. Wood, *Class Ideology and Ancient Political Theory*, Oxford, 1978, p. 227.

86. op. cit., bk. 6, 3:4–5.

87. op. cit., vol. 4, chap. 38, p. 402.

88. op. cit., p. 310.

89. op. cit., p. 312.

90. op. cit., *The Federalist* (no. 26), p. 126.

91. op. cit. (no. 63), p. 313.

92. op. cit. (no. 14), p. 71.

93. op. cit. (no. 2), pp. 14–15.

94. op. cit. (no. 14), p. 66.

95. op. cit. (no. 84), p. 420.

96. op. cit. (no. 33), p. 157.

97. op. cit., part 2, chap. 26, p. 335.

98. op. cit. (no. 78), p. 380.

99. op. cit. (no. 64), pp. 317–18.

100. A.P., January 18, 2017.

101. *New York Times*, January 13, 2018.

102. *New York Times*, June 26, 2018; *Military Times*, June 28, 2018.

103. op. cit. (no. 85), p. 428.

104. The Temple, l. 135, *The Complete English Poems*, Harmondsworth, 1992, p. 10.

105. Supreme Court Justice J. P. Stevens, in Van Orden v. Perry, no. 03–1500, June 27, 2005.

106. Exod., 20: 1–17; Deut., 5: 6–21.

107. op. cit., vol. 2, bk. 2, chap. 15, p. 242.

108. op. cit., 17:4.

109. Supreme Court Justice S. D. O'Connor, in McCreary County, Kentucky v. ACLU, no. 03-1693, June 27, 2005.

110. op. cit., p. 936.

111. op. cit., p. 976.

112. op. cit., p. 2.

113. qu. P. Miller, *The New England Mind*, Boston, 1961, p. 42.

114. [D. Digges], *An Answer to a Printed Book*, Oxford, 1642, p. 3, qu. W. Haller, *The Rise of Puritanism*, New York, 1957, p. 369.

115. op. cit., vol. 1, chap. 17, pp. 115, 118.

116. I. Goodwin, *Town Officer: Or Laws of Massachusetts Relative to the Duties of Municipal Officers*, Worcester, 1829, p. 25. My copy of this work was de Tocqueville's own, and has his signature on the fly-leaf.

117. Statute of 1799, chap. 87, qu. Goodwin, op. cit., p. 151.

118. R. Perry, *Fed Up! Our Fight to Save America from Washington*, New York, 2010, p. xviii.

119. Statute of 1785, chap. 75, para. 8, qu. Goodwin, op. cit., p. 268.

120. Preamble to Massachusetts Constitution, qu. Goodwin, op. cit., p. 2.

121. Ibid.

122. op. cit., vol. 1, chap. 2, p. 13.

123. op. cit., vol. 1, chap. 4, pp. 31, 35.

124. op. cit., vol. 1, chap. 2, p. 16.

125. S. C. Powell, *Puritan Village: The Formation of a New England Town*, New York, 1965, pp. 94, 115, 175.

126. Powell, op. cit., pp. 171, 178.

127. *The Politics*, 1280a34.

128. op. cit., part 2, chap. 20, p. 261.

129. op. cit., p. 98.

130. Powell, op. cit., pp. 109, 174.

131. Powell, op. cit., p. 109.

132. Statute of 1785, chap. 28, part 4, qu. Goodwin, op. cit., p. 265.

133. Goodwin, op. cit., pp. 98, 259.

134. Goodwin, op. cit., p. 194.

135. op. cit., vol. 1, chap. 13, p. 86.

136. A. M. Earle, *Customs and Fashions in Old New England*, Rutland, Vt., 1973, p. 166.

137. A.P., August 27, 2015; also Virginia Department of Alcoholic Beverage Control, qu. A.P., May 17, 2018.

138. *Telegraph*, June 12, 2012.

139. A.P., April 12, 2014.

140. *Columbus Dispatch*, March 24, 2016.

141. Friedman, op. cit., p. 292.

142. Friedman, op. cit., p. 157.

143. *The Politics*, 1337a11.

144. Mass. Rep., xvi.141, qu. Goodwin, op. cit., pp. 177–85.

145. Goodwin, op. cit., p. 178.

146. op. cit., p. 980.

147. op. cit., vol. 1, chap. 2, p. 16.

148. Ibid.

149. op. cit., p. 651.

150. Isaiah 60:2.

151. "A Preliminary Word," *Household Words*, London, 1850, vol. 1, no. 1, p. 1.

152. op. cit., 1:87–88.

153. Euripides, *Iphigenia in Aulis*, l.1096.

154. Herodotus, op. cit., bk. 1, 207:2.

155. Polybius, op. cit., bk. 6, l.51–54.

156. op. cit., part 2, chap. 29, p. 363.

157. B. Szydlo, speech to Polish Parliament, qu. wyborcza.pl, May 24, 2017, and A.P., May 24, 2017.

158. *The Rioters, or a Tale of Bad Times*, Wellington, 1827, p. 57.

159. Isaiah, 53:6.

160. op. cit., no. 58, p. 339.

161. op. cit., vol. 5, chap. 39, p. 31.

NOTE ON SOURCES

In addition to the works listed in the select bibliography, sources for *The Free Society in Crisis* include (1) the press in the United States, the United Kingdom, and elsewhere; (2) news agencies; (3) other media sources; (4) scientific journals; and (5) reports by governmental and nongovernmental institutions. Among them are the following:

1. Press Sources.

United States: *Advocate, Atlanta Journal-Constitution, Atlantic, Baltimore Sun, Boston Globe, Charleston Gazette-Mail, Chicago Sun-Times, Chicago Tribune, Christian Science Monitor, Columbus Dispatch, Courier-Journal, Dallas Morning News, Denver Post, Detroit News, Florida Today, Forbes, Fortune, Houston Chronicle, Indianapolis Star, Los Angeles Times, Louisville Courier Journal, Miami Herald, Milwaukee Journal Sentinel, National Catholic Register, National Catholic Reporter, New Hampshire Union Leader, New York Daily News, New York Daily Tribune, New York Post, New York Times, New Yorker, Newsweek, Orange County Register, Philadelphia Inquirer, Phoenix New Times, Portland Press Herald, Richmond Standard, San Francisco Chronicle, Seattle Times, Starkville Daily News, Tennessean, Time, Times Union, Tulsa World, USA Today, Wall Street Journal, Washington Post.*

United Kingdom: *Catholic Herald, Church Times, Daily Express, Daily Mail, Evening Standard, Financial Times, Guardian, Herald, Independent, Manchester Evening News, New Statesman, Observer, Scotsman, Spectator, Sunday Times, Telegraph, Times, Times Educational Supplement, Times Higher Education Supplement.*

Australia: *Australian, Newcastle Herald, Sydney Morning Herald*; Belgium: *La Libre*; Brazil: *Estado de S. Paulo*; Canada: *Globe and Mail, Ottawa Citizen, Toronto Sun*; China and Hong Kong: *Global Times, Hong Kong Free Press, People's Daily, South China Morning Post*; France: *Le Canard Enchainé, La Croix, L'Express, Le Figaro, France-Soir, Libéra- tion, Le Monde, Paris-Match, Le Parisien, Le Point, Le Soir, La Voix du Nord*; Germany: *Frankfurter Allgemeine Zeitung, Der Spiegel, Die West- falenpost, Die Zeit*; India: *Business Standard, Hindu, Hindustan Times, India Today, Times of India*; Israel: *Ha'aretz, Israel Hayom*; Italy: *Cor- riere della Sera, Il Giornale, Il Giorno, Libero, Il Mattino, Il Messaggero, Quotidiano Nazionale (QN), Quotidiano di Puglia, La Repubblica, La Stampa, Il Resto del Carlino*; Japan: *Japan Times, Kyoto News*; Kenya: *Star*; Malaysia: *Malaysia Today*; Netherlands: *Dagens Perspektiv, NRC Handelsblad*; New Zealand: *New Zealand Herald*; Pakistan: *Pakistan Observer*; Russia: *Moscow Times*; Turkey: *Hurriyet Daily News*.

2. News Agencies.

Agence France-Presse, ANSA (Italy), Associated Press (A.P.), Fars News Agency (Iran), Korean Central News Agency (KCNA, North Korea), Press Association, Press Trust of India, Reuters, Tasnim News Agency (Iran), Tass (Russia), Xinhua News Agency (China).

3. Other Media Sources.

abc.net (Australia), ABC News, Al-Arabiya (Dubai), Al Ghad Al Arabi TV (Egypt), aljazeera.com (Qatar), Almajd TV (Gulf States, Saudi Arabia), American Interest, ammonnews.net (Jordan), Arabic News Broadcast (ANBTV), Army Times, BBC, Bloomberg Politics, bre- itbart.com, Business Insider, buzzfeed.com, CBC News (Canada), CBN News, CBS News, chinadaily.com, China Military, CityNews Toronto, cleveland.com, CNBC, CNN, cnsnews.com, Dabiq (ISIS), Daily Caller, Daily Stormer, dallasnews.com, Deutsche Welle, Dip- lomat (Japan), Education Week, euobserver.com, Facebook, Federal

News Service, Fox News, Gallup News, goal.com, Hamas TV, Health Service Journal, Huffington Post, Ikhwanonline (Muslim Brotherhood), internazionale.it, Kiro TV, LBC, metro.co.uk, MidEast Church News, Military Times, mynorthwesst.com, NBC, National Journal, National Review, nknews.org, nwi.com, onreligion.co.uk, ONTD Political, openDemocracy, OpenSecrets.org, Pink News, Politico.com, Politics Home, Politifact, Press TV (Iran), Radio Maria (Italy), RT (Russia), Reader's Digest, Science Daily, Science News, spacedaily. com, statista.com, statnews.com, SVT Nyheter (Sweden), TalkRadio, Tempi.it, Townhall, UAWire (Ukraine), UPI, Vatican.va, Vice News, vox.com, Washington Examiner, WCPO Cincinnati, wkyt.com, World Population Review, Ynet News (Israel).

4. Scientific Journals.

American Journal of Bioethics, American Journal of Preventive Medicine, American Journal of Public Health, BMC Public Health, British Journal of General Practice, British Medical Journal, Cell, Child Development, Human Reproduction Update, JAMA: Journal of the American Medical Association, Journal of Medical Ethics, Journal of the Royal Society of Medicine, The Lancet, Nature, Nature Geoscience, New England Journal of Medicine, New Scientist, Physics Today, Proceedings of the National Academy of Sciences of the United States of America, Psychiatric Clinics of North America, Science, Science Advances.

5. Reports by Governmental and Nongovernmental Institutions.

In the United States: American Presidency Project, Anti-Defamation League, A.P.-NORC Center for Public Affairs Research, Association of Writers and Writing Programs, Brennan Center for Justice (New York University), Brookings Institution, Bureau of Justice Statistics, California Department of Public Health, Center for Competitive Politics, Center for Migration Studies, Center for Public Integrity, Center for Strategic and International Studies (CSIS), Center for the Study of Voting, Elections and Democracy, Centers for Disease Control and Prevention (CDC), Chicago Police Department, China Labor Watch, Common Sense Media, Drug Enforcement Administration, Economic Innovation Group, Environmental Protection Agency (EPA), Equilar, Everytown for Gun Safety, Federal Aviation Administration, Federal Bureau of Investigation (FBI), Federal Election Commission, Federal Highway Administration, Food and Drug Administration (FDA), Georgetown University Law Center, Gun Violence Archive, Guttmacher Institute, Home School Legal Defense Association, IMS Health, Institute for Children, Poverty and Homelessness, Institute for Health Metrics and Evaluation (University of Washington), Institute for Policy Studies, Institute for the Study of War, Learning Policy Institute, Lewin Group, National Academy of Sciences, National Aeronautics and Space Administration (NASA), National Alliance for Public Charter Schools, National Assessment of Educational Progress, National Center for Children in Poverty, National Center for Education Statistics, National Center on Family Homelessness, National Center for Health Statistics, National Center for Injury Prevention and Control, National Counterintelligence and Security Center, National Household Survey on Drug Use and Health, National Institute on Money in Politics, National Oceanic and Atmospheric Administration (NOAA), National Rifle Association (NRA), National Science Foundation, National Transportation Safety Board, New York City Department of Homeless Services, New York City Department of Investigation, New York City Independent Budget Office, New York City Police Department, New York State Comptroller, New York State Technical and Education Assistance Center, Office of the Press Secretary (White House), Oregon Office of Economic Analysis, Panama Papers, Pew Research Center, Public Policy Institute of California, Salk Institute, Stimson Center, Supplemental Nutrition Assistance Program (SNAP), Tax Justice Network, US Army Recruitment Command, US Bureau of Labor Statistics, US Census Bureau, US Council on Foreign Relations, US Customs and Border Protection Agency, US Defense Intelligence Agency (DIA), US Department of

Agriculture, US Department of Education, US Department of Health and Human Services, US Department of Homeland Security, US Department of Housing and Urban Development, US Department of Justice, US Department of Labor, US Department of State, US Department of Transport, US Global Change Research Program, US Government Executive, US House of Representatives Energy and Commerce Committee, Virginia Department of Alcoholic Beverage Control, US Internal Revenue Service, US Senate Homeland Security and Government Affairs Subcommittee, US Senate Permanent Committee on Investigations, US Treasury, Washington Department of Fish and Wildlife, Williams Institute (UCLA).

In the United Kingdom: Age UK, Alcohol Health Alliance, Association of Directors of Adult Social Services, Association of Teachers and Lecturers, Aviva, British Dietetic Association, British Medical Association, British Social Attitudes Survey, Bureau of Investigative Journalism, Cancer Research UK, Carehome.co.uk, Center for Diet and Activity Research (University of Cambridge), Centre for Economic and Social Inclusion, Centre for Economics and Business Research, Centre for Education and Monitoring, Centre for Policy Studies, Centre for Social Justice, Centre for Time Use Research (University of Oxford), Charity Commission, Chartered Institute of Personnel and Development, Child Poverty Action Group, Children's Society, ChildWise, Church of England Synod, Commission on Religion and Belief in Public Schools, Committee on Standards in Public Life, Community Security Trust, Department of Business, Energy and Industrial Strategy, Department for Communities and Local Government, Department of Education, Department of Health, Department for Work and Pensions, DrugWise, Enlightenment Foundation, Equality Trust, Family and Childcare Trust, Future of Humanity Institute (University of Oxford), Gingerbread, Girlguiding UK, GMB Union, Greenpeace, GSM Association, Headmasters' and Headmistresses' Conference, Health Foundation, Health and Social Care Information Centre, Health Survey for England (Department of Health), Her Majesty's

Inspectorate of Constabulary (HMIC), Her Majesty's Inspectorate of Prisons, High Pay Centre, Higher Education Statistics Agency, Home Office, House of Commons All-Party Parliamentary Group, House of Commons Defence Select Committee, House of Commons Home Affairs Select Committee, House of Commons Justice Committee, House of Commons Public Accounts Committee, House of Commons Public Administration Committee, House of Commons Science and Technology Committee, Human Rights Watch, ICM Research, Independent Age, Independent Food Aid Network, Independent Police Complaints Commission, Inland Revenue, Institute of Cognitive Neuroscience (University College, London), Institute of Education (University of London), Institute of Health Equity (University of London), Institute for Public Policy Research, Institute for Strategic Studies, Ipsos MORI, Joint Council for Qualifications (JCQ), The Key, Local Government Association, London Ambulance Service, Longevity Science Panel, Marriage Foundation, Mental Health Trusts England, Metropolitan Police, Ministry of Justice, National Association of Head Teachers, National Audit Office, National Centre for Social Research, National Child Measurement Programme, National Crime Agency, National Diet and Nutrition Survey, National Foundation for Educational Research, NFU Mutual, NHS Digital, NHS England, NHS Protect, NHS Scotland, National Offender Management Service, National Police Chiefs' Council, National Rural Crime Network, National Society for the Prevention of Cruelty to Children (NSPCC), National Union of Teachers, Nuffield Council on Bioethics, Nuffield Trust, Obesity Health Alliance, Ofcom, Office for National Statistics (ONS), Ofqual, Ofsted, OnePoll, Oxfam, Parent Zone, Place2BE, Police Federation of England and Wales, Poverty and Social Exclusion in the United Kingdom (PSE), Prince's Countryside Fund, Prison Reform Trust, Public Health England, Relate, Resolution Foundation, Joseph Rowntree Foundation, Royal College of Paediatrics and Child Health, Royal College of Psychiatrists, Royal Society of Medicine, Save the Children, Scottish Survey of Literacy and Numeracy, Shelter, Society of Authors, Stonewall, Sutton Trust,

Trussell Trust, Trust for London, UK Border Agency, UK Government Actuary's Department, UK Government Office for Science, UK Health Forum, UK Meteorological Office, Unison Scotland, Universities and Colleges Admissions Service (UCAS), Which?, Worldwide Responsible Accredited Production (WRAP), YouGov.

Other Institutions: Atomic Energy Organisation of Iran, Centre for Research on Globalisation (Canada), China National Space Administration, Conferenza Episcopale Italiana, European Congress on Obesity, European Foundation, European Monitoring Centre for Drugs and Drug Addiction, European Parliament Committee on Legal Affairs, Evangelical Church of Germany, Federal Statistics Office (Germany), Food and Agriculture Organization (FAO), Fred Hollows Foundation (Australia), German Ethics Council, German Federal Statistics Office, GfK (Germany), Global Nutrition Report, International AIDS Society, International Atomic Energy Agency (IAEA), International Congress on Physical Activity and Public Health, International Joint Conference on Artificial Intelligence (IJCAI), Irish National Teachers' Organization, Italian Statistical Service (Istat), Levada Center (Russia), McKinsey Global Institute, Médecins Sans Frontières, Muslim Brotherhood, OECD, Opera Italiana Pellegrinaggi, Program for International Student Assessment (PISA), Progress in International Reading Literacy Study (PIRLS), Russian Audit Chamber, Russian Statistical Service (Rosstat), Small Arms Survey (Switzerland), State Council (China), Statistics Canada, Tecnè Research Institute (Italy), Turin Advanced Neuromodulation Group, UNAIDS, UN Committee Against Torture, UN Department of Economic and Social Affairs, UN Habitat, UNICEF, UN Intergovernmental Panel for Climate Change (IPCC), UN Office on Drugs and Crime, UN Security Council, UN World Food Programme, United Nations University, Vatican Pontifical Council for Interreligious Dialogue, World Economic Forum, World Meteorological Organisation (WMO), World Wildlife Fund (WWF).

SELECT BIBLIOGRAPHY

T he Greek and Latin works cited in the book include the following:

1. Aeschines, *Against Timarchus*; Aeschylus, *Eumenides*; Aristotle, *Eudemian Ethics*, *The Politics*; Demosthenes, *Philippics*, *Prosecution of Aristogeiton*; Euripides, *Iphigenia in Aulis*; Herodotus, *Histories*; Hypereides, *Prosecution of Demosthenes*; Longinus, *On the Sublime*; Plato, *Apology*, *The Laws*, *The Republic*; Plutarch, *Political Precepts*; Polybius, *Histories*; Sophocles, *Antigone*, *Oedipus Rex*; Thucydides, *History of the Peloponnesian War*; Xenophon, *Agesilaus*.

2. Cicero, *On Duties*, *Letters to Brutus*; Horace, *Satires*; Juvenal, *Satires*; Livy, *History of Rome*; Lucan, *Pharsalia*; Lucretius, *On the Nature of Things*; Ovid, *Art of Love*; Petronius, *Satyricon*; Sallust, *Conspiracy of Catiline*; Seneca, *De Tranquillitate Animi (Of Peace of Mind)*; Suetonius, *Lives of the Caesars*; Tacitus, *Germania*; Tertullian, *The Apology*.

Adorno, T., *Contro l'Antisemitismo*, Rome, 1994.
Allen, W., *Killing No Murder*, London, 1689.
Anon., *A Helpe to Discourse*, London, 1635.
Anon., *A Relation or Journall of the Beginning and Proceedings of the English Plantation Settled at Plimoth*, London, 1622.
Anon., *An Answer to a Printed Book*, Oxford, 1642.
Aptheker, H., *The Colonial Era*, London, 1960.
Arnold, M., *Culture and Anarchy* (1869), Cambridge, 1971.
Ashley, M., *Oliver Cromwell and the Puritan Revolution*, London, 1958.
Bacon, F., *Of the Advancement and Proficiencie of Learning*, Oxford, 1640.

———, *The Essayes or Counsels, Civill and Morall*, London, 1639.

Barker, E., *Greek Political Theory*, London and New York, 1960.

Blakely, E. J., *Fortress America: Gated Communities in the United States*, Washington, 1997.

Bloom, A., *The Closing of the American Mind*, New York and London, 1988.

Bunyan, J., *The Pilgrim's Progress* (1678), Harmondsworth, 1970.

Burke, E., *Select Works*, ed. E. J. Payne, Oxford, 1885.

Carlyle, T., *On Heroes, Hero-Worship, and The Heroic in History* (1841), London, 1870.

———, *Past and Present* (1843), Berkeley and London, 2005.

Castiglione, B., *The Book of the Courtier* (1528), New York, 1959.

Chesterfield, Earl of, *Letters to His Son*, London, 1774.

Churchill, W., *Liberalism and the Social Question*, London, 1909.

———, *My Early Life*, London, 1930.

———, *The River War*, London, 1899.

Cobbett, W., *Advice to Young Men*, London, 1829.

Collins, A., *A Discourse of Free-Thinking*, London, 1713.

Cromwell, O., *Letters and Speeches*, ed. T. Carlyle, London, 1850.

Dickens, C., *David Copperfield* (1850), Oxford, 1983.

———, *Dombey and Son* (1848), London, 2012.

———, *Little Dorrit* (1855), Oxford, 1982.

Dover, K. J., *Greek Political Morality in the Times of Plato and Aristotle*, Oxford, 1974.

Earle, A. M., *Customs and Fashions in Old New England* (1893), Rutland, VT, 1973.

Erasmus, D., *Twenty Select Colloquies*, trans. R. L'Estrange, n.d.

Evelyn, J. ["J. E."], *Fumifugium*, London, 1661.

Federalist Papers, The (1787–89), ed. L. Goldman, Oxford, 2008.

Friedman, M., and R. Friedman, *Free to Choose: A Personal Statement*, New York and London, 1980.

Fukuyama, F., *The End of History and the Last Man*, London, 1992.

Gibbon, E., *The History of the Decline and Fall of the Roman Empire* (1776–1789), London, 1908.

Godwin, W., *Thoughts on Man*, London, 1831.

Goodwin, I., *Town Officer*, Worcester, 1829.

Greenawalt, K., *Religion and the Constitution*, Princeton, 2009.

Hale, M., *A Discourse Touching Provision for the Poor*, London, 1683.

Haller, W., *The Rise of Puritanism*, New York, 1957.

Handlin, O., and M. Handlin, *The Popular Sources of Political Authority*, Cambridge, 1966.

Hawthorne, N., *Our Old Home*, Edinburgh, 1865.

————, *Passages from the American Notebooks*, London, 1868.

Herbert, G., *The Complete English Poems*, Harmondsworth, 1992.

Hobbes, T., *Leviathan* (1657), Harmondsworth, 1981.

Hume, D., *Private Correspondence*, London, 1820.

Ibn Khaldun, *The Muqaddimah* (1377), Princeton, 1981.

Judd, D., *Radical Joe* (1993), London, 2010.

Keates, J., *Handel: The Man and His Music*, London, 2008.

Klemperer, V., *Diaries, 1933–1945*, London, 2000.

Lewis, S., *Babbitt* (1923), London, 1973.

Locke, J., *Two Treatises of Civil Government* (1690), London, 1962.

Martineau, H., *The Rioters, or a Tale of Bad Times*, Wellington, 1827.

Marx, K., *Grundrisse* (1857–1858), Harmondsworth, 1973.

————, *Selected Writings*, Oxford, 1978.

Masterman, C., *The Condition of England* (1909), London, 2009.

Maurois, A., *Disraeli: A Picture of the Victorian Age*, London, 1927.

Miller, P., *The New England Mind*, Boston, 1961.

Milton, J., *Paradise Lost* (1667), Oxford, 2008.

Montesquieu, C., *The Spirit of the Laws* (1848), Berkeley, 1977.

Mumford, L., *The City in History* (1961), New York, 1989.

Musil, R., *The Man Without Qualities* (1930–1932), London, 1954.

Orwell, G., *Collected Essays*, London, 1961.

————, *The Road to Wigan Pier*, London, 1937.

Oxberry, W., *Anecdotes of the Stage*, London, 1827.

Perry, R., *Fed Up! Our Fight to Save America from Washington*, New York, 2010.

Pope, A., *An Essay on Man*, 1733.

Powell, S. C., *Puritan Village: The Formation of a New England Town*, New York, 1965.

Rand, A., *Atlas Shrugged* (1957), New York, 1992.

————, *The Virtue of Selfishness*, New York, 1964.

Reid, M., *The Child Wife: A Tale of the Two Worlds*, London, 1868.

Rose, J., *The Intellectual Life of the British Working Classes*, New Haven, 2010.

Ross, A., *The Industries of the Future*, New York, 2016.

Seforim, M. M., *The Nag* (1873), New York, 1955.

Seldon, A., and D. Kavanaugh, *The Blair Effect, 2001–5*, Cambridge, 2005.

Selbourne, D., *Death of the Dark Hero: Eastern Europe, 1987–90*, London, 1990.

Sinclair, T. A., *A History of Greek Political Thought*, London, 1952.

Smith, A., *The Wealth of Nations* (1776), London, 1999.

Southey, R., *Letters from England*, London, 1807.

Tocqueville, A. de, *Democracy in America* (1835), London, 1998.

————, *The Old Regime and the French Revolution* (1856), New York, 2010.

Trollope, F., *Domestic Manners of the Americans*, London, 1832.

Turgot, A. R. J., *Oeuvres*, Paris, 1913–1923.

Waites, M., *The Age of Consent: Young People, Sexuality and Citizenship*, New York, 2005.

Webster, D., *A Discourse in Commemoration of the First Settlement of New England*, Boston, 1821.

Weil, S., *La Prima Radice*, Milan, 1996.

Whitelocke, B., *Memorials of English Affairs* (1682), Ann Arbor and Oxford, 2007.

Williams, M., *Parliament Ltd*, London, 2015.

Wolfe, T., *Hooking Up*, London, 2000.

Wood, E. M., and N. Wood, *Class Ideology and Ancient Political Theory*, Oxford, 1978.

Wortley, E. S., *Travels in the United States*, London, 1851.

Wright, T. ["The Journeyman Engineer"], *The Great Unwashed*, London, 1868.

———, *Johnny Robinson*, London, 1868.

Wright, T., *Our New Masters*, London, 1873.

Zimmern, A. E., *The Greek Commonwealth*, Oxford, 1911.

Zweig, S., *Erasmus of Rotterdam*, London, 1934.

———, *Marie Antoinette: The Portrait of an Average Woman*, London, 1933.

INDEX